W9-AYE-302

WRITING POEMS

Sixth Edition

Michelle Boisseau

University of Missouri–Kansas City

Robert Wallace

Late of Case Western Reserve University

PEARSON
Longman

New York   San Francisco   Boston
London   Toronto   Sydney   Tokyo   Singapore   Madrid
Mexico City   Munich   Paris   Cape Town   Hong Kong   Montreal

Vice President and Editor-in-Chief: Joseph Terry
Acquisitions Editor: Erika Berg
Associate Editor: Barbara Santoro
Senior Marketing Manager: Melanie Craig
Senior Supplements Editor: Donna Campion
Production Manager: Donna DeBenedictis
Project Coordination, Text Design, and Electronic Page Makeup:
    Elm Street Publishing Services, Inc.
Cover Designer/Manager: Wendy Ann Fredericks
Cover Photo: © Raphael Senzamici / Monsoon Images / PictureQuest
Manufacturing Buyer: Lucy Hebard
Printer and Binder: Courier Corporation/Stoughton
Cover Printer: Coral Graphic Services, Inc.

For permission to use copyrighted material, grateful acknowledgment is made to the
copyright holders on pp. 333–338, which are hereby made part of this copyright page.

Library of Congress Cataloging-in-Publication Data

Boisseau, Michelle, 1955–
    Writing poems / Michelle Boisseau, Robert Wallace—6th ed.
        p. cm.
    ISBN 0-321-09423-9
    1. Poetry—Authorship. I. Wallace, Robert, 1932–1999
    II. Title.
    PN1059.A9W34 2004
    808.1—dc21   2002043443

Copyright © 2004 by Michelle Boisseau and Christine Wallace

All rights reserved. No part of this publication may be reproduced, stored in a retrieval
system, or transmitted, in any form or by any means, electronic, mechanical, photocopying,
recording, or otherwise, without the prior written permission of the publisher. Printed in the
United States.

Please visit our website at http://www.ablongman.com

ISBN 0-321-09423-9

1 2 3 4 5 6 7 8 9 10–CRS–06 05 04 03

For Tom and Anna

CONTENTS

5   THE SOUND (AND LOOK) OF SENSE   100

Part II
CONTENT:
A Local Habitation and a Name   125

6 SUBJECT MATTER   127

9 BEYOND THE RATIONAL 210

Part III
PROCESS:
Making the Poem Happen   235

10 FINDING THE POEM   237

Poems to Consider

Poems to Consider

PREFACE

To the Teacher

Poets learn from poets. Like the earlier editions of *Writing Poems*, the sixth edition assumes that in the poetry already written lie the clues of how to write. In the poems of others, beginning poets apprehend the possibilities for their own work, joining a tradition of great poems even as they begin to create their own.

Since reading poems stimulates and guides the writing of poems, this book acts as a handy anthology (heavily weighted on poems written in the past twenty years), a friendly guide for the student, and a backup for you as the teacher. The book thoroughly covers fundamentals like lineation, imagery, and metaphor, so that you can spend class time focusing on the students' own poems, responding to the issues their poems pose, and illustrating what poems have to teach them about craft.

Enduring Features

- Combines **comprehensive instruction** and a **practical, student-friendly** approach.
- Offers a wealth of **writing exercises** to prompt students to write their own poetry.
- Contains an **anthology of over 250 classical and contemporary poems,** a diverse selection of examples, illustrations, and inspiration.
- Discusses **the writing process** throughout and encourages students to view poems as acts of revision.

Features New to This Edition

If you used the fifth edition, you will notice a few differences and additions to this edition, including:

- New exercises for inspiring student poems.
- A clarification and simplification of versification in Chapter 3 ("Making the Line [I]").
- A new section, "Memory," in Chapter 6 ("Subject Matter") that shows students the resources memories offer and suggests how students can draw on them to make poems.
- A new set of drafts examined in a section of Chapter 11 ("Drafts") that emphasizes how revision often comes from listening to the poem.
- A new student poet's development discussed in Chapter 12 ("Becoming a Poet") that explores the many routes a poet's growth can take.
- More emphasis on the revision process throughout the text to emphasize that writing poems means re-writing.
- A wider variety of poets—from C. D. Wright to Philip Larkin, from Kay Ryan to Al Young—to encourage students to see how varied the poetic universe is and the many possibilities they have for making their own poems.
- Quotation boxes have been integrated throughout the text. These brief quotations from experienced writers provide inspiration and illumination to the beginning student.
- A more thorough and easier-to-use glossary.
- More than seventy-five new poems have been added to *Writing Poems*, Sixth Edition, including new poems by the following list of poets. Poets who wrote their poems as students are marked with an asterisk.

Anonymous	Russell Edson	Josephine Miles
John Ashbery	Carol Frost	Lorine Niedecker
Jennifer Atkinson	Lucia Cordell Getsi	Michael Nelson*
Angela Ball	Margaret Gibson	William Olsen
Erin Belieu	R. S. Gwynn	Alicia Ostriker
Geoffrey Brock	Michael S. Harper	Eric Pankey
Travis Brown*	Jeffrey Harrison	Greg Pape
Christopher Buckley	Anthony Hecht	Molly Peacock
Andrea Hollander	Garrett Hongo	Sylvia Plath
Budy	Richard Jackson	Lizette Woodworth
Rafael Campo	Hettie Jones	Reese
Jared Carter	Allison Joseph	Trish Reeves
Kelly Cherry	Ashley Kaine*	Pattiann Rogers
Ye Chun*	Sarah Kennedy	Kay Ryan
David Citino	Roger Kirschbaum*	William Shakespeare
Amy Clampitt	Carrie Klok*	Arthur Smith
Patricia Clark	Philip Larkin	R. T. Smith
Samuel Taylor	Li-Young Lee	Maura Stanton
Coleridge	Cynthia MacDonald	Wallace Stevens
Martha Collins	Colleen J. McElroy	Robert Stewart
Adelaide Crapsey	Heather McHugh	Jonathan Swift
Emily Dickinson	Randall Mann	Luci Tapahonso

Janine Tran*   Christian Wiman   Charles Wright
William Trowbridge   Susan Wood   Al Young
Chase Twichell   Jeff Worley   Gary Young
Michael Waters   Baron Wormser
Charles Harper Webb   C. D. Wright

Strategies for Using This Book

In writing a poem, the poet aims to shape everything at once. But, of course, the teacher cannot address simultaneously every feature of a poem; therefore, consider this book's organization more a structural convenience than an agenda. This book divides poetry writing into large units called "Form," "Content," and "Process," and subdivides these into chapters, but these categories aren't tight: how can one separate form from content, process from form? The book organizes the material, not the course or, really, the variety of possible courses. Courses that use this text cross a wide spectrum of creative writing courses: from multi-genre courses that introduce students to creative writing to advanced and graduate courses. I encourage you to follow your own inclinations and priorities and move across the part divisions as you organize your approach.

- For introductory courses, you might best set off with Chapter 1 ("Starting Out") as it presents a few basics to get students quickly on their feet and engaged with the notion of what good writing is.
- In a course covering poetry and fiction writing, you might then turn to Chapter 7 ("Tale, Teller, Tone"), which focuses on features critical to both genres, such as narrative and point of view.
- For introductory classes where students have little experience with poetry, the course might turn to Chapter 2 ("Verse") early on so that students understand at the outset that attention to the line makes poems. Next the course can go on to Chapter 6 ("Subject Matter"), which emphasizes how poems are built from detail and imagery, from things, as William Carlos Williams says, that lie close to the nose.
- In classes in which you want to encourage student experimentation, you may next want to move them on to Chapter 8 ("Metaphor"), Chapter 9 ("Beyond the Rational"), and Chapter 10 ("Finding the Poem"), which emphasize the play of language and the uses of the imagination.
- More advanced classes may want to begin with the more technical chapters on meter (Chapter 3, "Making the Line [I]") and free verse (Chapter 4, "Making the Line [II]"), and then move on to Chapter 11 ("Devising and Revising"), since trusting in the revision process marks the more advanced writer.
- You might also encourage more advanced—or more adventurous—classes to try out some of the forms described in Appendix I ("A Brief Glossary of Forms") and to explore the websites and literary journals mentioned in Chapter 12 and the reading suggestions in Appendix III.

- Classes that include majors and minors in creative writing will find that covering the section "The Growth of the Poet" in Chapter 12 ("Becoming a Poet") early in the term can inspire students to push their work over the next threshold of their development.

Often, as you get to know your students in a particular term, you may want to adjust your approach. A class with many staid or timid poets, for instance, might be urged to open up and take risks through Chapter 9 ("Beyond the Rational"). Similarly, an undisciplined group might reap the most benefits if early on the students understand, through chapters 10–12, that the vision of poems comes from revision. Whatever approach you take, feel free to mix chapters from the three parts, thus raising simultaneous matters more or less simultaneously.

If you allow a little extra time for the condensed technical information in Chapter 3 (on meter), the twelve chapters make a comfortable fit for a semester course. For a shorter course, sections of some chapters may be assigned selectively; for example, the section "Alliteration and Assonance" from Chapter 5 ("The Sound [and Look] of Sense") or the section "Exploring" from Chapter 11 ("Devising and Revising"). A section may be relevant for a particular student (e.g., "Emotion and Thought" in Chapter 10) and can be assigned individually and discussed in conference.

In workshop courses, *Writing Poems* allows you to put the emphasis on student poems and to let the book cover basics like syntax and sentimentality. In that case, you'll want to spend a few minutes early in the course encouraging students to think of the book as a friendly guide they can explore on their own. Point out a particularly riveting poem or two among the "Poems to Consider" in a chapter you won't be teaching soon, or an exercise in the "Questions and Suggestions" that might give students a boost when they are searching for ideas for poems. Encourage them to browse through "A Brief Glossary of Forms" and "Index of Terms." Students noodling around in the appendices might become intrigued by the rondeau and try one of their own.

On the first day of class the students seated around the room are usually unsure but eager, so the challenge is less to inspire them than to provide the continuing stimulus of fresh ideas and new information. In workshop courses, especially, when students are reading each other's poems, they need to be asking W. H. Auden's practical questions: Here is a verbal contraption. How does it work? as well as, What can I use?

Because students are rarely familiar with much recent poetry, sometimes only with Shel Silverstein and pop lyrics, the poetry selections lean strongly toward recent poems. Poems included by students (whose names are marked by asterisks in the list on pages xvi–xvii) offer models of what student poets can accomplish. Usually the poems that appear in the "Poems to Consider" sections at the end of each chapter exemplify matters raised in that chapter, but as every good poem does a thousand things at once, many might appear anywhere in the text. The "Questions and Suggestions" section of each chapter offers a variety of exercises and discussion topics, meant as supplements, not replacements, for your own hands-on instigations and direction.

All poets write (and learn from) their own weaker poems, hence examples of bad student poems do not appear here. Early versions of poems, particularly in chapters 1, 11, and 12, offer instances of the clumsy or wrongheaded as well as assurance for aspiring poets that problems can be solved. As Ben Jonson urges,

> No more would I tell a green writer all his faults, lest I should make him grieve and faint, and at last despair. For nothing doth more hurt, than to make him so afraid of all things, as he can endeavor nothing. . . . Therefore a master should temper his own powers, and descend to the other's infirmity. If you pour a glut of water upon a bottle, it receives little of it; but with a funnel, and by degrees, you shall fill many of them.

Acknowledgments

For their suggestions and corrections, I owe deep thanks to many students, teachers, poets, and colleagues, and in particular to my own students, who have been game to try the new and willing to challenge the useless. Thanks go to Lorrie Carano, Amy Lucas, and especially Xu Ge for help with proofing and permissions. Special thanks go to Deborah Kroman for her sharp eyes and sound judgment, and to Anna Boisseau and Tom Stroik, whose patience and understanding made this revision possible.

I also wish to thank the formal reviewers who have reviewed this book during various stages of development: Angela Ball, University of Southern Mississippi; Martin Baum, Jamestown Community College; Michael Collier, University of Maryland; Robert Collins, University of Alabama–Birmingham; Keith Coplin, Colby Community College; Jim Daniels, Carnegie Mellon University; Ren Draya, Blackburn College; Neal Dwyer, College of Southern Maryland; Vince Gotera, University of Northern Iowa; Angela Green, Lee College; Randall Huff, Iowa State University; Steve Jaech, Pierce College; Leslie Jenike, Ohio State University; Lance Larsen, Brigham Young University; George Looney, Bowling Green State University; Michael McFee, University of North Carolina–Chapel Hill; Robert Miltner, Kent State University–Stark; Darrell Peters, University of North Carolina–Pembroke; Marianne Taylor, Kirkwood Community College; Karen Wallace, West Valley College; Michael Warren, Maple Woods Community College; and Charles Webb, California State University–Long Beach.

And, finally, most of all, I want to remember the originator of *Writing Poems*, Robert Wallace, who died in April 1999. Bob was a fine poet, an inspiring teacher, a discriminating critic, and a generous friend. Bob and I met not long after the release of the third edition of *Writing Poems*; when he brought me in as co-author with the fourth edition, I was a young poet who had just published her first book. His confidence in me bolstered me then and now, and I hope that this book continues to express his good sense, clear vision, and large spirit which I felt throughout the preparation of this edition.

—M. B.

A Note from the Publisher

Supplements Available with *Writing Poems*, Sixth Edition

A Student's Guide to Getting Published (ISBN: 0-321-11779-4)
This clear and concise "how-to" guide takes writers of all genres through the process of publishing their work—including the considerations of submission, how to research markets, the processes of self-editing and being edited, and how to produce a "well-wrought manuscript," among other useful and practical information. Available free when value-packed with *Writing Poems*.

A Workshop Guide to Creative Writing (ISBN: 0-321-09539-1)
This laminated reference offers suggestions and tips for students to keep in mind in a workshop situation—both as participant and presenter. Blank space is provided for students to record additional guidelines provided by their instructor. Available free when value-packed with *Writing Poems*.

The Longman Journal for Creative Writing (ISBN: 0-321-09540-5)
This journal provides students with their own personal space for writing. Helpful writing prompts and strategies are included as well as guidelines for participating in a workshop. Available free when value-packed with *Writing Poems*.

Responding to Literature: A Writer's Journal (ISBN: 0-321-09542-1)
This journal provides students with their own personal space for writing. Prompts for responding to fiction, poetry, and drama are integrated throughout. Available free when value-packed with *Writing Poems*.

Glossary of Literary and Critical Terms (ISBN: 0-321-12691-2)
This handy glossary includes definitions, explanations, and examples for more than 100 literary and critical terms that students commonly encounter in literature classes. Available free when value-packed with *Writing Poems*.

1

STARTING OUT

An Introduction

This was a Poet—It is That
Distills amazing sense
From ordinary Meanings—

—EMILY DICKINSON

Writing poems is nearly as old as humanity itself. Poetry is so interwoven with the human story that we can follow its origins into the dimmest reaches of our roots. We can easily imagine how not long after we began to structure the sounds that we could make into the words of language, we began tinkering with that language, making it memorable, making poems. The earliest generations of poets played with poems, made discoveries, and invented new poems, as did the next generation and the next, all the way down to us. People from cultures all over the globe trace their origins through poems. From Iceland to Cameroon, on rickety tables in apartment complexes, around campfires on windy plains, in the some five thousand human languages, people use poems to express who they are, what they believe, what they have done, and, most of all, what it feels like to be alive.

Ezra Pound urges poets to "make it new." The very simplicity of his statement tells us how fundamental the "new" is to making poems. Though human truth may reach back millennia, we will always need new poems because that truth must be reimagined and revived in poetry so that we can feel again its power. What strikes one era as innovative and exciting may often strike a later generation as worn and dated. As Mary Kinzie says, "Pretty soon the surprises do not surprise us any more." At the same time, poets must stay attentive to what earlier poets wrought. As a poet you can only know what remains to be written if you know what is already in poems. As T. S. Eliot points out, the poet "lives in what is not merely the present, but the present moment of the past, unless [the poet] is conscious, not of what is dead, but of what is already living." The poet must take to heart the poems that persist.

Starting to write poems, then, inevitably mixes what the beginning poet learns of poetry's craft, its possibilities, and what only each new writer can bring to the adventure—new subjects, attitudes, insights: "a place for the genuine," as Marianne Moore says. A teacher, like the authors of this book, can lead you toward writing poems, but expect to follow only so far. Each poet must learn (and learn and relearn) how to write his or her own poems. Learning to write poetry means exploring. It means not only recording what you think or feel but investigating those thoughts, digging deep, striving for a new shivery understanding. Howard Nemerov wryly defines writing poems as a spiritual exercise "having for its chief object the discovery or invention of one's character."

A course called "Creative Writing" might better be called "Experimental Writing." Faced with the daunting specter of a blank page, the poet may feel intimidated by the injunction to *be creative; create*. But, being told to *experiment, to try something out* can be more attractive. Even on a bad day when all you can seem to do is thrash around with a stubborn poem, you *can* experiment. Put a few words down, reorder them, find words that are more precise, shape an arresting sentence. Form it into the first line of a poem. What might the poem's *next* line say?

The poem you end up with may not be what you expected—and all the better. We make experiments in order to surprise ourselves, to find out what we don't know, to clarify what we're trying to discover. Each experiment teaches us how to venture better the next time—how to pose a problem more sharply, how to comprehend more thoroughly what we are looking for. The great German poet Rainer Maria Rilke in his *Letters to a Young Poet* offers this advice:

> Being an artist means: not numbering and counting, but ripening like a tree, which doesn't force its sap, and stands confidently in the storms of spring, not afraid that afterward summer may not come. It does come. But it comes only to those who are patient . . . . *patience* is everything!

Writing—trying to dig up one's deepest feelings and to untangle one's most intricate view of the world—will always be an intimate, vulnerable activity. You may be hard on your poems, but go easy on yourself.

We learn to write poems from reading (and rereading) poems we like, the poems that encourage us to write poems in the first place. That's how poets trained themselves before creative writing courses, and that's how they still learn. Elizabeth Bishop's advice to an aspiring poet in the 1960s still holds today:

Read a lot of poetry—all the time. . . . Read Campion, Herbert, Pope,
Tennyson, Coleridge—anything at all almost that's any good, from the past—
until you find out what you really like, by yourself. Even if you try to imitate it
exactly—it will come out quite different. Then the great poets of our own
century—Marianne Moore, Auden, Wallace Stevens—and not just 2 or 3
poems, each, in anthologies—read ALL of somebody.

When you meet a poem that speaks to you, in this book or elsewhere, see what else
by the poet you can find in your bookstore, in the library, in journals, on the Internet.
These poets will help you realize places your own poems might go.

And as you write, make sure you're having fun. Keep your sense of humor lively, as
the poet Sharon Bryan (b. 1943) does in this celebration of words:

Sweater Weather: A Love Song to Language

Never better, mad as a hatter,
right as rain, might and main,
hanky-panky, hot toddy,

hoity-toity, cold shoulder,
bowled over, rolling in clover,   5
low blow, no soap, hope

against hope, pay the piper,
liar liar pants on fire,
high and dry, shoo-fly pie,

fiddle-faddle, fit as a fiddle,   10
sultan of swat, muskrat
ramble, fat and sassy,

flimflam, happy as a clam,
cat's pajamas, bee's knees,
peas in a pod, pleased as punch,   15

pretty as a picture, nothing much,
lift the latch, double Dutch,
helter-skelter, hurdy-gurdy,

early bird, feathered friend,
dumb cluck, buck up,   20
shilly-shally, willy-nilly,

roly-poly, holy moly,
loose lips sink ships,
spitting image, nip in the air,

hale and hearty, part and parcel,   25
upsy-daisy, lazy days,
maybe baby, up to snuff,

flibbertigibbet, honky-tonk,
spic and span, handyman,
cool as a cucumber, blue moon,   30

high as a kite, night and noon,
love me or leave me, seventh heaven,
up and about, over and out.

Bryan's poem develops by mining the riches of English idiom, by staying alert to associations that sounds and images suggest. The poem keeps us leaping from one phrase to the next, so that the double "l" sounds in "shilly-shally, willy-nilly," in line 21 lead to more "l's" repeated in the following stanza which lead to an echoing of "o" followed by short "i" sounds:

roly-poly, holy moly,
loose lips sink ships,
spitting image, nip in the air

Often student poets start out writing a poem with a firm statement in mind about what they want to say, approaching the poem as if it were to be developed logically, like an essay or report, and the process of writing a poem as nailing down those first notions. Starting a poem with a fixed notion, however, can quickly frustrate you because what you wanted to say inevitably changes as it is translated to the page. If instead of holding fast to a starting idea, you relax your grip on the poem and concentrate on the words as they come—paying attention to how one image suggests others—you can let the poem develop more naturally and in unexpected directions. And in the end you'll have more fun, an excruciating fun, perhaps, but a real engagement with poetry. Robert Frost once said, "No surprise for the poet, no surprise for the reader." If in writing the poem, the poet doesn't find out something new and stay curious about where a poem might lead, why would a reader? Of course, the poet is the poem's most important reader, but external readers are also essential. They keep us honest. We may convince ourselves that the poem we have labored over says brilliantly what we mean it to say, but an objective reader will test those convictions. As you listen closely to what other readers have to say about your poems—and as you, too, articulate your readings of other poets—your critical skills will slowly, but surely, become sharpened, and you will be able to direct a keener critical eye to your own poems. That critical eye is essential to writing poems.

Word Magic

The joy that painters find in messing around with paint, poets find in words, as Sharon Bryan's "Sweater Weather" demonstrates. You may find it helpful to picture the words of your poems fluid as paint—you can choose them, change them, blend them, layer them. Because we use words in the humdrum of our lives—buying a burger, answering the phone—we can sometimes forget what power they wield. As far back as we can go, we find humanity testing and sharpening that power. The oldest poems we have are the spells, prayers, curses, and incantations that accompanied the magical rites of ancient cultures. Words blessed apple trees and warriors' weapons, healed boils, cast out demons, and drove away swarms of bees. Through chants ancient people sanctified the newlyweds' first bed, celebrated a birth, cursed the rich and powerful, strengthened medicinal herbs, and sent the dead to the next life.

Like all effective poems, magic spells are precise. It's the specificity of *toe*, *wool*, *tongue*, and *blindworm* that makes the repulsive potion of *Macbeth*'s witches:

> Eye of newt, and toe of frog,
> Wool of bat, and tongue of dog,
> Adder's fork, and blindworm's sting,
> Lizard's leg, and howlet's wing—
> For a charm of pow'rful trouble.   5
> Like a hell-broth boil and bubble.
> Double, double, toil and trouble,
> Fire burn and cauldron bubble.

The word "spell" itself suggests how potent words are. As part of the curative, ancient peoples often literally spelled out the charm—something like a physician's prescription. An old charm in England against rabies called for writing down the spell on a piece of paper and feeding it to the mad dog. As part of a magic formula, soothsayers often spelled out in a triangle the occult word "abracadabra," and so evoked the essential power of language, of the ABC's.

As with all kinds of magic, the first criterion of word magic is that those who wield it and those affected by it must believe in its power. Evidently in the antebellum South, a slave who could convince masters that he or she held magical powers could be given special treatment and allowed to intercede for others. Knowing magic could bring income. This love spell, recorded by the Federal Writers' Project in the 1930s, was part of the repertoire of a former slave:

> Little pinch o' pepper,
> Little bunch o' wool.
>
> Mumbledy-mumbledy.
>
> Two, three Pammy Christy beans,
> Little piece o' rusty iron.   5
> Mumbledy-mumbledy.
>
> Wrop it in a rag and tie it with hair,
> Two from a hoss and one from a mare.
> Mumbledy, mumbledy, mumbledy.

Wet it in whiskey   10
Boughten with silver;
That make you wash so hard your sweat pop out,
And he come to pass, sure!

Oddly, the charm's ending seems off–rhythm. Perhaps the transcriber made an error or, more intriguing, the man deliberately gave the wrong verse in order to protect the magic.

We resort to magic and prayer when science and human effort fail us. We have a better treatment now for rabies, but struggle to understand as much as anyone who lived a hundred years ago why someone falls in love with one person instead of another, and so we may still count off on the petals of a daisy, "loves me, loves me not."

Children are great believers in word magic. From the toddler chirping out "Pat-a-cake," to the older parodist sneering at authority, "Glory, glory, hallelujah, / Teacher hit me with a ruler," children love language. From generation to generation, songs and charms are passed along because children believe in their power. Children govern their groups with rhyme ("One potato, two potato, three potato, four"); wish with it ("Star light, star bright, first star I see tonight"); threaten with it ("See this finger, see this thumb? / See this fist, you better run"); and accuse with it ("Liar, liar, pants on fire"). And when cornered, they make their defense, "I'm rubber, you're glue / What you say bounces off me and sticks to you." Like all preliterate peoples, children delight in words, find them powerful, and fear and respect them.

Most don't like to admit it, but adults aren't much different. Certain words remain taboo, and though we all know them, we avoid them in public, and they can't be printed in this paragraph. We use magical words in church, in court, and when we quarrel. With pledges, oaths, and vows, people become wives and husbands, nuns, physicians, presidents, witnesses, and citizens. In uttering the words we cross a threshold; we are not exactly the same person as before we pronounced them.

The ancient forms of language itself, its glacial mass and lightning flash, give shape to every new thought and discovery that our poems can make. Poets need not, perhaps should not, concern themselves too directly with the sources of poetry's magic. It is enough to know that when writing well we may tap into this energy as we flip on a light without considering how the power came from plants and animals that lived eons ago and from which, through dynamos and copper wires, ancient light arrives in the lamp on our desk.

Diction

As we have been seeing, **diction,** or word choice, is one of the poet's greatest tools. By choosing the *exact* word, not merely something close, the poet convinces and draws a reader into a poem. Through shrewd attention to the **denotative,** or literal, meaning of words, the poet makes explicit the world of the poem. A word used unwittingly, such as *liquidate* for *melt*, can quickly confuse and even ruin a poem.

Poets take every advantage words offer them; while working on the drafts of his poem "Among School Children," Yeats accidentally substituted "a *mess* of shadows" for "a *mass* of shadows" and immediately recognized the subtler possibilities that accompanied the choice.

As you write, you will find a good dictionary valuable, not only for checking spelling and usage but also for locating a word's etymology (the history of its development). Such etymologies can lead you to a word's **connotative** meanings—its figurative meanings—as well as the overtones and nuances that a word or phrase suggests. For example, since the etymology of *nuance* leads back to *nue*, or cloud, a "nuance" can be likened to the subtle shading, the dip in temperature a cloud gives the landscape of a poem.

Since poems operate in small spaces, the layers that lie beneath the surface—the poems' **implications**—have profound importance. In this poem, notice how the poet's diction shapes the world of the speaker and implies her deeper, unstated concerns.

Cold as Heaven   1995
JUDITH ORTIZ COFER (b. 1952)

Before there is a breeze again
before the cooling days of Lent, she may be gone.
My grandmother asks me to tell her
again about the snow.
We sit on her white bed   5
in this white room, while outside
the Caribbean sun winds up the world
like an old alarm clock. I tell her
about the enveloping blizzard I lived through
that made everything and everyone the same;   10
how we lost ourselves in drifts so tall
we fell through our own footprints;
how wrapped like mummies in layers of wool
that almost immobilized us, we could only
take hesitant steps like toddlers   15
toward food, warmth, shelter.
I talk winter real for her,
as she would once conjure for me to dream
at sweltering siesta time,
cool stone castles in lands far north.   20
Her eyes wander to the window,
to the teeming scene of children
pouring out of a yellow bus, then to the bottle
dripping minutes through a tube
into her veins. When her eyes return to me,   25
I can see she's waiting to hear more

about the purifying nature of ice,
how snow makes way for a body,
how you can make yourself an angel
by just lying down and waving your arms   30
as you do when you say
good-bye.

Ortiz Cofer's *details*—the trudging through snow, the dripping IV bottle, the making of snow angels—bring the scene to life, make it *realized*. Because she *shows* us, instead of *tells* us, we respond more directly. We can sense the coldness of the snow, the hot sun outside, the noisy children pouring from the bus, and the speaker's dread. Without explaining her feelings directly (which would seem both unnatural and intrusive), the speaker of the poem shows us how close she feels to her grandmother and how great her loss will be when her grandmother dies. By drawing on our basic humanity and our interest in our own families, the poem lets us participate in its drama. It doesn't *tell* us to think or feel a thing. And yet we do.

By using the word "conjure" Ortiz Cofer threads into the poem a suggestion that an element of magic lies within the scene. Derived from Latin and meaning "to swear together," *conjure* once meant "to entreat earnestly" and later "to summon supernatural spirits"; through "conjure," the poem implies that the grandmother once wielded a special power through storytelling.

A good thesaurus (the name comes from the Greek word meaning "treasury") can lead to scores of synonyms for a word. Substitutions for the verb *touch* include *feel, caress, massage, twiddle, paw, poke, grope, grapple, run the fingers over, fumble, sift, brush, pinch, prick, stroke, handle, manipulate, contact, rummage, frisk, hit, graze, tickle,* and *goose.* It will also take us to *touch upon, discuss, ventilate, dissertate, go into,* and *critique.* The omnivorousness of English—which has taken in words from many languages—offers us a host of choices to fit exactly what we mean, or, often more important, to help us to focus what we mean, even to distill the elusive ideas and feelings that come to us.

In making your poems, try to rely on precise nouns and verbs—language's bones—rather than on modifiers. Loading modifiers onto your poems won't make them seem more appealing, just overdecorated, like a room crammed with too many knick-knacks. Consider the difference between "She walked away furiously" and "She stomped off," between "I pawed the jacket" and "I touched the jacket harshly."

In choosing words, balance their meaning and nuance with how they fit the situation or attitude of the poem. If a love poem declares, "Let me integrate my life with yours," we will question the speaker's seriousness or wonder why the lover has chosen the tone of a job application. A poem's levels of diction (e.g., formal, informal, neutral, colloquial, vulgar) help to establish its **tone,** the poem's attitude toward its subject. Notice how most of Ortiz Cofer's diction is quiet and neutral; it sets a simple stage on which the intense emotions of the poem can play out. A fancy polysyllable might make us doubt the speaker's sincerity and might suggest she is showing off verbal fireworks rather than showing her concern for her grandmother. Were the speaker to claim she would like "to declaim on frozen rain," she would sound preposterous.

Sometimes an odd word provides exactly the sense and surprise the poet is after. Consider, for instance, Louise Glück's "coagulate" in "Racer's Widow" (p. 38) or Robert Hayden's (1913–1980) "austere and lonely offices" in the last line of this poem:

Those Winter Sundays

Sundays too my father got up early
and put his clothes on in the blueblack cold,
then with cracked hands that ached
from labor in the weekday weather made
banked fires blaze. No one ever thanked him.   5

I'd wake and hear the cold splintering, breaking.
When the rooms were warm, he'd call,
and slowly I would rise and dress,
fearing the chronic angers of that house,

Speaking indifferently to him,   10
who had driven out the cold
and polished my good shoes as well.
What did I know, what did I know
of love's austere and lonely offices?

The denotative meaning of "offices" is "tasks or duties," but the word's connotations remind us of the authority and trust that we associate with fatherhood. The word also carries great psychological weight. In choosing "offices" Hayden registers ambivalence; the son feels strong remorse for belatedly recognizing his father's efforts, and yet the son, despite what he knows, still feels emotionally distant. Some deep pain still haunts him. Notice, also, how much the simple word "too" placed in the first line tells us; *every* day, even on the day of rest, his father labored for his family.

As we work through a poem to explore ideas, feelings, and experiences, we might resort to using **clichés**—stale, too familiar words, phrases, and metaphors. The language of poetry pays attention; by its nature a cliché does not. You can test for a cliché by asking yourself whether the word, phrase, or image you are using is particular or generic. If you're writing about a rainbow, do you see a real rainbow with all its translucence, transience, and tenuousness? No rainbow looks exactly like another. Or do you see the commercial artist's generic sentimental symbol: neat little arches lined up according to the spectrum, red to violet, in flat unreal colors?

Another test for a cliché is to ask yourself if you really know what the word, phrase, or image means. Isn't *hated her with a passion* redundant? If you say you're eating *humble pie*, what's in that pie? Does it have anything to do with the deer innards that the king's huntsmen ate instead of the choice venison reserved for the nobility? Also, ask yourself if you get a sensation when you use the phrase, or whether you are only transmitting general impressions. A poem should be able to use every suggestion available to it; if you use *cool as a cucumber*, what suggestion can you draw from the cucumber? Because of its overuse, *cold as ice* isn't very intense, while Ortiz Cofer's "Cold as Heaven" intrigues. Does *light as a feather* recall the ticklish, wispy barbs? Be careful not to confuse clichéd and formulaic writing with idiomatic writing. *Idioms* are expressions that have become fixed in a language as constructions deemed natural. English speakers say, "I am going *to* Italy," not, as in other languages, "I am going *in* Italy." Tampering with idiomatic expressions doesn't freshen language; it makes it sound laughable, like the wild and crazy guys in old *Saturday Night Live* routines.

> U*se all the clichés possible, such as "He had a gleam in his eye," or "Her teeth were white as pearls."*
>
> —Langston Hughes, from "How to be a Bad Writer (In Ten Easy Lessons)"

Each age has its own stale formulas; our special curse includes *hard truth, revisit, phenomenal, hardliner, download, in denial, meeting one's needs,* and *poetry in motion.* Poetry often generates a kind of cliché all its own, **poetic diction**—fancy or contrived language that gets used and reused until it becomes dull and tries a reader's patience. American poets of the 1960s and 1970s had a particular affinity for *stone, dark, alone, dance* and titles that included gerunds such as *rising, diving, spinning.* The words *o'er* for *over, ere* for *before,* or *thou* for *you* were the poetic clichés of an earlier time, and using them now makes a poet sound stiff, starched, and goofy as a cartoon. As Pound advises, don't use in a poem a word that you wouldn't use in speech—or at least weigh your purpose carefully.

Syntax

Syntax is the structure of phrases, clauses, and sentences. The word *syntax* comes from the Greek *syn* ("together") and *tassein* ("to arrange"): "to arrange together." Also from *tassein* comes the word *tactics,* suggesting the value of syntax to the poet in deploying forces. Syntax is the muscle of poetry.

The syntactical qualities of strong writing in general apply to poetry, including these principles:

1. Place main ideas in main clauses and subordinate ideas in subordinate clauses.
2. Use parallel structures for parallel ideas.
3. Put modifiers next to the nouns they modify.
4. Use active voice.
5. Vary sentence structure.
6. Set the most significant part of a sentence at the end.
7. Use unusual syntax only when appropriate to meaning.
8. Break any rule that makes you sound ludicrous.

If you're unsure about syntax, devote some time to paying attention to it. A writing guide such as Strunk and White's classic *The Elements of Style* can help, as well as an ear attuned to the ways the poems you come across marshal meaning and emotion through syntax.

In her elated "Sweater Weather: A Love Song to Language," Sharon Bryan overcomes the rule against using sentence fragments by aligning the celebratory phrases in a parallel list. Her careful coordination of the phrases keeps us from getting tangled in fragments, and her interplay of the poem's sounds helps it cohere and progress. For example, in the last two lines, "love me or leave me, seventh heaven, / up and about, over and out" (lines 32–33), the phrases are balanced, allowing the "o," "e," and "v" sounds to resonate and hold the parts together.

By opening "Cold as Heaven" with the repeated prepositional structure, "Before there is a breeze . . . before the cooling days," Ortiz Cofer suspends—holds off—the main clause ("she may be gone"), enacting the grandmother's tenuous hold on life. Ortiz Cofer varies the type (e.g., simple, compound, complex) and length of her sentences to speed and slow the poem's movement, manifesting the speaker's train of thought as she considers what she is telling her grandmother. Following the long parallel clauses of the poem's third sentence (lines 7–13), the simpler fourth sentence ("I talk winter real for her . . . .") seems to erupt, as if the speaker had suddenly grasped why she describes the snow.

Notice in the first stanza of "Those Winter Sundays" how Hayden deploys his sentences to create a startling emotional impact. Following the four-and-a-half-line opening sentence that lists the father's chores ("Sundays too my father got up early / and put his clothes on in the blueblack cold . . . ."), the son delivers a short sentence that comes like a heavy blow: "No one ever thanked him." The brevity of the admission helps us feel how little effort—even to express thanks—the other family members took. Try rewriting that stanza—either combining both sentences into one long sentence or breaking them apart into a series of short ones—and you'll quickly see how Hayden's syntax is responsible for much of the poem's emotional depth.

As syntax is a poem's muscle, flexing or relaxing those muscles lends the poem its strength and agility. In "Barbed Wire" (p. 74) Henry Taylor manages all twenty-four lines of the poem through one sentence, driving home a sense that nothing can stop the accident. Robert Francis's "Excellence" (p. 56) compresses two sentences into one line: "From poor to good is great. From good to best is small." The terse sentences seem to register the exactitude we hope for in truth.

Robert Frost (1874–1963) was a master of coaxing both music and meaning out of syntax. Listen to the inversions, repetitions, and emphases in this poem:

Old Man's Winter Night

All out-of-doors looked darkly in at him
Through the thin frost almost in separate stars,
That gathers on the pane in empty rooms.
What kept his eyes from giving back the gaze
Was the lamp tilted near them in his hand.   5
What kept him from remembering what it was
That brought him to that creaking room was age.
He stood with barrels round him—at a loss.

And having scared the cellar under him
In clomping here, he scared it once again   10
In clomping off;—and scared the outer night,
Which has its sounds, familiar, like the roar
Of trees and crack of branches, common things,
But nothing so like beating on a box.
A light he was to no one but himself   15
Where now he sat, concerned with he knew what,
A quiet light, and then not even that.
He consigned to the moon, such as she was,
So late-arising, to the broken moon
As better than the sun in any case   20
For such a charge, his snow upon the roof,
His icicles along the wall to keep;
And slept. The log that shifted with a jolt
Once in the stove, disturbed him and he shifted,
And eased his heavy breathing, but still slept.   25
One aged man—one man—can't keep a house,
A farm, a countryside, or if he can,
It's thus he does it of a winter night.

Through frequent inversions, as when he places the complement before the verb
("A light he was to no one but himself," line 15), Frost presents the old man's world
as slightly off-kilter; he is losing touch. The second sentence, which begins on line 4
with "What kept his eyes . . . ," leads us through a long series of the results of his
uncertainty before we get to its cause in line 7, "age." Lines 6–9, which repeat "him"
four times, work to a minor climax within the turning and returning syntax that creates a rhythm to the old man's wandering through the house.

A few words on grammar and mechanics: Sometimes inexperienced writers labor
under the delusion that knowing grammar might dry up their creative juices. But not
knowing the rules will dry up your readers. To paraphrase Byron, easy writing makes
hard reading. As a carpenter knows when to use which screwdriver and a cook when
to use garlic, good writers know the tools at their disposal, and don't, for instance, use
a semicolon in place of a colon. Similarly, though we don't notice correct spelling, a
poem blotched with a misspelling distracts and destroys the illusion of the poet's
control. When a speaker steps on stage with an unzipped fly, the audience won't be
paying much attention to the words.

Pruning and Weeding

Like a coiled spring, much of a poem's power comes from its compression. We don't
mean that all poems should be epigrams, or that, at the expense of clarity or grace,
a poem should be clogged, cramped, or written in robot-speak. Cutting out the articles in a poem, for instance, doesn't make it tighter, just wooden. But the poet
should follow the principle of not using two words when the poem calls for one.

Don't state the obvious but show enough that the reader can gather a strong impression. Everything need not be said. Notice in "Those Winter Sundays" how powerfully we feel the son's sense of regret and longing because he doesn't overtly state these emotions. Ernest Hemingway notes that when thoroughly engaged in a subject the writer can leave out things, and the reader

> if the writer is writing truly enough, will have a feeling of these things as strongly as though the writer had stated them. The dignity of movement of an iceberg is due to only one-eighth of it being above water.

Poets think of poetry as an art of revision. By constantly sifting the words and gauging each sentence, the poet allows what lies beneath the surface—the implications—to propel the poem. Often a poem goes wrong when the poet overlooks what a word or a sentence pattern implies. Getting words down on the page, like poking seeds into the ground, is just the first step. The seeds may sprout, but unless the gardener thins the plants and weeds them, the garden will become a choked mess.

As you play around with a poem, look for redundancies, for what you can clear out of the way. Cynthia Macdonald advises students to think of what she calls the "Small Elephant Principle." We don't need to state an elephant is big; enormity naturally comes with our sense of that creature. If the elephant is small, however, that's worth mentioning. Apply this principle as you weigh choices like "winter snow," "nervous groom," or "delicious dessert."

Tightening the poem, seeing what can be dropped and what can be rearranged, often leads the poet to depict more dramatically the elements in a poem. Take a look at this poem Wilfred Owen (1893–1918) wrote from the trenches of World War I. He was killed in France just before the armistice.

Dulce et Decorum Est

Bent double, like old beggars under sacks,
Knock-kneed, coughing like hags, we cursed through sludge,
Till on the haunting flares we turned our backs
And towards our distant rest began to trudge.
Men marched asleep. Many had lost their boots   5
But limped on, blood-shod. All went lame; all blind;
Drunk with fatigue; deaf even to the hoots
Of tired, outstripped Five-Nines° that dropped behind.

Gas! Gas! Quick, boys!—An ecstasy of fumbling,
Fitting the clumsy helmets just in time;   10
But someone still was yelling out and stumbling,
And flound'ring like a man in fire or lime . . .
Dim, through the misty panes° and thick green light,
As under a green sea, I saw him drowning.

8 **Five-Nines:** 5.9-inch caliber shells.   13 **misty panes:** of the gas mask.

In all my dreams, before my helpless sight,   15
He plunges at me, guttering, choking, drowning.

If in some smothering dreams you too could pace
Behind the wagon that we flung him in,
And watch the white eyes writhing in his face,
His hanging face, like a devil's sick of sin;   20
If you could hear, at every jolt, the blood
Come gargling from the froth-corrupted lungs,
Obscene as cancer, bitter as the cud
Of vile, incurable sores on innocent tongues,—
My friend, you would not tell with such high zest   25
To children ardent for some desperate glory,
The old Lie: Dulce et decorum est
Pro patria mori.

The soldier's death by mustard gas makes a compelling case against the motto—popular during World War I—from the Latin poet Horace: "Dulce et decorum est pro patria mori," translated as "Sweet and fitting it is to die for one's country."

Owen's drafts of the poem (the originals are held in the British Museum) show how he coaxed this vivid picture from his material. In early drafts, he labored over these lines which appeared just before the startling second stanza:

Then somewhere near in front: Whew . . . fup, fup, fup,

Gas shells? Or duds? We loosened masks in case,—

And listened. ~~Nothing~~. Far rumouring of Krupp.
          ~~crawling~~ swoosh stung
Then ~~sudden~~ poison[s] ~~hit~~ us in the face.

The anxious soldiers listen for sounds that might indicate gas shells detonating and the poisonous gas drifting down on them. After fiddling with the lines for a while, Owen crossed all of them out; obviously he saw that beginning the stanza abruptly with "Gas! Gas! Quick, boys!" made the menace fiercer. The soldiers are suddenly engulfed.

Cutting and rearranging the elements of a poem can help you re-see it and allow you more room to include new discoveries. Consider this draft by a student, D. A. Fantauzzi:

Moorings

A collection of white, yellow, red
hulks of sailboats—
bugs with wings
folded down their backs,
tucked out of the wind,   5

sitting still.
Through the heart
a tall pin
sticks each to the blue-green mat.

This keenly observed poem presents a scene that might be invigorated if pruned. Here is the text again, with possible omissions shown by brackets:

[A collection of] white, yellow, red
[hulks of] sailboats—
bugs with wings
folded down their backs,
[tucked out of the wind,]   5
[sitting still.]
[Through the heart]
a tall pin
sticks each to the blue-green mat.

The plural "sailboats" is sharper without "A collection of." The analogy between sailboats and a display of pinned insects makes "collection" relevant, but since the phrase comes first, it has little force. In line 2 "hulks of" seems unnecessary and misleading (did he mean "hulls"?); "hulks" feels too lumbering for sailboats. The comparison of sails to wings seems accurate (both are means of propulsion by air) and necessary, and the sails are "folded down their backs," as insects' wings might be.

Yet "tucked out of the wind" makes the action sound too volitional since in the metaphor the insects are dead. In line 6 "sitting" appears too flat and motionless for sailboats moored on the water. Though the drama of "Through the heart" seems right, neither sailboats nor insects have hearts, so the line becomes sentimental.

Each of these potential deletions raises a question the poet should mull over. How necessary is this word or detail to the poem I am trying to write? What happens if I move this phrase? Here is the poem as the poet might rearrange and condense it:

White, yellow, red sailboats—
bugs with wings
folded down their backs.
A tall pin
sticks each to the blue-green mat.   5

The form above has the added benefit of suggesting—through its unbalanced, low, flat shapes—the folded-down sails of the boats. At this stage other phrases and details may occur to the poet. Might the word "collection" now go in somehow? Might "away from the wind"—an alteration of "tucked out of the wind"—work somewhere? What about the rhythm? Working through such questions, the poet writes the poem. Here is the poet's revision:

A collection of white, yellow, red
sailboats—bugs with wings
folded down their backs,
in rows.

A tall pin   5
sticks each to the blue-green mat.

The added detail—"in rows"—focuses the picture and helps support the metaphor. The poet decided to keep the phrase "A collection of," which sets up the metaphor and prevents a reader from imagining the sailboats as dispersed.

It's sometimes helpful to imagine the poem you are working on as a raft. It must be held together tightly and carry only what is necessary, or it will be swamped. Slack writing (wasted words, wasted motions) hinders the smooth movement of a poem. As Anton Chekhov notes: "when a person expends the least possible movement on a certain act, that is grace." Not all poems should be short, of course, nor as short as this poem by Ezra Pound (1885–1972) which, from a thirty-five-line draft, became a two-line poem. But every poem should be as short as possible.

In a Station of the Metro

The apparition of these faces in the crowd;
Petals on a wet, black bough.

Clarity, Obscurity, and Ambiguity

Nobody really champions **obscurity.** "It is not difficult to be difficult," Robert Francis quipped. If what you are saying is worth saying, nothing can be gained (and everything can be lost) by obscuring it. Yes, poems that handle complicated issues may be demanding. All the more reason to be as scrupulously clear as you can. However, if what you are saying turns out to be not really worth saying, readers will not find the poem more compelling if they have to slosh though a swamp. You may feel what you have to say just seems too obvious to state directly, but don't confuse clarity with the underdeveloped, the simplistic, or the unexamined.

In this poem Wallace Stevens (1879–1955) pokes fun at naysayers who simplistically insist "The world is ugly, and the people are sad," and blind themselves to the universe's marvels.

Gubbinal

That strange flower, the sun,
Is just what you say.
Have it your way.

The world is ugly
And the people are sad.   5

That tuft of jungle feathers,
That animal eye,
Is just what you say.

That savage of fire,
That seed,   10
Have it your way.

The world is ugly
And the people are sad.

Each new metaphor for the sun—"Strange flower," "tuft of jungle feathers," "animal eye," "savage of fire," "seed"—demonstrates the power and dazzle of the ordinary. You won't find "gubbinal" in a lot of dictionaries (Stevens loved odd words); a "gubbin" is a small fragment. Ironically, through sentence fragments such as "That seed," Stevens makes a full case against clichéd thinking, easy notions about the state of the world and its people.

Don't confuse obscurity with **ambiguity,** a poem's ability to offer more than one plausible reading at a time. The connotations of its words, its syntax, the multiple meanings enjambment suggests, the implications of its images, the strength of its metaphors, its use of allusion, its shape and sounds—every aspect of a poem enriches and creates poetry's depth and resonance so we return to a poem again and again, drawing more from it each time.

> *Insofar as poetry has a social function it is to awaken sleepers by other means than shock.*
> —Denise Levertov

Beginning poets learn that clarity is demanding, for what may seem obvious to the poet may be anything but obvious to the reader on the outside. We have often watched student poets squirm as class discussions about their poems lead to nutty conclusions about what they meant.

The fault lies sometimes with readers who don't pay close enough attention and so miss a signal. A poem of multiple layers lends itself to multiple readings. Responsible readers try to make sure that their reading of a poem accounts for, or at least does not contradict, each of the poem's features. It's unfair to ignore signals a poem gives about how it should be read in order to make another reading work. In the poem above, we do a rotten job as readers if we ignore the vigor of images like "tuft of jungle feathers" and take Stevens *literally* to mean that "the world is ugly and the people are sad."

Sometimes obscurity enters a poem accidentally, through a confusing sentence fragment or an infelicity of word choice that escaped the poet's scrutiny—for example, a pronoun that doesn't refer to what the poet thinks it does. When readings of a poem cancel each other out—or just lead in totally opposite directions—obscurity rears up. Given several mutually exclusive choices, a reader can become like the proverbial donkey between two piles of hay: It couldn't make up its mind which to eat and so starved to death.

But often the inexperienced poet, in a state of ingenious solitude, has so tangled and hidden the signals in the underbrush that no one can spot them. In this essay from 1965, Robert Francis describes a situation still common today among men and women apprentice poets:

The Indecipherable Poem

I have no love for the indecipherable poem, but for the indecipherable poet I have often a warm friendly feeling. He is usually a bright chap, perhaps brilliant, a good talker, someone worth knowing and worth watching. He is also often a college undergraduate majoring in English and in love with writing.

In his literature and writing courses it is taken for granted that the significant poets are the difficult ones. So, what less can an undergraduate poet do than be difficult himself?

Difficulty, of course, is not the only virtue of great poets. They give us passion, vision, originality. None of these the undergraduate poet probably has, but he can be difficult. He can be as difficult as he wants to be. He can be as difficult as anybody else. He need only give the words he uses a private set of meanings. It is not difficult to be difficult.

What I mean is, a poem that is very difficult to read may not have been at all difficult to write.

One poem sufficiently difficult can keep a creative writing class busy a whole hour. If its young author feels pleased with himself, can we blame him? He is human. He has produced something as difficult as anything by Ezra Pound. Why shouldn't he be pleased?

If he wants to, he can let his classmates pick away at his poem indefinitely and never set them straight. If his teacher ventures to criticize a phrase or a line, the author can say that the passage is exactly as he wants it. Is it awkward? Well, he intended it to be awkward since awkwardness was needed at that point. This would be clear, he murmurs, to anyone who understood the poem.

Nobody can touch him. Nobody at all. He is safe. In an ever-threatening world full of old perils and new, such security is to be envied. To be able to sit tight and pretty on top of your poem, impregnable like a little castle perched on a steep rock.

Although you may well feel pangs listening to others read your poem in ways you never imagined, try to listen intently. Such readings can show you better how to direct your poem and may lead you to just the insight your poem needs. As you reconsider and revise, avoid "analyzing" your own work; you can't spin around the dance floor if you're staring at your feet.

Bear in mind that readers read in a poem things you did not intend, as well as things you did. With any poem that touches readers, readers will tie in their own associations and feelings. These will never be exactly like the poet's, just as one person can never hope to convey to another person the *exact* mental picture of a particular place. (Even pointing out a particular star to someone is hard.) So long as the reader's "poem" doesn't violate or undermine the clues to the poet's "poem," the transaction works. When readers bring themselves to a poem and make it truly their own, they are doing precisely what any poet hopes they will, making the poem come alive.

QUESTIONS AND SUGGESTIONS

1. Write a poem that uses at least five words from side "A" of the list below and at least one word from side "B." Make the diction choices appropriate to the context. What happens to your poem when the more formal diction from side B enters the poem?

A		B
clump	limestone	pacify
grouse	blast	distinction
strict	spruce	survey
coat	tar	codify
cloud	water	postulant
battery	smear	quarantine
bungle	shirk	numinous
shrink	stopper	convolve
mash	smelt	refraction
wrangle	crumble	alacrity
sick	cube	sanguine
curb	ink	epoch

2. *For a group*: Each of you makes photocopies of three poems you really love. Next cut each poem into lines and phrases—don't leave more than a couple of lines together. Meet other members of the group at a classroom or your favorite pizza joint. It helps if one or two of you bring scissors, tape (in a dispenser makes it easier), and blank sheets of paper. In the center of a table everyone spills out their poem pieces and uses them to assemble their own poems. Feel free to break the poem pieces even further, and to adjust punctuation and capitalization. When you have finished, read the poems aloud to each other. Below is an example from a recent class. Your group will likely come up with poems equally outrageous, but that carry seeds of poems you might have the urge to take somewhere.

Climbing the Mountain Height

We shall not sleep
or set upon a golden bough to sing
of the photographed horse
though poppies grow
against the cliff behind the house.
We are the Dead
hung on barb and thorn
that teach the rustic moralist to die

streaming from lobbies
and a mystery. That is   10
how jocund
to hunt buffalo.
Come girls and women.
Our ashes live their wonted fires
beneath their sturdy stroke!   15
And there's a story in a book about it:
the children's house of make-believe,
the frail, illegal
curtains drawn.

3. Write a poem that begins with one or more long subordinate clauses and ends with a short declarative clause. For instance, "When my truck crossed the bridge, / when I rolled down the window, / when the river flashed beneath . . . I began to see . . .

4. Take the poem you wrote in exercise 1 or any other poem you have written, and tighten it. If you're feeling particularly daring, go through it and strike out every other line. (You can always put them back!) At least try to cut out all the adjectives and adverbs. Try to reduce the poem by one-fourth. Examine what you have left. Is a new poem developing? Try to pursue that poem: refine the diction, rearrange the lines. Can you cut out a fourth more?

5. Memorize a poem you really admire; best if it's one you don't completely understand yet. Say it aloud to yourself when you're stuck in traffic. Say it aloud to a group. When you really have it by heart, use its rhythms to fuel the beginning of your own poem. Try to avoid writing a parody.

6. In a poem *everything* happens for a reason, even if the "reason" can't be put easily into words. Examine "Famous" in "Poems to Consider" and consider what the poem would be like if the final line were missing. What if the order of the stanzas were changed? If the fourth stanza ("The tear") appeared where the first now does? What if the sixth stanza ("The bent photograph") opened the poem? You might want to copy the poem, cut the stanzas apart, and see if you can discover the "logic" of their order.

7. Write a prayer, curse, blessing, or magic spell. Craft it to a particular situation. A Curse for Microsoft? Prayer for My Skidding Car? A Spell against Lost Luggage?

8. With your notebook open to a clean page, think back to where you lived ten years ago. Look out your favorite window there. What do you see? Make it the first day of summer. Perhaps it's raining. What does it smell like? What do you hear? Are you wearing shoes? Close your eyes and for five minutes look out that window. When you're finished, jot down what you saw. Now look out another window, in some other year. It hasn't rained for weeks. Close your eyes, look, write it down. Then climb out the window and go for a walk. (And take notes.)

POEMS TO CONSIDER

Famous

1982

NAOMI SHIHAB NYE (b. 1952)

The river is famous to the fish.

The loud voice is famous to silence,
which knew it would inherit the earth
before anybody said so.

The cat sleeping on the fence is famous to the birds   5
watching him from the birdhouse.

The tear is famous, briefly, to the cheek.

The idea you carry close to your bosom
is famous to your bosom.

The boot is famous to the earth,   10
more famous than the dress shoe,
which is famous only to floors.

The bent photograph is famous to the one who carries it
and not at all famous to the one who is pictured.

I want to be famous to shuffling men   15
who smile while crossing streets,
sticky children in grocery lines,
famous as the one who smiled back.

I want to be famous in the way a pulley is famous,
or a buttonhole, not because it did anything spectacular,   20
but because it never forgot what it could do.

First Sight

1964

PHILIP LARKIN (1922–1985)

Lambs that learn to walk in snow
When their bleating clouds the air
Meet a vast unwelcome, know
Nothing but a sunless glare.
Newly stumbling to and fro   5
All they find, outside the fold,
Is a wretched width of cold.

As they wait beside the ewe,
Her fleeces wetly caked, there lies
Hidden round them, waiting too,   10
Earth's immeasurable surprise.
They could not grasp it if they knew,
What so soon will wake and grow
Utterly unlike the snow.

Sizing   1999
HEATHER McHUGH (b. 1948)

Where's my hairbrush? Where's the belt?
I want my switch. I need that cane. Just let me get
my hands upon that licking-stick, and then

we'll take the starch right out of you.
Your hide is fixing for a tanning. Just you wait.   5
What hit you you won't know. The future cannot help

but cut you down to size. Its feeling for you,
more and more apparently parental,
cannot help but grow.

We Three Kings   Unknown
ANONYMOUS

We three kings all orient are
one in a taxi one in a car
one on a scooter blowing his hooter
smoking a big cigar

oh star of wonder star of bright   5
sit on a box of dynamite
light the fuse and off we go
all the way to Mexico

Realism   1994
CZESLAW MILOSZ (b. 1911)

We are not so badly off if we can
Admire Dutch painting. For that means
We shrug off what we have been told
For a hundred, two hundred years. Though we lost

Much of our previous confidence. Now we agree   5
That those trees outside the window, which probably exist,
Only pretend to greenness and treeness
And that the language loses when it tries to cope
With clusters of molecules. And yet this here:
A jar, a tin plate, a half-peeled lemon,   10
Walnuts, a loaf of bread—last, and so strongly
It is hard not to believe in their lastingness.
And thus abstract art is brought to shame,
Even if we do not deserve any other.
Therefore I enter those landscapes   15
Under a cloudy sky from which a ray
Shoots out, and in the middle of dark plains
A spot of brightness glows. Or the shore
With huts, boats, and, on yellowish ice,
Tiny figures skating. All this   20
Is here eternally, just because once it was.
Splendor (certainly incomprehensible)
Touches a cracked wall, a refuse heap,
The floor of an inn, jerkins of the rustics,
A broom, and two fish bleeding on a board.   25
Rejoice! Give thanks! I raised my voice
To join them in their choral singing,
Amid their ruffles, collets, and silk skirts,
One of them already, who vanished long ago.
And our song soared up like smoke from a censer.   30

Translated, from the Polish, by the author and Robert Hass.

Difficult Daughters   2001
ANGELA BALL (b. 1952)

To have a poet for a daughter
Is to wonder why.

To have a TV for a daughter means frustration
On "Take a Daughter to Work Day."

To have a Kleenex for a daughter   5
Is to worry about colds.

To have the moon for a daughter
Is to be a nervous astrologer.

To have a highway for a daughter
Means you never rest.   10

If your daughter is a grocery store,
You make sure her aisles are gleaming
And her mice are tucked out of sight.

My daughter is a room. I throw roses
through her window.   15

My daughter is a satellite. I watch
For the star that moves.

My daughter is a locomotive. When the walls
Begin to vibrate, I fall to my knees,
I listen.   20

A Poem of Attrition   1986
ETHERIDGE KNIGHT (1931–1991)

I do not know if the color of the day
Was blue, pink, green, or August red.
I only know it was summer, a Thursday,
And the trestle above our heads
Sliced the sun into black and gold bars   5
That fell across our shiny backs
And shimmered like flat snakes on the water,
Worried by the swans, shrieks, jackknives,
And timid gainers—made bolder
As the day grew older.   10
Then Pooky Dee, naked chieftain, poised,
Feet gripping the black ribs of wood,
Knees bent, butt out, long arms
Looping the air, challenged
The great "two 'n' a half" gainer . . .   15
I have forgotten the sound of his capped
Skull as it struck the block . . .
The plop of a book dropped? The tear of a sheer blouse?
I do not know if the color of the day
Was blue, pink, green, or August red.   20
I only know the blood slithered, and
Our silence rolled like oil
Across the wide green water.

No   1993
MARK DOTY (b. 1953)

The children have brought their wood turtle
into the dining hall
because they want us to feel

the power they have
when they hold a house   5
in their own hands, want us to feel

alien lacquer and the little thrill
that he might, like God, show his face.
He's the color of ruined wallpaper,

of cognac, and he's closed,   10
pulled in as though he'll never come out;
nothing shows but the plummy leather

of the legs, his claws resembling clusters
of diminutive raspberries.
They know he makes night   15

anytime he wants, so perhaps
he feels at the center of everything,
as they do. His age,

greater than that of anyone
around the table, is a room   20
from which they are excluded,

though they don't mind,
since they can carry this perfect
building anywhere. They love

that he might poke out   25
his old, old face, but doesn't.
I think the children smell unopened,

like unlit candles, as they heft him
around the table, praise his secrecy,
holding to each adult face   30

his prayer,
the single word of the shell,
which is no.

David   1960

JOSEPHINE MILES (1911–1985)

Goliath stood up clear in the assumption of status,
Strong and unquestioning of himself and others,
Fully determined by the limits of his experience.
I have seen such a one among surgeons, sergeants,
Deans and giants, the power implicit,   5

Then there was David, who made few assumptions,
Had little experience, but for more was ready,
Testing and trying this pebble or that pebble,
This giant or that giant,
He is not infrequent.   10

How could Goliath guess, with his many assumptions,
The force of the slung shot of the pure-hearted?
How could David fear, with his few hypotheses,
The power of status which is but two-footed?
So he shot and he shouted!   15

For Hai Zi,° Who Calls Himself Son of the Sea   2001
YE CHUN*

> *There is nothing faraway but farness.*
> *—Hai Zi, "Faraway"*

I no longer want to birth a snowman—
It would soon bleed to death
in a strange land with unfriendly weather.

I no longer want to wash the wind out of my hair
or paint the river onto my forehead. I no longer   5
want to wear my badge of moon.

I no longer want to show my shoulders—
which have made boats sigh—to my lover
whose breasts are like icy mountains in Tibet.

I no longer want to wear clouds on my feet,   10
which would force me to turn and turn
and then pierce me through with raindrops.

I no longer want to take another look at the earth.
Its green, sometimes emerging
in my dreams, has long flooded my eyes.   15

I can no longer wait
for my gills and scales to grow back
so that I can go home again.

°Hai Zi, a Chinese poet, died in 1989 at 25 by throwing himself under a train.

*Poets who wrote their poems as students are marked with an asterisk throughout this book.

PART

I

FORM

The Necessary Nothing

Glass
Words of a poem should be glass
But glass so simple-subtle its shape
Is nothing but the shape of what it holds.

A glass spun for itself is empty,
Brittle, at best Venetian trinket.
Embossed glass hides the poem or its absence.

Words should be looked through, should be windows.
The best words were invisible.
The poem is the thing the poet thinks.

If the impossible were not
And if the glass, only the glass,
Could be removed, the poem would remain.

ROBERT FRANCIS

2

VERSE

When you open a book, you know at once whether you are looking at poetry or prose. Poetry is written in lines, as verse; it has a fluid right margin. Prose is rectangular and comes in blocks. Prose fills the page from the left margin to a straight right margin set arbitrarily, *externally*, by the printer, not by the writer. The printer determines when a new line begins, and the wider the page, the longer the line. Prose trains readers to ignore the movement from line to line.

Poetry, however, pays attention to that movement. When we want to write poems, we usually set out by writing verse, with one *line*—not to be confused with *sentence*—following another. But why does that help? **Verse** is a system of writing in which the right margin, the line turn, is set *internally*, by something in the line itself. Thus, no matter how wide the page, the line remains as the poet intended. The poet, not the printer, determines the line.

All verse, even what is called "free" verse, has a measure, some rationale or system by which the poet breaks lines. The choices may be trained or intuitive, but the nature of verse insists the poet consider the identity of each line, weigh what work each line does, even if the poet cannot articulate what the line is doing.

This vital aspect of verse appears in the etymology of the word itself. *Verse* comes from the Latin *versus*, which derives from the verb *versare*, meaning "to turn." (The root also appears in words like *reverse*, "to turn back," or *anniversary*, "year turn.") As a noun it came to mean *the turning of the plough*, which creates a *row* or *line*. Thus, the English word *verse* refers to the *deliberate turning from line to line* that distinguishes verse from prose. In this age-old image, like the farmer driving ox and plough, the poet plants the seeds of sound and meaning row by row, guided by the line just written, aware of the line to come, and so enabling the cross-pollination that enriches the poem for a reader's harvesting.

The deliberate turning of lines is essential to verse. Lines are what make a poem a poem. The rhythm of prose is simply the linear cadence of the voice, a flow patterned only by the phrases and clauses that are the units of sentences. In verse, however, the cadence of sentences also plays over the additional, relatively fixed unit of **line.** Reading verse, we pause ever so slightly at line ends—even when there is no punctuation there; this pausing gives the line ending relatively more emphasis than the words at the beginning and even more emphasis than words in the middle of the line. Handling this emphasis can give the poet multiple layers of meaning, and the line thus empowers the poet with a dynamic way to pattern and vary the flow of language.

> *I dwell in Possibility—*
> *A fairer House than Prose—*
> *More numerous of Windows—*
> *Superior—for Doors—*
> —Emily Dickinson

Line breaks may coincide with grammatical or syntactical units. Such breaks reinforce regularity and emphasize normal speech pauses as in these passages from Wallace Stevens's "Metaphors of a Magnifico" which we will turn to shortly:

> Twenty men crossing a bridge,
> Into a village,
> Are twenty men crossing twenty bridges,
> Into twenty villages,

When the end of a line coincides with a normal speech pause (usually at punctuation), the line is called **end-stopped,** as are the lines above.

Line breaks also may occur within grammatical or syntactical units, creating pauses and introducing unexpected emphases.

> The boots of the men clump
> On the boards of the bridge.
> The first white wall of the village
> Rises through fruit-trees.

Coming at the end of a line, "clump" seems louder than it might if the word came at another position in the line. Lines such as this, which end without any parallel to a normal speech pause, are called **enjambed** (noun: **enjambment**). These pairs of lines from Stevens's "Sunday Morning" are also enjambed, and contain an additional pause inside the line:

> Deer walk upon our mountain, ‖ and the quail
> Whistle about us their spontaneous cries . . .

> At evening, ‖ casual flocks of pigeons make
> Ambiguous undulations as they sink . . .

This additional pause is called a **caesura** (‖), a normal speech pause that occurs within a line. The caesura produces further variations of rhythm not possible in prose. By varying end-stop, enjambment, and caesura, and by playing sense, grammar, and syntax against them, the poet can create a momentum in the poem that can underscore, counterpoint, even contradict what is happening within the poem. Robert Browning draws us into "My Last Duchess" (p. 163) in the opening of the poem through his deft handling of pauses within and at the end of lines:

> That's my last duchess painted on the wall,
> Looking as if she were alive. ‖ I call
> That piece a wonder, now: ‖ Frà Pandolf's hands
> Worked busily a day, ‖ and there she stands.
> Will't please you sit and look at her? ‖ I said   5
> Frà Pandolf by design, ‖ for never read
> Strangers like you that pictured countenance,
> The depth and passion of its earnest glance,
> But to myself they turned ‖ (since none puts by
> The curtain I have drawn for you, ‖ but I)   10
> And seemed as they would ask me, ‖ if they durst,
> How such a glance came there . . .

An Italian Renaissance duke is speaking to the envoy of another nobleman whose daughter the duke seeks in marriage. But before he negotiates for a new duchess, he is showing off a painting of his last, whom, we come to understand further into the poem, he has had murdered. Note how rarely the duke's speech is end-stopped; each line creates momentum that pulls the poem forward as the duke launches a subtle justification for his cruelty. So powerful is the poem's drive forward and so deftly does Browning use enjambment, that many readers miss that the poem is rhymed in what we call **heroic couplets,** pairs of rhyming lines.

Line

The poet's deploying of lines accounts for a large part of what makes a poem a poem; as Paul Valery put it, poetry creates "a language within a language." Consider this quatrain written by an anonymous, sixteenth-century poet.

Western Wind

> Western wind, when wilt thou blow,
>   The small rain down can rain?
> Christ, if my love were in my arms
>   And I in my bed again!

In love and far from home, the speaker longs for spring when he and his lover will be reunited. His speaking *to* the wind suggests his isolation and loneliness. Both wind and the "small rain" are personified. (**Personification** means treating something inanimate as if it had the qualities of a person, such as gender—or here—volition.) So "can rain" implies that the rain shares the speaker's impatience. Direct address to the wind also suggests that the exclamatory "Christ" in line 3 is, in part, a prayer. The speaker's world is a world of forces—wind, rain, Christ—and his passion makes the human also a force among forces. The incomplete conditional of lines 3–4 ("if my love") conveys through implication the speaker's longing, rather than a explicit but passive phrase "then we will be in bed together."

The compression of verse calls for staying alert—word by word, line by line—paying attention in a way we rarely do with prose, which is habitually discursive and given to adding yet something further, drawing us onward to what is next and next. Prose, like a straight line, extends to the horizon. Verse draws us spiraling into itself.

This reflexiveness of verse causes us to *feel* a poem's rhythm as we seldom do with prose. All but two syllables in lines 1–2 (the second syllable of "Western" and "The") are heavy. The lines are slow, dense, and clogged, expressing the ponderousness of waiting. By contrast, lines 3–4 offer light syllables; only "Christ," "love," "arms," "I," and "bed" have real weight. The lines leap forward, expressing the speaker's passion. The poet's measuring of lines helps to measure feeling. Rhythm is meaning. The "equal" lines of verse differ tellingly from one another in a way that the looser elements of prose cannot imitate. The lover's yearning carries its own music with it.

Poems make us alert to each line. Writing in verse creates a spatial dimension that prose cannot imitate. Look at how Wallace Stevens (1879–1955) manages his lines here:

Metaphors of a Magnifico

Twenty men crossing a bridge,
Into a village,
Are twenty men crossing twenty bridges
Into twenty villages,
Or one man   5
Crossing a single bridge into a village.

This is old song
That will not declare itself . . .

Twenty men crossing a bridge,
Into a village,   10
Are
Twenty men crossing a bridge
Into a village.

That will not declare itself
Yet is certain as meaning . . .   15

The boots of the men clump
On the boards of the bridge.
The first white wall of the village
Rises through fruit-trees.

Of what was it I was thinking?   20

So the meaning escapes.

The first white wall of the village . . .
The fruit-trees. . . .

Stevens lays out his lines to present the poem as an equation. Depending on one's perception we can have twenty men or one man, twenty bridges or one. Looked at from
a distance, for instance, one might see a group of men moving over one bridge, but
within the group each man crosses just one bridge. Stevens rearranges his lines within
the stanzas to register these shifting perspectives, floating in the third stanza the
word "are" on a line by itself so it acts as a kind of equals sign. The stanza creates a
simple formula, which the next stanzas question and toy with as he explores how we
arrive at meaning through images, and how images seem to operate on a level beyond
meaning, enough in themselves to move us:

The boots of the men clump
On the boards of the bridge.
The first white wall of the village
Rises through fruit-trees.
Of what was it I was thinking?

So the meaning escapes.

The first white wall of the village . . .
The fruit-trees. . . .

The short stanzas that close the poem seem to register the stops and starts of the mind
turning over possibilities, bringing in sensual images that seem to overpower thought.

Form

When we consider form, we delve deeply into the mystery of every art. Balanced
proportions please us. As children we delighted in stacking colored blocks of wood,
and used rhythm to remember things like "Thirty days hath September . . . ." Form
preserves content, and at its best, *expresses* content. Ideally, it is the necessary
nothing, the pressure, that transforms the ordinary carbon into diamond.

We may think of poetic form as growing out of two kinds of strategies, metrical and
nonmetrical. Both make good poems. As the poet Robert Lowell remarks, "I can't
understand how any poet, who has written both metered and unmetered poems,
would be willing to settle for one and give up the other." The two turn out to be far
more alike than different, despite the oppositional, loaded terms sometimes used to
refer to them: "closed" and "open," "fixed" and "free," "solid" and "fluid" or "organic"
form. Such terms tend to misrepresent the way poems are actually written. The
process, in which scattered thoughts, phrases, images, insights, and so on gradually
come together into a poem, is always open, free, and fluid at the beginning and

becomes, as the poet realizes the poem's form, finally closed, fixed, and solid. Hayden's "Those Winter Sundays" (p. 9) is ultimately no more organic, no less artificial, than "Western Wind." All poems are *made* things.

As Paul Lake points out in "The Shape of Poetry," "the rules of formal poetry generate not static objects like vases, but the same kind of bottom-up, self-organizing processes seen in complex natural systems such as flocking birds, shifting sand dunes, and living trees." As Lake notes, the process is also top-down since the poet's ideas of what a poem is or might be—the poems he or she admires—enter the loop of self-adjustment and feedback. The poet inevitably borrows and varies, and so recreates formal elements that occur in earlier poems, as Hayden does, for instance, in handling enjambment, proportion, diction levels, and repetition. Whether in a traditional "fixed" form or in one the poet invented for the occasion, a **nonce** form, in every successful poem the poet actively *achieves* the final form.

Space here won't permit a full discussion of the many kinds of traditional forms poets have used in English (a brief description of some of them appears in Appendix I). Particular ages seem to be drawn to certain kinds of poems. The 1590s saw a spate of sonnet sequences, and the early seventeenth century delighted in complex invented forms. The eighteenth century honed the heroic couplet. The Romantics were intrigued by the possibilities of the ode. Since early in the twentieth century, poets have increasingly pushed the rules of fixed forms, invented new forms, and turned to traditions and forms earlier English poets used little, such as the blues (which originated in the African American South), the sestina (in twelfth century France), and the pantoum (in Malaysia). Art can leap over all boundaries.

Knowing the possibilities of form guides and challenges a poet in making a poem. The sestina—with its repeated end words—seems particularly suited for poems of obsessiveness. The heroic couplet has proved a shrewd vehicle for balanced, measured argumentation—and for farce. The more forms of poems you try, the more you'll know the resources available, and the more arrows you'll have in your quiver when you step up to shoot the target. And let the poem itself, not the just the form, direct how the poem develops.

> *The man who writes a good love sonnet needs not only to be enamored of a woman, but also to be enamored of the sonnet.*
> —C. S. Lewis

If the poem works best by breaking a rule (or two or more), break it. Every form started as an experiment on something that came before.

In Sonnet 73, William Shakespeare (1564–1616) both shapes the rhyming **quatrains** (groups of four lines) and couplet and uses them to find the shape of his material, in the way that a good interviewer probes a witness to create a clear picture. The sonnet form helps lay out and weigh the parts of his argument.

That time of year thou mayst in me behold
When yellow leaves, or none, or few, do hang
Upon those boughs which shake against the cold,
Bare ruined choirs° where late the sweet birds sang.
In me thou see'st the twilight of such day   5

4 choirs: choir lofts.

As after sunset fadeth in the west,
Which by-and-by black night doth take away,
Death's second self that seals up all in rest.
In me thou see'st the glowing of such fire
That on the ashes of his youth doth lie,   10
As the deathbed whereon it must expire,
Consumed with that which it was nourished by.
This thou perceiv'st, which makes thy love more strong,
To love that well which thou must leave ere long.

The form of the **English sonnet** itself (see Appendix I for more on the sonnet) encourages Shakespeare to find the stages of his poem's argument and then to turn and call the argument into account. The English sonnet is built of three quatrains of alternating rhyme which close with a **couplet,** with two rhyming lines. The closing couplet often registers a turn, a twist, a hefting of the ideas or feelings presented earlier.

In the successive quatrains, Shakespeare's speaker compares his aging to a different period of time: to autumn, the dying of the year; to twilight, the dying of the day; and to glowing ashes, the dying of the fire. The three quatrains emphasize the three-step comparison. The couplet at the end, which marks a shift in tone, presents a resolution to the problem offered in the quatrains. Form and content work together.

The order of the comparisons corresponds to a mounting anguish. The poem moves, first, from a bare winter daylight scene to a twilight scene, and then to a night scene, when a fire dies out. The progression from day to dusk to night emphasizes the image of night as "Death's second self" and possibly suggests night as the time one most fears dying.

Another progression moves through the three images. In the first two quatrains we are out of doors, looking up at the tree and sky; in the last we have come indoors where it is darker and more confined. The constraint of the sonnet form matches the speaker's attitude. He addresses the trouble of aging only indirectly, through inanimate images, as if to hold its personal implications at a distance. But his apparent composure deceives. Each of the three images begins with a more positive tone than it ends with. The increasingly self-diminishing revisions in line 2 offer a clear example: "yellow leaves, or none, or few." The yellow leaves, like the "twilight" and the "glowing" of the fire, attempt an optimism that the speaker cannot maintain. In each of the images he is compelled to say what he originally seems to have wanted to hold off from his own awareness.

Framed as a compliment to the person addressed, the couplet begins on a positive note: "This thou perceiv'st, which makes thy love more strong." But the next line betrays the speaker's fears because he does not say, as we might expect, "To love that well which thou must *lose* ere long"; rather, "To love that well which thou must *leave* ere long." He sees his death as his beloved leaving him, not the other way around. Throughout the poem, the speaker has expressed, not his self-image, but what he imagines to be his lover's image of him: "thou mayst in me behold," "In me thou see'st," and "This thou perceiv'st." By "leave" in line 14 he need not mean more than "leave behind," but the phrase carries a sense of betrayal.

The brevity of the couplet creates the force of the poem's closing. Within two lines he turns around an argument which he had built up in twelve. The sudden shift in approach or focus—which nevertheless stems from the preceding lines—creates part of the sonnet's tensions and one of the attractions that draw poets to the sonnet form. Its form registers the tensions of a healthy argument, its proportions the power of a winning one: because the couplet operates in a much smaller space than the quatrains, it has more punch and sounds more convincing.

The general proportions of the sonnet—a longer first part that is finished with a concise second—we see in many poems, indeed in many forms of art. The action comes to a head in the last twenty or thirty minutes of a movie. In a novel, the crisis typically happens in the penultimate or the last chapter. In a short story, the crucial moment unfolds in the last few pages; in a very short story, the last paragraph or even the last sentence. Of course, satisfying closure requires subtlety. A story that suddenly ends with the central characters killed off will seem disappointing and melodramatic unless risk has been carefully woven into the plot.

Recollect the sharp closing of Robert Hayden's "Those Winter Sundays": "What did I know, what did I know / of love's austere and lonely offices?" The final lines work like the closing of a sonnet. In a short space, they transport us to a higher level of emotional recognition, from his memory of his father's thankless work, to his sudden remorse for his indifference to his father's acts of love.

Look at the delicate precision of content and the shrewd sense of proportion Whitman creates in this nonmetrical poem:

A Noiseless Patient Spider
WALT WHITMAN (1819–1892)

A noiseless patient spider,
I marked where on a little promontory it stood isolated,
Marked how to explore the vacant vast surrounding,
It launched forth filament, filament, filament, out of itself,
Ever unreeling them, ever tirelessly speeding them.   5

And you O my soul where you stand,
Surrounded, detached, in measureless oceans of space,
Ceaselessly musing, venturing, throwing, seeking the spheres to connect them,
Till the bridge you will need be formed, till the ductile anchor hold,
Till the gossamer thread you fling catch somewhere, O my soul.   10

The lines unreel loosely out across the page, suggesting the long filaments the spider strings out into the wind when preparing to construct a web. The two stanzas—one for the spider, one for the soul's "musing, venturing, throwing, seeking"—shape the poem's central comparison.

Each stanza has five lines. Notably, the first line in each is shorter than the other four, as if to suggest the outward flinging and lengthening of the spider's filaments and of the soul's "gossamer thread." The form of the poem suggests the correspondence between spider and soul. The spider's activities, described in stanza 1, are neither explained nor resolved until the last line of stanza 2. The success of the soul's "gossamer thread," catching and anchoring, implies a similar success for the spider.

Through the two-part structure of his poem, Whitman can unveil the similarities between spider and soul and so discover truths about them both. Notice the verbal echoes between various words in the two stanzas: "stood"/"stand," "surrounding"/"Surrounded," "tirelessly"/"Ceaselessly." Similar links bridge the images, as in the contrast of small to grand scale with "on a little promontory," followed in stanza 2 by "measureless oceans of space." After "promontory" (a cliff jutting out into the ocean), the images of "oceans of space," "bridge," and "anchor" lend unity to the comparison. Like the spider's action, the poem's apparently random movement has a deeper purpose.

Like the closing couplet of Shakespeare's poem, Whitman's final two lines, parallel phrases that begin with "Till," help create a sense of the poem's culmination. After the soul's striving through the long sentences of the second stanza, it reaches completion as "the thread catch[es] somewhere." Grammatically, the poem could end there with "somewhere," but such an ending would suggest indecisiveness. The strong sounds of Whitman's final exclamation, "O my soul," suggest his spiritual arrival.

A poem's power depends less on a choice between metrical and nonmetrical, fixed or free, than on the poet's ingenuity and skill in taking full advantage of form as the poem takes shape.

Balance, Imbalance

By shaping and reshaping the form, the poet zeroes in on what the poem reveals, and brings to the reader's attention those revelations. Intense attention to what is materializing on the page lies at the heart of writing a poem. By concentrating on the line you are writing, you can weigh it, judge it, see its implications, and let it help you discover something about what your poem might reveal: that discovery is what you're after. It needn't be earth-shattering; modest revelations can stun us. Close scrutiny of the developing line, particularly its sense of balance or imbalance, permits the poet to sense the places the poem might go.

In his essay, "Listening and Making," Robert Hass points out the rhythmical imbalance in these lines from the opening section of Whitman's sweeping "Song of Myself":

I lóaf and invíte my sóul,   3

I léan and lóaf at my éase ‖ obsérving a spéar of súmmer gráss.   3/4

The numbers at the end of each line above indicate the number of stresses per syntactic unit. The rhythm of the first line (three stresses) is essentially repeated by the first part of the second line (three stresses); but the second part not only extends the line but does so by *four* stresses. Hass adds, "Had Whitman written *observing a spear of grass*, all three phrases would be nearly equivalent . . . ; instead he adds *summer*, the leaning and loafing season, and announces both at the level of sound and of content that this poem is going to be free and easy."

As a further example, Hass offers this brief poem by Whitman:

A Farm Picture

Through the ámple ópen dóor ‖ of the péaceful cóuntry bárn,	3/3
A súnlit pásture fíeld ‖ with cáttle and hórses féeding.	3/3
And háze and vísta, ‖ and the fár hórizon fáding awáy.	2/4

Each line has six stresses (marked with an ictus ´), divided (by a light phrasal pause, or caesura in line 3) as indicated. The asymmetry of line 3 (2/4) effectively resolves the pattern (as a 3/3 version of the line might not), releasing the tension, letting the rhythm come to rest in the longer, four-stress phrase, "and the far horizon fading away."

Looking even closer, we notice that lines 1 to 2 are not only linked by their parallel, balancing rhythms, but also make up one of the poem's two sentences; together they present the speaker's place: the frame of the open barn doorway, "the cattle and horses feeding" seen at a middle distance. Whitman offers a scene of order and plenty; the barn is "ample," "peaceful," the pasture "sunlit." However, if we can intuit the speaker's feelings in the symmetric rhythms of the verbless, actionless sentence, the scene seems also static and unsatisfying.

The asymmetry of rhythm in line 3, the elongation created by the phrase "and the far horizon fading away," suggests he is drawn to the uncertain and far-off, because it represents possibilities either longed for or unrealized ("fading"). Perhaps he pauses from his work and looks out, his attention lingering on the distant and vanishing.

In the previous examples, lines are end-stopped and create a sense of peacefulness and vague yearning. In this poem by Louise Glück (b. 1943), however, a number of lines break violently. Observe how the enjambment interacts with the lines' often striking imbalance:

The Racer's Widow

The elements have merged into solicitude.
Spasms of violets rise above the mud
And weed and soon the birds and ancients
Will be starting to arrive, bereaving points
South. But never mind. It is not painful to discuss   5
His death. I have been primed for this,
For separation, for so long. But still his face assaults
Me, I can hear that car careen again, the crowd coagulate on asphalt
In my sleep. And watching him, I feel my legs like snow

That let him finally let him go   10
As he lies draining there. And see
How even he did not get to keep that lovely body.

Look at how sentences break at line ends, then stop abruptly at the beginning of lines (like "But still his face assaults / Me"), giving the rhythm an effect of jerking forward and then dead-ending, of careening around corners, like a car going out of control. The device also appears monosyllabically in "bereaving points / South." And it occurs less sharply in "above the mud / And weed," "discuss / His death," "on asphalt / In my sleep," and—going the other way, from a caesura near line end—in "And see / How even he." The poem's rhythm seems quite off-balance, especially in these lines:

For séparátion, ‖ for só lóng. ‖ But stíll his fáce assáults   2/2/3

Mé, ‖ I héar that cár caréen agáin, ‖ the crówd coágulate on ásphált   1/4/5

In my sléep. ‖ And wátching hím, ‖ I féel my légs like snów   1/2/3

That lét him fínally lét him gó   4

The repetition in line 10—"That let him finally let him go"—needs, but has no punctuation, and so appears syntactically incoherent. The "snow-go" rhyme makes us aware the poem rhymes in couplets, in slant rhymes—"solicitude-mud," "ancients-points." The dissonance that slant rhyme can suggest heightens the sense of trauma.

The widow contradicts her claim that "It is not painful to discuss / His death." The lurching rhythm, wrenching imagery ("Spasms of violets"), and almost compulsive alliteration ("I can hear the car careen again, the crowd coagulate . . .") suggest she is barely managing. These choices allow Glück to convey the widow's struggle, her repressed but ill-concealed emotional turmoil.

A quite different impression emerges in the rhythm of the following poem by Elizabeth Spires (b. 1952). The speaker, three months pregnant, meditates languorously.

Letter in July

My life slows and deepens.
I am thirty-eight, neither here nor there.
It is a morning in July, hot and clear.
Out in the field, a bird repeats its quaternary call,
four notes insisting, *I'm here, I'm here.*   5
The field is unmowed, summer's wreckage everywhere.
Even this early, all is expectancy.

It is as if I float on a still pond,
drowsing in the bottom of a rowboat,

curled like a leaf into myself.   10
The water laps at its old wooden sides
as the sun beats down on my body,
a wand, an enchantment, shaping it
into something languid and new.

A year ago, two, I dreamed I held   15
a mirror to your unborn face and saw you,
in the warped watery glass, not as a child
but as you will be twenty years from now.
I woke, a light breeze lifting the curtain,
as if touched by a ghost's thin hand,   20
light filling the room, coming from nowhere.

I know the time, the place of our meeting.
It will be January, the coldest night
of the year. You will be carrying a lantern
as you enter the world crying,   25
and I cry to hear you cry.
A moment that, even now,
I carry in my body.

Through a strong sense of rhythmic stasis, Spires's poem presents a speaker at ease. Of the twenty-eight lines, twenty-two are end-stopped; five of the seven lines in stanza 1 are complete sentences. Scanning lines 1 and 2 shows:

Mў lífe slóws ănd déepĕns.   3

Í ăm thírtў-éight, ‖ néithĕr hére nŏr thére.   3/3

Not only do the two phrases of line 2 repeat the three-stress pattern of line 1, but, as the breves (˘) indicating unstressed syllables show, the pacing of the three stresses in each phrase is the same. The poem ends with a similar balance:

Ă mómĕnt thát, ‖ évĕn nów,   2/2

Ĭ cárrў ín mў bódў.   3

The poem closes with a regular pattern of stressed and unstressed syllables: She is poised for the next stage.

Even in its use of enjambment, the poem is relaxed; note the break between lines 11 and 12, which connects full clauses. Caesuras usually occur midline, suggesting balance. One exception, line 13—"a wand, an enchantment, shaping it"—evokes balance in a different way by framing the central phrase. Also, the enjambment of "shaping it / into something languid and new" seems quietly expressive, implying transformation. So, too, with the early caesura in line 19, "I wake," where the imbalance suggests the sudden waking to the wafting curtain.

Spires builds her poem in four seven-line stanzas. The balanced form evokes the order and serenity the speaker feels in the expectancy around and within her. It is July, the middle of the year, the middle of the summer, and she too is in the middle, "thirty-eight, neither here nor there." Anchored solidly in the present, she can contemplate how her life "slows and deepens" and can move through time. Her imagination climbs from the vivid present in stanza 1, to the drowsiness within her in stanza 2, to a memory of a dream a year ago in stanza 3, then arrives in stanza 4 at the anticipation of January, winter, a new year, and the child's birth: the future she holds within her. Each stanza contains a stage and yet leads naturally to the next, just as each part of her pregnancy leads naturally to birth. The form of the poem contains and creates its meaning.

QUESTIONS AND SUGGESTIONS

1. Here are two poems printed as prose. Experiment with turning them into verse by dividing the lines in different ways. What different effects can you create? The originals, as well as all further notes to the Questions and Suggestions, can be found in Appendix II.

   a) **Night Winds**
      The old old winds that blew when chaos was, what do they tell the clattered trees that I should weep?

   b) **Liu Ch'e**
      The rustling of the silk is discontinued, dust drifts over the court-yard, there is no sound of foot-fall, and the leaves scurry into heaps and lie still, and she the rejoicer of the heart is beneath them: a wet leaf that clings to the threshold.

2. In the "Poems to Consider" section that follows, look thoroughly at how William Stafford's use of stanzas paces his "Traveling Through the Dark." Consider in particular how each stanza marks a different stage in the speaker's experience with the deer, showing his deepening response and leading to his final decision. Notice, too, that he lets the details show us how he feels rather than telling us directly. What effect does Stafford create by closing the poem with a shorter stanza? Write a poem of similar length and stanza form about a similar subject in which a speaker comes upon an animal unexpectedly, looks closely at it, and reacts in some way. Concentrate on letting the responses be suggested through the imagery.

3. Here is a favorite technique of the French Dadaists and Surrealists. Create a **found poem:** find a piece of prose that you find evocative, troubling, or amusing (one of the first found poems was taken from a travel book about Tonga) and try shaping it into a poem in verse. Below is a memo from IBM that the poet Jeff Worley discovered. You might try shaping it yourself. The poem he created, and later published in *The Southern Poetry Review*, appears in Appendix II, p. 321.

IBM Memo: Mouse Balls Available as Field Replacement Unit (FRU)

Mouse balls are now available as FRU. Therefore, if a mouse fails to operate or begins to perform erratically, it may need a ball replacement. Because of the delicate nature of this procedure, replacement of mouse balls should only be attempted by properly trained personnel. Before proceeding, determine the type of mouse balls by examining the underside of the mouse. Domestic balls will be larger and harder than foreign balls. Ball removal procedures differ. Foreign balls can be replaced using the pop-off method. Replace domestic balls using the twist-off method. Mouse balls are usually not static sensitive; however, excessive handling can result in sudden discharge. Upon completion of ball replacement, the mouse may be used immediately. It is recommended that each replacer have a pair of spare balls for maintaining optimum customer satisfaction, and that any customer missing his balls should suspect local personnel of removing these necessary items for their own unofficial use.

4. Benjamin Franklin described training himself as a writer by reading carefully several times, but not memorizing, a passage of prose he admired; then, after putting it aside for a time, *writing it himself in his own words*. Comparing his version with the original was illuminating—and occasionally he'd improved upon the original. Try this experiment with a *poem* you like but don't know very well.

5. Choose a poem of your own that you aren't satisfied with but aren't sure how to improve, and experiment with its form. Rearrange the sentences into lines either much shorter or much longer than in the original version. Try breaking the poem into stanzas of two, then three lines, and so on. If something *feels right*, you may have found a way to reawaken the poem.

6. Write a poem either (a) in strictly alternating lines of seven and five *words* in length, or (b) in stanzas progressively one line shorter or one line longer than the first one. What difficulties do you find? What opportunities? Such merely arbitrary, mechanical patterns (to work with or against) can often be a helpful control in composition.

7. Browse an encyclopedia or surf the Web to find an item that intrigues you, and write a poem using the information. Maybe: manatee, ice shelf, armored catfish, Lake Texcoco, or "Cool Papa" Bell.

8. Locate a reproduction of Gustav Klimt's famous painting *The Kiss*. Is Marta Tomes's poem (p. 46) faithful to it? Might a painting give you a good subject for a poem? (*Voices in the Gallery*, Dannie and Joan Abse, eds., The Tate Gallery, 1986, is a lively collection of poems and the works of art on which they are based.)

POEMS TO CONSIDER

Traveling through the Dark   1960
WILLIAM STAFFORD (1914–1993)

Traveling through the dark I found a deer
dead on the edge of the Wilson River road.
It is usually best to roll them into the canyon:
that road is narrow; to swerve might make more dead.

By glow of the tail-light I stumbled back of the car   5
and stood by the heap, a doe, a recent killing;
she had stiffened already, almost cold.
I dragged her off; she was large in the belly.

My fingers touching her side brought me the reason—
her side was warm; her fawn lay there waiting,   10
alive, still, never to be born.
Beside that mountain road I hesitated.

The car aimed ahead its lowered parking lights;
under the hood purred the steady engine.
I stood in the glare of the warm exhaust turning red;   15
around our group I could hear the wilderness listen.

I thought hard for us all—my only swerving—,
then pushed her over the edge into the river.

April   2002
HETTIE JONES (b. 1934)

one robin, one yellow willow
love braving the rain on the wrong highway—
honestly, I don't know what to think!

a Canada goose, a headlong cloud

Open the window!   5
under my hand, your wet skin
you looking?

thirty April mornings

one white tulip, one red

one precise interior   10
one persistent stem

2

cherry blossom, silver bridge

don't ever take my sweet
for weak

peaches! peaches! April   15
has no way to get there yet

quiet room, roaring sky
April, I'm almost over you again

One Heart   2000
LI-YOUNG LEE (b. 1957)

Look at the birds. Even flying
is born

out of nothing. The first sky
is inside you, Friend, open

at either end of day.   5
The work of wings

was always freedom, fastening
one heart to every falling thing.

Mulroney   2000
BARON WORMSER (b. 1948)

Where the hell do these people come from?
Mulroney asked me.
We were crumpling up a Sunday *New York Times*
That had found its way into the pile of papers
We used as packing filler for glass jars of honey.   5
We were wadding up the wedding notices—
Young lawyers in love with account executives.
Their fathers were surgeons and vice-presidents;
Their mothers were psychologists and counselors.

We were working as prep cooks at a ski resort   10
And packing boxes at a place down in the valley
To make a couple extra bucks.

Mulroney didn't know anything except
Eat, fuck, sleep, ski. A regular physical guy,
He barely knew what Vietnam was   15
And it was 1975.
He could have lived any time, any place,
And for all ostensible purposes he was.
He'd wake up in the morning in the cabin
We shared and it was cold and he'd curse   20
And try to coax whatever woman he was sleeping
With to start the fire in the woodstove.
I could hear him cooing in his gravelly
Flattened brogue of a voice.
A few mornings the woman would get up, most   25
Mornings not. Defeats and victories and
Sunlight licking the frosted windows
And Mulroney full of the dumb sap of time
And scratching his balls.

Where the hell do these people come from?   30
He asked me.
Mulroney, you dim honky ass, I said.
They are groomed to run the show
And he looked down at the crumpled vivacity
Of the young brides in newsprint   35
And he broke into an almost lovely smile
And he said in a voice that could have
Passed for thoughtful, How sad.

Celebrating the Freak   1980
CYNTHIA MACDONALD (b. 1928)

—for May Swenson

The freak is	the other
The freak is	wrapped in lamb cloth because
It is precious	
The freak is	precious
The freak is	the other 5
Alarming us	when it talks through the crook in
	its arm as it has no mouth
Astounding us	when it threads its legless, armless
	body through the eye of a needle
Amazing us	when it plays a violin concerto with 10
	its feet
The German freak	replaces vaccine for the Germans
The Finnish freak	swims the Baltic for the Finns

The Armenian freak	disarms the cruelest Armenians	
The Polish freak	is a totem for the Poles	15
The freak wears	well	
Though it dies early		
The freak wears	silk and velvet to promote its nobility	
The freak wears	on the outside what we conceal	
The freak wears	down. It becomes tired of being	20
The freak. It retires	to a country home built to its	
Freak specifications:	low toilets or moving staircases or	
	beds the size of billiard tables	
The freak leaves us	bereft, forcing a little	
Mutilation somewhere	to set things right	25
To wreak	penance	
To set	the freak flags flying.	

The Kiss   1995
MARTA TOMES*

He knows he is irresistible. No doubt he has
looked in the mirror wearing his stained glass robe

and seen the cropped curls and stately shoulders
of Marc Antony. He cups my head like an infant

and lifts my chin toward him. He thinks I am shy;   5
my eyes are closed, my face turned away. He thinks

that this arm slung about his neck is my embrace,
that I've shrunken my shoulders forward so the dress

slides down my white arms just for him. This swirling
pekoe aura around me, he believes, exudes   10

my great excitement. I am trapped on my knees
on a cliff of flowers, and I've braced myself.

My bare toes tense forward, stiff as triggers.

In the Beginning   2002
SARAH KENNEDY (b. 1960)

When the man I'd only met twice sat me
beside him at the dinner before his wedding
to my runaway older sister, it had long since
begun. Fourteen, I could only wonder why
he offered me raw oysters from a spoon,   5
Just to watch you swallow. My father
was reaching toward some young woman

while my mother looked away, but I'd known
for years never to question parents; I'd heard
the stories, passed down by the older girls   10
with their worn dresses; I almost remembered
Dad slapping me in my highchair, again
and again, for sealing my lips against
breakfast oranges. When my brother-in-law
whispered, weeks later, Let's keep this   15
in the family, laughing and pouring me
vodka, when my sister shrugged, humor him,
all men act like that, it was already bred into me
to do as he said. When he laid me down
in his old pickup — What you need is to learn   20
to love — it had already begun, years before,
it was like lying, new-born again,
in my father's hands.

❖ Names of Horses   1977
DONALD HALL (b. 1928)

All winter your brute shoulders strained against collars, padding
and steerhide over the ash hames, to haul
sledges of cordwood for drying through spring and summer,
for the Glenwood stove next winter, and for the simmering range.

In April you pulled cartloads of manure to spread on the fields,   5
dark manure of Holsteins, and knobs of your own clustered with oats.
All summer you mowed the grass in meadow and hayfield,
    the mowing machine
clacketing beside you, while the sun walked high in the morning;

and after noon's heat, you pulled a clawed rake through the same acres,
gathering stacks, and dragged the wagon from stack to stack,   10
and the built hayrack back, uphill to the chaffy barn,
three loads of hay a day from standing grass in the morning.

Sundays you trotted the two miles to church with the light load
of a leather quartertop buggy, and grazed in the sound of hymns.
Generation on generation, your neck rubbed the windowsill   15
of the stall, smoothing the wood as the sea smooths glass.

When you were old and lame, when your shoulders hurt bending
    to graze,
one October the man, who fed you and kept you, and harnessed you
    every morning,
led you through corn stubble to sandy ground above Eagle Pond,
and dug a hole beside you where you stood shuddering in your skin,   20

and lay the shotgun's muzzle in the boneless hollow behind your ear,
and fired the slug into your brain, and felled you into your grave,
shoveling sand to cover you, setting goldenrod upright above you,
where by next summer a dent in the ground made your monument.

For a hundred and fifty years, in the pasture of dead horses,   25
roots of pine trees pushed through the pale curves of your ribs,
yellow blossoms flourished above you in autumn, and in winter
frost heaved your bones in the ground—old toilers, soil makers:

O Roger, Mackerel, Riley, Ned, Nellie, Chester, Lady Ghost.

A Grave   1924
MARIANNE MOORE (1887–1972)

Man looking into the sea,
taking the view from those who have as much right to it as you
    have to it yourself,
it is human nature to stand in the middle of a thing,
but you cannot stand in the middle of this;
the sea has nothing to give but a well excavated grave.   5
The firs stand in a procession, each with an emerald turkey-foot
    at the top,
reserved as their contours, saying nothing;
repression, however, is not the most obvious characteristic of the sea;
the sea is a collector, quick to return a rapacious look.
There are others besides you who have worn that look—   10
whose expression is no longer a protest, the fish no longer investigate
    them
for their bones have not lasted:
men lower nets, unconscious of the fact that they are desecrating a grave,
and row quickly away—the blades of the oars
moving together like the feet of water-spiders as if there were no such
    thing as death.   15
The wrinkles progress among themselves in a phalanx—beautiful
    under networks of foam,
and fade breathlessly while the sea rustles in and out of the seaweed;
the birds swim through the air at top speed, emitting cat-calls as
    heretofore—
the tortoise-shell scourges about the feet of the cliffs, in motion
    beneath them
and the ocean, under the pulsation of lighthouses and noise of
    bell-buoys,
advances as usual, looking as if it were not that ocean in which   20
    dropped things are bound to sink—
in which they turn and twist, it is neither with volition nor consciousness.

Storm Window

CONRAD HILBERRY (b. 1928)

1980

At the top of the ladder, a gust catches the glass
and he is falling. He and the window topple
backwards like a piece of deception slowly
coming undone. After the instant of terror,
he feels easy, as though he were a boy   5
falling back on his own bed. For years,
he has clamped his hands to railings, balanced
against the pitch of balconies and cliffs
and fire towers. For years, he has feared falling.
At last, he falls. Still holding the frame,   10
he sees the sky and trees come clear
in the wavering glass. In another second
the pane will shatter over his whole length,
but now, he lies back on air, falling.

3

MAKING THE LINE (I)

The universe is rhythmic. Light arrives from the sun in waves. The sounds of a passing car reach us in waves. And if that car isn't moving smoothly through traffic, if it weaves and sputters, we notice immediately, and sense something is amiss (and so might a cop). In most things, our bodies naturally fall into a rhythm, from breathing, to running, to washing windows, to rowing a boat. When we hear another's voice, we tune in to the rising and falling rhythm of speech. We hear something very different when a person dashes from a house yelling, "Help me! Lord, help me!" than we hear when someone murmurs the same words as she slides a spoon into an oozing Kahlua mocha mousse in chocolate sauce. Poetry exploits what we know of the natural rhythms of spoken language.

To create a line with a regular rhythm, the poet capitalizes on some prominent element in the language and repeats it relatively regularly. Languages differ; each has its own distinctive rhythm and from it develops the ways it makes its lines. Latin verse, for example, uses the duration of vowels, long or short, as the controlling element. Chinese, in which all words are monosyllabic, counts syllables. As it developed, English poetry counted stresses, which we can hear as beats, and since the Renaissance, English has also traditionally counted syllables. This counting is **meter,** which means measurement; in making a line a poet makes a **measure** of beats. We hear, even *feel*, the rhythm immediately. From infancy we've responded to it:

Round and round the mulberry bush,
The monkey chased the weasel.
Round and round the mulberry bush,
Pop! goes the weasel.

A small child hearing this sung doesn't need to know what a mulberry bush, a weasel, or a monkey is (or that they make a rare trio!), yet because the rhythm sets up an expectation, the child will giggle when she hears the surprise of "Pop!" You'll not get the same response if you say, "Repeatedly the monkey chased the weasel around a mulberry bush and then the weasel popped up." We might sketch out the rhythm of the verse by using waves, marking stressed syllables with the peaks of waves and unstressed syllables with troughs:

Round and round the mulberry bush

The monkey chased the weasel,

Round and round the mulberry bush

Pop! goes the weasel.

The wave pattern shows us what our ears register: a relatively regular pattern of rising and falling emphasized by how the lines break the phrases. Normally, singing this verse to a child, we make a dramatic stop after "Pop!" that substitutes for an unstressed syllable and allows the meter to resume with "goes." Alternating between stressed and unstressed syllables in English sounds natural and rhythmic. When unstressed and stressed syllables don't seem to alternate, when many stressed or many unstressed syllables pile up together we begin to hear dissonance, as in this example: "The insidious monkey chased the agitated weasel again and again around the mulberry bush and then the weasel surprised him and popped out." Decorating a sentence with modifiers often hobbles its sound.

In making lines of verse in English, poets have traditionally used what we call **syllable-stress,** or "accentual-syllabic," meter which counts syllables and stresses. Dominant from Shakespeare in the sixteenth century to Yeats and Frost early in the twentieth century, syllable-stress meter remains vital in the work of many poets writing today; poets such as Marilyn Hacker, Molly Peacock, Henry Taylor, Mark Jarman, Marilyn Nelson, and Rafael Campo have explored its resources. But with increasing popularity throughout the twentieth century, other ways of conceiving the line sprang up; since what unites them is that they *aren't* systematically metrical, they are usually summed up vaguely as "free" verse. We looked at several poems in these measures in Chapter 2, and we will turn to others in Chapter 4. First, though, what is this meter poems are "free" from?

Syllable-Stress Meter

As the name implies, syllable-stress meter counts both the number of stresses and the number of syllables. For metrical purposes we count only two levels of stress: a syllable is either relatively stressed or relatively unstressed. The stress is *relative* to the context in which we hear the syllable. We call the *pattern* that the unstressed and stressed syllables form the meter. The basic unit, one wave, is called a **foot.** It's like one step in a dance. In English, the most common kind of foot is an unstressed syllable followed by a stressed syllable, called an **iamb,** the meter **iambic:** te TUM, as in "a foot" or "will bloom" or "the monkey chased the weasel." The last example illustrates two points. First, when the pattern ends on an unstressed syllable, as with "weasel," we normally don't take that syllable into account as part of the meter. Second, the metrical pattern can move across words; a word may be part of two separate feet as the last syllable of "monkey" begins the second iamb.

Several iambs strung together produce the pattern or meter of a line as in the opening lines from Housman's "Loveliest of Trees" (p. 70). Read them out loud:

Lóvelĭĕst | ŏf trées, | thĕ chér|rў nów

Ĭs húng | wĭth blóom | ălóng | thĕ bóugh

You'll pick up the distinctions between stressed and unstressed syllables more readily if you read aloud passages in which we discuss meter. As linguist Derek Attridge says,

> Poetry *takes place* in time; its movement through time . . . is its *rhythm.* It should be read aloud whenever possible, and even when read silently it should take up the same amount of time that reading aloud would give it.

In general, stress falls on the most significant syllables, on "content" words, those that offer the most meaning: on nouns, verbs, adverbs, and adjectives. In the lines above we easily hear these syllables stressed: "love-" (in "loveliest"), "tree," "cher-" (in "cherry") "hung," "bloom," and "bough" above. Function words—those that depend on other words for meaning—are usually unstressed; these are articles ("the"), prepositions ("of," "with"), conjunctions ("and," "when"), pronouns ("it," "we"), auxiliary verbs ("is" in "is hung"), demonstratives ("that"), and adverbs that accompany adjectives and adverbs ("so," "more").

Because Housman's lines above are cast in iambic meter, we also place stress on the syllables "now" and "-long" in "along." Polysyllabic words usually take stress on at least one syllable. In the preposition "along" within Housman's line, the syllable "-long" becomes stressed because just before and after it we have syllables we hear as unstressed, and these syllables themselves come before and after syllables that receive a lot of stress ("<u>BLOOM</u> a<u>LONG</u> the <u>BOUGH</u>"). Stress is often a matter of degree and context. A syllable that is not stressed in one context might naturally be in another. The word "now" receives stress in the line above both because it follows the unstressed syllable "y" in "cherry," and it is the last sound in an iambic line. But in another context, "now" might not be stressed:

Now grab your keys and leave my house.
You lied to me, you nasty louse.

In the passage above the pronoun "you" isn't stressed, but "me" is; pronouns take stress depending on their relationship to the syllables around them. As you read out loud the lines below from Shakespeare's Sonnet 73, listen for where you hear syllables stressed.

That time of year thou mayst in me behold
When yellow leaves, or none, or few, do hang
Upon those boughs that shake against the cold,
Bare ruined choirs where late the sweet birds sang.

Now copy these lines out, and then, starting at the end of each line and moving backward, mark the places that sound stressed to you by placing a stress mark (´) above the first vowel in each stressed syllable ("boughs"). If you're not sure if a syllable will be stressed, skip and go on to a syllable you feel sure is stressed. Start with content words that normally get stressed. A good dictionary (indispensable to any poet) will indicate the primary accent of polysyllabic words. After you have marked the syllables you're sure about, look at those you skipped. Do they come before or after an unstressed syllable? Then they may be stressed, especially if stressing them naturally allows for an iamb. In Appendix II you'll find a scansion for Shakespeare's lines.

> Most *arts attain their effects by using a fixed element and a variable.*
>
> —Ezra Pound

Because iambs are the typical (and thus most neutral) foot, iambic meter serves as the norm in English metrical verse. When we come upon a metrical poem, we can normally assume that most of it will be written in iambs. But not all of it. Poets use many substitute rhythms and varied feet to create nuances of tone, emotion, and emphasis and to make a statement or an image quieter, stronger, stranger, or funnier. In two phrases in the fourth line of his poem above, "Bare ruined choirs" and "sweet birds sang," Shakespeare places content words ("bare" and "birds") where unstressed syllables would normally appear in an iambic line, making these phrases more emphatic. Compared with the rhythmic regularity of the opening lines, the greater stress makes the bare trees seem starker, the speaker's anguish more intense.

Rhythm

Something wonderful happens when the words of a poem flow through a metrical pattern. We hear a human voice at a heightened moment, speaking a rhythm that is never precisely regular or mechanical. The usual stresses of words, their varying importance or placement in lines, their sounds, as well as the pauses and syntactic links among them, all work to give each line an individual movement and flavor, a distinct rhythm.

Poetic rhythm comes from blending the fixed (meter) and the flexible (speech). It's neither precisely the *te TUM te TUM* of meter nor a reproduction of idiomatic speech. A poem is read as something between the two. We may show the relationship this way:

$$\frac{\text{speech}}{\text{meter (line)}} \;=\; \text{poetic rhythm}$$

The flow of speech slows, becoming more distinct, as we listen for the binary values (unstressed, stressed) that flow into the meter. Subtleties we may be unaware of, in the hurry of speech, become magnified and we then perceive them. A line of iambs can create an exacting rhythmic character, if we listen.

Consider a simple sentence (which is part of the first line of Richard Wilbur's "Juggler": "A ball will bounce, but less and less." We would be as wrong to read the line mechanically, emphasizing each stressed syllable the same ("a BALL will BOUNCE, but LESS and LESS") as we would be wrong to read it as we might normally speak it ("a ball will BOUNCE, but less and less"). In conversation and in prose, we zip through everything except the key elements. In fact, depending on what we mean to say, we might place the primary stress on *any* of the eight words in the sentence. To distinguish a ball from a bottle, for instance, we might say, "a <u>BALL</u> will bounce, but less and less." In distinguishing one ball from a box of balls, we might say, "<u>A</u> ball will bounce, but less and less." Similarly, we might find a perfectly good reason for saying "a ball <u>WILL</u> bounce, but less and less" and so on, depending on what we are trying to stress.

Because this sentence appears in a poem, however, we read it neither in rigid rhythm nor in the usual dash of speech. In the poem the meter changes the speech-run a little, giving the sentence a more measured movement; the speech-run of the sentence loosens the march-step of the meter. The result is distinctive: rhythm. *Speech flowing over meter produces rhythm.*

Wilbur's four perfectly regular iambs, *te* TUM *te* TUM *te* TUM *te* TUM, create their own deliciously distinctive rhythm. Within regularity or, rather, because of it, small differences in stress give the effect of less and less force and so seem to imitate the way a ball slows to a stop in smaller and smaller arcs. The difference in stress from "A" to "ball" is relatively great, that from "will" to "bounce" somewhat less great, and so on through the line. The *difference* between each unstressed syllable and the following stressed syllable diminishes in succession. No two iambs sound the same. If we draw the difference of stress in each foot, it might look something like this:

A ball will bounce, but less and less

Using the conventions of scansion, we would mark it:

Ă báll wĭll bóunce bŭt léss ănd léss.

The first depiction shows the flexibility of the rhythm, the second its steadiness. The meter is regular, yet fluid as the ball's motion.

The Lengths of Metrical Lines

In English most lines in meter are four or five feet long, but a poet can form a line of any length, short or long, to create particular effects. Let's look at some passages that exemplify different line lengths which meter measures, each of which has a name. Take it slowly. Read the lines aloud. Don't worry about the occasional feet that aren't iambs—we'll explain them in a moment.

> *Formal poetry should continually remain in contact with the speech and the life around it . . . .*
> —Louise Bogan

Monometer, a line consisting of one ("mono") foot (˘ ´)—one metrical unit—rarely occurs except in stanzas of mixed line lengths, nor does **dimeter,** a line of two ("di") feet (˘ ´ ˘ ´). George Herbert uses both (along with lines of other lengths) in his "Easter Wings" (p. 105) in which he addresses God about humanity's diminishment by sin and enlargement by grace. In stanza 2 we find these lines (don't let the seventeenth century spelling throw you):

Thŏu dídst | sŏ pún|ĭsh sínne

    Thăt Í |bĕcáme

    Mŏst thínne.

    Wĭth thée

Lĕt mé | cŏmbíne

Ănd féel | thĭs dáy | thў víc|tŏrĭe . . .

Note: Parentheses indicate syllables that could be interpreted equally the other way, as here we are aware that some readers might hear "Most" as stressed; by counting it as unstressed, we are emphasizing the iamb.

To create a sense of shrinking, Herbert creates shorter and shorter lines, then turns the poem and creates lines of longer and longer lengths to express how he grows through grace.

The passage from Herbert begins and ends with **trimeter** lines, those of three feet (˘ ´ ˘ ´ ˘ ´) which poets use more commonly. For Theodore Roethke in "My Papa's Waltz," trimeter echoes the beats of a rolling waltz (p. 136). In this stanza Emily Dickinson (1830–1886) uses the line's brevity to express something distilled to its essence:

Súccĕss | ĭs cóun|tĕd sweet|ĕst

Bў thŏse | whŏ né'er | súccĕed.

Tŏ cóm|prĕhénd | ă néc|tăr

Rĕquír|ĕs sór|ĕst néed.

Tetrameter, a very common and serviceable meter, uses a line of four feet (˘ ´ ˘ ´ ˘ ´ ˘ ´). Here Paul Laurence Dunbar uses it in the opening of "We Wear the Mask" (p. 191) to create a terse, and ironic declaration:

Wĕ wéar | thĕ másk | thăt gríns | ănd líes,

Ĭt hídes | oŭr chéeks | ănd shádes | ŏur éyes,

Thĭs débt | wĕ páy | tŏ hú|măn guíle;

Wĭth tórn | ănd bléed|ĭng héarts | wĕ smíle,

Ănd móuth | wĭth mý|rĭăd | súbtlĕ|tĭes.

Pentameter is a line of five feet (˘ ´ ˘ ´ ˘ ´ ˘ ´ ˘ ´). Iambic pentameter, more flexibile than tetrameter, has been the standard line of verse in English from Shakespeare to the present. Unrhymed, iambic pentameter is called **blank verse.** Here Claude McKay, in the first stanza of "The Tropics in New York," employs the richness of pentameter to create a West Indian's longing for home as he looks at the bounty of a fruit stand:

Băná|năs rípe | ănd gréen, | ănd gín|gĕr-róot,

  Cócŏa | ĭn póds | ănd ál|lĭ gá|tŏr péars,

Ănd tán|gĕrínes | ănd man|gŏes ănd | grápe frúit,

  Fít fŏr | thĕ hígh|ĕst príze | ăt pár|ĭsh fáirs,

Hexameter (or **Alexandrine**) is a line of six feet (˘ ´ ˘ ´ ˘ ´ ˘ ´ ˘ ´ ˘ ´). Hexameter is not used frequently, but for Robert Francis (1901–1987) in "Excellence" its longer line becomes a fluid vehicle for showing the high jumper's arc:

ˣÉx|cĕllénce | ĭs míl|lĭmét|ĕrs ănd | nót míles.

Frŏm póor | tŏ góod | ĭs gréat. ‖ Frŏm góod | tŏ bést | ĭs smáll.

Frŏm ál‖mŏst bést | tŏ bést | sŏmetímes | nŏt méa‖sŭráb‖lĕ.

Thĕ mán | whŏ léaps | thĕ hígh‖ĕst léaps | pĕrháps | ăn ínch

Ăbóve | thĕ rún‖nĕr-úp. ‖ Hŏw glór‖ĭoús | thăt ínch

Ănd thát | splít-sé‖cŏnd lóng‖ĕr ín | thĕ aír | bĕfóre | thĕ fáll.

Note: The superscript x above the first word marks the dropped unstressed syllable at the beginning of a line.

Heptameter, a line of seven feet, is rare, as are octameter and so on. T. S. Eliot (1888–1965) opens a stanza from "The Love Song of J. Alfred Prufrock" by repeating a heptameter line and following it with pentameter and hexameter lines:

Thĕ yél‖lŏw fóg | thăt rúbs | ĭts báck | ŭpón | thĕ wín‖dŏw pánes,

Thĕ yél‖lŏw fóg | thăt rúbs | ĭts múz‖zlĕ ón | thĕ wín‖dŏw pánes,

Licked its tongue into the corners of the evening,

Lingered upon the pools that stand in drains,

Let fall upon its back the soot that falls from chimneys,

Slipped by the terrace, made a sudden leap,

And seeing that it was a soft October night,

Curled once about the house, and fell asleep.

As an exercise, perhaps mark above or on a sheet of scratch paper the stressed and unstressed syllables above. We will discuss some of these lines later in the chapter; a fuller scansion appears in Appendix II (p. 322).

To clarify some of these points, let's try out some basics. On a sheet of paper write out four lines with marks for four lines of iambic tetrameter, leaving a space between them, like this:

⌣ ⁄ ⌣ ⁄ ⌣ ⁄ ⌣ ⁄

⌣ ⁄ ⌣ ⁄ ⌣ ⁄ ⌣ ⁄

⏑ ⁄   ⏑ ⁄   ⏑ ⁄   ⏑ ⁄

⏑ ⁄   ⏑ ⁄   ⏑ ⁄   ⏑ ⁄

Next write short sentences to fit into the pattern. Don't worry as much about what you say as getting the lines to move naturally. Try to make a pronounced difference in emphasis between stressed and unstressed syllables. At first you may find it easier to rely on one- and two-syllable words. If you get stuck, try another topic. Stay loose and open. You should end up with four simple lines, something like this:

Ă blízzărd róarĕd thróugh tówn lăst níght.

Wĕ héard ĭt blást ăgaínst thĕ róof.

Ăt dáwn wĕ wóke tŏ héavў drífts

thăt cóverĕd éverўthíng wĭth snów.

Hardly high art, but this is just practice. Now go back to your four lines and try making each one longer by one iamb. First try something simple: "A sudden blizzard roared through town last night." Then try shifting words and attempting more dramatic changes: "All night we heard the blizzard's roaring wind / but woke in morning to a spacious calm." When you feel comfortable with iambic pentameter lines, try trimeter lines; try shortening the lines to three feet, and maybe add a rhyme or slant rhyme:

The blizzard roared through town
and beat our roof last night.
At dawn we found the drifts
had covered all in white.

With some tinkering, you will find ways to enjamb a line or two:

In morning heavy drifts
had smothered cars in white.

Feel free to keep playing with your draft. Save it; we will return to it later.

Substitution and Variations

Writing in meter for the first time may feel stiff, but like learning to drive a stick shift, one soon gets the hang of it, enjoys the control, and loses the suspicion that meter gets in the way.

When working in meter, poets have many ways of creating flexibility; varying line line lengths is a simple way, as Eliot does in the stanza describing fog through cat images and as does Frost to create the speaker's daze in "After Apple-Picking" (p. 111), where lines range from monometer to hexameter. Herbert in "Easter Wings" (p. 105) and Wilbur in "Hamlen Brook" (p. 72) invent stanzas. Notice how Wilbur's use of shorter lines before and after the stanza's single pentameter suggests the parallel (and sometimes reflecting) worlds above and below the surface of the water.

Another rich source of rhythmic flexibility in the metrical line is **substitution.** As we noted, the iamb (*te TUM*) is the basic foot. Substitution simply means that another kind of foot replaces an iamb in a line. You may have noticed a number of substitutions in the passages we scanned previously to illustrate line lengths. Some of the substitute feet are:

- **Trochee** (trochaic): stressed syllable followed by unstressed syllable: *TUM te*; as this foot is just an inverted iamb, it is sometimes called an *inversion*.

    Fit for   choirs where   Rotten

- **Spondee** (spondaic): two stressed syllables together: *TUM TUM.*

    not miles   bare ruined   grape fruit

- **Pyrrhic:** two unstressed syllables: *te te;* usually appears with a spondee.

    at the front door   hidden in tall   as it ran light

- **Anapest** (anapestic): two unstressed syllables followed by a stressed syllable: *te te TUM.*

    intervene   of a love   never believed

- **Dactyl** (dactylic): stressed followed by two unstressed syllables: *TUM te te.*

    Loveliest   slow as a   Useful to

There are many other kinds of feet, from **bacchic,** *te TUM TUM* (˘ ´ ´), to **amphibrach** *te TUM te* (˘ ´ ˘), to even four syllable feet taken from Greek prosody. Try not to let the terminology rankle. Just bear in mind that in English the normal metrical line is between seven and eleven syllables, usually eight or ten, which alternate between unstressed and stressed syllables. Generally speaking, a poet may at times vary the rhythm by varying the line length; by inverting unstressed and stressed syllables; by substituting a stressed syllable for an unstressed one (or vice versa); by adding an unstressed syllable (at the end of a line, for instance, or in substituting an anapest for an iamb); or even by dropping an unstressed syllable (usually at the beginning of a line). As long as the poet's substitutions aren't too frequent and the lines around them are relatively regular, the meter doesn't get lost.

Let's briefly elaborate on a few of these points, including duple endings, anacrusis, and promotion. When an extra unstressed syllable ends a line of iambic meter we have a **duple ending** (also called extra-syllable or feminine), which we see in the duple rhyme of this short iambic pentameter poem by Timothy Steele (b. 1948):

Epitaph

Hĕre líes Sĭr Táct, ă diplŏmátĭc fél‖lŏw

Whŏse sílence wás nŏt góldĕn, bŭt jŭst yél‖lŏw.

The unstressed endings close the line on a down note, emphasizing Tact's lack of bravery. As we said earlier, for the purposes of meter, we don't count the extra syllable. When two unstressed syllables end an iambic line, we have a **triple ending,** rare except for comic effects, as in these lines from Byron's *Don Juan*:

Hĕ léarn'd thĕ árts ŏf rídĭng, féncĭng, gún‖nĕrў,

Ănd hów tŏ scále ă fórtrĕss—ŏr ă nún‖nĕrў.

The added syllables don't keep the line from being iambic hexameter.

Although not counted in assessing meter, duple (and triple) endings often contribute significantly to rhythm. Look at these lines of Shakespeare's Sonnet 29:

Háplў Ĭ thínk ŏn thĕe—ănd thén mў státe,

Líke tŏ | thĕ lárk | ăt bréak | ŏf dáy | ărís‖ĭng

Frŏm súl‖lĕn éarth,| sĭngs hýmns | ăt héav‖ĕn's gáte;

In the second line here, the extra unstressed syllable adds to the speed or sweep of Shakespeare's enjambment, after which the sentence comes to its main verb in the emphatic spondee "sings hymns . . . ." The rhythmic *lift* of the lines evokes the speaker's rising spirits.

When the unstressed syllable that begins an iambic line is dropped, we have **anacrusis,** marked in scansion by a superscript ^{x}, as in Eliot's

^{x}Lícked | ĭts tóngue | ⁽ʹ⁾íntŏ | thĕ córnĕrs ⁽ʹ⁾ŏf | thĕ évĕn‖ĭng,

Língĕred | ŭpón | thĕ póols | thăt stánd | ĭn dráins,

Anacrusis is distinct from substitution of an initial trochee, as in the second line, although the effects sound similar—starting a line on a stressed syllable. Counted like regular iambs, anacruses create minor variations and, like duple endings, do not change the metrical count. Anacrusis may help through rhythm to suggest force, abruptness, or speed. Francis's use of it to open "Excellence" ("ˣExcellence is millimeters and not miles") registers how small increments can make a high jumper the winner. In "Loveliest of Trees" (p. 70), Housman uses it to depict fleeting time:

Now of | my three|score years | and ten,

ˣTwen|ty will | not come | again,

As we discussed early in the chapter, under certain conditions, we may credit as stressed, or **promote,** syllables that would normally be unstressed in speech. (Crediting them doesn't imply that we fully stress or emphasize the syllable woodenly, instead we give the syllable a full pronunciation.) **Promotion** occurs when a normally unstressed syllable appears in a normally stressed position and the syllables before and after it are unstressed. Consider "on" and "of" in this line you will recall from Sonnet 73 (p. 34):

That on the ashes of his youth doth lie,

In speech, these prepositions would receive little or no stress. For the purposes of scansion, however, both count as stressed and are marked in parentheses to indicate the promotion. Promotion comes about because the iambic norm creates an expectation. So with very little (if any) differential in stress, we are able to sense the meter ticking along regularly within the speech rhythm and to hear "on" and "of" as stressed syllables.

Because meter has only two values (unstressed and stressed), it simplifies the many levels of stress we hear in speech. This simplification lets us perceive the common pattern in rhythms that vary but are similar. We count syllables as unstressed or stressed only *relatively*, that is, by listening and comparing adjacent syllables, not by some absolute measurement. Thus, meter trains us to be aware of subtleties. We sort and weigh, as we usually do not when reading or writing prose. The taut web responds to the slightest touch.

Now return to the drafts of your quatrain. Try a few substitutions. First go for the easy and natural substitution of starting a line with a trochee instead of an iamb:

Over our roof the blizzard roared . . .

Or substitute a pyrrhic foot and a spondee for two iambs:

As the storm roared into our town . . .

You might go back to the trimeter lines you made and see if you can adjust them into pentameter lines. Highlighted below are the substitutions. We have an enjambment (line 1), a substituted spondee (line 2), a substituted anapest (line 3), and a substituted trochee (line 4):

> Although we heard the blizzard roar and beat
> our roof all night, at dawn we saw calm drifts
> had blanketed cars, erased the widest streets,
> and left a muffled white world in its wake.

Now try out a new quatrain, and see where you can take it. The close discipline of adding and subtracting feet, rearranging words and phrases, trying different approaches will often help you discover opportunities that normally wouldn't have occurred to you. Because working in meter requires us to weigh our words and examine their relationships carefully, poets value the rigors of meter. It often leads us down more fruitful paths than we would have found without it.

A Little Scanning

Through **scansion,** identifying the meter of a passage, we find those *divergences* from the norm (variations, substitutions, anomalies) that reveal a poem's individual rhythm, which, of course, includes other elements such as rhyme and phrasing. It doesn't matter, indeed it may be valuable for insights, if we hear or interpret a passage somewhat differently.

In scanning, listen to the poem. Don't impose a metrical pattern on it. Read each line aloud slowly, naturally, more than once. Perhaps scan several lines tentatively before marking any, to determine the norm. (This may help resolve difficult or ambiguous spots elsewhere in the poem.) Mark ambiguous syllables (those you can imagine counting two ways) with your preferred interpretation in parentheses. Like substitutions, such feet often provide a key to the subtleties in the rhythm. In general, scan to find the lowest common denominator: that is, what is closest to the iambic base, with the fewest or least complicated variations. And don't just begin by marking off feet from the beginning of lines—you'll quickly run into difficulties.

Let's scan two brief passages from this poem by Robert Frost (1874–1963). Its title appears in quotation marks because it is an **allusion** (a reference, in this case to a famous soliloquy in Shakespeare's *Macbeth*: "Out, out, brief candle"). As you read, notice a line or two that seem easily regular, to find the norm.

"Out, Out—"

The buzz saw snarled and rattled in the yard
And made dust and dropped stove-length sticks of wood,
Sweet-scented stuff when the breeze drew across it.
And from there those that lifted eyes could count
Five mountain ranges one behind the other

Under the sunset far into Vermont.
And the saw snarled and rattled, snarled and rattled,
As it ran light, or had to bear a load.
And nothing happened: day was all but done.
Call it a day, I wish they might have said   10
To please the boy by giving him the half hour
That a boy counts so much when saved from work.
His sister stood beside them in her apron
To tell them "Supper." At the word, the saw,
As if to prove saws knew what supper meant,   15
Leaped out at the boy's hand, or seemed to leap—
He must have given the hand. However it was,
Neither refused the meeting. But the hand!
The boy's first outcry was a rueful laugh,
As he swung toward them holding up the hand,   20
Half in appeal, but half as if to keep
The life from spilling. Then the boy saw all—
Since he was old enough to know, big boy
Doing a man's work, though a child at heart—
He saw all spoiled. "Don't let him cut my hand off—   25
The doctor, when he comes. Don't let him, sister!"
So. But the hand was gone already.
The doctor put him in the dark of ether.
He lay and puffed his lips out with his breath.
And then—the watcher at his pulse took fright.   30
No one believed. They listened at his heart.
Little—less—nothing!—and that ended it.
No more to build on there. And they, since they
Were not the one dead, turned to their affairs.

Take this first passage

And the saw snarled and rattled, snarled and rattled,

As it ran light, or had to bear a load.

and begin by marking the main (often the root) syllables of each noun, verb, and adjective. (If you are in doubt, a dictionary will show both main and secondary stresses for polysyllabic words, both of which are speech stresses and usually marked in scanning.) Also, *always* set off a duple ending, since a line's meter anchors on its final *stressed* syllable. So we have:

And the sáw snárled ănd ráttlĕd, snárlĕd ănd ráttlĕd,

As it rán líght, ŏr hád tŏ béar ă lóad.

To be safe, work backward through the line. Here, with single-syllable, function words between the marked stresses, it is pretty clear that both lines end in three iambs. So we mark:

And the sáw snárled | and rát|tlĕd, snárled | ănd rát|tled,

As it rán líght, | ŏr hád | tŏ béar | ă lóad.

The second foot of each line, having two stressed syllables, will probably count as spondees. In line 1, if so, we would be left with "And the" as a foot. Since "And" here carries no particular implication in the narrative, we would probably conclude, weighing the line's first four syllables, to mark a pyrrhic:

Ănd thĕ | sáw snárled | ănd rát|tlĕd, snárled | ănd rát|tlĕd,

Similarly, in line 2, "As it," no strong rhetorical emphasis lands on "as" or "it," though the stress on "it" may seem slightly heavier than on "As," but still distinctly less than on the "ran" that follows. So scanning *either* a muted iamb or a pyrrhic will be accurate:

Ăs ĭt | rán líght|, ŏr hád | tŏ béar | ă lóad.

Notice that snarling and rattling describe two rhythms of the buzz saw in operation. It *snarls* as wood to be cut is pressed into the whirling teeth of the blade, producing sharp noise. Then, idling, the saw *rattles* as the engine, belt, and blade run slack. The repetition in the first line—"snarled and rattled, snarled and rattled"—expresses the repetitiousness of the job the boy is doing as he cuts firewood. And the rhythm of the second line perhaps suggests the two actions of the saw: first, in "As it ran light," the speeding up when the blade spins freely; then, in the reengaged iambs of "or had to bear a load," the snarling as wood is again fed against the blade. The slight rhythmic difference in the two parts of the line matches this difference in denotation. So scanning a pyrrhic for "As it" may be somewhat preferable, as well as simpler.

> *Design and invention are the father and mother of all the arts.*
> —Giorgio Vasari

Before going on to the second passage, we may look at a faulty scansion. If we just mark off feet from the beginning of a line, the first foot might *seem* an anapest, and then we would get four trochees in the first line and three trochees and a problem in the second:

Ănd thĕ sáw | snárled ănd | ráttlĕd, | snárled ănd | ráttlĕd,

Ăs ĭt rán | líght, ŏr | hád tŏ | béar ă | lóad.

We avoid this problem if we first set off the duple ending and then key the scansion to the line's final stress. Here is another passage. Read it aloud and then try marking the lines lightly in pencil before moving on.

And then—the watcher of his pulse took fright.

No one believed. They listened at his heart.

Little—less—nothing—and that ended it.

No more to build on there. And they, since they

Were not the one dead, turned to their affairs.

The iambs in the first two lines are fairly regular; "of," following the "-er" in "watcher" would probably be promoted, as would "at" in the next line. And "took" would also probably be stressed, creating three consecutive stresses to close the line and signal "the watcher's" alarm:

And then—|the watch|er of | his pulse | took fright.

No one | believed. | They lis|tened at | his heart.

"No one" might also be easily heard as a spondaic substitution:

No one | believed.

With such a reading we would have five syllables stressed in a row, all the more emphasizing the sudden fright as the boy's life fades away. The third line begins with a trochee, followed by a spondee, and then, as the boy's heart stops beating, a pyrrhic foot to register the silence.

Little—|less—no|thing—and | that end|ed it.

Steady iambs return until the final line where we seem to have a spondee and a pyrrhic to create another effect.

No more | to build | on there. | And they, | since they

Were not | the one | dead, turned| to their | affairs.

After the three stresses of "one dead, turned," we speed over the unstressed sylla-bles in "*to their af*fairs," suggesting how quickly the survivors return to their lives. The cool tone that the word "affairs" supplies makes the survivors' attitude all the more chilling.

QUESTIONS AND SUGGESTIONS

1. Take the following passage, from Virginia Woolf's *To the Lighthouse* (or another interesting paragraph), and cast it into blank verse (unrhymed iambic pen-tameter) with substitutions and variations akin to those we see in Frost's "Out, Out." As much as you can, stick with the language of the original, but adjust it to fit the meter by rephrasing, stretching, compressing, and rearranging the words. Perhaps you can add your own stamp to it.

> So with the lamps all put out, the moon sunk, and a thin rain drum-ming on the roof a downpouring of immense darkness began. Nothing, it seemed, could survive the flood, the profusion of darkness which, creeping in at keyholes and crevices, stole round the window blinds, came into bedrooms, swallowed up here a jug and basin, there a bowl of red and yellow dahlias, there the sharp edges and firm bulk of a chest of drawers.

You might begin: "With lamps put out, the moon sunk down, and rain . . . ."

2. *For a group.* Write a "poem" together. Pick a simple subject—a familiar but unusual animal works well, for instance. Then, using the edges of a large blackboard as a "mind," think of and group as many details, ideas, and metaphors, especially metaphors, as you can. Start with whatever easy met-rical form comes to hand, perhaps trimeter and tetrameter quatrains rhyming *a b c b*; let possible rhymes suggest a scene or scenario. Begin the poem in the center of the blackboard *and keep going.*

    One group's poem came up with the image of a skunk "waddling like a tanker / that trails a plume of black smoke." Another group's began, "A snake's slow flowing stopped / Suddenly in the grass . . . ," and ended:

> Like a tiny pitchfork of lightning,
> Its tongue sparked in the socket.
> It looked as slim and mean
> As a hissing, countdown rocket.
>
> Eyes glowing like a switchboard
> That showed all systems on,
> It scared me—and I scared it,
> For suddenly it was gone.

3. Write a sonnet using rhyme words you start with, or those suggested below. The scheme below is for the English (or Shakesperean) sonnet; the letters represent rhymes:

a	drift
b	leave
a	sift
b	weave
c	shack
d	crumb
c	attack
d	drum
e	slight
f	glutted
e	tight
f	rutted
g	brake
g	take

Let the starting words be guide ropes, but by no means feel bound to them. If something really appealing shows up, go for it.

5. Instead of rhymed words, try a sonnet whose lines end with repeated words. Sir Philip Sidney wrote a fourteen-line "sonnet" with the words *day* and *night* repeated. Perhaps try a poem in which these words (or others) appear in an English sonnet pattern: wind, sea, wind, sea; dune, sand, dune, sand; foam, cold, foam, cold; stop, stop. You might want to have a look how at how Randall Mann in his "Fiduciary" (p. 74) builds a poem on repeated end words formed as couplets.

6. Scan the following poems and consider the effects of the rhythmic variations and substitutions. For comparison, scansions appear in Appendix II.

a) **Delight in Disorder**
   ROBERT HERRICK (1591–1674)

   A sweet disorder in the dress

   Kindles in clothes a wantonness;

   A lawn about the shoulders thrown

   Into a fine distraction,

   An erring lace, which here and there,   5

   Enthralls the crimson stomacher,

   A cuff neglectful, and thereby

   Ribbands to flow confusedly;

A winning wave, deserving note,

In the tempestuous petticoat,   10

A careless shoe-string, in whose tie

I see a wild civility,

Do more bewitch me than when art

Is too precise in every part.

b)   **#328**
     EMILY DICKINSON (1830–1886)

A Bird came down the Walk—

He did not know I saw—

He bit an Angleworm in halves

And ate the fellow, raw,

And then he drank a Dew   5

From a convenient Grass—

And then hopped sidewise to the Wall

To let a Beetle pass—

He glanced with rapid eyes

That hurried all around—   10

They looked like frightened Beads, I thought—

He stirred his Velvet Head

Like one in danger, Cautious,

I offered him a Crumb

And he unrolled his feathers   15

And rowed him softer home—

Than Oars divide the Ocean,

Too silver for a seam—

Or Butterflies, off Banks of Noon,

Leap, plashless as they swim   20

c) **Anecdote of the Jar**
    WALLACE STEVENS (1879–1955)

    I placed a jar in Tennessee,

    And round it was, upon a hill.

    It made the slovenly wilderness

    Surround that hill.

    The wilderness rose up to it,   5

    And sprawled around, no longer wild.

    The jar was round upon the ground

    And tall and of a port in air.

    It took dominion everywhere.

    The jar was gray and bare.   10

    It did not give of bird or bush,

    Like nothing else in Tennessee.

d) **For My Contemporaries**
    J. V. CUNNINGHAM (1911–1985)

    How time reverses

    The proud in heart!

    I now make verses

    Who aimed at art.

    But I sleep well.   5

    Ambitious boys

    Whose big lines swell

    With spiritual noise,

    Despise me not!

    And be not queasy   10

    To praise somewhat:

    Verse is not easy.

But rage who will.

Time that procured me

Good sense and skill   15

Of madness cured me.

POEMS TO CONSIDER

Loveliest of Trees   1896
A. E. HOUSMAN (1859–1936)

Loveliest of trees, the cherry now
Is hung with bloom along the bough,
And stands about the woodland ride
Wearing white for Eastertide.

Now, of my threescore years and ten,   5
Twenty will not come again,
And take from seventy springs a score,
It only leaves me fifty more.

And since to look at things in bloom
Fifty springs are little room,   10
About the woodlands I will go
To see the cherry hung with snow.

Crows   1930
LIZETTE WOODWORTH REESE (1856–1935)

Earth is raw with this one note,
    This tattered making of a song,
Narrowed down to a crow's throat,
    Above the willow-trees that throng

The crooking field from end to end,   5
    Fixed as the sun, the grave, this sound;
Of what the weather has to spend
    As much a part as sky or ground.

The primal yellow of that flower,
    The tansy making August plain;   10
And the stored wildness of this hour
    It sucks up like a bitter rain.

Miss it we would, were it not here,
  Simple as water, rough as spring,
It hurls us at the point of spear,   15
  Back to some naked, early thing.

Listen now. As with a hoof
  It stamps an image on the gust;
Chimney by chimney a lost roof
  Starts for a moment from its dust.   20

Balance   1990
MARILYN NELSON (b. 1946)

He watch her like a coonhound watch a tree.
What might explain the metamorphosis
he underwent when she paraded by
with tea-cakes, in her fresh and shabby dress?
(As one would carry water from a well—   5
straight-backed, high-headed, like a diadem,
with careful grace so that no drop will spill—
she balanced, almost brimming, her one name.)

She think she something, stuck-up island bitch.
Chopping wood, hanging laundry on the line,   10
And tantalizingly within his reach,
she honed his body's yearning to a keen,
sharp point. And on that point she balanced life.
That hoe Diverne think she Marse Tyler's wife.

Sonnet 116   1609
WILLIAM SHAKESPEARE (1564–1616)

Let me not to the marriage of true minds
Admit impediments. Love is not love
Which alters when it alteration finds,
Or bends with the remover to remove:
Oh, no! It is an ever-fixéd mark   5
That looks on tempests and is never shaken;
It is the star to every wand'ring bark,
Whose worth's unknown although his height be taken.
Love's not Time's fool, though rosy lips and cheeks
Within his bending sickle's compass come;   10
Love alters not with his brief hours and weeks,
But bears it out even to the edge of doom.
If this be error, and upon me proved,
I never writ, nor no man ever loved.

Scavenging the Wall   2000
R. T. SMITH (b. 1947)

When fall brought the graders to Atlas Road,
I drove through gray dust thick as battle
and saw the ditch freshly scattered with gravel.

Leveling, shaving on the bevel, the blade
and fanged scraper had summoned sleepers—   5
limestone loaves and blue slate, skulls of quartz

not even early freeze had roused. Some rocks
were large as buckets, others just a scone
tumbled up and into light the first time

in ages. Loose, sharp, they were a hazard   10
to anyone passing. So I gathered
what I could, scooped them into the bed

and trucked my freight away under birdsong
in my own life's autumn. I was eager
to add to the snaggled wall bordering   15

my single acre, to be safe, to be still
and watch the planet's purposeful turning
behind a cairn of roughly balanced stones.

Uprooted, scarred, weather-gray of bones,
I love their old smell, the familiar unknown.   20
To be sure this time I know where I belong

I have brought, at last, the vagrant road home.

Hamlen Brook   1982
RICHARD WILBUR (b. 1921)

At the alder-darkened brink
Where the stream slows to a lucid jet
I lean to the water, dinting its top with sweat,
And see, before I can drink,

A startled inchling trout   5
Of spotted near-transparency,
Trawling a shadow solider than he.
He swerves now, darting out

To where, in a flicked slew
Of sparks and glittering silt, he weaves   10
Through stream-bed rocks, disturbing foundered leaves,
And butts then out of view

> Beneath a sliding glass
> Crazed by the skimming of a brace
> Of burnished dragon-flies across its face, 15
> In which deep cloudlets pass
>
> And a white precipice
> Of mirrored birch-trees plunges down
> Toward where the azures of the zenith drown.
> How shall I drink all this? 20
>
> Joy's trick is to supply
> Dry lips with what can cool and slake,
> Leaving them dumbstruck also with an ache
> Nothing can satisfy.

Move 1998

GEOFFREY BROCK (b. 1964)

> Try driving twenty hours in a truck,
> your life a sprawl of boxes behind you,
> only a few of them light. Add bad luck:
>
> the radio doesn't work; the cat with whom
> you share the cab decides, in hour one, 5
> to piss in her cage (she is, we might assume,
>
> as scared as you); and—since these streaks run
> in threes—it starts to rain. Now, with a mere
> thousand miles to go, with the vague sun
>
> rising in your eyes, grip the wheel and steer. 10

Her Web 2000

ERIN BELIEU (b. 1965)

> Spirit of the ratio
> one above and one below,
> she takes figures in a script
> that haunts the cryptic willow.
>
> Spoken in the dialect 5
> known to every architect,
> her cathedrals made of string
> hold the stirring circumspect.
>
> The web, a clock stitched from will,
> chronologs which hours to kill; 10
> when she rests, it's just a clause
> in her gauzy codicil.

And when readying her bed,
she feels a pulse down the thread
current through the living weave,   15
she pins her sleeve to the dead.

Fiduciary   2002
RANDALL MANN (b. 1972)

the relationship between
    blackbird and fencepost, between
the cow and its egret, the field
    and wildflowers overrunning the field—
so little depends upon their trust.   5

    Here, in God we trust
to keep our cash and thoughts in line—
    in the sky, an unexplained white line
could be the first of many omens.
    But this is no country for omens,   10

the line as chalky as the moon,
    bleak and useless as the moon
now rising like a breath of cold air . . .
    There is gullibility in the air.

Barbed Wire   1985
HENRY TAYLOR (b. 1942)

One summer afternoon when nothing much
was happening, they were standing around
a tractor beside the barn while a horse
in the field poked his head between two strands
of the barbed-wire fence to get at the grass   5
along the lane, when it happened—something

they passed around the wood stove late at night
for years, but never could explain—someone
may have dropped a wrench into the toolbox
or made a sudden move, or merely thought   10
what might happen if the horse got scared, and
then he did get scared, jumped sideways and ran

down the fence line, leaving chunks of his throat
skin and hair on every barb for ten feet
before he pulled free and ran a short way   15
into the field, stopped and planted his hoofs
wide apart like a sawhorse, hung his head
down as if to watch his blood running out,

almost as if he were about to speak
to them, who almost thought he could regret   20
that he no longer had the strength to stand,
then shuddered to his knees, fell on his side,
and gave up breathing while the dripping wire
hummed like a bowstring in the splintered air.

The Payoff   2000
ALLISON JOSEPH (b. 1967)

Instant riches, lucky numbers, my father knew
those games—horse races, scratch-off cards—
his fever rose as jackpots grew.

Not one ticket, not merely two,
he bought as many as he could hoard.   5
Instant riches, lucky numbers, my father knew

a life of trying to accrue
the kind of luck he couldn't afford.
His fever rose as his jackpots grew.

Every night he would review   10
a pile of tickets he'd discard.
Instant riches, lucky numbers, my father knew

the lure of easy revenue—
compulsion hit my father hard.
His fever rose as jackpots grew.   15

He spent his cash as bills came due
with losing tickets his reward.
Instant riches, lucky numbers, my father knew
his fever would rise as jackpots grew.

Learning by Doing   1967
HOWARD NEMEROV (1920–1991)

They're taking down a tree at the front door,
The power saw is snarling at some nerves,
Whining at others. Now and then it grunts,
And sawdust falls like snow or a drift of seeds.
Rotten, they tell us, at the fork, and one   5
Big wind would bring it down. So what they do
They do, as usual, to do us good.
Whatever cannot carry its own weight
Has got to go, and so on; you expect
To hear them talking next about survival   10

And the values of a free society.
For in the explanations people give
On these occasions there is generally some
Mean-spirited moral point, and everyone
Privately wonders if his neighbors plan   15
To saw him up before he falls on them.

Maybe a hundred years in sun and shower
Dismantled in a morning and let down
Out of itself a finger at a time
And then an arm, and so down to the trunk,   20
Until there's nothing left to hold on to
Or snub the splintery holding rope around,
And where those big green divagations were
So loftily with shadows interleaved
The absent-minded blue rains in on us.   25

Now that they've got it sectioned on the ground
It looks as though somebody made a plain
Error in diagnosis, for the wood
Looks sweet and sound throughout. You couldn't know,
Of course, until you took it down. That's what   30
Experts are for, and these experts stand round
The giant pieces of tree as though expecting
An instruction booklet from the factory
Before they try to put it back together.

Anyhow, there it isn't, on the ground.   35
Next come the tractor and the crowbar crew
To extirpate what's left and fill the grave.
Maybe tomorrow grass seed will be sown.
There's some mean-spirited moral point in that
As well: you learn to bury your mistakes,   40
Though for a while at dusk the darkening air
Will be with many shadows interleaved,
And pierced with a bewilderment of birds.

4

MAKING THE LINE (II)

Although it takes many forms, nonmetrical verse falls under the catchall term **free verse.** Borrowed from the French *vers libre*, the term is attractive since everyone likes freedom but it doesn't tell us much—only what such verse is *not* (metrical) and nothing at all about what it is.

No verse is free, T. S. Eliot says, "for the poet who wants to do a good job." Another great American innovator in free verse, William Carlos Williams, was quite certain that "there is no such thing as free verse. It's a contradiction in terms. The verse is measured. No measure can be free." The nature of verse itself means that we pay attention to the way lines cut across and measure the flowing phrases and sentences of speech.

However, scant practical descriptions of free verse exist. Poets writing free verse successfully have done so mostly by intuition—often adapting traditional forms and techniques to free verse. A well-tuned ear—a delicate sensitivity to idiom—finds the unique form, the unique rhythm, which in Ezra Pound's words "corresponds exactly to the emotion or shade of emotion to be expressed." Denise Levertov puts the aim this way: "there is a form in all things (and in our experience) which the poet can discover and reveal." Much free verse falls short, she notes, because "the attention of the writer has been switched off too soon, before the intrinsic form of the experience has been revealed." The riskiest temptation for the poet writing in free verse may be to settle for the easy spontaneity the term seems to promise.

Until we have an adequate theory of nonmetrical verse, rough distinctions will help. As poems like "Those Winter Sundays" (p. 9) and "Traveling through the Dark" (p. 43) remind us, many free verse poems look and move like metrical verse. Although the composition of their lines is nonmetrical, how those lines interact with other features, like enjambment and syntax, can create tensions much like those in traditional verse and make a free verse poem as powerful a construction as any more formal creation. Many principles developed through formal verse apply to free verse. For instance, whether the poem's stresses are regular or not, many stressed syllables bunched together create a feeling of density, slowness, or weight (e.g., "in the blueblack cold," in "Those Winter Sundays"). And a series of lightly stressed syllables evokes lightness, swiftness, or precariousness (e.g., "at the top of the ladder" in "Storm Window.")

Nature has no outline. Imagination has.

—William Blake

Although most free verse grew out of metrical verse, some types of free verse stand out as distinctive. These are poems written in *very long* lines (like Whitman's), in *very short* lines (like William Carlos Williams's), or in lines of *greatly varying* or uneven lengths. They offer the poet differing opportunities, and, since by nature or definition lines cannot be established by meter, each creates somewhat different ways of organizing or using the unit of the line.

These three types of nonmetrical verse developed, logically enough, to exploit the possibilities in areas where metrical verse operates minimally. At the center of the traditional poetic spectrum are poems in lines of about eight to ten syllables (corresponding to tetrameters and pentameters); less frequently, but common, are poems of around six syllables or twelve syllables (corresponding to trimeters and hexameters). Lines shorter or longer than these seldom show up in metrical verse. Moreover, poems in meter often keep to one line length throughout, or vary only a little. In these areas where verse in meter is rarest, poets have found ways to create new forms of the nonmetrical poetic line.

In this chapter, we will discuss these three fairly open-ended types, as well as syllabics and the prose poem.

Nonmetrical Verse: Longer Lines

Walt Whitman is the great originator of the poem of long lines although he had antecedents in the "verse" of Psalms and Ecclesiastes in the King James Bible (1611) and poems by Christopher Smart, William Blake, and others. Whitman's "A Noiseless Patient Spider," discussed in Chapter 2 (pp. 36–37), exemplifies free verse in longer lines. Lines as long as Whitman's are usually end-stopped, breaking at natural syntactic or grammatical pauses or intervals. Structured by these pauses, the rhythm may then be modulated by caesural pauses, internal breaks, within the lines. The cadence of such verse derives from the tension between these two kinds of pauses. The rolling rhythm we hear in long-lined verse dwindles with shorter lines. In the extreme—where every syntactic unit is given a line—the tension disappears and all that remains is chopped up prose. Suppose lines of "A Noiseless Patient Spider" were rearranged:

Surrounded,
Detached,
In measureless oceans of space,
Ceaselessly musing,

Venturing,
Throwing,
Seeking the spheres to connect them . . .

The lineation now merely repeats the phrasal pauses of prose and the tension evaporates. Beginners sometimes divide lines this way and miss the opportunity of creating texture. The lines of a poem must somehow cut across the flow of sentences, at least often enough to create a new rhythm.

Let's look at another example of nonmetrical verse in longer lines, also by Whitman:

When I Heard the Learn'd Astronomer

When I heard the learn'd astronomer,
When the proofs, the figures, were ranged in columns before me,
When I was shown the charts and diagrams, to add, divide, and measure them,
When I sitting heard the astronomer where he lectured with much applause in
    the lecture-room,
How soon unaccountable I became tired and sick,   5
Till rising and gliding out I wander'd off by myself,
In the mystical moist night-air, and from time to time,
Look'd up in perfect silence at the stars.

All one sentence, the poem gets its rhythmic force through Whitman's handling of syntax. Lines 1 to 4, describing the lecture, lack a main clause, and so seem indecisive, repetitious, and bogged down in details, like a boring lecture. Whitman begins these lines with a device called **anaphora,** organizing lines or sentences by repeating a word or phrase at the start, as with "When" here. The verbs in lines 2 and 3 are passive and "*When I* sitting *heard*" in line 4 repeats the structure of line 1. We almost feel, in the awkward syntax, the speaker's fidgeting on a hard seat and his boredom in the redundant thump of "*lectured* . . . in the *lecture*-room." The rhythm enacts his discomfort, as it does again in line 5. The adverb "unaccount*ably*" would make sense, but we get instead the displaced adjective "unaccount*able* I." Bored by the lecture, the speaker suggests that he too can no more be counted in figures and columns than are the infinite stars.

Now let's look at a stresses-per-phrase scansion:

When I Heard the Learn'd Astronomer

When I héard the léarn'd astrónomer,   3

When the próofs, ‖ the fígures, ‖ were ránged in cólumns before mé,   1/4

When Í was shówn the chárts and diagráms, ‖ to ádd, ‖ divíde, ‖ and

    méasure thém,   5/1/1/2

When I sitting heard the astronomer ‖ where he lectured with much

    applause in the lecture-room,   4/5

How soon unaccountable I became tired and sick,   6

Till rising and gliding out ‖ I wander'd off by myself,   3/3

In the mystical moist night-air, ‖ and from time to time,   4/2

Look'd up in perfect silence at the stars.   5

Whitman's use of repetition and modification in lines 2 to 4 create a dense and dull lecture. The syntax of line 2 (short clause followed by a long one) is reversed in line 3 (long clause followed by short ones); *two* long clauses in line 4 make plain the lecturer's tediousness.

After the complex opening lines, both syntax and rhythm begin to clarify—even in line 5 where, despite the awkward construction, the single clause shows the speaker recognizing the cause of his distress. Shorter lines express unity. The adjectives "rising" and "gliding" are familiar terms for heavenly motion; "wander'd" recalls the literal meaning (*wanderer*) of the Greek root of the English word *planet*. The balancing rhythm in line 6 parallels the speaker's growing awareness of himself as part of the universal whole. The poem's sentence culminates in the phrasal unity of line 8—which also happens to be iambic pentameter:

Look'd up in perfect silence at the stars.

The line's familiar rhythmic music evokes the natural experience of standing beneath the stars.

Nonmetrical Verse: Lines of Mixed Length

The category of nonmetrical verse of mixed-length lines falls between that of verse in longer lines and that of verse in shorter. We can look at it here by considering this straightforward poem by Robinson Jeffers (1887–1962):

People and a Heron

A desert of weed and water-darkened stone under my western windows
The ebb lasted all afternoon,
And many pieces of humanity, men, women, and children, gathering shellfish,
Swarmed with voices of gulls the sea-breach.
At twilight they went off together, the verge was left vacant, an evening heron 5
Bent broad wings over the black ebb,
And left me wondering why a lone bird was dearer to me than many people.

Well: rare is dear: but also I suppose
Well reconciled with the world but not with our own natures we
   grudge to see them
Reflected on the world for a mirror.   10

Overlooking a pebbly beach as the tide ebbs, the speaker muses about why he prefers the lone heron to the families "gathering shellfish." He presents the people indifferently, as "pieces of humanity" that "swarmed" like insects, hinting at his misanthropy. He offers two explanations for this response. The first—"rare is dear"—implies an objectivity he doesn't seem to feel, so he considers a second reason. We may be "well reconciled with"—at peace with—the physical world, but not "our own natures," he says, though he doesn't explain that deep dissatisfaction.

Scanning the poem shows *regular alternation* between longer and shorter lines that reflect the poem's crucial oppositions: tidal flow and ebb, many and one, nature and human nature, self and mirror. The poem is about two states of mind, the solitary and the communal—*and* is of two minds about them. Lines 5 and 6 demonstrate this:

At twilight they went off together, ‖ the verge was left vacant, ‖

  an evening heron   5/3/2

Bent broad wings over the black ebb,   6

Through its expressive enjambment and phrasal unity, line 6 characterizes the lone heron as it sails down to replace people on the beach. Alliteration, *v*'s in line 5 and *b*'s in line 6, suggests in sound the fittingness of the lone bird's arrival. Except for line 8, the shorter lines have phrasal unity. By contrast, the longer lines, through the stopping and starting of caesuras, suggest multiplicity and busyness. The syntax of line 3, which describes the people, is the most frenetic in the poem: 3/1/1/1/3.

The shorter lines, and indeed the shorter second stanza, of the following poem by a student, Sheila Heinrich, appropriately suggest the poem's theme:

disappearances

was a man of many disguises
was a man of few words and
one day when they looked where he had been
they found

and no one said   5
so no one ever

The omitted name or pronoun at the beginning of line 1 and the omitted punctuation at its end signal what is coming. The man seems already elusive or mysterious before the significantly missing clauses of lines 4 to 6. The poem's form makes its statement.

Consider, too, this amusing poem by Jim Daniels (b. 1956):

Short-Order Cook

An average joe comes in
and orders thirty cheeseburgers and thirty fries.

I wait for him to pay before I start cooking.
He pays.
He ain't no average joe.   5

The grill is just big enough for ten rows of three.
I slap the burgers down
throw two buckets of fries in the deep frier
and they pop pop spit spit . . .
psss . . .   10
The counter girls laugh.
I concentrate.
It is the crucial point—
they are ready for the cheese:
my fingers shake as I tear off slices   15
toss them on the burgers/fries done/dump/
refill buckets/burgers ready/flip into buns/
beat that melting cheese/wrap burgers in plastic/
into paper bags/fries done/dump/fill thirty bags/
bring them to the counter/wipe sweat on sleeve   20
and smile at the counter girls.
I puff my chest out and bellow:
"Thirty cheeseburgers, thirty fries!"
They look at me funny.
I grab a handful of ice, toss it in my mouth   25
do a little dance and walk back to the grill.
Pressure, responsibility, success,
thirty cheeseburgers, thirty fries.

Lines range from one stressed syllable ("psss . . . ") to twelve syllables with nine stresses:

into páper bágs/fríes dóne/dúmp/fíll thírty bágs/

Daniels uses a series of repetitions to organize the poem; later lines answer earlier lines "I wait for him to pay . . . / He pays." Line 1, "An average joe comes in," is answered by line 5, "He ain't no average joe." This device also focuses the little internal drama. Line 11, "The counter girls laugh," corresponds to line 21, "and smile at the counter girls," and to line 24, "They look at me funny." The noun phrase of line 2, "and orders thirty cheeseburgers and thirty fries," acts like a refrain, recurring in line 23, and expressing satisfaction in line 28. The cook appreciates his triumph, whether or not the counter girls do.

The first half of the poem mixes short, medium, and long lines about equally, and randomly, creating an easygoing norm. The lines tighten as the pressure grows:

psss . . .

The counter girls laugh.

I concentrate.

It is the crucial point—

And the lines lengthen steadily up to the crisis (lines 16–20) when spatula-like slashes replace commas and the action is recounted in telegraphic style. The poem then relaxes into lines of mostly medium length with "and smile at the counter girls." Except for the action lines with slashes, few lines in the poem have caesuras until the last four:

I grab a handful of ice, ‖ toss it in my mouth	3/3
do a little dance ‖ and walk back to the grill.	3/3
Pressure, ‖ responsibility, ‖ success,	1/2/1
thirty cheeseburgers, ‖ thirty fries.	3/2

The balanced rhythm helps create the cook's sense of accomplishment and self-assurance. We may also be hearing a muted pentameter and tetrameter concealed in his rhythm:

Pressure, | respon|sibil|ity, |success,

thirty | cheeseburg|ers, thir|ty fries.

Since iambic lines sound natural in English, poets often use them in free verse to create a sense of fulfillment or orderliness. Thom Gunn notes in an interview, "If you look at most of my contemporaries and most new poems, they write something that's not quite free verse and not quite meter." We can discover iambs even in longer lines like Whitman's

When I | was shown | the charts | and di|agrams, | to add, | divide, | and

meas|ure them

The poet writing free verse understands that metrical cadences are one of the resources.

Nonmetrical Verse: Shorter Lines

We can think of verse in shorter lines as being, loosely, of two kinds. The simpler may be called *phrasal verse*, because the poet divides lines at phrase or clause boundaries. Most of what was thought of as "free verse" early in the twentieth century was of this kind—following almost literally Pound's injunction "to compose in the sequence of the musical phrase, not in sequence of a metronome." This poem by William Carlos Williams shows the potential of phrasal verse:

Pastoral

When I was younger
it was plain to me
I must make something of myself.
Older now
I walk back streets   5
admiring the houses
of the very poor:
roof out of line with sides
the yards cluttered
with old chicken wire, ashes,   10
furniture gone wrong;
the fences and outhouses
built of barrel-staves
and parts of boxes, all,
if I am fortunate,   15
smeared a bluish green
that properly weathered
pleases me best
of all colors.
        No one
will believe this   20
of vast import to the nation.

In a few places the lines might have been broken somewhat differently: "admiring / the houses of the very poor," for instance, or "admiring / the houses / of the very poor." But poets writing phrasal verse have limited options. Caesuras will inevitably be rare. In the scansion below, caesuras appear only in lines 10, 14, and 19. In the last, the dropped-line sets off and emphasizes the last sentence, very much as a stanza break would.

To look closely at what Williams's short free verse lines achieve, we turn now to another informal kind of notation for *drag*, *advance*, and *balance*. **Drag** identifies a line whose weight lies primarily on its beginning (stressed syllables running to unstressed syllables), and we mark it with an arrow pointing left (←); **advance** identifies a line whose weight lies primarily at the end (unstressed syllables running to stressed syllables), and we mark it with an arrow pointing right (→); **balance** identifies a line whose stressed syllables are distributed fairly symmetrically, and we identify it by an arrow that points both ways (↔). In a dragged line, then, stressed syllables predominate in the first half of the line; in an advanced line they predominate in the second half; in a balanced line they are about equal. With this notation tool, let's turn back to Williams's "Pastoral."

The norm is two to three stresses per line; there are nine lines of each. Three lines have four stresses (lines 8, 10, and 19). In general, nothing fancy—plain vanilla, in keeping with Williams's belief in "the American idiom." We also note drag/balance/advance.

Whĕn Í wăs yóungĕr	↔
ĭt wăs pláin tŏ mé	→
Ĭ mŭst máke sómethĭng (´) ŏf mўsélf.	→
Óldĕr nów	↔
Ĭ wálk báck stréets	→
ădmírĭng thĕ hóusĕs	↔
ŏf thĕ vérў póor:	→
róof óut ŏf líne wĭth sídes	←
thĕ yárds clúttĕred	↔
wĭth óld chíckĕn wíre, ‖ áshĕs,	↔
fúrnĭtŭre góne wróng;	→
thĕ féncĕs ănd óuthóusĕs	→
búilt ŏf bárrĕl-stáves	↔
ănd párts ŏf bóxĕs, ‖ áll,	→
ĭf Í ăm fórtŭnăte,	←
sméarĕd ă blúĭsh gréen	↔

that prŏpérlў wéathĕred   ↔

pléasĕs mĕ bést   ↔

ŏf áll cólŏrs.‖

        Nó óne   ⌐↳

wĭll bĕlíeve thís   →

ŏf vást ímpŏrt tó thĕ nátiŏn.   ↔

In the poem's first and last thirds Williams uses mostly two-stress lines, but uses only one in lines 8 to 14 where the rhythm is appropriately denser when presenting the cluttered landscape. Nine lines showing advance and ten balance are spread out fairly evenly through the poem. The poem's end shows balance, registering the speaker's notion that others will not recognize the importance of this urban scene, which despite its poverty kindles in him admiration (line 6) and aesthetic pleasure (line 18). These values oppose the more typically American ambition, recalled in line 3, to make something of himself. Also, though the speaker does not argue his preference, the title "Pastoral" suggests the idyllic world of the pastoral poetry tradition. We may find meaning and beauty now, Williams implies, not among happy shepherds, but in such gritty everyday scenes the poem shows us.

The other kind of nonmetrical verse in shorter lines may be called *radically enjambed*. The poet breaks some or many of the lines at radical or dramatic points *within* phrases—between adjective and noun, for example, or even between preposition and article, article and noun, and so on. Ezra Pound pioneered the device in "The Return" (p. 92) in which these lines appear:

> See, they return; ah, see the tentative
>   Movements, and the slow feet,
>   The trouble in the pace and the uncertain
>   Wavering!

The rhythmic character of the passage derives from the abrupt enjambment between adjectives and nouns: "The tentative / Movements" and "the uncertain / Wavering!" Both force a slight, abnormal pause, and this extra hesitation rhythmically evokes the tentative, uncertain feeling. Alone in a line, "Wavering!" unexpectedly ends the stanza's momentum, leaving it on an appropriately awkward diminuendo.

Pause or delay creates only part of the effect, however. In addition, paradoxically, we feel a slight *speeding up* as the momentum of the interrupted phrase and sentence reasserts itself and seems to pull the voice around the corner into the next line. Read Pound's lines aloud several times, and listen carefully. You should feel, first, a slight pause or hesitation as voice and eye reach the unexpected break in the sentence's flow; then, second, as if to catch up, a slight hurrying as the voice curves into the new line and continues. In the last line break we feel a frustration of that hurrying as the voice jams up in "Wavering!" because the sentence ends. Radical enjambment releases a lot of energy, but overused the device can quickly seem a coy mannerism.

Robert Hass suggests that training readers to re-see was one of Williams's goals in his poems:

> A lot of William Carlos Williams's individual perceptions are a form of iambic music, but he has arranged them so that the eye breaks the iambic habit. The phrase—"a dust of snow in the wheeltracks"—becomes
>
>   a dust of
>   snow in
>   the wheeltracks
>
> and people must have felt: "yes, that is what it is like; not one-TWO, one-TWO. A dust of / snow in / the wheeltracks. That is how perception is. It is that light and quick." The effect depends largely on traditional expectation. The reader had to be able to hear what he was not hearing.

Presumably Williams is aware of, and counts on his readers hearing, the iambs that the enjambments mute.

Especially when enjambment impels a sentence forward, shorter lines often produce rhythmic speed, as in Cornelius Eady's "The Wrong Street" (p. 95). But this isn't always the case. The cat in Williams's "Poem," in spite of radical enjambments, moves in slow motion:

Poem

As the cat
climbed over
the top of

the jamcloset
first the right   5
forefoot

carefully
then the hind
stepped down

into the pit of   10
the empty
flowerpot

One notable detail: The poem is unpunctuated. This omission of the cogs of commas and periods opens the sentence to the white space of the page. End stops become muted or softened, as in line 4, where we would expect a comma, or in the last line where the almost seamless motion seems poised to continue. Williams can omit the punctuation because he manages his sentence deftly. Scansion shows a norm of one or two stresses per line:

Ăs thĕ cát	→
clímbed óvĕr	←
thĕ tóp ŏf	↔
thĕ jámclósĕt	↔
fírst thĕ ríght	↔
fórefóot	↔
cárefŭllў	←
thén thĕ hínd	↔
stépped dówn	↔
íntŏ thĕ pít ŏf	↔
thĕ émptў	↔
flówĕrpót	↔

The drag-advance notation reveals that only line 1 shows advance. Lines 2 and 7 show drag, and the rest—*nine* of the poem's twelve lines—show balance. This preponderance of lines in balance, these symmetrical rhythms, produce a feeling of stasis that even the momentum of radical enjambments can scarcely overcome.

Poems, of course, aren't written through calculation or complicated analysis. No doubt Williams, a doctor, wrote "Poem" rapidly, on the back of a prescription pad. But he had trained himself to listen for the rhythm he needed among the words that were suggesting themselves.

Syllabics and Prose Poems

Syllabics, a form which counts the number of syllables in each line, is often a variant of radically enjambed verse. As developed with great success by Marianne Moore (1887–1972), syllable count links corresponding lines of often complex stanzas. Consider this example by Moore.

To a Steam Roller

The illustration
is nothing to you without the application.
　　You lack half wit. You crush all the particles down
　　　　into close conformity, and then walk back and forth on them.

Sparkling chips of rock 　　　　　　　　　　　　　　　　　　　　5
are crushed down to the level of the parent block.
　　Were not "impersonal judgment in aesthetic
　　　　matters, a metaphysical impossibility," you

might fairly achieve
it. As for butterflies, I can hardly conceive 　　　　　　　　　10
　　of one's attending upon you, but no question
　　　　the congruence of the complement is vain, if it exists.

Moore's poem is an example of **quantitative** syllabics: the number of syllables per line varies. You probably first met syllabics in writing haiku in elementary school. In quantitative syllabics, each stanza repeats the syllabic pattern of the first. Here each first line has five syllables; each second line, twelve; each third line, twelve; and each fourth line, fifteen. Especially in stanzas 1 and 3, the longer last lines mimic, both visually and rhythmically, the effect of something rolled and flattened by a steamroller. And the rhyme in each stanza's lines 1 and 2 (on top, like the too-thorough steamroller) is followed by no rhyme in lines 3 and 4, as if the last two rhymes had been squashed down. Even the chopped off "achieve / it" seems an effect of steamrolling. Another example of Moore's delightful syllabics, "The Fish," appears in Chapter 11 (p. 270).

Another kind of syllabics is **normative:** each line has the same number of syllables. Sometimes a significant line of the poem becomes the baseline around which the poet builds the poem. Or a poet may choose a particularly significant number and write the poem's syllabics around that number. Donald Hall wrote a series of poems about baseball which had nine syllables per line, nine lines to a stanza, and nine stanzas. Later he wrote a series of three "Extra Innings" with—you guessed it—the syllabics organized around ten, eleven, and twelve. Whatever shape syllabics take, poets find them attractive not because they offer a particular rhythm, but because they offer a discipline—though a light one—around which the poet can create the poem. The poet trains the poem onto the syllabic structure as a vine climbs a trellis.

> [A *poem is] a kind of machine
> for producing the poetic state of
> mind by means of words.*
> —Paul Valéry

Prose poems, as one might infer, aren't verse at all, but short compositions in prose that ask for (and reward) the concentrated attention usually given to poetry. Prose poems can remind us that besides the architecture of line, stanza, and form, poems are also structured around the interplay of ideas, feelings, images, and metaphor. An example by Robert Bly (b. 1926):

Looking at a Dead Wren in My Hand

Forgive the hours spent listening to radios, and the words of gratitude I did not say to teachers. I love your tiny rice-like legs, that are bars of music played in an empty church, and the feminine tail, where no worms of Empire have ever slept, and the intense yellow chest that makes tears come. Your tail feathers open like a picket fence, and your bill is brown, with the sorrow of an old Jew whose daughter has married an athlete. The black spot on your head is your own mourning cap.

In subject, tone, and imagery—as well as in length—"Looking at a Dead Wren in My Hand" differs considerably from what we expect in a short story or essay or, for that matter, natural history. Bly begins with emotion, with the shock of personal seriousness the dead wren in his hand prompts, and even in that his approach is oblique: "Forgive the hours spent listening to radios, and the words of gratitude I did not say to teachers." Only gradually and indirectly can he come to an empathy that properly expresses his grief—for the bird, and no longer for the realization of his own inevitable death. Other prose poems are Gary Young's "The stillborn calf" (p. 99), Russell Edson's "A Man Who Writes" (p. 234), and Erica Pankey's "Improvisations" (p. 311).

QUESTIONS AND SUGGESTIONS

1. To test the integrity and possible effects of lines, try out as many free verse versions of a prose sentence as you can think of. You'll find dozens of possibilities. Below are some shapes that the following sentence might take: "The rain dribbled down the window panes and pooled on the window sill." We might emphasize the phrasing:

   The rain dribbled
   down the window pane
   and pooled
   on the window sill.

   Or use syllabics to organize it and create the visual effect of a rivulet:

   The rain
   dribbled
   down the
   window
   pane and
   pooled on
   the win-
   dow sill.

   Or use indentation and white space:

> The rain
>   dribbled down
>   the window
>   pane
>   and
>   pooled
>   on the window
>   sill.

Some versions are bound to seem artificial and strained, but that's half the point. You're looking for possibilities.

2. Take a free verse poem by a poet you admire (Elizabeth Bishop works well), type it up as prose, and put it aside for a day or two. Then, without looking at the original, put the poem back into lines. Compare your version with the original. What choices did the poet make that are different from yours? See if you can determine why the poet chose to break the lines where he or she did.

3. Choose a simple object—a stone, a seed, a leaf, a wristwatch, for example— and study it slowly and carefully with each of your five senses in turn. Don't be shy about tasting a watch or listening to a twig! Then write a sentence or two of description for each sense. Comparisons are fine. ("It feels like a flat, closed bowl or box. Heavy. There's a little toothed wheel on the side.") Any surprises? Might there be a poem in it?

4. Write a poem in syllabics. Either try repeating a stanza pattern of different line lengths or establishing one length and developing the poem around that.

5. Below is the first draft of a poem called "In One Place." Consider ways you might revise it. What's the poem's essential discovery? What might be refined? What is unnecessary? What might be implicit? You'll find the final version in Appendix II.

In One Place

The tree grows in one place.

A seed goes down, and something
holds up two or three leaves
the first year.

            Then the spindling   5
goes on climbing, branching,
up, up, up

      until birds
live in it and no one can
remember it wasn't there.   10

The tree stands always here.

6. Look closely at the selections in the "Poems to Consider" section that follows, and consider how the poets' use of line, stanza, and form help carry the poems' subject, tone, and imagery. How do the radically shaped "Amaryllis" and "Moon" earn their eccentric appearances? Take one of the poems that particularly appeals to you and type it up on a computer. Now recast the lines, making them longer, then shorter, then of mixed lengths. How do the different lineation strategies affect the poem? Next try casting the poem in syllabics and as a prose poem. What else do you notice?

POEMS TO CONSIDER

The Return   1912
EZRA POUND (1885–1972)

See, they return; ah, see the tentative
   Movements, and the slow feet,
   The trouble in the pace and the uncertain
   Wavering!

See, they return, one, and by one,   5
With fear, as half-awakened;
As if the snow should hesitate
And murmur in the wind,
         and half turn back;
These were the "Wing'd-with-Awe,"   10
    Inviolable.

Gods of the wingèd shoe!
With them the silver hounds,
     sniffing the trace of air!

Haie! Haie!   15
   These were the swift to harry;
These the keen-scented;
These were the souls of blood.

Slow on the leash,
       pallid the leash-men!   20

Balloons   1963
SYLVIA PLATH (1932–1963)

Since Christmas they have lived with us,
Guileless and clear,

Oval soul-animals,
Taking up half the space,
Moving and rubbing on the silk   5

Invisible air drifts,
Giving a shriek and pop
When attacked, then scooting to rest, barely trembling.
Yellow cathead, blue fish—
Such queer moons we live with   10

Instead of dead furniture!
Straw mats, white walls
And these traveling
Globes of thin air, red, green,
Delighting   15

The heart like wishes or free
Peacocks blessing
Old ground with a feather
Beaten in starry metals.
Your small   20

Brother is making
His balloon squeak like a cat.
Seeming to see
A funny pink world he might eat on the other side of it,
He bites,   25

Then sits
Back, fat jug
Contemplating a world clear as water.
A red
Shred in his little fist.   30

Amaryllis   2001
MARGARET GIBSON (b. 1944)

God in the near
onion, in the wintered song sparrow
in the long-gone scarlet tanagers, God in the school of orange
carp and the dark amber of watery
weeds, God   5
in the tissue of chaste berry and skullcap—
God, I have been looking for you
months of waiting
since the last flamboyant flame of leafing
on the worn-down   10

> amaryllis
> whose seven red trumpets
> could have blown down the walls of Jericho
> and raised up the rubble
> had I known how to play them   15
> had I known how to let
> them play me—
> God in the up-welling
> phase of green reeds, ungainly God
> a strut of green   20
> from the bulb, like a cockscomb
> God in the last green flare left
> to thirst in the sun,
> the arc and graceful swoop of it
> the startled brow of the invisible   25
> all-seeing
> eye of the boundless—
> God in the bulb, God in the faceless dark
> this morning my hands
> lift you   30
> scaly and dry, squat, used as you are to the ease
> of unlit corners in the cool closet where
> winter apples and oranges
> ember—
> God, I give you back to the bonfire sun   35
> and to the new pot, to tap water and the tamped soil
> of repeated generation, not knowing
> what to make of this your
> tenderness, God in these hands that do
> not know how to say   40
> otherwise—
> blinding God, hear this prayer
> amaryllis.

A Simple Experiment   1973
MURIEL RUKEYSER (1913–1980)

When a magnet is
struck by a hammer
the magnetism spills out of
the iron.

The molecules   5
are jarred,
they are a mob going
in all directions

The magnet is
shocked back   10
it is no magnet but
simple iron.

There is no more
of its former
kind of accord   15
or force.

But if you take
another magnet
and stroke the iron
with this,   20

it can be
remagnetized
if you stroke it
and stroke it,

stroke it   25
stroke it,
the molecules
can be given
their tending grace

by a strong magnet   30
stroking stroking
always in the same direction,
of course.

The Wrong Street   1991
CORNELIUS EADY (b. 1954)

If you could shuck your skin and watch
The action from a safe vantage point,
You might find a weird beauty in this,
An egoless moment, but for
These young white men at your back.   5
Your dilemma is how to stay away from
That three to five second shot
On the evening news of the place
Where you stumble, or they catch
Their second wind, or you run up   10
To the fence, discover that
You are not breeze, or light,
Or a dream that might argue
Itself through the links. Your responsibility

Is not to fall bankrupt, a   15
Chalk-marked silhouette faintly
Replaying its amazement to
The folks tuning in, fist to
Back, bullet to mid-section.
Your car breaks down   20
And gives you up. A friend's
Lazy directions miss
The restaurant by two
Important blocks. All of this
Happened. None of this   25
Happened. Part of this
Happened. (You dream it
After an ordinary day.) Something
Different happened, but now
You run in an   30
Old story, now you learn
Your name.

◎ The Long Marriage   1997
MAXINE KUMIN (b. 1925)

The sweet jazz
of their college days
spools over them
where they lie
on the dark lake   5
of night growing
old unevenly:
the sexual thrill
of PeeWee Russell's
clarinet; Jack   10
Teagarden's trombone
half syrup, half
sobbing slide;
Erroll Garner's
rusty hum-along   15
over the ivories;
and Glenn Miller's
plane going down
again before sleep
repossess them . . .   20

Türschlusspanik.
Of course
the Germans have

a word for it,
the shutting of   25
the door,
the bowels' terror
that one will go
before
the other as   30
the clattering horse-
hooves near.

Moon   2001
CAROL FROST (b. 1948)

Grief again, the turntable left on
and the needle set at the beginning
of our song before the rebuff, you gone

back to your life. The lopsided moon sings
outside on the trellis its style of song,   5
and I can hear, ghostly, the little rhymes

that rhyme with sad. I haven't the heart
to close the blinds. They stay as they are left.
Shadows pile in the corners, a part

of the night, the speckled air adrift   10
and filling with the soft valley mist
for morning. I call it my season

for misery, like watching winter come,
cold rain blown, hardening into snow,
then lasting too long. When rain trickles from   15

the eaves, I'll go where least shadows
lie, moon-tossed, at the garden end, a sparrow
in the tree with its three notes, and hear him.

my sweet old etcetera   1922
E. E. CUMMINGS (1894–1962)

my sweet old etcetera
aunt lucy during the recent

war could and what
is more did tell you just
what everybody was fighting

for,   5
my sister

isabel created hundreds
(and
hundreds) of socks not to   10
mention shirts fleaproof earwarmers

etcetera wristers etcetera, my
mother hoped that

i would die etcetera
bravely of course my father used   15
to become hoarse talking about how it was
a privilege and if only he
could meanwhile my

self etcetera lay quietly
in the deep mud et   20

cetera
(dreaming,
et
   cetera, of
Your smile   25
eyes knees and of your Etcetera)

Meeting the Occasion   1992
LUCIA CORDELL GETSI (b. 1944)

Friends come in relays to the hospital
to read you mail and stories, bathe
your face, decorate your walls, to chase
away young residents curious to view
this rare disease, to hold your hand   5
while needles probe for veins. They cook
for you, then spoon tiny bites
onto your tongue that relearns how
to swallow. They stay away
when they are sick,   10

                        all but one

who wears malaise like a threadbare
robe. She wilts like a flower
by your bed. Her sad face gray
with fatigue or martyrdom, I say   15
nothing, but my body forks like a rod
to divine where the danger is, one hand
extended in greeting, the other
knifing in between,

nothing will get through   20

me. I grow heads taller than myself
until my hair sweeps the ceiling
clean of rising germs. I bend at the waist
and spread out—I am a mosquito net,
a spider web, an awning, a tent for you   25
to live in, a tidal wave of will
that washes her out the door.

Early Dawn   2001
JANINE TRAN*

The scent of jasmine
rice early
in the morning.
Its curl of steam
like a finger   5
beckoning
to days when my father
rose with the dawn.
He carried
the metal lunch tin   10
lightly, the packed
rice inside colored orange
by the dried shrimp
my mom made
at four a.m.   15

The stillborn calf   1997
GARY YOUNG (b. 1951)

The stillborn calf lies near the fence where its mother licked the damp body, then left it. All afternoon she has stood beside a large, white rock in the middle of the pasture. She nuzzles it with her heavy neck and will not be lured away. This must be her purest intelligence, to accept what she expected, something sure, intractable, the whole focus of the afternoon's pale light.

5

THE SOUND
(AND LOOK) OF SENSE

Before printing was developed in the fifteenth century, poetry was primarily an oral art. Instead of seeing it on the page, the audience heard it in songs, ballads, recited epics, and tales. Formal meters, with countable stresses, helped the poet compose and remember the poem and allowed a poem's form to be followed by its hearers; rhyme signaled line ends like a typewriter bell. Since the sixteenth century, and especially after the rise of general literacy in the nineteenth century, poetry has increasingly emphasized the visual. Today we are more accustomed to seeing a poem than to hearing it, and we must remind ourselves to read poems aloud lest we miss their essential music.

In this famous passage from his "An Essay on Criticism," Alexander Pope (1688–1744) shows some of the tricks verse can perform while he calls to task poets who plod along by writing only by the "numbers," by meter and rhyme alone.

> But most by numbers judge a poet's song;
> And smooth or rough, with them, is right or wrong:
> In the bright muse though thousand charms conspire,
> Her voice is all these tuneful fools admire;
> Who haunt Parnassus° but to please their ear,   5
> Not mend their minds; as some to church repair,
> Not for the doctrine, but the music there.

5 Parnassus: Greek mountain, sacred to the Muses.

These equal syllables alone require,
Though oft the ear the open vowels tire;
While expletives their feeble aid do join;   10
And ten low words oft creep in one dull line:
While they ring round the same unvaried chimes,
With sure returns of still expected rhymes;
Where'er you find "the cooling western breeze,"
In the next line, it "whispers through the trees":   15
If crystal streams "with pleasing murmurs creep,"
The reader's threatened (not in vain) with "sleep":
Then, at the last and only couplet fraught
With some unmeaning thing they call a thought,
A needless Alexandrine ends the song,   20
That, like a wounded snake, drags its slow length along.

The passage constitutes a library of poetic effects. In mentioning the tediousness of too many open vowels, he provides a line of them: "Though oft the ear the open vowels tire," (line 9). He illustrates how filler words such as "do" make awkward lines through "While expletives their feeble aid do join." Or how monotonously monosyllables can move: "And ten low words oft creep in one dull line." He makes an illustrative hexameter (the "Alexandrine") sinuously sluggish with the line, "That, like a wounded snake, drags its slow length along." Further on in his "Essay," Pope demonstrates how sound should echo sense:

True ease in writing comes from art, not chance,
As those move easiest who have learned to dance.
'Tis not enough no harshness gives offense,
The sound must seem an echo to the sense:
Soft is the strain when Zephyr° gently blows,   30
And the smooth stream in smoother numbers flows;
But when loud surges lash the sounding shore,
The hoarse, rough verse should like the torrent roar:
When Ajax strives some rock's vast weight to throw,
The line too labors, and the words move slow;   35
Not so, when swift Camilla scours the plain,
Flies o'er th' unbending corn, and skims along the main.

30 **Zephyr:** the west wind.

Pope's lines show the difference between a "smooth stream" and "loud surges," between the heaving of strongman Ajax and the graceful stride of Camilla, who was said to be able to run so fast the stalks of grain wouldn't move under her feet.

In this chapter we will examine the effects produced by a poem's visible shape and by its sounds: *visible form, repetition, onomatopoeia, alliteration, assonance,* and *rhyme.*

Visible Form

As poets in the past century turned more and more to nonmetrical verse they relied more heavily on the visual dimension of poetry. With such verse, we *see* line breaks; the measure shapes itself on the page, before the eye. The visual, of course, does not replace the oral (poetry always draws on speech for its vigor) but complements it, opening new formal possibilities.

On the page every poem has a visible form, a shape that conveys a message, at least subliminally, of tone or theme, heft or airiness, difficulty or informality, quiet or agitation, and so on. Is the poem slender, bony, quick? Solid, heavy, full? Are the lines even, orderly, smooth? Or raggedy, jumpy, anxious, mixing long and short lines? Or perhaps lines get gradually longer, or shorter, as the poem goes along? Are some lines indented? Irregularly or in a pattern?

Does the poem use stanzas? Of the same or of a varying number of lines? Narrow stanzas, like couplets? Plumper ones? Do the stanzas have a distinctive shape, like those of Wilbur's "Hamlen Brook" (p. 72) or Moore's "To a Steam Roller" (p. 89)?

In short, will the visible form give readers an accurate first impression of the poem? Like a good title, appearance can be informative, as well as attractive and enticing. Further, does the visible form help readers respond to the poem?

> [O]ne of the pleasures of poetry is] its ability to give us a sense of community: as we think along with someone else, the boundaries between two minds come down. Form itself is communal . . . .
>
> —Marilyn Nelson

Stanzas, for instance, can express—often create—a poem's organization. They may be "closed," ending with a completed sentence, or "open," continuing a sentence across the stanza break. Like paragraphs in prose, stanzas may correspond to segments of an idea or argument, as in Whitman's "A Noiseless Patient Spider" (p. 36) where they present the comparison of venturing spider and venturing soul, or stanzas can delineate the steps in a process, as in Muriel Rukeyser's "A Simple Experiment" (p. 94). Open stanzas help Williams express the cat's poise and hesitancy in "Poem" (p. 87) and help Moore express the fluid underseascape of "The Fish" (p. 270). In writing, the careful poet seizes the opportunities visible form presents.

Fixed stanzas of a certain number of lines can often help, like a trellis, over which the poem can grow. In Donald Hall's "The Names of Horses" (p. 47), for example, the long-lined unrhymed quatrains create a stable unit in which Hall can narrate the horses' lives, making possible the emphasis created by the closing one-line stanza where he lists their evocative names: "O Roger, Mackerel, Riley, Ned, Nellie, Chester, Lady Ghost."

In this poem, Liz Rosenberg (b. 1955) uses increasingly shorter stanzas to suggest the silencing of women:

The Silence of Women

Old men, as time goes on, grow softer, sweeter,
while their wives get angrier.

you see them hauling the men across the mall
or pushing them down on chairs,
"Sit there! and don't you move!"   5
A lifetime of *yes* has left them
hissing bent as snakes.
It seems even their bones will turn
against them, once the fruitful years are gone.
Something snaps off the houselights,   10
and the cells go dim;
the chicken hatching back into the egg.

Oh lifetime of silence!
words scattered like a sybil's leaves.
Voice thrown into a baritone storm—   15
whose shrilling is a soulful wind
blown through an instrument
that cannot beat time

but must make music
any way it can.   20

Women have words, but they have been scattered; they have a voice, but it has been
drowned out by men's "baritone storm" and turned into "a soulful wind" that "must
make music / any way it can." The poem realizes this suppression visually in the
dwindling of stanzas from twelve to six, then to two lines, as well as in the shortening
of the lines. The poem's shape acts as an emblem of its meaning.

Consider how stanzas create the gestures that Bruce Bennett (b. 1940) uses in
this poem:

Smart

like the fox
who grabs a stick
and wades
into the water

deep   5
and deeper
till only his muzzle's
above it
his fleas

leap   10
up and up
onto his head
out onto the stick

which he lets go

off it floats   15
as he swims back
and shakes himself dry

The poem's lack of capitalization and punctuation partially disguises its three sentences and gives an impression of uninterrupted motion. The first stanza break, stretching the sentence over it, helps to suggest the "deep / and deeper" water; and the second, how "his fleas // leap / up and up . . . ." The third and fourth stanza breaks isolate "which he lets go," floating the one-line stanza on the page, visually like the stick adrift on the water.

Other sorts of visual choreographing use typography and spacing on the page, including indentation or dropped-line we see in E. E. Cummings's "my sweet old etcetera" (p. 97), based on his experience in World War I. The spaces in Christopher Buckley's "Perseid Meteor Shower" (p. 116) seem to mimic its subject's surprise, randomness, and brilliance.

Dropped-line is a convention that probably originated in dramatic usage. In printing Shakespeare's plays, for instance, when a single pentameter line is divided between two speakers, the second part of the line is shown as "dropped":

Hamlet: Did you not speak to it?
Horatio: My lord, I did,
            But answer made it none. Yet once methought . . . .

Dropped-line produces rhythmical variation and emphasis, as in these lines from Richard Wilbur's "Love Calls Us to the Things of This World" (p. 282):

And the heaviest nuns walk in a pure floating
Of dark habit,
                keeping their difficult balance.

In Charles Wright's "January II" (p. 118), dropped lines suggest alternative paths, asides, and modifications the mind makes as it considers and responds to a winter scene. In the following poem, Nancy Eimers (b. 1954) uses dropped-line or indentation to indicate rhythmic subordination, guiding both eye and voice:

A Night Without Stars

And the lake was a dark spot
                on a lung.
Some part of its peace was dead; the rest was temporary. Sleeping ducks
        and geese,
goose shit underfoot   5
            and wet gray blades of grass.
The fingerlings like sleeping bullets

hung deep in the troughs of the hatchery
and cold traveled each one end to end,
such cold,   10
    such distances.

We lay down in the grass on our backs—
beyond the hatchery the streetlights were mired in fog and so
there were no stars,
        or stars would say there was no earth   15

Just a single homesick firefly lit on a grass blade.
Just our fingers
    curled and clutching grass,
this dark our outmost hide, and under it
        true skin.   20

The speaker and a companion go to a fish hatchery where the fog, eerie, disappointing, seems like a lung and the lake is an ominous spot. The tiny fish are "like sleeping bullets" and the speaker interprets the lone firefly as "homesick." The outing is a failure. They can't lie romantically on the grass and watch stars.

In a general way, the device of dropped-line registers this disjunction between expectation and event. We read, for instance,

such cold,
    such distances,

somewhat differently than we would if the second phrase appeared either on the same line with the first or as a completely separate line flush left. The device suggests a remoteness, a dropping of the voice. Each of the eight dropped-lines or indentations has its own singular tone or effect. The combined length of lines 7 and 8, for instance, suggests the long rectangular pools or troughs in which the young fish are raised, and the dropping of line 8 implies the depth fingerlings lie beneath the surface of the water. Facing the current that runs from end to end of the troughs, the fish seem in touch with distances as well as the chill, fresh water. The brevity of the dropped-line—"true skin"—helps register the vulnerability the speaker feels beneath the foggy darkness that seems close as "our outmost hide."

For a very small class of poems, the visual or spatial element dominates and becomes explicitly pictorial. "Easter Wings" by George Herbert (1593–1633), written in meter, is an early example of this tradition:

Easter Wings

Lord, who createdst man in wealth and store,
  Though foolishly he lost the same,
    Decaying more and more
      Till he became
        Most poore;   5
        With thee

O let me rise
  As larks, harmoniously,
    And sing this day thy victories;
Then shall the fall further the flight in me.   10

My tender age in sorrow did beginne;
  And still with sicknesses and shame
    Thou didst so punish sinne,
      That I became
        Most thinne.   15
      With thee
    Let me combine,
  And feel this day thy victorie;
For if I imp° my wing on thine,
Affliction shall advance the flight in me.   20

19 imp: to graft. Alludes to a term in falconry.

The lines of each stanza decrease and then increase by one foot, to make the poem look like two pairs of angels' wings (turn the book on its side to see them) and also embody in rhythm its theme of how grace gives him flight. Poets have used the shapes of a Coca-Cola bottle, key, fireplug, umbrella, lightbulb, New York State, and even a swan and its reflection.

Often the shape of a poem offers a subtle undercurrent to a poem, like this famous William Carlos Williams' poem:

The Red Wheelbarrow

so much depends
upon

a red wheel
barrow

glazed with rain   5
water

beside the white
chickens

One might view each stanza as a miniature wheelbarrow in side view, with the longer first line suggesting the handle. Visual and rhythmic forms combine. This tiny still life catches energy in stasis, a vital moment at rest.

Repetition

Repetition lies at the heart of all the arts. Consider, for instance, how necessary both repetition and variation are to making music. In poetry we find repetition in the small echo sounded in rhyme, in the larger rhyme schemes in a poem, and in the concept of *verse* itself, which turns and returns on the line. Repeating elements—whether a rhyme scheme, a chorus, or a catalogue of heroes—helped oral poets compose by ear. Repeating shapes—or even avoiding repeating them—helps poets today form the poem on the page.

In poems written in fixed forms, a particular kind of repetition often defines the form. The **villanelle** is based on repeating the poem's first and third lines in alternating stanzas. The first stanza of a **sestina** establishes end words that are repeated in a different order in the next stanzas. The **ghazal** repeats an end word established in its first couplet. In the **pantoum,** the second and fourth lines of a quatrain recur as the first and third lines of subsequent stanzas. A fuller discussion of these and other forms appears in Appendix I.

In nonfixed forms, repetition often serves as a structural device in a variety of ways, as in E. E. Cummings's "my sweet old etcetera" (p. 97), Langston Hughes's "Aunt Sue's Stories" (p. 180), and Robin Becker's "When Someone Dies Young" (p. 166). More formally, repetition becomes the **refrain** often found in songs. The refrain is the line or lines regularly repeated from stanza to stanza, usually at the end. Often we remember only the refrain of a song. In "Recuerdo" (Spanish for *recollection* or *memory*), Edna St. Vincent Millay (1892–1950) organizes the poem by beginning the stanzas with a refrain:

> *E*very part of a short poem is
> large, just as every part of a
> large poem is small . . . .
> —Paul Fussell

Recuerdo

We were very tired, we were very merry—
We had gone back and forth all night on the ferry.
It was bare and bright, and smelled like a stable—
But we looked into a fire, we leaned across a table,
We lay on a hill-top underneath the moon;   5
And the whistles kept blowing, and the dawn came soon.

We were very tired, we were very merry—
We had gone back and forth all night on the ferry;
And you ate an apple, and I ate a pear,
From a dozen of each we had bought somewhere;   10
And the sky went wan, and the wind came cold,
And the sun rose dripping, a bucketful of gold.

We were very tired, we were very merry,
We had gone back and forth all night on the ferry.
We hailed, "Good morrow, mother!" to a shawl-covered head,   15
And bought a morning paper, which neither of us read;
And she wept, "God bless you!" for the apples and pears,
And we gave her all our money but our subway fares.

Of course, as her poem suggests, memory is itself a form of repetition. The refrain mimics how we roll in our minds a powerful memory and draw from it the images that stick.

Simply repeating a word or phrase, perhaps with variations, can lend a tune to a passage, as in Howard Nemerov's "Learning by Doing" (p. 75): "So what they do / They do, as usual, to do us good"; or in Robert Hayden's "Those Winter Sundays" (p. 9), we hear emotion in the doubled phrase: "What did I know, what did I know / of love's austere and lonely offices?" In "The Wrong Street" (p. 95), Cornelius Eady breaks the repeated narrative to create the close of the poem:

> . . . All of this
> Happened. None of this
> Happened. Part of this
> Happened. (You dream it
> After an ordinary day.) Something
> Different happened, but now
> You run in an
> Old story, now you learn
> Your name.

"Something / Different happened" and since the day was ordinary, whatever it was wasn't overtly dangerous, but nonetheless can precipitate—"now . . . now . . ."—the very real fear and the identity that the "Old story" holds for the speaker. Repetition focuses the poem's emotions.

Relentless repetition helps convey the hectic scene in this poem by Richmond Lattimore (1906–1983):

Catania to Rome

The later the train was at every station,
the more people were waiting to get on,
and the fuller the train got, the more time it lost,

and the slower it went, all night, station to station,
the more people were on it, and the more people   5
were on it, the more people wanted to get on it,

waiting at every twilight midnight and half-daylight
station, crouched like runners, with a big suitcase
in each hand, and the corridor was all elbows armpits

knees and hams, permessos and per favores, and a suitcase   10
always blocking half the corridor, and the next station
nobody got off but a great many came aboard.

When we came to our station we had to fight to get off.

The ever-branching, delaying, crowded sentence of lines 1 through 12 captures the frustration of the long train journey in repeating and repeating: *station, more people, more, waiting, get* (and *got*), *on, all* and *always, suitcase, corridor, came,* and ultimately *off,* not to mention eight *and*'s. It is a sentence crowded with commas and is equally crowded because it does not include commas where we expect them: "twilight midnight and half-daylight" as well as "all elbows armpits // knees and hams." Line 13 is a relief, although missing its needed comma after "station," the sentence has to push its way to its end.

Alliteration and Assonance

Alliteration is the repetition of consonant sounds in several words in a passage; **assonance** the repetition of vowel sounds. Initial alliteration usually jumps out at us. In Pope's line, "But when loud surges lash the sounding shore," the *l*'s of "*l*oud" and "*l*ash" and the *s*'s of the "*s*urges" and "*s*ounding" are unmistakable. Harder to notice is the alliteration of "la*sh*" and "*sh*ore," since the first of the pair doesn't start the syllable's sound. For a similar reason, assonance may also be subtle, as in "l*ou*d" and "s*ou*nding," where it links the noise of surf and breakers striking the shore—echoing, too, in the *d*'s following the vowel sounds.

Consider another line in Pope's passage:

The line | too la|bors, and | the words | move slow.

An impression of dragging stems from the two spondees and from the promoted stress on "and," which (after the caesura) makes it awkward for the voice to regain momentum. Long vowels and alliterating *l*'s in "line," "too," "labors," "move," and "slow" increase the effect, though probably the assonance in "too" and "move" most impedes the sentence's progress.

With the same devices Howard Nemerov creates a very different music in these lines from "The Fourth of July":

> It is, indeed, splendid:
> Showers of roses in the sky, fountains
> Of emeralds, and those profusely scattered zircons
> Falling, and falling, flowering as they fall
> And followed distantly by a noise of thunder.
> My eyes are half-afloat in happy tears.

The flowing alliteration of *f*'s and *l*'s center on the repetitions in "Falling and falling, flowering as they fall." The assonance in "Showers" and "fountains," which frames the first full line, shows up two lines below as internal rhyme in "flowering"—which also picks up the *er* sound in "emeralds," "scattered," "zircons," and then in "thunder." Assonance and internal rhyme also link "roses," "those," and "profusely," and both alliteration and assonance link "*half-*" and "*happy*" in the last line. Readers may not notice that the line about the profusion of zircons has six feet, but poets will who want to know how effects happen.

Alliterative pairing can emphasize either comparison, as in Pope's "The sound must seem an echo to the sense," or contrast, as in Francis's "Excellence is millimeters and not miles." Like rhyme, alliteration or assonance may serve both as a musical and as an organizing device. Howard Nemerov gets the last word:

Power to the People
Why are the stamps adorned with kings and presidents?
That we may lick their hinder parts and thump their heads.

Alliteration precisely links "hinder parts" and "heads"; the assonance in "presidents" and "heads" helps make the couplet seem formally complete, nearly rhyming.

Rhyme

By definition, **rhyme** repeats stressed vowel sounds and the following consonants. Examples of *exact* rhymes include *Jane-restrain, groan-bone, ensnare-hair, applause-gauze,* and *priest-yeast.* Rhymes usually fall on stressed syllables. Duple (also called extra-syllable or feminine) rhymes normally fall on a stressed and unstressed syllable: *tumble-fumble, ankle-rankle;* but they may fall on two stressed syllables, as in *ping-pong, sing-song.* Triple rhymes are *cranium-geranium* and *hairiness-wariness.* There are a few natural four-syllable rhymes, such as *trivially-convivially.*

Unlike the mellifluous Romance languages, English is difficult to rhyme. Many common words have no natural rhymes, such as "circle" or "month." For some words, there is only one natural rhyme: *strength-length* and *fountain-mountain* are examples. *Gloves* and *doves* have often reared up in love poems only because of rhyme. Also, because many rhymes in English have become cliché, poets find it hard to make fresh exact rhymes and consequently turn to **blank verse** (unrhymed iambic pentameter) and to **slant-** or **off-rhyme** (inexact rhyme).

Slant rhymes can be inventive, created through terminal alliteration, for instance, as in *love-move, brain-gone, bath-truth, chill-full;* or through **consonance** (identity of consonants with different main vowels), as in *sad-sod, bell-bull, point-pint,* or *pillow-palor;* or near consonance as in *firm-room, love-loathe,* or *balk-park.* Assonance can also create a vocalic echo as in *bean-sweet* or *how-cloud.* Emily Dickinson has even made length of vowel work, as in "*be-fly*" or the fainter "*day-eternity.*"

Another slant rhyme technique involves rhyming stressed with unstressed (or secondarily stressed) syllables, as in *see-pretty, though-fellow, full-eagle, fish-polish, them-solemn,* and *under-stir.*

Whereas exact rhyme can give us an impression of rightness, precision, or fulfillment, off-rhyme can give us a sense of something amiss, as in the rhyme of "wished-vanished" that closes Christian Wiman's "Poŝtolka" (p. 121) or in the following

World War I poem by Wilfred Owen. The poem's persistent refusal to rhyme gives it an off-key sound that fits its ironic theme.

Arms and the Boy

Let the boy try along this bayonet-blade
How cold steel is, and keen with hunger of blood;
Blue with all malice, like a madman's flash;
And thinly drawn with famishing for flesh.

Lend him to stroke these blind, blunt bullet-leads   5
Which long to nuzzle in the hearts of lads,
Or give him cartridges of fine zinc teeth,
Sharp with the sharpness of grief and death.

For his teeth seem for laughing round an apple.
There lurk no claws behind his fingers supple;   10
And God will grow no talons at his heels,
Nor antlers through the thickness of his curls.

Rhymes also can occur randomly as here Robert Frost varies line length and rhyme pattern in "After Apple-Picking":

After Apple-Picking

My long two-pointed ladder's sticking through a tree
Toward heaven still,
And there's a barrel that I didn't fill
Beside it, and there may be two or three
Apples I didn't pick upon some bough.   5
But I am done with apple-picking now.
Essence of winter sleep is on the night,
The scent of apples: I am drowsing off.
I cannot rub the strangeness from my sight
I got from looking through a pane of glass   10
I skimmed this morning from the drinking trough
And held against the world of hoary grass.
It melted, and I let it fall and break.
But I was well
Upon my way to sleep before it fell,   15
And I could tell
What form my dreaming was about to take.
Magnified apples appear and disappear,
Stem end and blossom end.
And every fleck of russet showing clear.   20

My instep arch not only keeps the ache,
It keeps the pressure of a ladder-round.
I feel the ladder sway as the boughs bend.
And I keep hearing from the cellar bin
The rumbling sound   25
Of load on load of apples coming in.
For I have had too much
Of apple-picking: I am overtired
Of the great harvest I myself desired.
There were ten thousand thousand fruit to touch,   30
Cherish in hand, lift down, and not let fall.
For all
That struck the earth,
No matter if not bruised or spiked with stubble,
Went surely to the cider-apple heap   35
As of no worth.
One can see what will trouble
This sleep of mine, whatever sleep it is.
Were he not gone,
The woodchuck could say whether it's like his   40
Long sleep, as I describe its coming on,
Or just some human sleep.

Although they occur sometimes in adjacent lines, the rhymes may be separated by as many as three other lines, as are "break-take" in lines 13 and 17 and "end-bend" in lines 19 and 23. The triple-rhyme "well-fell-tell" in the quickly turning lines 14–16 helps to convey the indefinable transition from waking to dreaming.

Near the end of the poem, "heap" in line 35 doesn't find its end-rhyme until, after seven lines, "sleep" in line 42, although the word teasingly occurs three times *within* intervening lines. Unlike end-rhyme, such **internal rhyme,** may occur anywhere within lines for expressive effects as the "*um*" sound rumbles through these lines:

And I keep hearing *from* the cellar bin
The *rum*bling sound
Of load on load of apples *com*ing in.

Internal rhyme may be overt and corny as in the old song's "the *lazy*, *hazy*, *crazy days* of summer" or subtle as in these lines of Richard Wilbur's "Year's End":

I've known the wind by water banks to shake
The late leaves down, which frozen where they fell
And held in ice as dancers in a spell
Fluttered all winter long into a lake . . .

The whirling sound within the "which" clause mainly results from the internal rhyme of "h*eld*," which links the end-rhyme "f*ell*" and spins the voice toward the end-rhyme "spell." The quick movement is intensified by the only technically stressed "in" of "as dancers in a spell," with three essentially unstressed syllables speeding the line. Although hardly noticeable, the "rhyme" of two *in*'s—one unstressed, the other technically stressed—in "in ice as dancers in a spell" also produces the feeling of whirling, as does the light, hidden rhyme in "And" and "dancers."

The best rhymes uncover subliminal connections between emotions and ideas in a poem. Renaissance poets quickly seized the implications that rhymes such as *womb-tomb* and *birth-earth* made, but such rhymes became too expected for later generations to use. The advantage of working in rhyme is that it can help you think beyond the logical and obvious, urge you toward a word or sound that wouldn't otherwise come to mind, into unchartered territory. But when the poet writes only for the rhyme, the poem will likely thud. Robert Frost tested for rhymes by seeing if he could detect which had occurred to the poet first. Both words had to seem equally natural, equally called for by what was being said. If one or the other seemed dragged in more for rhyme than sense, he considered the rhyming a failure. This is a hard but useful test. If you sometimes have to settle for a slightly weak rhyme, put the weaker of the pair *first*; then, when the rhyme bell sounds in the ear with the second, it will be calling attention to the more suitable and natural word.

Onomatopoeia

Words can have sound effects built in: *clunk, snarl, buzz, hiss, rattle, snap, crunch, whirr, murmur, roar, boing*. Such words, called onomatopoetic (noun: **onomatopoeia**), imitate their meaning. They will often imitate sounds, like those just listed, but also express size, motion, touch, and other qualities. Notice *thin, skimpy, slim, skinny, spindly*, or *fat, brawny, plump, rotund, gross, humongous, pudge-pot*. Notice how lightly *delicate* hits its syllables, how heavily *ponderous* does. Feel how your mouth says *pinched, shut, open, round, hard, soft, smooth*.

We can overemphasize the connection; many words don't sound at all like their meanings: consider *cat, suddenly, pink*. We often respond to the association as much as to the sound for words such as *tip* and *top* or *slip* and *slide*—though there are also *slice, slick, slight, slime, sling, slink, slit, slither, sliver*. As Dr. Johnson put it, "on many occasions we make the music we imagine ourselves to hear."

A familiar example of onomatopoeia is Tennyson's

The moan of doves in immemorial elms
And murmuring of innumerable bees

Overdoing it is the fun of this poem by John Updike (b. 1932):

Player Piano

My stick fingers click with a snicker
And, chuckling, they knuckle the keys;
Light-footed, my steel feelers flicker
And pluck from these keys melodies.

My paper can caper; abandon   5
Is broadcast by dint of my din,
And no man or band has a hand in
The tones I turn on from within.

At times I'm a jumble of rumbles,
At others I'm light like the moon,   10
But never my numb plunker fumbles,
Misstrums me, or tries a new tune.

The density of onomatopoetic diction and sound effects—alliteration, assonance, rhyme, and even rhythm—create the mechanical music of a piano played without the musician's sensitivity. Updike's poem wittily captures how too many sound effects can be risky and can, like too much eye shadow, make the poem seem artificial and fake. *Ars celare artem*, as Horace said. The art is to hide the art.

QUESTIONS AND SUGGESTIONS

1. Either write a love poem that uses words that sound harsh or repugnant (e.g., *screech, sludge, pus, wretched, frump*) or a poem that goes on the attack with sweet or gentle sounds (e.g., *breeze, sway, glide, loft, smooth*). Let the sounds guide the poem. What difficulties do you run up against? What delights?

2. Write out the lyrics of a song you enjoy. What formal devices do you detect? Try writing a verse with your own lyrics.

3. Because there are words for which no natural exact rhymes exist, such as "scarce," "census," and "broccoli," poets are tempted to invent comic rhymes for them. Ogden Nash (1902–1971) reported, for instance, that kids eat spinach "inach by inach" and remarked that a man who teases a cobra will soon be "a sadder he, and sobra." Anonymous worked around "rhinoceros" this way:

> If ever, outside a zoo,
> You meet a rhinoceros
> And you *cross her, fuss*
> Is exactly what she'll do.

Have a try at "umbrella" or "lionesses" before looking in Appendix II to see what poets did with them. If you find the game amusing, go on to some puzzlers of your own.

4. Recalling "Easter Wings," use shape to form a picture poem of your own. Try an ice cream cone, a kite, a gun, a mouse, a cigar, a state with a recognizable shape, for instance.

5. After checking the technicalities of the sestina in Appendix I, try writing one of your own. Michael Heffernan's "Famous Last Words" (p. 119) demonstrates the advantage of choosing an obsessive subject or speaker. An in-class variant suggested by poet Susan Thornton involves using six randomly chosen words. Everyone (including the teacher) writes a sestina before the period ends and reads the result aloud. One class used *raining, chalkboard, watermelon, ordeal, zoo,* and *needle.* As an alternative, if the general subject and point of view are determined at the outset (e.g., first person during a summer storm in the park), each student, or group of students, can take up a particular stanza.

6. Read aloud many of the poems in the "Poems to Consider" section in order not to miss the sound effects of repetition, rhyme, alliteration, and assonance. Jean Toomer's "Reapers" and John Keats's "To Autumn" offer plentiful examples of deliciously patterned sound. In the former, you'll notice the alliteration of "*Black,*" "*bleeds,*" "*blade,*" and "*Blood*" in lines 5 to 8, but don't stop with that. "To Autumn" is the most charming of Keats's great odes, with its subtle texturing of diction, syntax, sound, and indentation. For instance, what do you make of the phrase "full-grown lambs"? What word does Keats avoid? How does this choice help to set up the tone of the ending?

POEMS TO CONSIDER

Laundromat   1964
LORINE NIEDECKER (1903–1970)

Once again a public wedding
a casual, sudsy
social affair
at the tubs

After all, ecstasy   5
can't be constant

Perseid Meteor Shower   1993
CHRISTOPHER BUCKLEY (b. 1948)

Ucross, Wyoming

Out late in the wide dark field,
                looking into the domed wide dark,
a moonless sky clearer even than
                the planetarium from our air-
brushed and illuminated youth,   5
                we spotted Cassiopeia, its W̲ pointing
like lamp posts to Perseus
                and there that black window
through which meteors
                would rain down. For a minute, only   10
blank incessant space
            fell through,
                then faintly we could see
the misty band of the Milky Way
                turning with us   15
                  as our fingers
on the air traced the Northern Cross,
                the Big Dipper's steely pan
before the jazzy, unsynched bursts
                and strings of flame cross-hatched   20
the circuit board of stars.
              The thickest yellow streaks and burns
were like wooden safety matches
                pulled parallel over the horizon
and hill's slow length—   25
             then a few high darts like sparks popping off
welding with acetylene.
             In two hours, the sky ignited with something
like thirty shooting stars,
              and my Dutch friend recalled that in Amsterdam   30
last year
        a meteorite the size of a briquet broke through a family's roof
and cooled in a bowl of soup—
                other pieces, they figured, pockmarked
the Siberian snow.   35
             Between flashes, we guessed at their blazing cause,
then moved on to
             Einstein's matter and traveling light—and there,
invisible

in that dark space, it was almost as if we weren't   40
                                                   made up of both
or diminished by the distance of the stars. We only knew
                                          that we were moving
outward, away from each other,
                                 toward no place we could name, with the   45
                                 view
to our galaxy's jeweled heart
                              kept from us, dimmed by a starry dust cloud
dense in Sagittarius.
                       But, while things seemed set   50
                                      above us, it was magnificent
to find a place in this cold and abstract whirl
                                 and take what fire we were given.

⬡ Don't Look Back   2000
KAY RYAN (b. 1945)

This is not
a problem
for the neckless.
Fish cannot
recklessly   5
swivel their heads
to check
on their fry;
no one expects
this. They are   10
torpedoes of
disinterest,
compact capsules
that rely
on the odds   15
for survival,
unfollowed by
the exact and modest
number of goslings
the S-necked   20
goose is—
who if she
looks back
acknowledges losses
and if she does not   25
also loses.

January II   2002
CHARLES WRIGHT (b. 1935)

A cold draft blows steadily from a crack in the window jamb.
It's good for the soul.
For some reason, it makes me think of monuments in the high desert,
                                          and what dissembles them.

We're all born with a one-way ticket, of course,   5
Thus do we take our deaths up on our shoulders and walk and walk,
Trying to get back.

We'd like to move as the water moves.
We'd like to cover the earth
                          the way the wind covers the earth.   10
We'd like to burn our way there, like fire.

It's not in the cards.
Uncertainty harbors us like winter mist—
                          the further we go, the deeper it gets.
Sundown now, and wind from the northwest.   15

The month is abandoned.
                          Volvos go wandering to and fro
Like lost polar bears. The landscape is simple and brown.
The future's behind us, panting, lolling its black tongue.

Battle Scene   2002
KELLY CHERRY (b. 1940)

The blacksmith sun hammered the empty plain
Into a great gold plate: a mere mountain

Wouldn't withstand that onslaught day in and out.
Horse hooves striking the bright rock rang like cut

Glass, and a scorpion darted, like a tongue,   5
Back and forth, about to sting or having stung.

This was the scene of battle; on either side
Of the plain, in ranked rows, the soldiers tried

To clear their minds and concentrate on death—
Not their own but someone else's valued breath   10

Brought back like loot. Their shields mirrored the sun,
The sun tipped the head of each javelin

With flame, and in pairs the first line mounted
Chariots drawn by creatures since hunted

To extinction. The reins the driver held   15
Were painstakingly worked from precious gold,

Silver and lapis lazuli, and where
He drove, his cohort hurled a lighted spear.

By the time the shadows lengthened, cooling
The land like streams of water and pooling   20

Into darkness, bodies lay everywhere
As if beaten back by the muscular air

Into a vanished age. The scholars dig
Their grave. The dead soldiers' tactical rig

Spins around a painted wall in a frieze   25
And still spins, after centuries.

Famous Last Words   1979
MICHAEL HEFFERNAN (b. 1942)

Is it a question, then, of getting up
the will to move from one place to the next?
I'm undecided, largely, at the start,
as always, though I guess I'm apt to see
a good bit better once I've had a drink.   5
It's still too soon for that yet. I can wait.

Sometimes I have to laugh: the more you wait,
the more you end up wishing you could up
and have a look at what will happen next.
Where did it ever get you, from the start,   10
the time or two you said you'd wait and see,
when all you really wanted was to drink

it all in, all of it, in one long drink
that would relieve you of the need to wait
for the Right Moment? A man's time is up   15
too soon in this quick world. As for the next,
I think I have a theory: first you start
to notice how you can't move, think, or see,

and this alarms you, so you try to see
what a person has to do to get a drink   20
in this place. No one drinks here, so you wait
a long time trying to figure out what's up—
a very long time, well into the next
two or three thousand years, until you start

to feel more lonely than you were to start   25
with, and you stay this way forever. See,
I'm realistic. And I need a drink.
The will to move is only the will to wait
in different terms: moving is when you're up
and ready for whatever happens next;   30

waiting is what you do when you're the next
in line and several others got the start
on up ahead of you and you can see
their dust rise off them. If I had a drink
instead of breakfast, I could stand the wait.   35
They'd probably like to know what held me up.

Maybe they'll send a man up here to see
what keeps me waiting. Maybe he'll say I'm next.
Maybe he'd like a drink before we start.

The Guilt   1996
GERALD BARRAX (b. 1933)

He made himself her compost heap and hoped
Something old or something new would grow
Where he kept the guilt always in the best light
For her tending, fertilized with bile and bone meal
Ashes shaken through the grate in her heart.   5
She used her privilege of a good woman done wrong
And opened him up at will to nurse and prune
It, until the habit of their make-do lives
One day lulled them off guard into a casual quarrel,
And she turned at bay with her *cri de coeur*,   10
"I will never forgive you, never." He set his face
To muffle its shout of deliverance
When his seahorse womb aborted the misshapen thing
And, midwife to himself, he became a something new.

Ronda   1997
GLORIA VANDO (b. 1936)

On Tuesday they moved my father's
body from its temporary quarters
run by the state to a private plot
on the outskirts of San Juan. "Not

too far away," my sister assures me.   5
"When you come this summer we'll
visit. I think you'll like it better."
My stepmother spent the year

making *coquito* out of coconut
milk and rum. She sold enough bottles   10
at Christmas to raise the $350 it cost
to move my father's body across

town. I marvel at her zeal,
but think, too, of his impending ordeal,
of his bones having to make fresh   15
indentations in the soil, his flesh

having to warm the land around him.
Even in death he seems condemned
to suffer life's transgressions—
forced to break in a final mattress,   20

to take in a final mistress.

Poŝtolka (Prague)   2002
CHRISTIAN WIMAN (b. 1966)

When I was learning words
and you were in the bath
there was a flurry of small birds
and in the aftermath

of all that panicked flight,   5
as if the red dusk willed
a concentration of its light:
a falcon on the sill.

It scanned the orchard's bowers,
then pane by pane it eyed   10
the stories facing ours
but never looked inside.

I called you in to see.
And when you steamed the room
and naked next to me   15
stood dripping, as a bloom

of blood formed in your cheek
and slowly seemed to melt,
I could almost speak
the love I almost felt.   20

Wish for something, you said.
A shiver pricked your spine.
The falcon turned its head
and locked its eyes on mine.

For a long moment I'm still in   25
I wished and wished and wished
the moment would not end.
And just like that it vanished.

Reapers   1923
JEAN TOOMER (1894–1967)

Black reapers with the sound of steel on stones
Are sharpening scythes. I see them place the hones
In their hip-pocket as a thing that's done,
And start their silent swinging, one by one.
Black horses drive a mower through the weeds,   5
And there, a field rat, startled, squealing bleeds,
His belly close to ground. I see the blade,
Blood-stained, continue cutting weeds and shade.

To Autumn   1819
JOHN KEATS (1795–1821)

Season of mists and mellow fruitfulness,
    Close bosom-friend of the maturing sun;
Conspiring with him how to load and bless
    With fruit the vines that round the thatch-eves run;
To bend with apples the moss'd cottage-trees,   5
    And fill all fruit with ripeness to the core;
        To swell the gourd, and plump the hazel shells
    With a sweet kernel; to set budding more,
And still more, later flowers for the bees,
Until they think warm days will never cease,   10
        For summer has o'er-brimm'd their clammy cells.

Who hath not seen thee oft amid thy store?
    Sometimes whoever seeks abroad may find
Thee sitting careless on a granary floor,
    Thy hair soft-lifted by the winnowing wind;   15
Or on a half-reap'd furrow sound asleep,
    Drows'd with the fume of poppies, while thy hook
        Spares the next swath and all its twinèd flowers:

And sometimes like a gleaner thou dost keep
   Steady thy laden head across a brook;   20
   Or by a cider-press, with patient look,
      Thou watchest the last oozings hours by hours.

Where are the songs of spring? Ay, where are they?
   Think not of them, thou hast thy music too,—
While barred clouds bloom the soft-dying day,   25
   And touch the stubble-plains with rosy hue;
Then in a wailful choir the small gnats mourn
   Among the river sallows, borne aloft
      Or sinking as the light wind lives or dies;
And full-grown lambs loud bleat from hilly bourn;   30
   Hedge-crickets sing; and now with treble soft
   The red-breast whistles from a garden-croft;
      And gathering swallows twitter in the skies.

PART

II

CONTENT

A Local Habitation and a Name

And as imagination bodies forth
The forms of things unknown, the poet's pen
Turns them to shapes and gives to airy nothing
A local habitation and a name.
Such tricks hath strong imagination,
That, if it would but apprehend some joy,
It comprehends some bringer of that joy;
Or in the night, imagining some fear,
How easy is a bush supposed a bear!

—WILLIAM SHAKESPEARE
from *A Midsummer Night's Dream* (V, i)

6

SUBJECT MATTER

Though almost no subject today is off-limits to the poet, several misconceptions can blind the beginning poet to the freedom of subject matter. Sometimes students assume that poems should be about traditional or momentous subjects like the seasons, love (especially a lost love), and "the meaning of life," or that a powerful subject will automatically inspire a poem, and the poet just needs to get it down on the page. Similarly, beginning poets suppose the ordinary, everyday things that we experience—things close to the nose, as William Carlos Williams says—aren't proper subjects. Writing under such assumptions, the poet misses scores of opportunities. As filmmaker and writer Jean Cocteau said, "Take a commonplace, clean and polish it, light it so that it produces the same effect of youth and freshness and spontaneity as it did originally, and you have done a poet's job."

Pay attention to the everyday world we usually ignore, and you will find ripe subjects for poems. The common sparrows in the backyard, a construction site at night, a reclusive neighbor, or a cat stepping carefully into and out of a pot can offer you as much raw material as any elaborate subject can.

Also blinding for the beginning poet is the assumption that poetry is mainly direct self-expression: what happened to *me*, what *I feel*. Poets risk psychobabble—merely reporting their own feelings, their own experiences (only because it's their experience), without transforming those experiences. Looking only inward can keep poets from looking outward. If they notice the construction site, the aging neighbor, or the cat, they rush on only to how such things affect them personally. When a poem begins, "The years march in step to a relentless beat," it will likely end with an overblown pronouncement about "the swiftness of time." Such poems emphasize a notion the poet starts with—often a generalized one—rather than reveal through

127

evocative images something a reader might experience. The poet determined to talk about "Time" isn't likely to notice how fast a tree's shadow moves in an hour or a vapor trail unraveling in the sky.

We're all tempted to write poems that spill out our feelings and proclaim our thoughts. And poets, of course, do express themselves, though rarely as directly as it may seem. Coming at a subject sidelong, through implication, can often help us fully engage it. In the following poem, notice how William Matthews (1942–1997) begins by deflecting attention away from himself, thereby taking in the scene's deeper significance:

Men at My Father's Funeral

The ones his age who shook my hand
on their way out sent fear along
my arm like heroin. These weren't
men mute about their feelings,
or what's a body language for?   5

and I, the glib one, who'd stood
with my back to my father's body
and praised the heart that attacked him?
I'd made my stab at elegy,
the flesh made word: the very spit   10

in my mouth was sour with ruth
and eloquence. What could be worse?
Silence, the anthem of my father's
new country. And thus this babble,
like a dial tone, from our bodies.   15

By decentering the son's grief (which nevertheless lies at the heart of this poem), Matthews can foreground the small gestures that reveal the mourners' hidden feelings: a mixture of generosity and selfishness. The older men lament the loss of their friend and at the same time fear for their own lives. Naturally, the men wouldn't admit or acknowledge, perhaps even to themselves, that they have such feelings, but the poet makes the feelings palpable in the awkward handshake between men and son which jolts his arm "like heroin"—powerful, dangerous, and forbidden.

Another poet might simply say he stood before his father's coffin to eulogize him, but Matthews says he stood with his *back* to his father's body, suggesting that he, too, wanted to shun the dead, perhaps because his father reminded him of the precariousness of his own life. The son, "the glib one," speaks the appropriate words of praise for his father, though they turn sour in his mouth for all that remains unsaid. All this noise—body language and spoken language, a babble meaningless as a "dial tone"— speaks of the survivors' desire to drown out the silence they feel hovering behind them. Matthews's poem shows how small commonplace actions speak more powerfully than grand pronouncements.

Subjects and Objects

New poets sometimes despair that everything has already been written. Love, loss, death, birth—the great universal themes of humanity have been written many times over. But the poets of each generation must explore them from their unique perspective in their own idiom and voice. The world is much the same place it has always been. We have cruelty and heroism, wars and famine, peace and bounty; we are selfish and narrow, generous and wise. We love, we work, we try to make sense of life. But we experience all these things somewhat differently from other ages. Our relationship with the natural world, for instance, has changed since the environment has changed, and few of us do much hunting or harvesting. And slightly changed are the relationships between men and women, children and parents, citizens and governments. We live with adult day-care centers, surveillance cameras, GPS systems, sea-farming, and slum malls.

> P*oetry is not the record of an event: it is an event.*
> ——Robert Lowell

Find what is close to your nose. Venture into parts of your neighborhood you have always passed up. Step into the bingo hall, bait shop, or paint store. Talk to the butcher at the supermarket or your elderly cousin. Hang out in the barbershop and listen to the banter, or start up a conversation at a yard sale.

Explore what makes you unique—your point of view, your particular upbringing, your heritage. Family stories may open out into vivid landscapes as they did for Rita Dove (b. 1952) in her Pulitzer-Prize-winning sequence about her grandparents, *Thomas and Beulah* (1986). Dove began with a story her grandmother told about her grandfather "when he was young, coming up on a riverboat to Akron, Ohio, my hometown." And her curiosity led, poem by poem, to a re-creation of the African American experience in the industrial Midwest. "Because I ran out of real fact, in order to keep going, I made up facts . . . ." Like old photographs coming to life, poems such as Dove's that follows show how to explore a subject. Notice how the Depression of the 1930s provides background:

A Hill of Beans

One spring the circus gave
free passes and there was music,
the screens unlatched
to let in starlight. At the well,
a monkey tipped her his fine red hat   5
and drank from a china cup.
By mid-morning her cobblers
were cooling on the sill.
Then the tents folded and the grass

grew back with a path   10
torn waist-high to the railroad
where the hoboes jumped the slow curve
just outside Union Station.

She fed them while they talked,
easy in their rags. *Any two points*   15
make a line, they'd say,
and we're gonna ride them all.

Cat hairs
came up with the dipper;
Thomas tossed on his pillow   20
as if at sea. When money failed
for peaches, she pulled
rhubarb at the edge of the field.
Then another man showed up
in her kitchen and she smelled   25
fear in his grimy overalls,
the pale eyes bright as salt.

There wasn't even pork
for the navy beans. But he ate
straight down to the blue   30
bottom of the pot and rested
there a moment, hardly breathing.
That night she made Thomas
board up the well.
Beyond the tracks, the city blazed   35
as if looks were everything.

Like all of us, these people live among things. The objects in the poem—the screen
door, the monkey with the red cap, the waist-high grass, the cat hairs, overalls, and
navy beans—make it feel authentic. When the couple can't afford peaches for cobblers, the wife gathers rhubarb at the edge of the field. They enjoy the brief wonder of
the circus, then return to their routines of eking out a living and helping out those
worse off. Unlike the hoboes Beulah feeds—who at least enjoy their freedom—the
man in the grimy overalls reeks of fear, suggesting he's on the run; from what or
whom, Dove doesn't reveal. Instead, she allows the tension his secret creates to per-
colate through the lives of her characters.

Anything can become a fertile subject, if you dig into it. As William Matthews says
in his essay "Dull Subjects," "It is not, of course, the subject that is or isn't dull, but the
quality of attention that we do or do not pay to it . . . . Dull subjects are those we have
failed." Cathy Song (b. 1955) puts a spotlight on young mothers taking their babies
out in strollers and makes the familiar seem wonderfully strange:

Primary Colors

They come out in warm weather
like termites
crawling out of the woodwork.

The young mothers chauffeuring
these bright bundles in toy carriages.   5
Bundles shaped like pumpkin seeds.

All last winter,
the world was grown up,
gray figures hurrying along
as lean as umbrellas;   10
empty of infants,
though I heard them at night
whimpering through a succession
of rooms and walls;
felt the tired, awakened hand   15
grope out from the dark
to clamp over the cries.

For a while, even the animals vanished,
the cats stayed close to the kitchens.
Their pincushion paws left padded tracks   20
around the perimeters of houses
locked in heat.
Yet, there were hints of children
hiding somewhere,
threatening to break loose.   25
Displaced tricycles and pubescent dolls
with flaxen hair and limbs askew
were abandoned dangerously on sidewalks.
The difficult walk of pregnant mothers.
Basketfuls of plastic eggs   30
nestled in cellophane grass
appeared one day at the grocer's
above the lettuce and the carrot bins.

When the first crocuses
pushed their purple tongues   35
through the skin of the earth,
it was the striking of a match.
The grass lit up, quickly,
spreading the fire.
The flowers yelled out   40
yellow, red, and green.
All the clanging colors of crayolas
lined like candles in a box.
Then the babies stormed the streets,
sailing by in their runaway carriages,   45
having yanked the wind

out from under their mothers.
Diapers drooped on laundry lines.
The petals of their tiny lungs
burgeoning with reinvented air.   50

Song turns inside out a commonplace subject and makes it riveting. Images normally suggestive of fruitfulness take on a menacing attitude. Babies, young mothers, spring flowers, the sudden growth of grass—the speaker turns a keen eye to these typical sights of spring and connects them with termites, clanging crayons, and fire, suggesting that behind the most familiar world lurks something potent and threatening. The poem's scene seems alien to the speaker and so she renders it as foreign and sinister. For instance, she says, "plastic eggs / nestled in cellophane grass / appeared one day at the grocer's" as if she had never seen Easter decorations before. The hidden children of stanza 3 are "*threatening* to break loose"; in stanza 4 the "flowers *yelled out* / yellow, red, and green"; "the babies *stormed* the streets." Such observations create an insidious undercurrent that suggests the speaker feels a mixture of disgust and delight in children and spring.

Uncovering a productive subject may be partly luck, but luck comes to poets who are alert, who keep their antennae out. In the words of that accidental wit Yogi Berra, "You can observe a lot just by watching." As other poets' poems remind us, the subjects for poetry are boundless, especially when one allows poems to sprout from a noticed detail, a stray connection, something forgotten. Pay attention. Look at things. Examine the tiny furrows in your T-shirt, for instance; really see it and then write about what you notice. Free yourself of clichés about the shirt on your back and how cotton was king. Look at the shirt, the threads, the fine filaments. Like the purloined letter in Edgar Allan Poe's story, the secret is hidden in the open.

Focusing only on what everybody else sees is easy. The result is cliché—not only clichés of language, but clichés of observation, of thought, and even of feeling. We all fall victim to them, and the result is a dead subject. In retelling the story of Romeo and Juliet or the assassination of JFK, the poem that merely reports what we already know won't interest a reader. The poem must see the subject from a unique perspective. What about Juliet's mother at a niece's wedding? What about the auto shop in Dallas that towed the blood-stained car?

Trying to see something fresh stands at the center of making good poems. Insights don't have to be large. Indeed, most of the original ones are small. In "Primary Colors," Cathy Song describes the bundled babies as "shaped like pumpkin seeds." Rita Dove gives us "pale eyes bright as salt." Matthews calls the "babble" of mourners a "dial tone."

Go in fear of abstractions. Don't retell in mediocre verse what has already been done in good prose.
——Ezra Pound

Poems compete with everything else for our attention. As E. E. Cummings says, "It is with roses and locomotives (not to mention acrobats Spring electricity Coney Island the 4th of July the eyes of mice and Niagara Falls) that my 'poems' are competing. They are also competing with each other, with elephants, and with El Greco." Poems must be interesting, or we'll leave them half-read. And *subject matter* can grab our attention like nothing else. Especially for the beginning poet, a subject handled in an arresting manner can make up for any number of technical blunders. If you have special knowledge of a subject (rock climbing, I-10 through Louisiana, how a landfill works, your grandmother's snow boots, your messy car, the origin of your name), exploit it and fascinate a reader.

Occasionally a poet will stumble upon a subject that seems to ask to be written. In 1991, while visiting the Hermitage Museum in St. Petersburg, Miller Williams heard the story that "The Curator" (p. 181) tells. Unable to use a tape recorder or take notes, Williams rushed back to the bus and jotted down three or four pages of vivid recollections. The poem, he remarks, though it went through many revisions, "is as literally true as told to me as any other poem I ever wrote."

Memory

Although poems are neither immediate as diaries nor factual as news reports, they can draw from the vast ocean of personal memory. But the poet doesn't just pull up the bucket, pour out the memory, and Eureka! the poem. Memory doesn't work that way. Although the metaphor of photography is popular, even the most vivid memories aren't snapshots, aren't complete, self-contained units with set boundaries. Memories come to us protean and mysterious, trailing ties to everything else we remember, everything else we are. For a memory to feed a poem, it must be investigated and shaped. Discovering how to approach a memory, exploring its significance, often urges the poet to write the poem in the first place. Consider this poem by Mark Jarman (b. 1952).

Ground Swell

Is nothing real but when I was fifteen,
Going on sixteen, like a corny song?
I see myself so clearly then, and painfully—
Knees bleeding through my usher's uniform
Behind the candy counter in the theater   5
After a morning's surfing; paddling frantically
To top the brisk outsiders coming to wreck me,
Trundle me clumsily along the beach floor's
Gravel and sand; my knees ached with salt.
Is that all that I have to write about?   10
You write about the life that's vividest,
And if that is your own, that is your subject,
And if the years before and after sixteen
Are colorless as salt and taste like sand—
Return to those remembered chilly mornings,   15
The light spreading like a great skin on the water,
And the blue water scalloped with wind-ridges,
And—what was it exactly?—that slow waiting

When, to invigorate yourself you peed
Inside your bathing suit and felt the warmth   20
Crawl all around your hips and thighs,
And the first set rolled in and the water level
Rose in expectancy, and the sun struck
The water surface like a brassy palm,
Flat and gonglike, and the wave face formed.   25
Yes. But that was a summer so removed
In time, so specially peculiar to my life,
Why would I want to write about it again?
There was a day or two when, paddling out,
An older boy who had just graduated   30
And grown a great blond moustache, like a walrus,
Skimmed past me like a smooth machine on the water,
And said my name. I was so much younger,
To be identified by one like him—
The easy deference of a kind of god   35
Who also went to church where I did—made me
Reconsider my worth. I had been noticed.
He soon was a small figure crossing waves,
The shawling crest surrounding him with spray,
Whiter than gull feathers. He had said my name   40
Without scorn, just with a bit of surprise
To notice me among those trying the big waves
Of the morning break. His name is carved now
On the black wall in Washington, the frozen wave
That grievers cross to find a name or names.   45
I knew him as I say I knew him, then,
Which wasn't very well. My father preached
His funeral. He came home in a bag
That may have mixed in pieces of his squad.
Yes, I can write about a lot of things   50
Besides the summer that I turned sixteen.
But that's my ground swell. I must start
Where things began to happen and I knew it.

About this poem, Jarman says:

The poem "Ground Swell" is a record of its own composition. Finding myself
writing again about Santa Monica Bay, where I grew up, I wondered to myself if
I had nothing else to write about, since the landscape of the beach and the
waves continued to be one memory that could always move me to write and
since I continued returning to it as a subject, often nostalgically. As I asked
myself this question, the boy I describe in the poem came skimming into my
mind, paddling past me during the summer of 1968, out into the morning surf,

headed toward the larger swells. Everything I say about him in the poem is true, that is, he was a couple of years older than I, had just graduated from high school, attended my church, was about to go into the army, and had grown a moustache. But for the purposes of composition, his appearance in my memory was crucial. I realized that his death in the Vietnam War, just about a year later, had an enormous effect on my church, my family, and my father. And the memory of him, bringing along with it such historical significance, answered my question. I return to Santa Monica Bay as a subject, again and again, because that is where I first discovered I was connected to history and a larger world. Incidentally, I've visited his name twice at the Vietnam War Memorial in D.C., along with the name of another boy who attended my high school.

The poem's authenticity stems from its steeping in fact and in the years when its memories became distilled. Returning to a memory can give a poem authenticity, but let yourself be fluid in how you use what you remember and how the poem remembers.

Some poems, like Jarman's, may develop out of several related events. But a memory may also simply supply the *context* of a poem in which the poet imagines the events. In the poem below, Philip Levine (b. 1928) takes one of his memories and imagines it through the poet Miguel Hernández. In 1965 Levine made his first visit to Orihuela, Spain, hometown to Hernández. During the Spanish Civil War, Hernández sympathized with the Republican forces that opposed the fascist Francisco Franco, and Hernández paid direly for his opposition. He died in prison at the age of thirty-one. When Levine first visited the region of Hernández's birth, Hernández's wife and son were still living there, and some thirty years later he wrote the following poem that imagined the poet returning from exile "had exile been possible," returning to that world Levine saw on his first visit. The poem asks *What if . . . ?*

The Return: Orihuela, 1965

for Miguel Hernández

You come over a slight rise
in the narrow winding road
and the white village broods
in the valley below. A breeze
silvers the cold leaves   5
of the olives, just as you knew
it would or as you saw
it in dreams. How many days
have you waited for this day?
Soon you must face a son grown   10
to manhood, a wife to old age,
the tiny, sealed house of memory.
A lone crow flies into the sun,
the fields whisper their courage.

Levine's poem is an act of generosity. Although Hernández didn't live to return to his white village with its silver olive trees or see his son grown and his wife old, in the poem he does. Levine shapes his own lively memories of the place and lets the dead poet live in them.

Presenting

Emotions, in themselves, are not subject matter. Being in love, or scared, or lonely, or feeling fantastic because it is spring, these are common experiences. Poems that merely state these emotions won't be very interesting. We respect such statements, but aren't deeply moved by them. To present a poem's complex emotional world, poets rely on the **image,** a representation of a sense impression. While we often think of imagery as visual, images can register any sense; they can be aural (sound), tactile (touch), gustatory (taste), and olfactory (smell). Poems that excite many of our senses draw us in and convince us. We can live inside them. In this poem, Theodore Roethke (1908–1963) brings many kinds of images into play to create an intense memory poem.

My Papa's Waltz

The whiskey on your breath
Could make a small boy dizzy;
But I hung on like death:
Such waltzing was not easy.

We romped until the pans   5
Slid from the kitchen shelf;
My mother's countenance
Could not unfrown itself.

The hand that held my wrist
Was battered on one knuckle;   10
At every step you missed
My right ear scraped a buckle.

You beat time on my head
With a palm caked hard by dirt,
Then waltzed me off to bed   15
Still clinging to your shirt.

We see the pans slide from the shelves and hear them bang on the floor. We feel the rollicking dance of the father, hear and feel him beating time. We can even smell the whiskey. Roethke doesn't state his feelings about his father in "My Papa's Waltz"; he doesn't need to. He lets us feel for ourselves by presenting us with the particular scene out of which the feelings came. While emotions in general aren't subject matter, the *circumstances* of a particular emotion, the scene or events out of which it comes, however, are subject matter. Don't tell the emotion; show the context. When a poem makes manifest—presents through images—a scene, the poem not only convinces the reader of its authenticity, the reader also dramatically *feels* it.

In "Ground Swell," the speaker doesn't say he admired the older surfer, he shows what his admiration meant to him that morning. For Levine details such as "a slight rise / in the narrow winding road" and the breeze that "silvers the cold leaves / of the olives" let him transport us to a place where something might physically happen, where the poet might return. In "A Hill of Beans," Dove doesn't tell us the circus felt magical. She says "the screens unlatched / to let in starlight."

Showing the scene will often be the only adequate way of making your point or presenting the emotion. What word or list of words that describes the emotions of love, fear, pain, mischief, panic, delight, and helplessness could begin to sum up what the boy (and the grown man) feel in (and about) the little scene in "My Papa's Waltz"?

The key is *presenting*; not to *tell* about, but to *show*. To enact, not summarize. Put in the poem how "the sun struck / the water surface like a brassy palm." Put the god-like older surfer with a "great blond mustache, like a walrus" into the poem. Put the circus monkey *into* the poem. Put the handshake between mourners *into* the poem.

And present the subject sharply. Accurate information, details, and terminology make a poem convincing. As a good liar knows, if you're going to say you were late because you had a flat tire, you'd better give a vivid description of your struggling with jack, lug bolts, and traffic whizzing by, and have a good explanation for your clean hands. Whether writing about genetics, antique rifles, Asian elephants, surfing, Finland, or the physics of hurricanes, the poet should know enough, or find out enough, to be reasonably authoritative. Potatoes originated in the New World. Whales aren't fish. Jackie Joyner-Kersee was a track-and-field Olympic gold medalist. Common knowledge, careful observation, and a keen memory are usually enough. Good reference books and field guides help, too. Jarman knows how fatalities were shipped during the Vietnam War. Levine knows the kind of trees that grow in Spain. Though Song sees the spring day from an odd angle, she is still accurate about when termites come out and crocuses bloom and what Easter displays look like. Sometimes poets come upon a subject that sends them to the library and requires their becoming something of a specialist.

In presenting subject matter, *particulars* offer overtones of thought and emotion to a poem, giving it depth and substance. We don't need (or want) *every* detail to make a poem vivid and moving. We need details that are significant and resonant. A poem will bore us with inconsequence if it places us at 51 degrees latitude and 4 degrees longitude on January 17th at 2:28 p.m. beside a 118-year-old willow near a farm pond owned by Mr. John Johnson. The right detail in the right place moves us. Here Thomas Hardy (1840–1928) deftly handles details to create an atmosphere of loss:

Neutral Tones

We stood by a pond that winter day,
And the sun was white, as though chidden of God,
And a few leaves lay on the starving sod;
    —They had fallen from an ash, and were gray.

Your eyes on me were as eyes that rove   5
Over tedious riddles of years ago;
And some words played between us to and fro
    On which lost the more by our love.

The smile on your mouth was the deadest thing
Alive enough to have strength to die;   10
And a grin of bitterness swept thereby
    Like an ominous bird a-wing. . . .

Since then, keen lessons that love deceives,
And wrings with wrong, have shaped to me
Your face, and the God-curst sun, and a tree,   15
    And a pond edged with grayish leaves.

The white sun, the ash tree, the unspecified words that "played" between the lovers, the grayish leaves—Hardy's discrimination, his careful selection of which details to include and which to ignore, presents the bleak memory, the neutral tones of the last moment of a love affair. Consider the difference between saying "a pale sky" and saying "the sun was white," between saying "tree" and saying "ash," or "oak," or "blossoming pear," or "hemlock."

In Roethke's "My Papa's Waltz," the detail about the "pans" sliding from the "kitchen shelf" does more than indicate the rowdiness of the drunken father's dancing. It tells us something about the working-class family—a kitchen neither large nor elegant. More importantly, it sets the scene in the kitchen. The father (affectionately "Papa" in the title) who works with his hands ("a palm caked hard by dirt") has come home late from work, after a bit of whiskey. He has come through the back door into the kitchen. Dinner is over and the pans back on the shelf, but the boy and his mother are still in the kitchen. That they have not held dinner for the father, or waited longer, measures the mother's stored-up anger, as does the word "countenance," which suggests how formidably she has prepared herself. She is "mother" not "mama." The incongruity of the father's merriment is all the stronger because the waltzing begins, so inappropriately, in the kitchen.

As the novelist Elizabeth Bowen observed, "Nothing can happen nowhere. The *locale* of the happening always colors the happening, and often, to a degree, shapes it." As you work your way into a poem—through imagination, memory, or both—anchor it somewhere in space. Even if the scene ends up sketchy, like the funeral in William Matthews's poem, placing the poem in a physical place will help you shape it.

Implication and Focus

Particulars can give a poem a striking singularity and place the reader within the world of the poem. They may also, implicitly, provide a sort of running commentary on the subject or action—and on the speaker's attitude about either. Consider the selection of detail in this poem by Elizabeth Bishop (1911–1979):

First Death in Nova Scotia

In the cold, cold parlor
my mother laid out Arthur
beneath the chromographs:
Edward, Prince of Wales,
with Princess Alexandra,   5
and King George with Queen Mary.
Below them on the table
stood a stuffed loon
shot and stuffed by Uncle
Arthur, Arthur's father.   10

Since Uncle Arthur fired
a bullet into him,
he hadn't said a word.
He kept his own counsel
on his white, frozen lake,   15
the marble-topped table.
His breast was deep and white,
cold and caressable;
his eyes were red glass,
much to be desired.   20

"Come," said my mother,
"Come and say good-bye
to your little cousin Arthur."
I was lifted up and given
one lily of the valley   25
to put in Arthur's hand.
Arthur's coffin was
a little frosted cake,
and the red-eyed loon eyed it
from his white, frozen lake.   30

Arthur was very small.
He was all white, like a doll
that hadn't been painted yet.
Jack Frost had started to paint him
the way he always painted   35
the Maple Leaf (Forever).
He had just begun on his hair,
a few red strokes, and then
Jack Frost had dropped the brush
and left him white, forever.   40

The gracious royal couples
were warm in red and ermine;

their feet were well wrapped up
in the ladies' ermine trains.
They invited Arthur to be   45
the smallest page at court.
But how could Arthur go,
clutching his tiny lily,
with his eyes shut up so tight
and the roads deep in snow?   50

Her first experience with death so absorbs the speaker that she mentions almost nothing outside the "cold, cold parlor"; the details radiate around Arthur in his coffin, the color lithographs of the royal family, and the stuffed loon on its marble-topped table. No other furnishings appear in the poem, and yet from these we can draw the impression of a rather formal room, as well as a sense that the household values patriotism, family loyalty, and propriety.

The pattern of Bishop's imagery links the poem's details. Like Arthur himself and his coffin ("a little frosted cake"), the loon and the chromographs of the royal family are studies in white and red. The loon's breast and the "frozen lake" of the marble-topped table are white; his glass eyes red. Similarly the "gracious royal couples" look "warm in red and ermine." Arthur is "white, forever," except for the "few red strokes" of his hair. The red and white of the loon (killed by her uncle) and of the chromographs (in which the royal family keeps warm wearing other dead animals) seem to connect in the girl's mind with her dead cousin. Such connections create the poem's icy, rich unity: red and white; warm (royal family) and cold (loon).

The nature of the girl's associations embody her limited experience as, for instance, in how the coffin reminds her of a "little frosted cake." The loon is not dead so much as silenced: "Since Uncle Arthur fired / a bullet into him, / he hadn't said a word." Like the girl, the loon is cautious; he "kept his own counsel" and only "eyed" little Arthur's coffin. Struggling to find comfort in the scene, she shifts her attention from Arthur's corpse to the familiar loon and chromographs. The girl's fantasy that the royal family had "invited Arthur to be / the smallest page at court" shows her translating her cousin's death into what she knows. "Jack Frost" suggests the storybook dimensions of that experience. Her mother's whimsical invitation to " 'Come and say good-bye / to your little cousin Arthur' " encourages the fantasy.

Although the girl doesn't understand, she senses that the confusion between life (red) and death (white) will resolve itself ominously: "But how could Arthur go, / clutching his tiny lily, / with his eyes shut up so tight / and the roads deep in snow?" This question implies the fragility of her defense against the grim truth. The final lines shift from the close-up view of Arthur, eyes shut, "clutching his tiny lily," to the wide-angle shot of "roads deep in snow." The distance sets the small boy against a forbidding landscape; both children are up against great, strange forces.

Thinking of visual detail as *cinematography* can remind you of your options as you explore a scene; think of camera angle or location, close-up or distant shot, fade-in or fade-out, panning, montage, and so on. Bishop first presents a frozen lake, and then superimposes the marble-topped table, when she says that the stuffed loon

> kept his own counsel
> on his white, frozen lake,
> the marble-topped table.

The lake becomes a table. The metaphor is simple enough and, in reading, the transformation happens so fast that we scarcely notice. The poet no doubt manages such things intuitively, absorbed by the scene in the inner eye, but nonetheless picking angle, distance, and focus. In "My Papa's Waltz" we never glimpse the father's face. We see his *hand* twice, however: close-ups of the hand on the boy's wrist, the battered knuckle, and of the "palm caked hard by dirt." We see close-ups of the buckle and the shirt. The camera is *at the boy's eye-level*, sees what he sees; the man now speaking sees again what he saw as a boy. Note, incidentally, that he says "My right ear scraped a buckle," not the expected reverse: "His buckle scraped my right ear." How perfectly we see that he cannot blame his father for anything!

As another instance of camera work, consider again Shakespeare's quatrain from Sonnet 73 (p. 34):

> That time of year thou mayst in me behold
> When yellow leaves, or none, or few, do hang
> Upon those boughs which shake against the cold,
> Bare ruined choirs, where late the sweet birds sang.

Line 2 shows us first the yellow leaves of fall, then the later absence of leaves. We're given a distant shot; we don't see a particular tree, simply yellow leaves in the aggregate. But as the camera seems to pan from "yellow leaves" to "none," it seems to stop and move in for a close-up: "or few." So close are we to a few leaves, we are probably seeing a single tree. The sense of loss is intensified; the few hanging leaves seem more desolate than the simplicity of "none."

In line 3, "Boughs" also seems a close-up, looking *up* into the branches. In line 4, the branches are compared to "Bare ruined choirs"; that is, choir lofts of a ruined and roofless church. For a moment we have the impression of standing inside such a church, looking upward through its buttresses (like the branches) at the sky. The film word for the effect might be a "dissolve." It is only momentary, however; in the last half of line 4 we focus on the early winter boughs again, but this time with a superimposed shot of the same boughs in summer, with birds in them. The musical association between the songbirds and the choir lofts supports the shift. Good description means not only choosing effective details but also visualizing them effectively, from the right angle and the right distance.

Details—like the props on the stage and the characters' costumes—bring a scene to life, not just for the reader but for the poet, too, struggling to discover the poem. Details like Bishop's dead loon and Hardy's "ominous bird a-wing" can carry with them a psychological or dramatic undercurrent. Notice, however, that none, if any, of the poems we have been discussing is wholly or mainly descriptive. Purely descriptive poems, though we are tempted to write them, are likely to be tedious, like a video of someone's Hawaiian vacation. As everything in a poem needs to do more than one job, description needs some dramatic or thematic thrust to carry it. Philip Levine in "The Return" renders the village of Orihuela through the eyes of a political exile who has longed for home; the description does emotional work—it *doesn't decorate*. In trying to render a scene's authenticity, poets often go wrong by overdecorating. Particularly when a poem grows out of a strong memory, you may feel inclined to include *everything* you can remember, from every bit of clothing you were wearing to every piece of furniture in the room to every relative who patted you on the head. Consider that if you want to fix your car, you're better off hiring a few skilled mechanics than twenty friends who just want to hang out. So, too, it's best to choose the most evocative details, as Bishop does with the minimal furnishings that suggest the entire psychological realm of the speaker.

While the right detail can convince, careless abstraction can undermine the reader's confidence in the poet. In the work of many beginning poets, words like *love, truth, war, poverty, innocence,* and *evil* ring as hollow and sound as pretentious as political speeches. Trust William Carlos Williams's famous dictum, "No ideas but in things." He does not mean *no* ideas, but rather ideas arrived at through particulars. Not the one or the other, but the inductive relationship between the two. In a general sense, the subjects of "Ground Swell" are memory, growing up, surfing, war, teen aspirations, identity, and lost innocence, but such inert abstractions can't touch us as the poem's details do.

The difference between statement and implication is crucial. Abstractions state a meaning, whereas particulars convey it. Abstractions fail when they draw conclusions unwarranted by example. Abstractions that are earned, distilled from details, convince readers. The details of Hardy's scene in "Neutral Tones" prepare us for the haunting paradox in the middle of the poem: "The smile on your mouth was the deadest thing / Alive enough to have strength to die." (**Paradox:** a seemingly self-contradictory statement that nonetheless expresses some truth.) The speaker abstracts the "keen lessons that love deceives / And wrings with wrong" from his exploration of the particulars of the lovers' last moments together.

QUESTIONS AND SUGGESTIONS

1. After thoroughly examining a slice of bread, a snapped pencil, your knuckle (or some other common object) for twenty minutes or so, write a description of it. Concentrate on what you see, but include smell, touch, taste, and sound if you can.

2. Write a poem about one of the following, or a similarly odd or unique subject (a little research will help). Flesh it out with carefully chosen details.

wringer washer	tattoo parlor	bone fractures
tether ball	skating backwards	sugar cane
bayonets	fire ants	pistachios

3. Here is a poem that has been rewritten so that abstractions and clichés replace imagery, detail, and implication. Freely revise it (including the title), keeping with the same narrative, but inventing images and details you feel might be evocative. Compare your poem with those by others in your writing group (and with the original in Appendix II). How similar do the poems seem?

Our Parents' Wedding

With the silk of her groom's parachute
from World War II, she made her dress.
She felt so vulnerable and exposed
as she stood ready to march
down the aisle with everyone watching,   5
to march into a future spread before her,
a future when we would be born.
She was wide-eyed as a baby deer
and wanted a marriage like in old movies,
her hero a loving husband.   10
They were both so young and innocent.
Her hands shook so hard her bouquet
trembled. She felt she might faint.
Things had been so different
during the war—all the young men   15
were gone,
but now they had returned, the church
overflowing with handsome men
turning to see her coming down
the aisle like a queen. She thought   20
about the reception when the men
would swirl her around the dance floor.
She loved their sexy military haircuts.
Her mother's warnings rang in her ears.
The men looked at her wearing the parachute   25
and remembered the horrible dangers
they had survived.

4. The contemporary references in Maura Stanton's "Handwriting" (p. 150) and Alice Friman's "Diapers for My Father" (p. 208) are among their attractions. Take a detail, device, event, activity, scene that has appeared relatively recently in American life, and see how you might explore it in a

poem. Some possibilities are snowboarding, e-mail chain letters, bubble tea, airport security, West Nile virus, or some recent event in the news.

5. As Judson Mitcham's "An Introduction" (p. 145) and Elizabeth Holmes's "What She Could Do" (below) make abundantly clear, we get to know people in poems by where and how we find them. Write a poem about someone you know well (or someone you invent) by evoking your subject's particular talents, interests, and experiences, for example, "She was runner-up for Miss Daytona Beach in 1972," or "He slept in the bathtub."

6. Take a hobby, talent, or interest you have and plunder it for the subject of a poem. For examples, take a look at the "Poems to Consider" section following and consider how these poets exploit the particulars of their subjects to create poems: Pattiann Rogers, biology; William Olsen, physiology; Al Young, his hometown (Detroit); and Charles Harper Webb, his own name. What special knowledge do you have, or would you like to explore?

POEMS TO CONSIDER

What She Could Do   1997
ELIZABETH HOLMES (b. 1957)

> Swing some good licks
> with a hoe or an axe.
> Scatter sheep manure, doom
> dandelions. Mulch
> with bark and batting.   5
> Name lilies in Latin.
>
> Render pot liquor, turkey-neck
> broth, enormous
> grape-juice fruitcakes—batter
> dripping from fingers.   10
>
> Get her mouth around hymns,
> young Lochinvar, tintinnabulation
> of bells. Be the eensy spider,
> or voice of God. Walk
> blunt. Laugh big. Pinch   15
> with her long white toes.

⬚ An Introduction

JUDSON MITCHAM (b. 1949)

1996

> You who break the dark all night, whisper and shout,
> who travel in and out of all the rooms,
> who come with pill or needle, vial or chart,
> with bedding, mop and bucket, tray of food;
> who turn, clean, pull, read, record, pat, and go;   5
> who see her hair matted by the pillow, greasy white
> wild short hair that will shock
> anyone from home who hasn't seen her for a while—
> shocking like her bones, showing now,
> like the plum-colored bruises on her arms, like her face   10
> when she first comes to and what it says, like her mouth
> and the anything it says: *Call thé bird dogs*, or
> *I've got to go to school*, or *Tonight y'all roll*
> *that wagon wheel all the way to Mexico*; you
> who have seen three children—unbelieving, unresigned—   15
> in all these rooms, full of anger and of prayer;
> you who change her diaper, empty pans
> of green and gold bile she has puked up; you
> who cannot help breathing her decay,
>
> I would like to introduce you to our mother,   20
> who was beautiful, her eyes like nightshade,
> her wavy brown hair with a trace of gold. Myrtle,
> whose alto flowed through the smooth
> baritone our father used to sing;
> our mother, who would make us cut a switch,   25
> but who rocked us and who held us and who kissed us;
> Myrtle, wizard typist, sharp with figures,
> masterful with roses and with roast beef;
> who worked for the New Deal Seed Loan Program,
> for the school, local paper, county agent, and the church;   30
>
> who cared long years for her own failing mother
> (whom she worries for now—you may have heard her);
> who was tender to a fault, maybe gullible,
> as the truly good and trusting often are; and even so,
> who could move beyond fools, though foolishness itself   35
> delighted her—a double take, words turned around,
> a silly dance—and when our mother laughed
> (I tell you this because you haven't heard it),
> the world could change, as though the sun could shine
> inside our very bones.   40

And where it's written in Isaiah
that the briar won't rise, but the myrtle tree,
there's a promise unfulfilled:
she will not go out with joy.
Still, if you had known her, you yourselves,   45
like Isaiah's hills, would sing. You'd understand
why it says that *all the trees*
of the field shall clap their hands.

The Fold-Out Atlas of the Human Body   2002
A Three-Dimensional Book for Readers of All Ages
WILLIAM OLSEN (b. 1954)

The vertebrae are a ladder of moonlight
up and out of the perpetual nocturne of the body.

I open myself with the casualness
of a man having a smoke on a hotel roof.

The legs flip down   5
like ironing boards, and when I turn the page

each bone is numbered and charted and named in a dead language.
When the skeleton folds back, there are the organs—

the lungs, two punctured footballs; the tire-tread tendons;
fold out the lungs, and a jungle of bronchioles   10

must be macheted through
to reach the vertebrae espaliered by arteries.

Here and there a floral wreath of hissing nerves.
When the last tears are secreted,

and the eyes must be avulsed from the skull,   15
whoever will speak in praise of the passing face?

Whoever guessed the prayer book was flesh?
The tongue turned all night like a sleeper in his bed,

having been possessed
And there below the endlessly crouched ilium   20

is the place where the groin is missing out of tact.
The beginning embarrasses us all:

the red lights of our musculature are bad enough.
Blood washes its hands of blood,

there's nothing behind it,   25

and as for the heart,
there is a little door you can open

and reach inside:
bison drawings, cavemen, mothers, mud.

It has dreamed these things we never believed it would.   30

On the Way to Early Morning Mass   2001
PATTIANN ROGERS (b. 1940)

I entered the sea on the way
to early morning mass, walked
down deep along the rims of rock
coral caverns where my misstep
and consequent falling was most   5
slow and careful flying. I passed
over fields of slender, swaying
tubes of cuttlefish nests, supple
sheaves white and iridescent as pearl,
moved among the swift metal precision   10
of barracuda passion and shears.
A scatter of rain on the ceiling
of the sea above me appeared a sky-wide
scatter of stars struck to light
and snuffed in the same moment.   15

I rose from the sea on the way
to early morning mass, walked along
the wet stones of the path, through
the sunken-blue-eyed grasses and cat
peas of the pasture gauzed with drizzled   20
webs, shrouds and shells of beeflies
and seeds clinging to my feet,
along the two-rutted road, its frost-
fringed skims of water in shallow
delves, the fence ragged and tipsy   25
with wild rose, stripped blossoms,
crusty yellow leaves black-spotted.

On the way to early morning mass,
I entered the soft-spun skull inside
the curlew's egg, heard the echo   30
of chimes in that electric cellar
of sun, entered the knot of the witch's
pit, the sweet pulp pit of the lover's

intention, the knot of felicity,
the pit of vagary. Nothing was blacker   35
fire than the government of summer
collapsed in the knot of the coal.

I passed once a fragrance
of strawberries and orange simmering
for jam, once lavender and cedar   40
as from a spinster's trunk long
locked and suddenly opened, once
a sage wind down from the tops
of the pines. A door blew shut,
and a mongrel bitch on her chain   45
yipped to an empty window, circled
twice on her measured length.

On the way to early morning mass,
I followed the invisible corridor
of sky forged by swallows from river-   50
bank to bluff, followed the way
of my hand along the bones of his sleep
in the bed beside me, followed the way
of my eye following the way of winter
rain down the icy runnels of budded   55
oak, and every remembered motion
of succeeding motion was providential,
the way of making the way sanctum,
the proceeding the arrival,
the service continuing on   60
the continuing.

Charles Harper Webb   2001
CHARLES HARPER WEBB (b. 1952)

"Manly," my mother said my first name meant.
I enjoyed sharing it with kings, but had nightmares
about black-hooded axmen lifting bloody heads.

I loved the concept of Charlemagne, and inked
it on my baseball glove and basketball.   5
I learned that females pronounce "Charles" easily;

males rebel. Their faces twitch, turn red as stutterers.
Finally they spit out Charlie or Chuck.
Charles is a butler's name, or a hairdresser's, they explain.

(I'll bet Charles Manson would straighten   10
those guys' tails. I'll bet he'd fix their hair just right.)
My name contains its own plural, its own possessive.

Unlike Bob or Bill or Jim, it won't just rhyme with anything.
I told Miss Pratt, my eighth-grade French teacher,
"Charles sounds like a wimp." I switched to German to be Karl.   15

Of all possible speech, I hear "Charles" best.
I pluck it from a sea of noise the way an osprey plucks a fish.
In print, it leaps out before even sex-words do.

My ears twitch, eager as a dog's. What sweet terror
in the sound: Is Charles there? Oh, Charles.   20
Oh, Charles. Oh, Charles. Charles, see me after class.

Get in this house, Charles Harper Webb!
Harper—nag, angel, medieval musician.
Webb, from Middle English webbe, weaver (as in the web

of my least favorite crawling thing), my pale ancestors   25
stoop-shouldered, with sneezing allergies,
stupefied by the loom's endless clack clack clack,

squatting in dirt-floored cottages year after year,
poking out every decade or so to see brawny men in armor gallop past,
followed by the purple passage of a king.   30

The Tropics in New York   1920
CLAUDE McKAY (1890–1948)

Bananas ripe and green, and ginger-root,
   Cocoa in pods and alligator pears,
And tangerines and mangoes and grape fruit,
   Fit for the highest prize at parish fairs,

Set in the window, bringing memories   5
   Of fruit-trees laden by low-singing rills,
And dewy dawns, and mystical blue skies
   In benediction over nun-like hills.

My eyes grew dim, and I could no more gaze;
   A wave of longing through my body swept,   10
And, hungry for the old, familiar ways,
   I turned aside and bowed my head and wept.

Handwriting   2001

MAURA STANTON (b. 1946)

My sleeve soaked by the automatic spray
Misting the curly endive, my wire cart
Wedged by the potato bin, I'm puzzling
Over my own grocery list. Reams and silk
For supper? Pest food? Some tango chips,   5
A bottle of red wave? I think my brain
Needs other food than what my stomach craves,
And twists my hand into this messy scrawl—
Why waste time on useful cheese and rye
When I could search the aisles for chirps   10
In cellophane bags, buy loaves of rhyme bread,
Every slice exact? Once in grade school
I let my handwriting shrink, almost vanish.
No one but me could read the faint squiggles
Floating above blue lines of tablet paper.   15
At first I just wrote tiny, taking care
To shape each miniature letter perfectly,
But when I realized the teacher couldn't read
My homework answers in such little script,
(WRITE BIGGER! she scrawled across the top)   20
I faked whole lines, giving the illusion
Of sense with all my tiny dots and spirals.
Why? I don't know. I knew the answers.
"Can you read this?" she asked once, pointing,
And I did, extemporizing, so that   25
My homework counted. That's when she gave me
A wooden ruler, and forced me to write
So all my letters fit a measured height.
Glancing now at my list, I see I do
Write large—the lesson stuck—but no more   30
Clearly than before. Shall I put margins
On my toast, add cruelty to salads,
Drink orange joy? As I dig for blurberries
In the frozen food bin, turning up bags
Of rhubarb and black cherries, my fingers   35
Burn with frost, searching for something new
On sale today, maybe ziz-zags of lightning
Some merchant harvested with a thousand kites
And trucked to my town, cubed, still radiant.

My Attempt to Slow Down the World   2001
ROGER KIRSCHBAUM*

On the last night of visitation, we came together
in the shallow home of the much-respected physician
to down beers and close the last chapter in his father's life.
Lois, who had never learned to drive a car, sat beside
herself while we refused to tell the stories of Lyle she   5
so needed to hear; there were plenty of nights left for that.
Cups of coffee steamed on small plates, attempting to strengthen
resolve as we stood weary of our confidence in God.
Family and friends slid past each other politely, touching
hands and faces to bestow upon the other this life;   10
Lois touched them all—the banker, the coke dealer, the stock
broker, the candy striper, the instructor, the stripper.
In the kitchen, the physician and his brothers conferred
and a room upstairs was prepared, tables bruised into place,
lights aimed in interrogation as if to slow down the world;   15
fives and tens were elicited from the men who clamored
near the sink when the plan was broadcast: the stripper would strip
if we wanted her to. We held our hands open and laughed.
We are often wrong about what we think will sustain us.

Détroit Moi   1999
AL YOUNG (b. 1939)

I.

Who says the autumn sonata is not the loveliest of all?
In ancient Detroit, French exploiters like Antoine de la Mothe,
Sieur de Cadillac and Father Richard knew

the meaning of Rolling on the River centuries before
Creedence Clearwater hunked it out. When October rain came   5
to Lake Ponchartrain, how Great Lakes winds blew cold

across and bowed the strings of a Stradivarius, hushed, blasé!
Cadillac knew he didn't have much time to sweat it;
his big gig as Governor of Louisiana was coming up.

The fix was in. To hell with all the wild pigs out there   10
uprooting Belle Isle! Nobody knew the trouble they'd see.
Nobody knew how ruthlessly the troublesome Negroes

would migrate, would move Louisiana, Texas, Arkansas,
Mississippi, chicken bones, spareribs and all, straight up
to Michigan. And with them—packed, billed out and bound to go—   15

your red and white and blue people, your purple mountain
majesty people, some fruitfully, some truthfully plain.
O Lady Be Good. And the Lady of Our Profit was good.

The Cream of Michigan Café, 12th Street, its prehistoric
gleam distilled with raw gangster moonlight in the pull-down   20
Purple Gang nights, sang her virtues. This was Jewish splendor,

this was life that came down heavily on the side of live
(as in give and let give, get and let get). Friends and lovers
in the dharma, how easy it is to forget that every mouth

you twitch to kiss, each cheek you speak your half of stories to,   25
and every body you long to hold magnificently belongs.
To someone nestled in the somewhere they come from,

they return in dreams, in daydreams, in the ways they walk
or worry, hold their mouths, or gaze across a ruined café, or smoke.
Those many somewheres do not sit alone; their someones leave   30

to start new families by design, or on the fly. A song,
a rhapsody, a blacked-out blues, a softening autumn sonata
can take you up to Canada and back, the watery crawl a cry away.

The émigré who danced or listened hard to dreams escaped.
Endurance wasn't measured by the mapped rabbit's leap   35
above the glove, but by which peninsula of Michigan you reached.

II.

Autumn sonata. 1937. When Henry Ford sent a payroll of goons
to break the union ties, to crack the onion heads of strikers
and their ilk, the rusting stream of red at River Rouge grew thick.

All down between the cracks, all up and down, the earth was bled.   40
Gone Russia shone with blood, Brown shirts were turning black.
Back in Detroit the car to be somebody in became a Cadillac.

And so Ferdinand Destouches sailed into Big D. as Céline.
Now we know there was a woman involved, a nurse, no, a Detroiter
who ended up becoming his obsession. By profession, the Nazi   45

strain of things unlinked and let this solid block of properties become
the Arsenal of Democracy. If the Czechs construct that Monument
to the Victims of Communism, someone will have to build another:

Monument to the Victims of Capitalism. Bohunks of the world, unite!
You have nothing to lose but your tedious prejudices. When they ask   50
and you can't site the home turf of a colorful American, say Detroit.

Say Robert Hayden, Lily Tomlin, Gladys Knight, Madonna,
Marge Piercy, Mitch Ryder, Philip Levine, Diana Ross, Joe Henderson,
Marvin Gaye, Elmore Leonard, Aretha Franklin, Michael Moore,

Smokey Robinson, Malcolm X, Lawrence Joseph, Barry Harris,   55
Paul Chambers, John Sinclair, Yusef Lateef, Stevie Wonder—
and if your blue sonata thrills like Detroit in the fall, call Al Young.

7

TALE, TELLER, AND TONE

Every poem begins with a voice, a **speaker,** the person who tells us whatever we hear or read. Usually the poet speaks, but often someone else does. Just as anything can serve as the subject of a poem, so too anyone, indeed, any*thing* can serve as the speaker. A mermaid, whose song seduced sailors into shipwreck, speaks in this poem by Amy Gerstler (b. 1956):

Siren

I have a fish's tail, so I'm not qualified to love you.
But I do. Pale as an August sky, pale as flour milled
a thousand times, pale as the icebergs I have never seen,
and twice as numb—my skin is such a contrast to the rough
rocks I lie on, that from far away it looks like I'm a baby   5
riding a dinosaur. The turn of centuries or the turn
of a page means the same to me, little or nothing.
I have teeth in places you'd never suspect. Come. Kiss me
and die soon. I slap my tail in the shallows—which is to say
I appreciate nature. You see my sisters and me perched   10
on rocks and tiny islands here and there for miles:
untangling our hair with our fingers, eating seaweed.

As the siren talks, she characterizes herself and presents the scene where we find her stretched out on a rock, munching on seaweed. Her cool diction ("not qualified," "I appreciate nature") supports her cool temperament—and temperature. Her skin is "pale as icebergs." She says, matter of factly, "Kiss me / and die soon." She fits our assumptions about a mermaid/siren, but the details of her portrait—her phrasing, her tail slapping the water, her disinterest in passing time, her diet—sharpen and complicate the picture.

We can think of a poem as a miniature play. The speaker steps out and begins to address us, or someone else, and thereby creates a person and a context. As when we see a character step on to a stage, when we see a poem on the page our expectations are heightened: We expect that what follows will somehow be significant (even if what's said is simple), that what's said will be a *distillation* of thought, emotion, events, not merely someone's prosaic ramblings. (Even when a poem appears to capture the inner stream of someone's consciousness, the poem presents particular associations of a particular mind at a particular time, not accidental musings). After all, a poem that charms us with its seeming artlessness is still a poem, a work of art; it aims for the permanent, not the merely expedient, like a phone call. The scene in which we find a speaker can be just as various as a poem's speaker. We may find the complex world of Miller Williams's "The Curator" (p. 181) which takes many turns over many lines, telling the story of the Hermitage Museum during World War II. Or we find the more direct but less realistic circumstances of "Siren." But for the speaker's circumstances to matter to us, something must be at stake in them: They must be dynamic. In "The Curator," artistic masterpieces and the spirit of a people are at stake. In "Siren," what's at stake is implicit—the lives of the sailors.

Consider the simple, yet dynamic, circumstances, of this quiet poem:

Adlestrop
EDWARD THOMAS (1878–1917)

Yes, I remember Adlestrop—
The name, because one afternoon
Of heat the express-train drew up there
Unwontedly. It was late June.

The steam hissed. Someone cleared his throat.　　　　　　　　　5
No one left and no one came
On the bare platform. What I saw
Was Adlestrop—only the name

And willows, willow-herb, and grass,
And meadowsweet, and haycocks dry,　　　　　　　　　　　10
No whit less still and lonely fair
Than the high cloudlets in the sky.

And for that minute a blackbird sang
Close by, and round him, mistier,
Farther and farther, all the birds　　　　　　　　　　　　15
Of Oxfordshire and Gloucestershire.

No one would mistake this for a Hollywood action flick, but notice the poem opens dynamically, with a **motivating incident,** something that prompts the poem: Apparently the speaker has just been asked if he has ever heard of the town Adlestrop, and he responds with this memory.

Look how the circumstances change and how much is at stake though nothing dramatic *happens*. We're presented with a little mystery—why the express halts at an unlikely place for no apparent reason. The train "hissed," as if impatient. Someone almost speaks, but doesn't. After the first sentence, running three and a half lines, we get three short sentences expressing stasis as we anticipate something happening. Then, although the *train* doesn't move, the *sentences* begin to. The bluster and rush of the express train give way to the quiet affirmation of the wildflowers and then, gradually, the birds' singing. For the moment of quiet, the speaker seems to *hear* "Farther and farther," until this spot of nowhere, with no town visible, enters a birdsong-filled stillness that spreads out across two counties. Of course he remembers Adlestrop.

Narration and Action

Many poems are **narratives**; they tell (or imply) stories. Books of poetry can be novel-like: Robert Browning's crime thriller *The Ring and the Book* (1868–1869), Vikram Seth's *The Golden Gate* (1986), Andrew Hudgins's *After the Lost War* (1988), Mark Jarman's *Iris* (1992), Margaret Gibson's *The Vigil* (1993), and Anne Carson's *The Autobiography of Red* (1998). And poets have written striking short stories in verse, from Chaucer's tales to Christina Rossetti's "Goblin Market" to Frost's "Witch of Coös" (p. 173).

Like fiction writers, poets, too, can deploy narrative techniques to spin an arresting tale. Consider this poem by Marilyn Nelson (b. 1946):

Minor Miracle

Which reminds me of another knock-on-wood
memory. I was cycling with a male friend,
through a small midwestern town. We came to a 4-way
stop and stopped, chatting. As we started again,
a rusty old pick-up truck, ignoring the stop sign,   5
hurricaned past scant inches from our front wheels.
My partner called, "Hey, that was a 4-way stop!"
The truck driver, stringy blond hair a long fringe
under his brand-name beer cap, looked back and yelled,
       "You fucking niggers!"   10
and sped off.
My friend and I looked at each other and shook our heads.
We remounted our bikes and headed out of town.
We were pedaling through a clear blue afternoon
between two fields of almost-ripened wheat   15
bordered by cornflowers and Queen Anne's lace

when we heard an unmuffled motor, a honk-honking.
We stopped, closed ranks, made fists.
It was the same truck. It pulled over.
A tall, very much in shape young white guy slid out: 20
greasy jeans, homemade finger tattoos, probably
Marine Corps boot-camp footlockerful
of martial arts techniques.

"What did you say back there!" he shouted.
My friend said, "I said it was a 4-way stop.   25
You went through it."
"And what did I say?" the white guy asked.
"You said: 'You fucking niggers.'"
The afternoon froze.

"Well," said the white guy,   30
shoving his hands into his pockets
and pushing dirt around with the pointed toe of his boot,
"I just want to say I'm sorry."
He climbed back into his truck
and drove away.   35

Paying attention to the fundamentals of good narrative allows a poet to choose what to include and what to leave out, when to summarize details and when to depict the action moment by moment; that is, how to control the poem's *pacing*. Nelson's deft handling of the narrative derives from her pacing, her control of the poem's sense of *time*. She starts her story very close to the center of the action, not with the beginning of the bike ride but with the confrontation with the man. The poem's conversational tone draws us in. Then she presents the crucial circumstances of the story: cycling, small Midwestern town, four-way stop. When the driver "hurricanes past," the action speeds up, the details grow menacing, then erupt.

After the driver hurls the racial slur at them, Nelson slows the action down again by turning the camera on the countryside, building suspense. In rendering the lush natural world around them, in "writing off the subject" as Richard Hugo called the technique, Nelson sharpens the scene's contrast with the threatening man and his loud machine. When the driver looms up again, he intrudes upon the peaceful meadows which (we come to realize) anticipate the amazing turnaround we later see in the driver's character. Through stanza breaks and by focusing in on details like the pointed toes of the man's boots, Nelson holds off this final revelation and so intensifies the payoff.

A seemingly unimportant feature, *verb form*, helps control the action. Most of "Minor Miracle" takes place in the simple past tense, also called the *narrative past*: "stopped," "started," "yelled," "slid out," "shouted," "climbed back," "drove away." But the past progressive marks crucial moments; the central story begins with "I was cycling," signaling that the action will soon shift. Look at the point after they remount their bikes: "We were pedaling through a clear blue afternoon . . . when we heard an unmuffled motor . . ." (lines 14–17). This past progressive indicates something is about to happen. Similarly at the end, before the man makes his apology, we see him "shoving his hands in his pockets / and pushing dirt." And did you notice that the entire poem is framed within the present tense, within the phrase, "Which reminds me . . ."? Such a frame helps supply the poem's motivating incident: spurred by something in conversation, the speaker recounts the story.

> *We make out of the quarrel with others, rhetoric, but of the quarrel with ourselves, poetry.*
> —W. B. Yeats

For telling a story or even relating a short anecdote, the storyteller must handle verb form attentively. As we can see in Nelson's poem, the verbs help us keep track of where the action is going, where it has been, and where it's headed. Use of the past tense indicates completed action and suggests, therefore, that the speaker has had time to reflect, as Wordsworth says, *to recollect in tranquility*, to weigh the events. Marilyn Nelson's title suggests such reflection: The man's surprising apology was a "Minor Miracle."

For creating immediacy and intensity the present tense usually works best. You will often find that when a poem *feels* cool and remote that casting it in present tense can warm it up. The present tense also controls the realm of eternal truths, as in Whitman's "A Noiseless, Patient Spider" (p. 36), and that of discovered truths, like those of Liz Rosenberg's "The Silence of Women" (p. 102). Gerstler's siren lives in an eternal, remorseless present.

As we might expect, the future tense belongs to the realms of the imagined and desired; it controls prophecy poems such as Nina Cassian's "Ordeal" (p. 220) and Donald Justice's "Variations on a Text by Vallejo" (p. 240).

Carefully handled, verbless fragments can be effective "sentences." Sharon Bryan's "Sweater Weather" strings such fragments into a "Love Song to Language" (p. 3). The first stanza of Keats's "To Autumn" (p. 122) contains only *verbals*, such as "maturing" or "to bend." The stanza itself acts like a long address to the season, helping Keats personify it as a beautiful woman. But use verbless sentences with care. A passage without verbs surrenders a significant marker. As you work on your poems, carefully weigh your decisions about verb form; try out different tenses to see what effect they have on your subject. Consider how "Adlestrop" cast entirely in the present tense would lose its poignancy, as would "Siren" cast in the past tense. The skilled writer minds a poem's verbs as a shrewd gambler keeps track of the betting around the table. This sly poem about storytelling makes the point clear:

Understanding Fiction
HENRY TAYLOR (b. 1942)

What brings it to mind this time? The decal
from East Stroudsburg State in the window
ahead of me as traffic winds to the airport?

Maybe we pass the Stroudwater Landing apartments.
Whatever it is, you who are with me get to hear it   5
all over again: how once, just out of college

or maybe a year or two later, into the first
teaching job, some circumstance found me
in the home of an old friend, one of the mentors

to whom I owe what I am, on one of those days   10
when the airwaves are filled with football.
We remember it now as four games, and swear

to one another, and to others, that this
is what happened. In the second game,   15
as men unpiled from a crowded scramble,

a calm voice remarked that Mike Stroud
had been in on the tackle, and we told
ourselves that we had heard the same thing

in the first game. Odd. So we listened,
or claimed to be listening, and drank,   20
and took what we were pleased to call notice.

Never an isolating or identifying shot,
just these brief observation of crowds:
Mike Stroud was in all four games.

An astonishing trick, a terrific story—   25
some plot of the color commentators,
a tribute to a friend with a birthday,

or maybe just a joke on the world.
I tell it at least four times a year,   30
and each time it is longer ago.

Mike Stroud, if he ever played football,
does not do so now, but he might
even have played only one game

that late fall day in—oh, 1967, let's say.
We were drinking. God knows what we heard.   35
But I tell it again, and see how

to help you believe it, so I make
some adjustment of voice or detail,
and the story strides into the future.

Persona

The poet's ability to imagine and to project underlies what Keats called **negative capability.** In a letter he described this as the capability "of being in uncertainties, Mysteries, doubts, without any irritable reaching after fact & reason." In another letter he talks about

the chameleon Poet . . . the most unpoetical of anything in existence, because
he has no Identity—he is continually in for [informing] and filling some other
Body—The Sun, the Moon, the Sea and Men and Women.

Through negative capability poets can empty the self, suspend judgments, and so
imagine others from the inside out. Keats wrote, "if a sparrow come before my window,
I take part in its existence and pick about the gravel," and that he could conceive that
"a billiard Ball . . . may have a sense of delight from its own roundness, smoothness
volubility & the rapidity of its motion."

The following poem shows how the poet can get inside the existence of others and
manifest their inner reality. While touring an abandoned coal mine in Wales, the
speaker imagines the strange sunless world of the ponies his guide describes.

Pit Pony
WILLIAM GREENWAY (b. 1947)

There are only a few left, he says,
kept by old Welsh miners, souvenirs, like
gallstones or gold teeth, torn
from this "pit," so cold and wet my
breath comes out a soul up   5
into my helmet's lantern
beam, anthracite walls running,
gleaming, and the floors iron-rutted
with tram tracks, the almost pure
rust that grows and waves like   10
orange moss in the gutters of water
that used to rise and drown.
He makes us turn all lights off, almost
a mile down. While children scream
I try to see anything, my hand touching   15
my nose, my wife beside me—darkness palpable,
velvet sack over our heads, even the glow
of watches left behind. This is where
they were born, into this nothing, felt
first with their cold noses for the shaggy   20
side and warm bag of black
milk, pulled their trams for twenty
years through pitch, past birds
that didn't sing, through doors
opened by five-year-olds who sat   25
in the cheap, complete blackness listening
for steps, a knock. And they
died down here, generation after
generation. The last one, when it
dies in the hills, not quite blind, the mines   30

closed forever, will it die strangely? Will it
wonder dimly why it was exiled from the rest
of its race, from the dark flanks of the soft
mother, what these timbers are that hold up
nothing but blue? If this is the beginning   35
of death, this wind, these stars?

The poem moves us from the present, to the past, then—as the poet explores the
weird world of creatures shut away from the open air—to the future. By moving us
through these three time periods, Greenway gives the
impression of having made a wide swoop through
time, projecting a sad dignity to the forgotten ponies
and overcoming the limited vision that a poem set
solely in the present tense might risk.

> *P*oetry is the supreme fiction.
> —Wallace Stevens

When a poem's speaker is clearly someone other than the poet, we often refer to it
as a **persona poem:** a poem in which a fictional, mythic, historic, or other figure
speaks. As if dressing up for a costume party, the poet takes on the mask of another
character. The speaker need not be important, nor even human.

Daisies
LOUISE GLÜCK (b. 1943)

Go ahead: say what you're thinking. The garden
is not the real world. Machines
are the real world. Say frankly what any fool
could read in your face: it makes sense
to avoid us, to resist   5
nostalgia. It is
not modern enough, the sound the wind makes
stirring a meadow of daisies: the mind
cannot shine following it. And the mind
wants to shine, plainly, as   10
machines shine, and not
grow deep, as, for example, roots. It is very touching,
all the same, to see you cautiously
approaching the meadow's border in early morning,
when no one could possibly   15
be watching you. The longer you stand at the edge,
the more nervous you seem. No one wants to hear
impressions of the natural world: you will be
laughed at again; scorn will be piled on you.
As for what you're actually   20
hearing this morning: think twice
before you tell anyone what was said in this field
and by whom.

These bright, articulate, and witty daisies see through the poet's nervousness and seem to mock her internal struggle: "It is very touching," they say. They apparently have recognized that the poet resists them as poetic subject—even though she is drawn to them—because the daisies are "not modern enough." The poet feels she "will be / laughed at again; scorn will be piled on" her if she offers "impressions of the natural world." The daisies act as the vehicle that identifies the poet's misgivings and exposes the tangle of voices inside a poet when writing a poem: "think twice," the daisies advise, "before you tell anyone what was said in this field / and by whom."

In a sense a persona operates in most, if not all, poems. After all, for readers who don't know the poet personally, any poem involves the perception of a presented character, real or otherwise. Thus, even the poet writing or trying to write in his or her own voice creates a self, by presenting a *particular* tone, stance, circumstance, and theme; otherwise, the poem drifts in the generic. As in life we show different faces to different people and in different situations (at the beach, in church), so in writing, often without realizing it, we adjust the voice we use, naturally adopting somewhat different *personae*. Yeats called such versions of the self the poet's *masks*. In writing a poem, the poet puts on a mask, adopts a *persona* who speaks the poem. This process of taking on a mask, when the issues are serious, may even amount to exploring one's identity, ethnicity, gender, or heritage; that is, to self-discovery.

Through looking at a version of the self, poets challenge their assumptions and enlarge their perceptions—along with a reader's. The imagination of this poem leads the speaker through a spiritual exercise.

Among the Cows
ENID SHOMER (b. 1944)

Advised to breathe with the Holsteins
    as a form of meditation,
I open a window in my
    mind and let their vast humid breath,
sticky flanks, the mantric switching   5
    of their tails drift through. I lie down
with them while they crop the weedy
    mansions, my breasts muffled like the
snouts of foxes run to ground. I
    need to comfort the cows, the way   10
heart patients stroke cats and the grief
    of childhood is shed for dogs. I
offer them fans of grass under
    a sky whose grey may be the hide
of some huge browser with sun and   15
    moon for wayward eyes. It begins

to rain. How they sway, their heavy
    necks lift and strain. Then, like patches
of night glimpsed through a bank of clouds,

they move toward four o'clock, the dark 20
fragrant stalls where dawn will break first
    as the curved pink rim of their lips.
I want to believe I could live
    this close to the earth, could move with
a languor so resolute it 25
    passes for will, my heart riding
low in my body, not this flag
    in my chest snapped by the lightest
breeze. Now my breath escapes with theirs
    like doused flames or a prayer made 30
visible: May our gender bear
    us gracefully through in these cumbrous frames.

Choosing cows for a poem about contemplation makes fine sense. Cows are classified with other cud-chewers as "ruminants," related to the word "ruminate." When we ponder something we're said to chew on it. The languorous cows show her a way to be "close to the earth." Imagining the cows' "vast humid breath, / sticky flanks, the mantric switching / of their tails," she arrives at the notion that cows see the cosmos as a version of themselves: the gray sky may be "the hide of some huge browser with sun and / moon for wayward eyes." Similarly, the dawn breaks like the "curved pink rim of their lips." Gradually she seems to understand that if the world resembles ourselves, then by finding peace within, the world outside will become peaceful. The speaker finds that breath itself, in the simple act of breathing, becomes a prayer that she is praying, too: "May our gender bear / us gracefully through in these cumbrous frames."

Point of View

We call the angle from which a poem comes to us its **point of view.** In *first-person* point of view the "I" or "we" reports what happens; in *second* person the "you" reports; in *third* person "he," "she," or "they" reports. Although we use these three general categories, any point of view of any particular narrative involves fine gradations. As this devious speaker makes plain, control of the vantage point makes all the difference:

My Last Duchess
ROBERT BROWNING (1812–1889)

That's my last duchess painted on the wall,
Looking as if she were alive. I call
That piece a wonder, now: Frà° Pandolf's hands
Worked busily a day, and there she stands.

3 Frà: Friar, a monk; Browning has invented a Renaissance painter-monk, like Frà Angelico, for this poem. The sculptor of the poem's last line (Claus of Innsbruck) is also Browning's invention.

Will't please you sit and look at her? I said   5
"Frà Pandolf" by design, for never read
Strangers like you that pictured countenance,
The depth and passion of its earnest glance,
But to myself they turned (since none puts by
The curtain I have drawn for you, but I)   10
And seemed as they would ask me, if they durst,
How such a glance came there; so, not the first
Are you to turn and ask thus. Sir, 'twas not
Her husband's presence only, called that spot
Of joy into the Duchess' cheek: perhaps   15
Frà Pandolf chanced to say "Her mantle laps
Over my lady's wrist too much," or "Paint
Must never hope to reproduce the faint
Half-flush that dies along her throat": such stuff
Was courtesy, she thought, and cause enough   20
For calling up that spot of joy. She had
A heart—how shall I say?—too soon made glad,
Too easily impressed; she liked whate'er
She looked on, and her looks went everywhere.
Sir, 'twas all one! My favor at her breast,   25
The dropping of the daylight in the West,
The bough of cherries some officious fool
Broke in the orchard for her, the white mule
She rode with round the terrace—all and each
Would draw from her alike the approving speech,   30
Or blush, at least. She thanked men—good! but thanked
Somehow—I know not how—as if she ranked
My gift of a nine-hundred-years-old name
With anybody's gift. Who'd stoop to blame
This sort of trifling? Even had you skill   35
In speech—which I have not—to make your will
Quite clear to such an one, and say, "Just this
Or that in you disgusts me; here you miss,
Or there exceed the mark"—and if she let
Herself be lessoned so, nor plainly set   40
Her wits to yours, forsooth, and made excuse,
—E'en then would be some stooping; and I choose
Never to stoop. Oh sir, she smiled, no doubt,
Whene'er I passed her; but who passed without
Much the same smile? This grew; I gave commands;   45
Then all smiles stopped together. There she stands
As if alive. Will't please you rise? We'll meet
The company below, then. I repeat,
The Count your master's known munificence

Is ample warrant that no just pretense   50
Of mine for dowry will be disallowed;
Though his fair daughter's self, as I avowed
At starting, is my object. Nay, we'll go
Together down, sir. Notice Neptune, though,
Taming a sea-horse, thought a rarity,   55
Which Claus of Innsbruck cast in bronze for me!

By allowing this Renaissance duke to speak for himself, Browning reveals that within this eloquent, intelligent, cultivated man lurks greed, arrogance, cunning, and ruthlessness. The Duke of Ferrara is addressing a subordinate, an envoy from a count; they are negotiating the terms for the count's daughter to become the next duchess.

Just as he controls who will now look at his last duchess, the duke controls his words, all the while claiming he has no "skill / In speech." With prevaricating smoothness, he reveals that he had her murdered ("I gave commands; / Then all smiles stopped together," lines 45–46) because he felt, among other things, that she did not exhibit a high enough regard for him and his title ("as if she ranked / My gift of a nine-hundred-years-old name / With anybody's gift," lines 32–34). He puts a slick spin on his account of her.

When he comes to the delicate subject of the new dowry, notice how abstract his diction and how convoluted his syntax become ("no just pretense / Of mine for dowry will be disallowed," lines 50–51). The duke doesn't specify how much of a dowry he expects; instead he compliments the count's generosity and notes the expectations that munificence engenders.

When a character's speech creates a dramatic scene, like the Italian Renaissance world of "My Last Duchess," we often call the poem a **dramatic monologue.** Created by his speech, the duke appears as vividly as a character on stage. Besides monologues, poems can take the forms of letters, diary entries, prayers, internal meditations, definitions—any form that human utterance can take. Frost's "The Witch of Coös" (p. 173) combines two forms: A first person narrates a *dialogue* between a mother and son.

The first-person point of view has the advantages of creating immediacy, intensity, and sympathy. Call to mind the child-speaker in "First Death in Nova Scotia" (p. 139). Filtered through the girl's innocence and inexperience, the scene suggests the bizarre nature of death's rituals, and, ultimately, of death itself. Hearing the duke's story from his own mouth makes him a compelling, even perversely attractive, figure; we hear what he wants the envoy to hear although we perhaps end up knowing more about his ruthlessness than he intends. Perhaps. The duke's self-disclosure may be a tactic. Is he manipulating the envoy, planting a message for the new bride about what the duke demands—and what the consequences are if she doesn't comply? Or perhaps the duke doesn't care how much he reveals; perhaps he is merely relishing his power.

Like many first person narrators, the duke is unreliable; the reader must weigh his claims. First-person narrators may have intellectual, psychological, emotional, experiential, or even moral limits which color the picture they present. The duke's arrogance skews his description of his duchess who, we nonetheless understand, is guilty only of having had an easy and open nature. Typically, the closer a narrator is to the poem's central character or situation, the less psychic distance he or she will have and the less reliable the narrator will be. The closer we are to an event—temporally or psychologically—the less objective we tend to be. And, the farther from an event, the weaker our memory—as Henry Taylor's "Understanding Fiction" slyly attests.

The second-person point of view appears infrequently in stories, but more often in poetry than in prose fiction. The second person appears in the direct address of love poems and in imperatives—directions and directives—like Muriel Rukeyser's "A Simple Experiment" (p. 93), which tells someone how to unmake and remake a magnet. In American English, we often use "you" when the British would use "one," to describe habitual or typical action; such is the case with poems such as Cornelius Eady's "The Wrong Street" (p. 95) and Natasha Sajé's "Reading the Late Henry James" (p. 238). At times "you" may signify "I," as when you mutter to yourself, "You're going to be late for work." When speakers address themselves—advising, blaming, warning, motivating, reminding—we glimpse their inner struggle and can feel pulled into a common sympathy with the speaker:

When Someone Dies Young
ROBIN BECKER (b. 1951)

When someone dies young
a glass of water lives
in your grasp like a stream.
The stem of a flower
is a neck you could kiss.   5
When someone dies young
and you work steadily
at the kitchen table
in a house calmed by music
and animals' breath,   10
you falter at the future,
preferring the reliable past,
films you see over and over
to feel the inevitable
turning to parable, characters   15
marching with each viewing
to their doom.
When someone dies young
you want to make love furiously
and forgive yourself.   20
When someone dies young
the great religions welcome you,
a supplicant begging with your bowl.
When someone dies young
the mystery of your own   25

good luck finds a voice
in the bird at the feeder.
The strict moral lesson
of that life's suffering
takes your hand, like a ghost,   30
and vows companionship
when someone dies young.

The poem's distinctive details—such as the working at the kitchen table "in a house
calmed by music / and animals' breath"—suggest that the speaker is addressing herself,
and yet the poem's entire attitude includes the reader. In a sense the "you" calls us by
name and includes us, helping us remember—or imagine—our own feelings "when
someone dies young." The repetition of this subordinate clause forms a rhythm of sus-
pension and release that further involves the reader.

The third-person point of view covers a wide spectrum, from narrow to wide angles
of vision, from limited points of view that focus on a single character to wider, all-
knowing points of view. Such *omniscient* third-person points of view may display god-
like powers, jumping around in time and space, shifting from inside one character's
consciousness to another's, and understanding events, motives, and circumstances one
person would not.

The following poem takes a narrow point of view, that of a girl who is trying to avoid
thinking or feeling. Notice the point of view's detachment as it presents the scene.

Kitten
FLEDA BROWN (b. 1944)

She is thirteen. Her cat, Sneakers,
has just had another litter of kittens
to be chloroformed by her father
in the large cooking pot. "Keep whichever
you want," he says, "mother or kitten,   5
just one." She is sitting on her bed
petting the male kitten with thick
tan fur. She sits close to her Silvertone
radio, moves her mouth to the music.
A rifle cracks in the back yard,   10
then a scuffle like a rat
under the house. Sneakers has gotten
away, not quite dead, is crouched
in a far corner wailing a low
steady wail. She watches the square   15
knob on her dresser, lit with sun,
the back hairs of her kitten ablaze
in the sunlight like little spines.
Under her is the live crawlspace.

She holds the little paws of her kitten,   20
pushes her thumbs gently into the center
of the pads with almost divine
tenderness, watches the claws extend
involuntarily, translucent little hooks.
She has a vision of pushing until they fly   25
outward like darts, or rays of sun,
leaving the kitten with buff-
colored buttons of feet. She names it
Buffy, imagines buffing the DeSoto
with the kitten, rubbing him flat   30
as her grandmother's fox stole,
popping in little marbles for eyes
that would catch the light,
hard. Her father is calling kitty, here
kitty, his flashlight in the cat's   35
eyes. It is Jungle-Cat, leaping out
of a 3-D screen among arrows, flying
at the audience. She stretches out on
the bed and brushes her face across
her smooth animal. A dark creature passes   40
through the back chambers of her thought
like a shadow, enters a kingdom
of shadows, stirring and stirring.

The poem's omniscient narrator keeps her distance, cooly reporting what happens as we move between the girl's obsessive attention to the kitten to the father hunting down the doomed mother cat. Having established the scene, the point of view shifts to the girl's violent fantasies and reveals her as passive, floating in a wordless realm without deeply reflecting on the events around her. The images of hardness and sharpness suggest that this passiveness may be an armor she wears against her father's cruelty. Her manipulation of the kitten's claws hints at how the girl might repay her father as she grows up.

Tone

When we attempt to describe the **tone** of a poem, we are trying to identify its complex of attitudes toward its subject, including the attitudes of the speaker and the poet, which, as Brown's "Kitten" and Browning's "My Last Duchess" suggest, may be quite different. Poetry can range through all human attitudes and so register many tones—anger, elation, curiosity, hysteria, bliss, indifference, sorrow, terror, tenderness, skepticism, joy, anticipation, scorn, silliness. Since poems often trace moments of heightened awareness and intense emotions, the poet may take a reader on a roller-coaster ride of feelings. As long as the context supports the tone—or tones—a poet can express any attitude, even contradictory attitudes, in the course of a poem.

Consider the interplay of tones in this poem:

Lunch by the Grand Canal
RICHARD LYONS (b. 1951)

Harry Donaghy, an ex-priest, is telling us
that, after ten rounds, the welterweight was still panting
from a literal hole in his heart.
The fish the waiter lays before me on a white plate
is hissing through its eye, I swear it.   5
Harry spills out a carton of old photos
between the bread & the vials of vinegar.
The people in the pictures are friends of his aunt, whose body

he's signed for & released, now on a jet lifting from Rome.
He says he's always preferred Venice,   10
here a Bridge of Sighs separates this life from the next.
One of the photos, he thinks, is of his aunt,
she's no longer young having dropped a cotton dress at her feet

so the artist at arm's length might see her beauty
as if it had already slipped away. Across from me,   15
Paige Bloodworth is wearing a red hat, which looks good on her,
but she hasn't said a word, so pissed we missed the launch
to San Michele where Pound is buried.

For her, Harry's unidentified relatives
posing on the steps down to the Grand Canal   20
are lifting stones from their pockets
and pelting the poet's coffin as it eases out
on a black boat, chrysanthemums hoarding their perfumes.

I'm stroking the curved prow of a boat as if it were
the neck of a wild stallion rearing close   25
for a hidden cube of sugar or a slice of apple.
Miss Bloodworth's hat becomes a figure in memory's contract
as it lifts over water the color of tourmaline.
Harry's big hands trap all the photos, spilling the wine.
It's the winter of 1980, just warm enough   30
to sit outside as I remember. The rest of that year
no doubt is a lie.

The heterogeneous mix of people, motives, details, and time frames makes for a darkly funny poem and an ironic tone. The speaker seems to feel simultaneously intrigued by the strangeness and appalled at the meaninglessness of the circumstances he delineates. The aimless trio of Harry, Paige, and the narrator, sit around a common table, but have little in common, except perhaps a shared annoyance with things that might interrupt their diversions.

Quirky juxtapositions intensify the scene's incongruence. A welterweight boxer with a hole in his heart is set against a fish hissing through its eye. An ex-priest, apparently the surviving relative of an expatriate model, casually flips through what's left of her life at an outdoor café. A woman whose surname is *Blood*worth wears a red hat that "looks good on her" even though she is sulking because they missed a boat to see a famous poet's grave.

At the end, the rootlessness of the people and the discordance of other elements seem to be cosmically dismissed when the wind scatters the photographs and carries off the hat. Although Lyons writes the poem in present tense, the scene remains distant; that is, he establishes an ironic distance between himself and the poem's subject.

One feature of tone that deserves elaboration is **irony,** which generally indicates a discrepancy between the author's attitude and the attitude(s) expressed within the poem. The incongruous elements that Lyons assembles set up a disapproval of the self-centered, dislocated lives we glimpse in the poem. The poem's entire tone is ironic, and in the poem's closing the speaker levels that irony at himself, "The rest of that year / no doubt is a lie." In the last line Lyons shows his hand. He reports to us that he made the entire poem up. He had been encouraging his students to feel freer about using lies in their poems and wrote the poem to show how believable an invented story can be.

The term **verbal irony** identifies a discrepancy between what the speaker says and what the speaker means, as when wrestling with an umbrella in the rain you say, "What a lovely day." Nemerov's speaker in "Learning by Doing" (p. 75) uses the barb of irony to prick the mistaken experts who kill a perfectly sound tree: "what they do / They do, as usual, to do us good."

Dramatic irony marks a discrepancy between what the author and reader know and what the speaker or characters know. Hamlet does not kill the king when he is at prayer, lest the king in a state of grace go straight to heaven. Hamlet does not know what the audience has seen: that the king, burdened with guilt because he cannot regret his crime, is unable to pray. Dramatic irony solidifies the relationship between audience and writer, letting readers in on what remains hidden to the characters. Irony torques a poem's tension as readers become caught up wondering if the characters will catch on or fall for the trap.

On a simple level, we see dramatic irony in horror movies when someone in the audience yells at the bumbling teenager "Watch out!" as she reaches for the door that hides the maniac with his ax. On a more subtle level, dramatic irony allows the audience to become the moral voice in a poem. The girl in "Kitten" does not protest the heartless choice her father gives her, allowing us to condemn his callousness.

Often life itself is ironic. Our expectations meet unexpected twists. The deserted church is turned into a liquor store. The "D" math student becomes a physics genius. This poem by T. S. Eliot (1888–1965) exemplifies such **situational irony:**

Aunt Helen

Miss Helen Slingsby was my maiden aunt,
And lived in a small house near a fashionable square
Cared for by servants to the number of four.
Now when she died there was silence in heaven
And silence at her end of the street.   5
The shutters were drawn and the undertaker wiped his feet—
He was aware that this sort of thing had occurred before.
The dogs were handsomely provided for,
But shortly afterwards the parrot died too.
The Dresden clock continued ticking on the mantel-piece,   10
And the footman sat upon the dining-table
Holding the second housemaid on his knees—
Who had always been so careful while her mistress lived.

The speaker shows the aunt's character was defined by her concern for proprieties which now seem merely empty, whether observed (by the undertaker, who "wiped his feet") or flouted (by the footman and second housemaid). Though written in first person—through the eyes of the nephew—the point of view suggests omniscience. The detached nephew reports what goes on behind closed doors and even that "there was silence in heaven."

QUESTIONS AND SUGGESTIONS

1. Try writing a poem using one of the following as the speaker:

   a cat carrying its prey into the house
   a servant in the Duke of Ferrara's household
   the old woman who lived in a shoe and had so many children she didn't
      know what to do
   Elvis, in hiding
   the baffled ghost in Frost's "Witch of Coös" (p. 173)
   a bear in the zoo being harassed by kids on a field trip
   someone sneaking a cigarette at a funeral

   What might you need to know or find out, or invent, in order to make the poem convincing and interesting? Or imagine another speaker who in some way will help you explore some attitude. Here William Trowbridge (b. 1941) writes in the voice of a slug:

Slug
Silent as time, simple as snot,
I make my rounds among leaves and stems,
going in moonlight, morose and gray,
phlegmatic locomotion beneath your view.

Naked membrane, a meal for crows,   5
stomach-foot on a trail of slime,
ancient, limber, I ooze along
munching my way through your bed of roses.

I leave you notes in a rainbow film,
a drunk unraveling of loamy love   10
that's blind and patient, cold and moist,
dark as the dreams you don't remember.

2. Write a poem about your mother, father, or another close relative, using an anecdote (real or imagined) before you were born. An old photograph or high school yearbook might help. Let the poem help you find out something you didn't know.

3. Take a well-known story and retell it from a fresh point of view, for instance, one of Cinderella's mice recalling its night of transformation; the inhabitants of Hispaniola being "discovered" by Columbus; one of the girls Georgie Porgie kissed.

4. *For a group.* Form a circle. (a) On the top of a blank piece of paper each of you writes a brief description of a character (e.g., "A forty-eight-year-old produce manager . . ."). Pass the description to the person to your right and take the written description from the person on your left. (b) Now each of you should add a further detail about the character or the situation found on the piece of paper you receive (". . . cleaning up a load of spilled iceberg lettuce"). When you have added the detail, again pass the paper on to the person on your right. (c) Again each person adds another complication ("is thinking of her mother in the nursing home") and passes on the paper. (d) Then each person adds some detail that is occurring *while* the rest of this action is taking place—a moment of "writing off the subject" ("customers race in the door as a thunderstorm rolls through")—and passes the paper on. (e) Finally, out of the character and circumstances written on the paper in front of you, each of you tries to write a poem, using whatever point of view seems most effective.

5. Both Frost's "Witch of Coös" following in the "Poems to Consider" section and Nelson's "A Minor Miracle" are frame narratives—they tell a story within a story. How do the outer frames help the poets present the inner stories?

6. Take a poem of yours and change its point of view and its time reference. If it's in first person and present tense, try it in third person and past tense. If it has a wide point of view, try a narrower one. If the point of view knows a lot about the situation, try one that knows less.

POEMS TO CONSIDER

Personals   1991
C. D. WRIGHT (b. 1949)

Some nights I sleep with my dress on. My teeth
are small and even. I don't get headaches.
Since 1971 or before, I have hunted a bench
where I could eat my pimento cheese in peace.
If this were Tennessee and across that river, Arkansas,   5
I'd meet you in West Memphis tonight. We could
have a big time. Danger, shoulder soft.
Do not lie or lean on me. I am still trying to find a job
for which a simple machine isn't better suited.
I've seen people die of money. Look at Admiral Benbow. I wish   10
like certain fishes, we came equipped with light organs.
Which reminds me of a little known fact:
if we were going the speed of light, this dome
would be shrinking while we were gaining weight.
Isn't the road crooked and steep.   15
In this humidity, I make repairs by night. I'm not one
among millions who saw Monroe's face
in the moon. I go blank looking at that face.
If I could afford it I'd live in hotels. I won awards
in spelling and the Australian crawl. Long long ago.   20
Grandmother married a man named Ivan. The men called him
Eve. Stranger, to tell the truth, in dog years I am up there.

Witch of Coös   1923
ROBERT FROST (1874–1963)

I stayed the night for shelter at a farm
Behind the mountain, with a mother and son,
Two old believers. They did all the talking.

MOTHER.   Folks think a witch who has familiar spirits
She could call up to pass a winter evening,   5
But won't, should be burned at the stake or something.
Summoning spirits isn't "Button, button,
Who's got the button," I would have them know.

SON.   Mother can make a common table rear
And kick with two legs like an army mule.   10

MOTHER.   And when I've done it, what good have I done?
Rather than tip a table for you, let me
Tell you what Ralle the Sioux Control once told me.
He said the dead had souls, but when I asked him
How could that be—I thought the dead were souls—   15
He broke my trance. Don't that make you suspicious
That there's something the dead are keeping back?
Yes, there's something the dead are keeping back.

SON.   You wouldn't want to tell him what we have
Up attic, mother?   20

MOTHER.   Bones—a skeleton.

SON.   But the headboard of mother's bed is pushed
Against the attic door: the door is nailed.
It's harmless. Mother hears it in the night,
Halting perplexed behind the barrier   25
Of door and headboard. Where it wants to get
Is back into the cellar where it came from.

MOTHER.   We'll never let them, will we, son! We'll never!

SON.   It left the cellar forty years ago
And carried itself like a pile of dishes   30
Up one flight from the cellar to the kitchen,
Another from the kitchen to the bedroom,
Another from the bedroom to the attic,
Right past both father and mother, and neither stopped it.
Father had gone upstairs; mother was downstairs.   35
I was a baby: I don't know where I was.

MOTHER.   The only fault my husband found with me—
I went to sleep before I went to bed,
Especially in winter when the bed
Might just as well be ice and the clothes snow.   40
The night the bones came up the cellar stairs
Toffile had gone to bed alone and left me,
But left an open door to cool the room off
So as to sort of turn me out of it.

I was just coming to myself enough   45
To wonder where the cold was coming from,
When I heard Toffile upstairs in the bedroom
And thought I heard him downstairs in the cellar.
The board we had laid down to walk dry-shod on
When there was water in the cellar in spring   50
Struck the hard cellar bottom. And then someone
Began the stairs, two footsteps for each step,
The way a man with one leg and a crutch,
Or a little child, comes up. It wasn't Toffile:
It wasn't anyone who could be there.   55
The bulkhead double doors were double-locked
And swollen tight and buried under snow.
The cellar windows were banked up with sawdust
And swollen tight and buried under snow.
It was the bones. I knew them—and good reason.   60
My first impulse was to get to the knob
And hold the door. But the bones didn't try
The door; they halted helpless on the landing,
Waiting for things to happen in their favor.
The faintest restless rustling ran all through them.   65
I never could have done the thing I did
If the wish hadn't been too strong in me
To see how they were mounted for this walk.
I had a vision of them put together
Not like a man, but like a chandelier.   70
So suddenly I flung the door wide on him.
A moment he stood balancing with emotion,
And all but lost himself. (A tongue of fire
Flashed out and licked along his upper teeth.
Smoke rolled inside the sockets of his eyes.)   75
Then he came at me with one hand outstretched,
The way he did in life once; but this time
I struck the hand off brittle on the floor,
And fell back from him on the floor myself.
The finger-pieces slid in all directions.   80
(Where did I see one of those pieces lately?
Hand me my button box—it must be there.)
I sat up on the floor and shouted, "Toffile,
It's coming up to you." It had its choice
Of the door to the cellar or the hall.   85
It took the hall door for the novelty,
And set off briskly for so slow a thing,
Still going every which way in the joints, though,
So that it looked like lightning or a scribble,

From the slap I had just now given its hand.   90
I listened till it almost climbed the stairs
From the hall to the only finished bedroom,
Before I got up to do anything;
Then ran and shouted, "Shut the bedroom door,
Toffile, for my sake!" "Company?" he said,   95
"Don't make me get up; I'm too warm in bed."
So lying forward weakly on the handrail
I pushed myself upstairs, and in the light
(The kitchen had been dark) I had to own
I could see nothing. "Toffile, I don't see it.   100
It's with us in the room, though. It's the bones."
"What bones?" "The cellar bones—out of the grave."
That made him throw his bare legs out of bed
And sit up by me and take hold of me.
I wanted to put out the light and see   105
If I could see it, or else mow the room,
With our arms at the level of our knees,
And bring the chalk-pile down. "I'll tell you what—
It's looking for another door to try.
The uncommonly deep snow has made him think   110
Of his old song, 'The Wild Colonial Boy,'
He always used to sing along the tote road.
He's after an open door to get outdoors.
Let's trap him with an open door up attic."
Toffile agreed to that, and sure enough,   115
Almost the moment he was given an opening,
The steps began to climb the attic stairs.
I heard them. Toffile didn't seem to hear them.
"Quick!" I slammed to the door and held the knob.
"Toffile, get nails." I made him nail the door shut   120
And push the headboard of the bed against it.
Then we asked was there anything
Up attic that we'd ever want again.
The attic was less to us than the cellar.
If the bones liked the attic, let them have it.   125
Let them stay in the attic. When they sometimes
Come down the stairs at night and stand perplexed
Behind the door and headboard of the bed,
Brushing their chalky skull with chalky fingers,
With sounds like the dry rattling of a shutter,   130
That's what I sit up in the dark to say—
To no one anymore since Toffile died.
Let them stay in the attic since they went there.
I promised Toffile to be cruel to them

For helping them be cruel once to him.   135

SON.   We think they had a grave down in the cellar.

MOTHER.   We know they had a grave down in the cellar.

SON.   We never could find out whose bones they were.

MOTHER.   Yes, we could too, son. Tell the truth for once.
They were a man's his father killed for me.   140
I mean a man he killed instead of me.
The least I could do was help dig their grave.
We were about it one night in the cellar.
Son knows the story: but 'twas not for him
To tell the truth, suppose the time had come.   145
Son looks surprised to see me end a lie
We'd kept up all these years between ourselves
So as to have it ready for outsiders.
But tonight I don't care enough to lie—
I don't remember why I ever cared.   150
Toffile, if he were here, I don't believe
Could tell you why he ever cared himself . . . .

She hadn't found the finger-bone she wanted
Among the buttons poured out in her lap.
I verified the name next morning: Toffile.   155
The rural letter box said Toffile Lajway.

Antigone Today   2000
RICHARD JACKSON (b. 1946)

It turns out the whole sky is a wall.
It turns out we all drink from history's footprints.
One day the stones seemed to open like flowers
and I walked over the orphaned ground for my brother.
Even now I can count every barb in the wire.   5
The stars were covered with sand.
The sandstorm had almost covered the body.
I dug around him, covered him myself.
Today, each memory is a cemetery that must be
tended. You have to stand clear of the briars of anger.   10
You have to wash revenge from your eyes.
Sophocles kept seeing me as a bird
whose nest is robbed, screeching hysterically.
In another place a flock of birds tear themselves apart
to warn the king of what will happen to his state.   15
I don't know who I am. I hardly said a word.

I think Sophocles knew what I might mean,
and was afraid. Everything I did was under
one swoop of the owl's wing. Who is anything
in that time? And he never listened.   20
Even the sentry's words dropped their meanings
and fumbled like schoolboys forgetting their lessons.
What I dug up was a new word for justice,
a whole new dictionary for love. But why did my own
love desert me? He came too late. He was   25
another foolish gesture from another age. What I tried
to cover with dust was the past, was anger, was revenge.
Now you can see it all in mass graves everywhere.
You can see it in the torture chambers,
the broken mosques and churches, the sniper scopes.   30
You can see it in the women raped by the thousand.
Who is any one of us in all that?
Who was I? I've become someone's idea of me.
You can no longer read the wax seal of the sun.
The trees no longer mention anything about the wind.   35
I don't see who could play me later on.
It turns out I am buried myself.
It turns out we are all buried alive
in the chamber of someone else's heart.

A Cigarette's Iris in the Eye of a Candle   1999
MARTÍN ESPADA (b. 1957)
—for Sister Dianna Ortiz
Washington, DC, April 1996

The White House gleams at nightfall,
a kingdom after death where pillars and fountains
wrap themselves in robes of illumination.
Light bathes in water; water basks in light.

There is a vigil across the street: 5
Sister Dianna in a sleeping bag,
back swarming with a hundred cigarette burns,
one ember screwed into her skin
for every upside down question mark
dangled by the inquisitors of Guatemala.   10
None of them saw the candle's iris
in the smoldering eye of a cigarette,
yet tonight candles encircle her,
flames like blurred hummingbirds

around her face, cheekbones   15
the cliffs of a hunger strike.
A cardboard sign at her feet says:
Who is Alejandro?

The torturers called him Alejandro, boss,
wiped their hands to greet him.   20
After the cigarettes, they burned her body
with phallic torches, invited him to join
the interrogation of the ripped orifice,
lubricated with blood.
Instead he listened to the cries   25
like a doctor measuring breath. Later
she heard him curse in midwestern wheatfield English;
without the blindfold, she saw an Americano, white as ash.
She leapt from his car on the way to the Embassy,
refusing the ash smeared across her skin.   30

Sister Ortíz simulated the kidnapping,
violated the Eighth Commandment
against false witness, said the U.S. Ambassador.
A sadomasochistic lesbian nun,
said a State Department official.   35
A case of delicate nerves,
said the Guatemalan Minister of Defense.
The First Lady sat on a couch with her
beneath a constellation of cameras,
careful as a hostess with a wine-befuddled guest.   40
At the press conference a chorus of spies and bureaucrats
crooned in soprano: There is no Alejandro, no Americano.
In Guatemala, the pit where they dangled her
still writhes with rats and dying fingers,
the cordillera of skulls swells and ripples across the map.   45

Now Sister Dianna keeps vigil on Pennsylvania Avenue,
sheltered from the drizzle of ambassadors
by a cardboard sign, the vowels in *Alejandro*
becoming the eyes and mouths of the words
she once taught in the Mayan highlands.   50
Her silence is the bread she will not eat, her eyes
contemplating the cigarette's iris in the eye of a candle.
The White House is a burnished castle in the distance
where fountains thunder, but no one drinks,
where the word torture has been abolished.   55
From a high window someone peers,
a servant or the head of state, and curses in English.

Aunt Sue's Stories   1921
LANGSTON HUGHES (1902–1967)

Aunt Sue has a head full of stories.
Aunt Sue has a whole heart full of stories.
Summer nights on the front porch
Aunt Sue cuddles a brown-faced child to her bosom
And tells him stories.   5

Black slaves
Working in the hot sun,
And black slaves
Walking in the dewy night,
And black slaves   10
Singing sorrow songs on the banks of a mighty river
Mingle themselves softly
In the flow of old Aunt Sue's voice,
Mingle themselves softly
In the dark shadows that cross and recross   15
Aunt Sue's stories.

And the dark-haired child, listening,
Knows that Aunt Sue's stories are real stories.
He knows that Aunt Sue never got her stories
Out of any book at all,   20
But that they came
Right out of her own life.

The dark-faced child is quiet
Of a summer night
Listening to Aunt Sue's stories.   25

American Classic   1981
LOUIS SIMPSON (b. 1923)

It's a classic American scene—
a car stopped off the road
and a man trying to repair it.

The woman who stays in the car
in the classic American scene   5
stares back at the freeway traffic.

They look surprised, and ashamed
to be so helpless . . .
let down in the middle of the road!

To think that their car would do this!   10
They look like mountain people
whose son has gone against the law.

But every night they set out food
and the robber goes skulking back to the trees.
That's how it is with the car . . .   15

it's theirs, they're stuck with it.
Now they know what it's like to sit
and see the world go whizzing by.

In the fume of carbon monoxide and dust
they are not such good Americans   20
as they thought they were.

The feeling of being left out
through no fault of your own, is common.
That's why I say, an American classic.

The Curator   1992
MILLER WILLIAMS (b. 1930)

We thought it would come, we thought the Germans would come,
were almost certain they would. I was thirty-two,
the youngest assistant curator in the country.
I had some good ideas in those days.

Well, what we did was this. We had boxes   5
precisely built to every size of canvas.
We put the boxes in the basement and waited.

When word came that the Germans were coming in,
we got each painting put in the proper box
and out of Leningrad in less than a week.   10
They were stored somewhere in southern Russia.

But what we did, you see, besides the boxes
waiting in the basement, which was fine,
a grand idea, you'll agree, and it saved the art—
but what we did was leave the frames hanging,   15
so after the war it would be a simple thing
to put the paintings back where they belonged.

Nothing will seem surprised or sad again
compared to those imperious, vacant frames.

Well, the staff stayed on to clean the rubble   20
after the daily bombardments. We didn't dream—
You know it lasted nine hundred days.
Much of the roof was lost and snow would lie
sometimes a foot deep on this very floor,
but the walls stood firm and hardly a frame fell.
                                                                        25

Here is the story, now, that I want to tell you.
Early one day, a dark December morning,
we came on three young soldiers waiting outside,
pacing and swinging their arms against the cold.
They told us this: in three homes far from here   30
all dreamed of one day coming to Leningrad
to see the Hermitage, as they supposed
every Soviet citizen dreamed of doing.
Now they had been sent to defend the city,
a turn of fortune the three could hardly believe.   35

I had to tell them there was nothing to see
but hundreds and hundreds of frames where the paintings had hung.

"Please, sir," one of them said, "let us see them."

And so we did. It didn't seem any stranger
than all of us being here in the first place,   40
inside such a building, strolling in snow.

We led them around most of the major rooms,
what they could take the time for, wall by wall.
Now and then we stopped and tried to tell them
part of what they would see if they saw the paintings.   45
I told them how those colors would come together,
described a brushstroke here, a dollop there,
mentioned a model and why she seemed to pout
and why this painter got the roses wrong.

The next day a dozen waited for us,   50
then thirty or more, gathered in twos and threes.

Each of us took a group in a different direction:
Castagno, Caravaggio, Brueghel, Cezanne, Matisse,
Orozco, Manet, DaVinci, Goya, Vermeer,
Picasso, Uccello, your Whistler, Wood, and Gropper.   55
We pointed to more details about the paintings,
I venture to say, than if we had had them there,
some unexpected use of line or light,
balance or movement, facing the cluster of faces
the same way we'd done it every morning   60

before the war, but then we didn't pay
so much attention to what we talked about.
People could see for themselves. As a matter of fact
we'd sometimes said our lines as if they were learned
out of a book, with hardly a look at the paintings.   65

But now the guide and the listeners paid attention
to everything—the simple differences
between the first and post impressionists,
romantic and heroic, shade and shadow.

Maybe this was a way to forget the war   70
a little while. Maybe more than that.
Whatever it was, the people continued to come.
It came to be called The Unseen Collection.

Here. Here is the story I want to tell you.

Slowly, blind people began to come.   75
A few at first then more of them every morning,
some led and some alone, some swaying a little.
They leaned and listened hard, they screwed their faces,
they seemed to shift their eyes, those that had them,
to see better what was being said.   80
And a cock of the head. My God, they paid attention.

After the siege was lifted and the Germans left
and the roof was fixed and the paintings were in their places,
the blind never came again. Not like before.
This seems strange, but what I think it was,   85
they couldn't see the paintings anymore.
They could still have listened, but the lectures became
a little matter-of-fact. What can I say?
Confluences come when they will and they go away.

Sheep   2001

LINDA NEWTON*

The morning after some disturbance in the night we find the sheep,
some already still and stiff, mounds of red soaked wool
in the summer pasture. In white-eyed panic the wounded
survivors plunge to hide behind one another, crowding
their way to safety. Terror has made them forget   5
their tameness: hands that bottle-fed them now must
wrestle them down to salve their wounds.

Later we listen in the dark for the attackers to return—
nerves alert, fingers greasy on the trigger. A howl carries

through dampening air, then a distant bark, the drone of insects,   10
sudden beat of large wings. The sheep stir, spending nights
in the barn now, pacing in fear at the soft approach of predators,
sniffing around the cracks. We want to imagine wolves,
or even coyotes: it seems less gruesome somehow
to think of nature feeding on nature, but no,   15
we hear of a pack of dogs—runaway farm dogs, strays dumped
by the highway—banded and growing bold, lacking
that aversion to human scent that keeps the wild things wild.

Finding each other, they circle and snarl, heads down,
hackles raised, sensing which is the leader and must be obeyed.   20
Then they run, stretching their bony legs, outrunning
the rabbits they eat, and collies guarding farms, and farmers
who go for their guns. They drink from the creeks,
hide in the timber. By night, not hunger but blind memory
that rises like heat in the veins makes them chase, and lunge,   25
and tear at the soft throats, winning the ancient game
again and again. Sheep make that terrible bleating cry
and prance about on foolish tiny feet.

8

METAPHOR

"The greatest thing by far," Aristotle declared, "is to be a master of metaphor. It is the one thing that cannot be learned from others; and it is also a sign of genius, since a good metaphor implies an intuitive perception of the similarity in dissimilars." Perhaps more than any vehicle open to the poet, metaphor carries the greatest potential for creating a poem's psychological density; through its metaphors a poem reveals how the speaker's mind works. Inextricably entwined both with the ways we think and with the origin and nature of language itself, metaphor in theory seems a knot of complexity. Luckily, just as we can fry an egg without understanding the chemical reactions involved, we can make metaphors without understanding linguistic theory.

Robert Frost's definition suffices: "saying one thing in terms of another." **Metaphor** means (literally, from the Greek) *transference*: We transfer the qualities of one thing to another, something normally not considered related to the first thing, as in "The sun hangs like a bauble in the trees." Qualities of a bauble transfer to the sun. The center of our solar system, our source of heat, light, and food has been dethroned, and become weak, trivial, gaudy, and, perhaps, silly. Notice how much the particular choice of words contributes. An earring is also a bauble, but a sun that is an earring touches a very different emotional register.

We call the subject, the thing that undergoes transference, the **tenor** (sun) and the source of transferred qualities the **vehicle** (bauble). When the metaphor is stated directly, made explicit, we use the term **simile,** syntactically announced by *like* or *as* (or *as though, as if, the way that*). Simile denotes *similarity* between tenor and vehicle as in "The sun hangs like a bauble." The italicized phrases in the following lines are similes (when the full text of the poem appears in this book, the title is followed by a page number):

your own whiskers
that look rumpled *as if something's*
been in them already this morning
> —Pamela Alexander, from "Look Here," p. 189

Silent *as time*, simple *as snot*
> —William Trowbridge, "Slug," p. 172

their faces memorized *like perfect manners*
> —Eavan Boland, from "The Dolls
> Museum of Dublin"

sent fear along
my arm *like heroin.*
> —William Matthews, from "Men at My Father's Funeral," p. 128

The beach hisses *like fat.*
> —Elizabeth Bishop, from "Sandpiper"

Tom Andrews (1961–2001) makes lively use of similes in the following poem as he plays with a great Victorian poet's struggle to discover one thing in terms of another. What is Andrews suggesting about the resemblances (or lack of them) between language and film, artist and audience?

Cinema Vérité: The Death of Alfred, Lord Tennyson

The camera pans a gorgeous snow-filled landscape: rolling hills, large black trees, a frozen river. The snow falls and falls. The camera stops to find Tennyson, in an armchair, in the middle of a snowy field.

Tennyson:

It's snowing. The snow is like . . . the snow is like crushed aspirin,
like bits of paper . . . no, it's like gauze bandages, clean teeth, shoelaces,
      headlights . . . no.
I'm getting too old for this, it's like a huge T-shirt that's been chewed
      on by a dog,
it's like semen, confetti, chalk, sea shells, woodsmoke, ash, soap, trillium,
      solitude, daydreaming . . . Oh hell,
you can see for yourself! That's what I hate about film!

He dies.

When the transference is implicit, we use the term **metaphor.** A *metaphor* so compresses its elements that we *identify* the tenor with the vehicle; the connection happens in a flash: "The gun barked." "The sun is a bauble hung in the trees." "The ship ploughs the sea." Often we see in the compression its various elements and can untangle them: "The gun made a noise like a dog's bark" or "The ship cuts the water as sharply as a plough cuts the soil." As you work on your poems, strive for the intensity that metaphoric compression concocts, so that "Filled with elation, I quickly left the house" might become "I tangoed out the door." When metaphors flash before us, we can suddenly grasp new connections.

Metaphor often eludes exact translation; through its dense evocativeness, it not only compresses and compacts but also expresses the inexpressible—it tells it "like" it is. Metaphors are italicized in the following examples.

When I have fears that I may cease to be
Before my pen has *gleaned* my *teeming* brain
> —John Keats, from "When I Have Fears"

The words *are purposes.*
The words *are maps.*
> —Adrienne Rich, from "Diving into the Wreck"

My Life *had stood—a Loaded Gun—*
In Corners—till a Day
> —Emily Dickinson, from "My Life had stood"

[dreamers] *read about themselves—*
in colour, with their eye-lids shut.
> —Craig Raine, from "A Martian Sends a Postcard Home"

For I was tired of strange ghosts
Whose cool bones
Lived on the *green furnace of my blood.*
> —Lebert Bethune, from "A Juju of My Own"

The metaphors of this poem help carry the freight of its ambivalent attitudes:

The White Dress
LYNN EMANUEL (b. 1949)

What does it feel like to be this shroud
on a hanger, this storm cloud hanging
in the closet? We itch to feel it, it itches
to be felt, it feels like an itch—

encrusted with beading, it's an eczema   5
of sequins, rough, gullied, riven,
puckered with stitchery, a frosted window
against which we long to put our tongues,

a vase for holding the long-stemmed
bouquet of a woman's body.   10
Or it's armor and it fits like a glove.
The buttons run like rivets down the front.

When we're in it we're machinery,
a cutter nosing the ocean of a town.
Right now it's lonely locked up   15
in the closet; while we're busy

fussing at our vanity, it hangs there
in the drooping waterfall of itself,
a road with no one on it, bathed
in moonlight, rehearsing its lines.   20

Emanuel undercuts the somewhat pretty metaphors (*frosted window, vase, waterfall, bathed / in moonlight*) with unpleasant associations (*shroud, eczema, road with no one on it*). By playing the metaphors off each other, she goes beyond our received notions of tradition and of "whiteness" and offers the wedding dress as a kind of gorgeous trap.

In writing a poem, knowing the differences between simile and metaphor matters far less than recognizing their similarities. Because the way they link tenor and vehicle is explicit, similes may seem simpler and closer to the straightforward, logical uses of language. And metaphors, because their linkage is often buried, may seem more surprising. But the evocative quality of any metaphor or simile depends on context. The popular notion that metaphor is stronger than simile, more forceful or evocative, doesn't really hold up.

Consider these two lines from the poem above:

Or it's armor and it fits like a glove.
The buttons run like rivets down the front.

The metaphor of armor and the simile of a glove draw equally on notions of what we want our clothes to do for us; though it's certainly heavier, the armor doesn't do more work for the poem than the glove. The image of the buttons in the next line does. The line might easily be recast as metaphor: "The buttons are rivets running down the front" or "The buttons are rivets that run down the front." In substituting static "to be" verbs for the more dynamic "run," these metaphors, however, remove some of the line's energy. Another consideration: The original line carries the authority and grace of a natural line of iambic pentameter:

The bŭttŏns rún lĭke rívĕts dówn thĕ frónt.

Figuratively Speaking

Metaphors and similes fall into a larger group called *figures of speech* or *tropes.* Under this larger heading fall literary devices such as *irony, hyperbole,* and *understatement* that we mention in other chapters and which are so common we might forget they are "figures." Another device is **personification,** in which an inanimate object behaves like a person, as Emanuel's white dress "itches / to be felt" and feels "lonely locked up," or as one part of John Donne's compass "hearkens" after the other (p. 199).

A figure of speech similar to personification is **animism,** assigning animal characteristics to humans: "They were rolling on the floor like puppies" or "She snaked her arms around the flagpole." Consider the rollicking invective conjured up by the figures of speech in this poem by Pamela Alexander (b. 1948):

Look Here

Next time you walk by my place
in your bearcoat and mooseboots,
your hair all sticks and leaves
like an osprey's nest on a piling,
next time you walk across my shadow   5
with those swamp-stumping galoshes
below that grizzly coat and your own whiskers
that look rumpled as if something's
been in them already this morning
mussing and growling and kissing—   10
next time you pole the raft of you downriver
down River Street past my place
you could say hello, you canoe-footed fur-faced
musk ox, pockets full of cheese and acorns
and live fish and four-headed winds and sky, hello   15
is what human beings say when they meet each other
—if you can't say hello like a human don't
come down this street again and when you do don't
bring that she-bear, and if you do I'll know
even if I'm not on the steps putting my shadow   20
down like a welcome mat, I'll know.

On an immediate level, this poem presents a woman who has been rejected by a man for another woman (a "she-bear") and who now is delivering a tirade against him, calling him inhuman for his oafishness and boorishness. On a more fundamental level, the poem takes us on a ride where one delightful metaphor follows the next. The victim of this string of insults has hair "like an osprey's nest," stinks like a "musk ox" with "pockets full of cheese" and "live fish." The power of these inventive metaphors seems soothing. Though the angry speaker may be incensed by this man, she hasn't lost her spirit.

Classical rhetoricians list scores of figures of speech with which we needn't concern ourselves; a few common ones, however, bear comment. The first two, *metonymy* and *synecdoche*, involve substitution. In **metonymy** we substitute *one thing for something associated with it, or cause for effect or vice versa*. Metonyms can distill a notion down to its essentials as in "The White House was in a panic" or in "No turban walks across the lessened floors" (Wallace Stevens's "The Plain Sense of Things"). In his poem "Out, Out" (p. 62) Robert Frost deftly expresses the boy's desperate attempt to save himself by describing his holding up his arm, "to keep the *life* from spilling"; by substituting "life" for "blood" Frost emphasizes what's at stake. In **synecdoche** we substitute *a part for the whole or a whole for the part, genus for species*, or *vice versa*. Very like metonyms, synecdoches can capture the essence of an image: "The hired hand dug the potatoes," "She bought herself a new set of wheels," "There wasn't a dry eye at the funeral."

Through synecdoche and metonymy in "I heard a Fly buzz," Emily Dickinson (1831–1886) suggests a family, though gathered around a deathbed, that offers little comfort to the person dying:

I heard a Fly buzz—when I died—
The Stillness in the Room
Was like the Stillness in the Air—
Between the Heaves of Storm—

The Eyes around—had wrung them dry   5
And Breaths were gathering firm
For that last Onset—when the King
Be witnessed—in the Room—

I willed my Keepsakes—Signed away
What portion of me be   10
Assignable—and then it was
There interposed a Fly—

With Blue—uncertain stumbling Buzz—
Between the light—and me—
And then the Windows failed—and then   15
I could not see to see—

Dickinson sketches the gathered relatives (lines 5–6) as "Eyes around" (synecdoche) and "Breaths" (metonymy), highlighting how grief possesses them. The family and speaker anticipate the moment of death, a moment of revelation, "when the King / Be witnessed—in the Room." Whether the "King" is God or simply death, they all expect an apotheosis, but only a fly, associated with decay, "interposes."

A third figure of speech appears in the final stanza. The speaker fuses the visual with the aural as the fly knocks around the room "With Blue—uncertain stumbling Buzz." This device is **synesthesia:** the perception, or description, of one sense mode in terms of another, as when we describe language as "salty" or musical notes as "bright." Other elements in the poem suggest the speaker's failing senses. In line 15, as the speaker struggles with her loss of sight, she transfers the cause to the windows, reporting they, not her faculties, "failed."

The final lines seem to record the speaker's consciousness fading before it, too, goes out: "I could not see to see—" The final dash suggests her consciousness shuts down at the moment of the expected king's arrival, but whatever she finally experiences, she can't tell us.

Within their context, words fit somewhere on a scale between the purely literal and the purely figurative. If in conversation, you say, "I need more light to read this report," you are speaking literally. If, however, you say, "After I read the report, I saw the light about salmon farming," you mean *light* figuratively, as *comprehension*. Dickinson's poem uses "light" literally and figuratively; it evokes both the actual light coming from the windows, and implies the light of understanding, as well as the light of spirituality.

Because Dickinson has framed a clear picture, the hard questions the poem asks can hit us squarely. They don't get muddled as we grope to figure out the scene in front of us. Further enriched by associated images ("eyes" and "windows"—eyes have been called the "windows of the soul"), the light imagery helps construct a poem both direct and dense, able to provoke fundamental issues of epistemology and metaphysics even as the poem depicts a simple deathbed scene, and Dickinson does it all in sixteen lines.

Poems that operate only on a literal level risk seeming thin. Reading a poem that merely describes a dress ("an empire waist with a mother-of-pearl bodice and a gathered train of Belgian lace"), we're likely to shrug and say, "So what?" What about the lost opportunities, the "empire," "mother," and "train" embedded in the diction? In the same way, poems that operate wholly on a symbolic level often seem overblown and trite. A poem that makes passionate declarations with tired formulas ("I hungered for your touch as the sands of time sifted through my heart"), will more likely make us flinch than draw us in.

Even in highly symbolic poems like "I heard a Fly buzz," images let us respond to something real; we can *see* and *hear* a buzzing fly. Physical elements of Dickinson's poem—*light, fly, seeing, windows*—operate as **symbols** (they represent something else), but these symbols are grounded in, are a natural part of, the scene. The common housefly might represent death, but its presence is perfectly normal. How ludicrous—and obvious—the appearance of other death symbols would be: a turkey vulture perching on the windowsill or the branches outside the window forming a skull and crossbones. The one figure not grounded in the scene, "King," sticks out, emphasizing the speaker's and mourners' high-flown expectations.

Though it must be apt, a symbol can be generalized and still be powerful as are the masks in this poem by Paul Lawrence Dunbar (1872–1906).

We Wear the Mask

We wear the mask that grins and lies,
It hides our cheeks and shades our eyes,

This debt we pay to human guile;
With torn and bleeding hearts we smile,
And mouth with myriad subtleties.

Why should the world be overwise,   5
In counting all our tears and sighs?
Nay, let them only see us, while
    We wear the mask.

We smile, but, O great Christ, our cries   10
To thee from tortured souls arise.
We sing, but oh the clay is vile
Beneath our feet, and long the mile;
But let the world dream otherwise,
    We wear the mask!   15

The mask deceives onlooker and wearer; it hides the true self and hinders the wearer's abilities—it "shades our eyes." Knowing that Dunbar, the son of slaves, lived during a time of lynchings and the intensification of Jim Crow laws, we may infer that the poem describes the African American experience, but the symbol of a suffering group masking its pain with smiles is universal.

Poets needn't strain to find symbols. The images at hand make the most compelling figures—like Dickinson's light and fly, the snow and ice in "First Death in Nova Scotia" (p. 139), and the wedding gown in "The White Dress." Notice in Emanuel's poem she doesn't bring up notions of virginity and purity which the wedding dress conventionally symbolize—she knows we'll bring those associations to the poem. Instead the poem's metaphors invest the heavy symbolic wedding gown with strangeness and loneliness: the dress is "a road with no one on it, bathed / in moonlight, rehearsing its lines." The dress suggests the burden of becoming the symbolic bride. Set under the spotlight of original metaphor, the conventional symbol becomes fraught with psychological tension.

Although you can make just about any image serve as a symbol, don't get carried away. To paraphrase Freud, it's better sometimes to let a cigar be a cigar.

A Name for Everything

The roots of language lie in metaphor. We speak of *the eye* of a needle, *the spine* of a book, the *head* and *mouth* of a river (which are oddly at opposite ends), a flower *bed*, of *plunging* into a relationship, of *bouncing* a check, or of *going haywire*, without thinking of the buried metaphors—of faces, bodies, sleeping, swimming, or the tangly wire used for baling hay.

Dead metaphors (which include clichés) show a primary way language changes to accommodate new situations. Confronted with something new, for which we can find no word, we adapt an old word, and soon the new meaning seems perfectly literal. The part of a car that covers the engine, for instance, is a hood. On early cars, it was in fact rounded and looked very much like a hood; the use of the word survives, although now hoods are flat and look nothing like hoods. (They still cover the engines' heads.)

Without us, the world remains wordless. Adam's naming the animals of Eden stands as archetype for one of humanity's greatest concerns: naming things so we can talk about them. Whenever we invent something new, we find a new term or adapt an old one to express it—thus, the Internet, the World Wide Web, and *surfing*.

The classical Roman orator Quintillian praised metaphor for performing the supremely difficult task of "providing a name for everything." The more complex the issue, the more we need something else to explain it, as the double helix helps us understand DNA and the Möbius strip relativity. Metaphors work in an amazing variety of ways (no catalogue could be complete) and do an amazing variety of jobs. They may illustrate, explain, emphasize, heighten, or communicate information or ideas; they may carry a tone, feeling, or attitude. They may even work—Hart Crane's phrase is the "logic of metaphor"—as a mode of discourse, a sort of language of associations.

When a subject is abstract, such as the emotion in Emily Dickinson's "After great pain" (p. 245), metaphor allows the poet to express in particular terms what would otherwise remain vague and generalized. Dickinson ends that poem with exacting metaphors to evoke a *particular* feeling:

> This is the Hour of Lead—
> Remembered, if outlived,
> As Freezing persons, recollect the Snow—
> First—Chill—then Stupor—then the letting go—

As Marianne Moore wittily says, "Feeling at its deepest—as we all have reason to know—tends to be inarticulate." The more powerful the emotion, the more it requires metaphor to affect a reader; through metaphor Dickinson expresses the experience of deadness that follows "great pain."

We get frustrated with the general words for emotions—*love, hate, envy, awe, respect, rage*—because they don't express our *particular* feeling, and it is precisely their particularity that makes our emotions matter to us. For centuries, lovers have struggled to describe their particular feelings, grumbling that *words can't begin to express* their love, how their *love is beyond words,* and how *no one has ever felt* as they do.

> *If* you respect the reality of the world, you know that you can only approach that reality by indirect means.
>
> —Richard Wilbur

As we attempt to articulate what we feel, we turn to metaphor, borrowing the vocabulary of other things—in Dickinson's case, freezing to death—to say what no exact words say. Often finding the link between some abstract feeling and a physical sensation yields a vehicle that can explore complex emotions. For instance, in "A Noiseless, Patient Spider" (p. 36) Whitman takes the spider's throwing out its filaments as a means to understanding his soul's "musing, venturing, throwing, seeking."

In this poem Molly Peacock (b. 1947) navigates an abstract sea of emotion on the sturdy craft of metaphor:

Putting a Burden Down

Putting a burden down feels so empty
you almost want to hoist it up again,
for to carry nothing means there is no "me"

almost. Then freedom, like air, creeps in
as into a nearly airtight house, estranging   5
you and your burden, making a breach to leap in,

changing an airless place into a landscape,
an outdoors so full of air it leaves you breathless,
there's so much to breathe. Now you escape

what you didn't even know had held you.   10
It's so big, the outside! How will you ever carry it?
No, no, no, you are only meant to live in it.

This wide plain infused with a sunset? Here?
With distant mountains and a glittering sea?
With distant burdens and a glittering "me," here.   15

Peacock takes the metaphors that the phrase "putting a burden down" suggests and
uses them to open a complex of emotion. The "airless place," which burdens of heavy
responsibility and anxiety produce, gives way when "freedom, like air, creeps in" to a
"landscape, / an outdoors so full of air it leaves you breathless." In carrying us into this
landscape of "distant mountains and glittering sea" Peacock captures the startling
sense of release one feels after being stifled by worries. The metaphors unlock the
emotion.

Pattern and Motif

The distance between the two parts of a metaphor—between tenor and vehicle—
between their connotations, gives metaphor its resonance. In the best metaphors,
the meeting of tenor and vehicle acts like a small chemical reaction and creates a
flash of recognition. Tenor and vehicle too closely related (the sun *is a star*) won't
spark; metaphors too unrelated (the sun is *a tow truck*) may shimmer with their
strangeness only to leave a reader in the dark. A metaphor must do more than flash
and dazzle. It should establish a commitment that what follows the metaphor
somehow will be connected with it. If the bauble metaphor continued, "The sun
hung like a bauble stuck in the trees, its broken rockets / slippery as banana peels of
the gods," the reader would begin to suspect the poet was only showing off; mere
dazzle grows wearisome.

The unifying links, patterns, or motifs between and among the metaphors in a
poem must be somewhat conscious on the poet's part. But it is probably a matter more
of the poet recognizing and following the possibilities than of cold-bloodedly inventing or imposing them. Often the poet need only perceive the potential pattern in the

material, and as the poem develops, explore its possibilities. In this way metaphor can help a poet think. Consider this poem by Hart Crane (1899–1932):

My Grandmother's Love Letters

There are no stars tonight
But those of memory.
Yet how much room for memory there is
In the loose girdle° of soft rain.

There is even room enough   5
For the letters of my mother's mother,
Elizabeth,
That have been pressed so long
Into a corner of the roof
That they are brown and soft,   10
And liable to melt as snow.

Over the greatness of such space
Steps must be gentle.
It is all hung by an invisible white hair.
It trembles as birch limbs webbing the air.   15

And I ask myself:

"Are your fingers long enough to play
Old keys that are but echoes:
Is the silence strong enough
To carry back the music to its source   20
And back to you again
As though to her?"

Yet I would lead my grandmother by the hand
Through much of what she would not understand;
And so I stumble. And the rain continues on the roof   25
With such a sound of gently pitying laughter.

4 girdle: a sash or belt.

On a rainy night in an attic the speaker has come upon his grandmother's love letters. Notice how many ways—through similes, metaphors, images, connotations—Crane echoes what is tenuous, delicate, and precarious. The speaker's tone, his doubt about how he can cross the distance between his grandmother's intimate life and his own life, registers this delicacy.

The opening stanza builds a parallel between the stars that exist only in memory (for it is a rainy night) and the grandmother who lives on in the speaker's memory and in the love letters. Stars, of course, even on a clear night are themselves echoes, light that has traveled millions of light-years from its source; we know only what has reached us across great time and space.

Stanza 2 shifts the focus from the more general ruminations about memory to the care that entering the past requires. The closing phrase, "liable to melt as snow" (line 11), makes the letters so frail that even touching them (body heat quickly melts snow) could destroy them, much less opening them up and reading them. "Frail," "delicate," "flimsy," "friable"—none of these adjectives satisfies as the simile does. Notice how much we lose if the line were to rely on the metaphor alone: "and liable to melt."

Picking up on the "room for memory" in the "loose girdle of soft rain" (rain also melts snow) of stanza 1 and linking it with the fragile letters of stanza 2, stanza 3 leads to the realization that "Over the greatness of such space / Steps must be gentle." These "steps" offer multiple resonances, suggesting the stairs to the attic; the speaker's footsteps (setting up his stumbling in the last stanza); the stages in the process of remembering; and the tones and semitones—the steps—of the piano keys of stanza 5 (which, in turn, suggest *keys* that might unlock the grandmother's intimate life).

Images of whiteness underlie the poem, tying together its multiple strains: the white piano keys connect with the white starlight and the soft letters likened to snow. The "invisible white hair" that "trembles as birch limbs webbing the air" (lines 14–15) associates the delicacy of memory and the letters with the attic's fragile cobwebs, with the birch branches (apparently glimpsed outside the window), with the quiet sounds in the attic, with the piano's remembered sounds (an "air" is also a tune), and with the color of the grandmother's hair—invisible now, except in memory.

Through pattern and motif, Crane connects strength and delicacy, time and space, light and sound, distance and intimacy in a poem that itself subtly examines the nature of interconnections. Crane celebrates the fragile but persistent connection between himself and another generation now gone.

Metaphor says more in an instant than do pages of explication. Instantly the reader apprehends the pertinent elements and ignores the irrelevant. Our analysis of "My Grandmother's Love Letters" follows where intuition leads and enumerates the relevant qualities that Crane's metaphors suggest. But for any poem, the sum of the parts, however illuminating, rarely equals the effect of the metaphors as a whole.

Consider the associations prompted by the last stanza of Sylvia Plath's famous "Lady Lazarus":

> Out of the ash
> I rise with my red hair
> And I eat men like air.

We understand at once the speaker's bold claim, but what goes into our understanding? Eating something suggests we have power over it, and perhaps that we have killed it (or will when we eat it). Eating something "like air" further reduces it, making it inconsequential, common, negligible. Air, as Plath uses it, takes on a different tone than "air" as Dickinson uses it in this stanza of "After great pain" (p. 245):

The Feet, mechanical, go round—
Of Ground, or Air, or Ought—
A Wooden way Regardless grown,
A Quartz contentment, like a stone—

The speaker's indecisiveness or indifference in settling on one metaphor—"Ground, or Air, or Ought— / A Wooden way"—dramatizes how "Regardless" intense pain makes its victim. Plath's speaker exudes boundless energy; Dickinson's is down for the count—her feet are earth or air or wood or obligation or nothing ("ought" is a variation of "aught")—she doesn't seem to know or care. Crane's phrase "webbing the air" can allude to music since he has woven musical metaphors into the poem's texture. In each occurrence of "air" we screen out qualities that might undermine the metaphor. We don't consider how eating air might make Lady Lazarus hiccup, or that Dickinson's "mechanical feet" might be musical (except as a dirge!), or that "air"—the space of the attic air—is unimportant or negligible.

Dickinson's and Crane's poems build an extensive network of metaphor to express their speakers' feelings, but sometimes just a few light touches of metaphor can express what a speaker can't. Consider the images of weather and astronomy Greg Pape (b. 1947) works into this poem:

My Happiness

That spring day
I stood in the new grass
and watched the man cutting steel
with an arc welder—
the man my mother had just married.   5
I watched as he leaned in his welder's mask
and held a blue-white star
to a steel rod until it was glowing with heat.
A cloud drifted in front of the sun
and darkened the land   10
the way sweat darkened his back.
Then with some slip of the body
or misjudgment of a man
given over wholly to his work
a piece of glowing metal   15
fell like a tiny meteor into his boot.
His hand went down
his fingers seared.
Then the smell of burnt flesh,
a groan of pain, and the crazy hopping.   20
He fumbled in his pocket for a knife,
slit open the boot and swatted the hot metal

off his ankle. What could I do?
I ran for mother and a bucket of water.
And that spring day I remember my happiness   25
as I poured the cold water over his wound
and she put her arm around his neck
and the sun came out
and the mysterious healing began
and he was saying oh jeezus   30
and she was saying oh honey.

The shy, young speaker (he stands off to the side at first) does not have command over—or understand—his feelings of awe, yearning, hope, fear, pride, and, finally, joy that "the man my mother had just married" inspires in him. That the boy doesn't yet call the man by a name or title suggests the boy's uncertainty about their relationship. The poem opens with the speaker watching the strange man as he, with seeming god-like power, wields "a blue-white star." The boy, himself, wouldn't consciously assign the man such power; his choice of metaphor, however, suggests a young boy's admiration of an older, capable man.

As the man immerses himself in his work, the boy associates him with the larger forces of nature around them: a cloud "darkened the land / the way sweat darkened his back." The dark cloud prepares us for the step-father's momentary slip-up that drops a "tiny meteor" into his boot. In the scary moments that follow, the boy manages to come to the rescue, getting a bucket of healing water and his soothing mother. The world around them seems to respond as this new family passes its first test of family unity: he tells us that as they comforted each other, "the sun came out / and the mysterious healing began." Nature, too, seems to register the boy's happiness.

Conceits

When metaphors dominate or organize a passage or even a whole poem, we call them extended metaphors or **conceits.** Secondary metaphors and images spring from the first, controlling metaphor, as we can see in the metaphors of an airless house and an open landscape in "Putting a Burden Down" or of the volcano in Andrea Hollander Budy's "Giving Birth" (p. 206). To talk about sex, Carolyn Kizer takes us into "Shalimar Gardens" (p. 203) and Jeffrey Harrison takes us "Rowing" (p. 204).

The extended metaphor in the following poem by Mary Oliver (b. 1935) identifies music with a brother "Who has arrived from a long journey," a brother whose presence seems to tame the world's danger, the "maelstrom" outside the house.

Music at Night

Especially at night
It is the best kind of company—

A brother whose dark happiness fills the room,
Who has arrived from a long journey,
Who stands with his back to the windows   5
Beyond which the branches full of leaves
Are not trees only, but the maelstrom
Lashing, attentive and held in thrall
By the brawn in the rippling octaves,
And the teeth in the smile of the strings.   10

Oliver so densely weaves the conceit into the poem that we can't precisely state whether the trees outside the windows are part of the metaphorical description of the brother or part of the literal scene. The real and the imagined become one picture.

In this poem John Donne (1572–1631) urges his wife not to mourn their upcoming parting. To elevate their love, Donne seems to bring all his learning to bear on his "valediction," or farewell.

A Valediction: Forbidding Mourning

As virtuous men pass mildly away,
    And whisper to their souls to go,
Whilst some of their sad friends do say
    The breath goes now, and some say, No;

So let us melt, and make no noise,   5
    No tear-floods, nor sigh-tempests move,
'Twere profanation of our joys
    To tell the laity our love.

Moving of th' earth° brings harms and fears,
    Men reckon what it did and meant;   10
But trepidation of the spheres°
    Though greater far, is innocent.

Dull sublunary° lovers' love
    (Whose soul is sense) cannot admit
Absence, because it doth remove   15
    Those things which elemented° it.

But we by a love so much refined
    That our selves know not what it is,
Inter-assured of the mind,
    Care less, eyes, lips, and hands to miss.   20

9 **Moving of th' earth:** earthquakes.   11 **trepidation of the spheres:** irregular movements in the heavens.   13 **sublunary:** below the moon; hence, subject to change, weak.
16 **elemented:** composed.

Our two souls therefore, which are one,
   Though I must go, endure not yet
A breach, but an expansion,
   Like gold to airy thinness beat.

If they be two, they are two so   25
   As stiff twin compasses are two;
Thy soul, the fixed foot, makes no show
   To move, but doth, if th' other do.

And though it in the center sit,
   Yet when the other far doth roam,   30
It leans and hearkens after it,
   And grows erect, as that comes home.

Such wilt thou be to me, who must
   Like th' other foot, obliquely run;
Thy firmness makes my circle just,   35
   And makes me end where I begun.

Donne draws on theology to suggest that their parting should be like the peaceful deaths that the virtuous were believed to have. Then he turns to astronomy and geology to claim that their parting will be like the unharmful movements of the heavens ("trepidation of the spheres") in contrast to the quakes that harm the earthbound. Next he refers to metalurgy, to the fineness of gold which, even when hammered to "airy thinness," never breaks. In the poem's final conceit, he likens the lovers to a drawing compass. The whole world seems ransacked and brought to bear, to center, on these lovers, whose parting Donne makes as momentous as the metaphors that express it.

Part of Donne's accomplishment stems from how he manages to keep many subjects spinning at once without letting any drop at his feet. Not controlling or focusing the nuances of a metaphor can lead to **mixed metaphor,** a metaphor that combines unrelated, even contradictory, elements as in this sentence's mixing of military, baseball, and artistic metaphors: "If we're to marshal our forces, we'd better swing at every pitch and try to etch our cause into their consciousness." Mixed metaphors often occur when the poet ignores a metaphor's literal for its figurative meaning.

Metaphoric Implication

The simplest metaphors may work with an almost inexhaustible subtlety and work harder than either poet or reader may be aware. Even metaphors that are essentially nonimages—muted echoes, vague, shadowy partial shots, soft superimposition, or momentary flashes to a different scene—can work on our imaginations. Consider Shakespeare's Sonnet 30:

When to the sessions of sweet silent thought
I summon up remembrance of things past,
I sigh the lack of many a thing I sought,
And with old woes new wail my dear time's waste:
Then can I drown an eye, unused to flow,   5
For precious friends hid in death's dateless night,
And weep afresh love's long since cancelled woe,
And moan the expense of many a vanished sight:
Then can I grieve at grievances foregone,
And heavily from woe to woe tell o'er   10
The sad account of fore-bemoaned moan,
Which I new pay as if not paid before.
But if the while I think on thee, dear friend,
All losses are restored and sorrows end.

Shakespeare draws much of the poem's diction from the legal and quasilegal realms: "sessions," "summon," "dateless," "cancelled," "expense," "grievances," "account," "pay," "losses," and "restored." Together these images suggest a court proceeding over some financial matter (in Shakespeare's time debts were jailable offenses). The implicit metaphors make for a complex tone: a certain judicial solemnity, an irrecoverable loss, some technical injustice, which the miraculous appearance of the "dear friend" overturns. We see no definite courtroom and yet we feel the speaker's sense of relief—as though he'd been sprung from jail—when he thinks about his "dear friend."

When the speaker is someone other than the poet, metaphoric implication can allow the poet to explore the complexity of another consciousness without making the character seem overly self-conscious. Through her metaphors, the speaker in the following poem suggests—rather than reports—the depth of her feelings and scope of her insight.

> *I came to explore the wreck.*
> *The words are purposes.*
> *The words are maps.*
> —Adrienne Rich

The House Slave
RITA DOVE (b. 1952)

The first horn lifts its arm over the dew-lit grass
and in the slave quarters there is a rustling—
children are bundled into aprons, cornbread

and water gourds grabbed, a salt pork breakfast taken.
I watch them driven into the vague before-dawn   5
while their mistress sleeps like an ivory toothpick

and Massa dreams of asses, rum and slave-funk.
I cannot fall asleep again. At the second horn,
the whip curls across the backs of the laggards—

sometimes my sister's voice, unmistaken, among them.   10
"Oh! pray," she cries. "Oh! pray!" Those days
I lie on my cot, shivering in the early heat,

and as the fields unfold to whiteness,
and they spill like bees among the fat flowers,
I weep. It is not yet daylight.   15

The metaphors depict the disparity between the powerful and the powerless while folding in the implication that those in control have forfeited their humanity. The opening metonym—"The first horn lifts its arm"—reverses the normal order; the horn controls the arm rather than vice versa, suggesting the bugler who calls the slaves to work has submerged his identity in his job. Similarly, at the second horn, "the whip curls across the backs of the laggards": the whip seems to have a life independent of its wielder.

While she presents the masters as destructive and static, Dove presents the slaves as dynamic and productive. The sensual images associated with the slaves ("dew-lit grass," "children . . . bundled into aprons," "cornbread," "water gourds," "salt pork") put in relief the parasitic nature of the masters. The slaves rush about their cabins, gathering their babies and provisions for the day "while their mistress sleeps like an ivory toothpick" and "Massa dreams of asses, rum and slave-funk."

Dove's metaphors more convincingly testify against the slave system than pages of preaching can. Look how much the toothpick simile implies. The mistress appears frail and brittle and allied with death, for though ivory is precious and white, it is also the product of another massive exploitation of Africa. Also, by likening her to the negligible luxury of an ivory toothpick, Dove equates the mistress with an ornament; her role in the household pales against the active and vital slaves who "spill like bees among the fat flowers."

The speaker's choice of metaphor helps her articulate the sadness of her isolation and helplessness. Though her position in the house seems to cushion her from the toil in the fields and suffering from the whip, it also shuts her off from human contact, shuts her in a house associated with death. She cannot assuage her sister's or the others' pain, nor can she ask for—nor would she ask for—comfort from them. She can only lie on her cot, "shivering in the early heat," and listen to their cries. Dove closes the poem with the speaker's quiet desperation, "I weep. It is not yet daylight." The lonely day is still to come.

QUESTIONS AND SUGGESTIONS

1. Make up as many metaphors or similes as you can for a common object (remote control, pine cone, footprint, eyeglasses, toadstool, tree bark, pond scum, kitchen knife, or others). Develop the best in a poem.

2. Fill in the blanks below to create metaphors. The original phrases and the poems they appear in are listed in Appendix II.

   (a) A clear _____ of shadows / From huge umbrellas_____ the
               _{noun}   _{verb}
     pavement.

   (b) The sky's bright _____ peak through chinks in a barn.
                    _{noun}

   (c) Miraculous water, God's _____.
                        _{noun}

   (d) The road _____ between flat black fields.
              _{verb}

   (e) [L]ightning makes the clouds look like / _____ of _____.
                                      _{noun}   _{noun}

   (f) The great _____ of the head knows this.
                  _{noun}

3. As a group or on your own, list about twenty concrete but common nouns in one column and about twenty active, present-tense verbs in another; for example: dip, scoop, blade, crank, plug, cop, glaze, chain, axle, flag, bark, sleet, curdled, jar, barge, gravy, cup, gravel, trunk, tire, script, brace, tar, towel, clover. (Notice how many words can be either nouns or verbs.) Now, almost arbitrarily, draw lines to connect them, so that "the towels flag on the clothesline," or "the tire enscripts the tar," or "the gravy curdled." See what metaphors you can make. Try exploring the most evocative through a poem.

4. Recalling how Emanuel's poem explores weddings and Dove's slavery, take some issue, concern, or event about which you have strong feelings and explore it through metaphor.

POEMS TO CONSIDER

Shalimar Gardens   1998
CAROLYN KIZER (b. 1925)

    In the garden of earth a square of water;
    In the garden of waters a spirit stone.

    Here music rises: Barbelo! Barbelo!
    Marble pavilions border the water.

    Marble petals of lotus bevel   5
    The edge of the pool.

All about us a green benediction!
God's breath a germination, a viridescence.

From you the heavens move, the clouds rain,
The stones sweat dew, the earth gives greenness.   10

We shiver like peacock's tails
In the mist of a thousand colored fountains

Miraculous water, God's emissary,
Lighting our spring once more!

Here spirit is married to matter.   15
We are the holy hunger of matter for form.

Rowing   2001
JEFFREY HARRISON (b. 1957)

How many years have we been doing this together,
me in the bow rowing, you in the stern
lying back, dragging your hands in the water—
or, as now, the other way around, your body
moving toward me and away, your dark hair swinging   5
forward and back, your face flushed and lovely
against the green hills, the blues of lake and sky.

Soon nothing else matters but this pleasure,
your green eyes looking past me, far away,
then at me, then away, your lips I want to kiss   10
each time they come near me, your arms that reach
toward me gripping the handles as the blades
swing back dripping, two arcs of droplets
pearling on the surface before disappearing.

Sometimes I think we could do this forever,   15
like part of the vow we share, the rhythm
we find, the pull of each stroke on the muscles
of your arched back, your neck gorged and pulsing
with the work of it, your body rocking
more urgently now, your face straining with something   20
like pain you can hardly stand—then letting go,

the two of us gliding out over the water.

X

CARL PHILLIPS (b. 1959)

Several hours past that
of knife and fork

laid across one another
to say done, X

is still for the loose   5
stitch of beginners,

the newlywed
grinding next door

that says no one
but you, the pucker   10

of lips only, not yet
the wounds those lips

may be drawn to. X,
as in variable,

anyone's body, any set   15
of conditions, your

body scaling whatever
fence of chain-metal Xs

desire throws up, what
your spreadeagled limbs   20

suggest, falling, and
now, after. X, not

just for where in my
life you've landed,

but here too, where   25
your ass begins its

half-shy, half-weary
dividing, where I

sometimes lay my head
like a flower, and   30

think I mean something
by it. X is all I keep

meaning to cross out.

⬡ Giving Birth   2002

ANDREA HOLLANDER BUDY (b. 1947)

It's not so difficult—in time you won't even remember the pain.
—all the books on childbirth

On your back, heels locked in metal stirrups,
this immense volcanic shuddering
goes on against your will
as if it *were*, in fact, a volcano,
and your previous life merely a village of innocents   5
living on the island, used to it, barely mindful,
going about their daily repetitions, looking up
at each agitation only for a moment, thinking
it's nothing really, then returning
to their business, yanking the cord   10
of a lawnmower, mopping a kitchen floor,
licking stamps and sticking them one by one
onto a stack of sealed invitations.
And then again the mountain shudders.
Shudders again, this time violently.   15
But you are inside your breathing now, as you were taught,
and your husband's voice, his breath, that practiced duet now real,
the holding back, the pushing, the pain holding you
in its deep claws until there is nothing else.
And then the mountain erupts—you are sure of it—   20
erupts and erupts, its molten liquid
pushing beyond you, out, out
of your power, out, out. You wonder
where it will empty, what it will do
to those villagers who thought they had time.   25
Now there's no looking back, it's coming,
coming, and one of them
cries out—you hear him clearly, surely
as you heard your own pure cry moments ago,
or is this your own voice, or some part of your life   30
so distant it's barely attached even to memory, the way
volcanic ash showers cities hundreds of miles away,
where later the wind might shift
and a young man rising
onto the street from the metro   35
brushes a bit of soot from his face.

After Fighting for Hours   1995
KATE GLEASON (b. 1956)

When all else fails
we fall to making love,
our bodies like the pioneers
in rough covered wagons
whose oxen strained to cross the Rockies   5
until their hearts gave out trying,
those pioneers who had out-survived
fever, hunger, a run of broken luck,
those able-bodied men and women
who simply unlocked the animals   10
from their yokes, and taking
the hitches in their own hands, pulled
by the sheer desire of their bodies
their earthly goods over the divide.

The Elements   2001
TRISH REEVES (b. 1947)

There is a street in Kansas
where men stand with grain
in their hands, waiting.
When the wind whips down the street
they throw the grain with an upward arc   5
so that it falls downward
like snow
with the fast force of wind behind it.
The men stand with empty hands,
the grain stinging their faces.   10
They say, This is what life does to me
every day.

Cycladic Island Female Statue, British Museum   2001
ca. 2500–2300 B.C.E.
DAVID CITINO (b. 1947)

Breasts lifted high by hands in offering,
so far from the arms-folded-across pose
of my daughter on cold days

or in front of the boys clumped
like hunters, pawing at the ground   5
with their Nikes, caps low over their eyes,
at Hastings Middle School—as if
she wished to conceal the form
of the woman she woke to find.
(Her new blood is another thing   10
she can't discuss with a father.)

Carved of smooth, moony white marble,
for this is all about living forever.
A dark delta signifies the pubis.
The blessing of then and now,   15
woman nearly too ancient and new.
Two circles and a triangle, oldest code,
what we once knew was worthy
of all worship, before the male gods came
with their stones for throwing,   20
sharp-barbed arrow-tips, long spears,
hard altars, their hateful, bristling angels.

Diapers for My Father   1998
ALICE FRIMAN (b. 1933)

Pads or pull-ons—*that*
is the question. Whether to buy
pads dangled from straps
fastened with buttons or Velcro—
pads rising like a bully's cup   5
stiff as pommel with stickum backs
to stick in briefs. Or, dear God,
the whole thing rubberized,
size 38 in apple green, with
or without elastic leg. Or the kind,   10
I swear, with an inside pocket
to tuck a penis in—little resume
in a folder. Old mole, weeping
his one eye out at the tunnel's end.

The clerk is nothing but patience   15
practiced with sympathy.
Her eyes soak up everything.
In ten minutes she's my cotton batting,
my triple panel, triple shield—my Depends

against the hour of the mop: skeleton   20
with a sponge mouth dry as a grinning brick
waiting in the closet.

She carries my choices to the register,
sighing the floor with each step.
I follow, absorbed away to nothing.   25

How could Hamlet know what flesh is heir to?
Ask Claudius, panicky in his theft,
hiding in the garden where it all began
or behind the arras, stuffing furbelows
from Gertrude's old court dress into his codpiece.   30
Or better, ask Ophelia, daughter too
of a foolish, mean-mouthed father,
who launched herself like a boat of blotters
only to be pulled babbling under the runaway stream.

9

BEYOND THE RATIONAL

Mystery lies at the heart of all the arts. Something essential to their power always remains elusive, beyond craft or understanding. Toil as the artist must, the best usually just comes, like the gushing up of the sacred river in Coleridge's "Kubla Khan."

In their origins the arts were primitive and no doubt occult. Julian Jaynes, in *The Origin of Consciousness in the Breakdown of the Bicameral Mind* (1976), argues that poetry was originally the "divine knowledge" or "divine hallucinations" of primitive peoples. "The god-side of our ancient mentality . . . usually, or perhaps always, spoke in verse. . . . Poetry then," he adds, "was the language of the gods."

The Greeks explained the magic of poetry through the Muses. Nine goddesses aided and inspired writers and musicians, but the nine were hard to please and had to be courted and seduced. The Christian and Renaissance writers explained the magic through *inspiration* (from Latin, "to be breathed into"). The divine wind blows where it will. The Romantics looked to *genius*, some freak of nature or of the soul. Followers of Freud have regarded the subconscious as the magic's source, a bubbling up from hidden parts of the mind.

The Spanish poet Federico García Lorca uses the untranslatable term *duende*. It comes to the artist, an old musician told Lorca, not from the artist's conscious control or native talents but "from inside, up from the very soles of the feet." Researchers into creativity have found that people who tend toward the arts free-associate more easily than those in science and technology, but these psychologists can't identify what qualities of the mind, or the brain, create creativity.

The creative person, C. G. Jung says, "is a riddle that we may try to answer in various ways, but always in vain." The power remains unexpected and mysterious, even frightening. Randall Jarrell likens the magic of poetry to being struck by lightning. The poet may stand ready on high ground in a thunderstorm, but nothing guarantees the poet will be struck.

The Sense of Nonsense

At times we may get so bogged down in pondering the imponderabilities of language that we forget what any nursery rhyme, like this one, reminds us.

> Bat, bat,
>   Come under my hat,
> And I'll give you a slice of bacon;
>   And when I bake,
>   I'll give you a cake   5
> If I am not mistaken.

Nonsense is fun. Part of the magic of words stems from how often and how easily words give us pleasure without asking us to pay dues. A killjoy might ask why such incongruous images as "bat" and "bacon" appear in this verse. We're not irresponsible if we answer simply: because the words *sound good* together. What a delight to be led along by the string of bat-hat-bacon-bake-cake-mistaken. All the more fun because the elements are incongruous. In a post-Freudian, post-Marxist era, theorists might reason some hidden political and sexual agenda in phrases such as "the cow jumped over the moon" and "the dish ran away with the spoon." But nonsense wiggles out of the bonds of reason.

As you read this familiar example of nonsense poetry by Lewis Carroll (1832–1898), relax with its weirdness as you stay alert to how it affects you.

Jabberwocky

> 'Twas brillig, and the slithy toves
>   Did gyre and gimble in the wabe;
> All mimsy were the borogoves,
>   And the mome raths outgrabe.
>
> "Beware the Jabberwock, my son!   5
>   The jaws that bite, the claws that catch!
> Beware the Jubjub bird, and shun
>   The frumious Bandersnatch!"
>
> He took his vorpal sword in hand:
>   Long time the manxome foe he sought—   10
> So rested he by the Tumtum tree,
>   And stood awhile in thought.

And as in uffish thought he stood,
  The Jabberwock, with eyes of flame,
Came whiffling through the tulgey wood,   15
  And burbled as it came!

One, two! One, two! And through and through
  The vorpal blade went snicker-snack!
He left it dead, and with its head
  He went galumphing back.   20

"And hast thou slain the Jabberwock?
  Come to my arms, my beamish boy!
O frabjous day! Callooh! Callay!"
  He chortled in his joy.

'Twas brillig, and the slithy toves   25
  Did gyre and gimble in the wabe;
All mimsy were the borogoves,
  And the mome raths outgrabe.

In *Through the Looking Glass*, Humpty Dumpty heightens the poem's absurdity by informing Alice that "slithy" means "lithe and slimy," "mimsy" means "flimsy and miserable." And "toves" are "something like badgers . . . something like lizards—and . . . something like corkscrews" that "make their nests under sundials" and "live on cheese."

Though the words are nonsense, the story of "Jabberwocky" comes through clearly enough: A boy quests after the dreaded Jabberwock, slays it with his sword, and is hailed for his deeds. The story is archetypal, like the story of David and Goliath or Luke Skywalker and Darth Vadar. An **archetype** is a general or universal story, setting, character-type, or symbol that recurs in many cultures and eras. Because we recognize the archetypal pattern, we don't much concern ourselves with who the "beamish boy" is or that the "Jubjub bird" and "frumious Bandersnatch" still lurk out there. While cueing us in to the familiar, the poem can carry us through the unfamiliar, and celebrate language: its inventiveness, its whimsical sounds, its Jabberwock that "Came whiffling" and "burbled as it came."

> *True art can only spring from the intimate linking of the serious and the playful.*
> —J. W. Goethe

Like riddles, jokes, and other word games, nursery rhymes and poems like "Jabberwocky" remind us of the deep roots that join poetry—and all of the arts—to play. After all, the more common word for a dramatic composition is a *play*; we *play* musical instruments, and literary devices such as metaphors and puns *play* on words. The play of language juxtaposes all sorts of things from the palpably untrue to the delectably outrageous. The impossible happens. Grammatically, one noun can substitute for another so that "The cow jumps over the fence" becomes "The cow jumps over the moon." The cow can also "jump to conclusions" or "jump a jogger in the park." And if we're so inclined, the cow might "jump ship in Argentina on a silvery mission to choke the articulated artichokes of criminal post(age) stamps." The syntax of a sentence may seem to be clear while its meaning remains murky; the linguist Noam Chomsky offers this example: "Colorless green ideas sleep furiously."

Creating art certainly requires work. We speak of the finished product as a *work* of art, but we must also keep in mind that art grows out of play—goofing around, free-associating, seeing what happens next. If we read the following poem by James Tate (b. 1943) as a kind of game, we can avoid troubling ourselves too much about what it means and appreciate what it does—how it plays with patterns of words and phrases, shuffling them to create new patterns.

A Guide to the Stone Age

for Charles Simic

A heart that resembles a cave,
a throat of shavings,
an arm with no end and no beginning:

How about the telephone?
—Not yet.   5

The cave in your skull,
a throat with a crack in it,
a heart that still resembles a cave:

How about the knife?
—Later.   10

The fire in the cave of your skull,
a beast who died shaving,
a cave with no end and no beginning:

A big ship!
—Shut up.   15

Instructions which ask you to burn other instructions,
a circle with a crack in it,
a stone with an arm:

A hat?
—Not the hat.   20

A ship with a knife in it,
a telephone with a hat over it,
a cave with a heart:

The Stone Age?
—There is no end to it.   25

Despite the poem's strangeness, the poem shrewdly controls form: twenty-five lines of alternating three- and two-line stanzas. Each stanza type serves a different function. The tercets offer a kind of list; the following couplets a question and an answer. Each element in the first stanza reappears at least once in combinations with new items in the following tercets; for instance the parts of line 1, "A heart that resembles a cave," reappear in "The cave in your skull" (line 6), "a heart that still resembles a cave" (line 8), "The fire in the cave of your skull" (line 11), and then in the final tercet stanza, "a cave with a heart" (line 23). The last line reverses the order of the first line.

A colon closes each tercet and introduces the couplet that apparently proposes some item to be included (e.g., line 4: "How about the telephone?"). At first, each possibility (telephone, knife, ship, hat) is rejected; then in the final tercet all the rejected items are included in the first two lines while its last line rearranges the items of line 1. This closing stanza, unlike the others, uses only one method of creating the noun phrase: *Noun + with + noun + preposition + noun* in the first two lines, and in the last line, a simplification, *noun + with + noun*.

The final couplet—its first line echoes the title—seems to comment on the poem itself: "There is no end to it," that is, the process of combining and recombining could go on endlessly. This ending, of course, is part of the poem's playfulness, for the poem *does end* just as it claims, "There is no end to it."

The poem takes care that we appreciate its jocularity. The Abbott and Costello bantering in the couplets seems to come to a head with the central couplet (lines 14–15). "A big ship!" the interjector proposes. And the respondent, as if out of exasperation, rejoins, with a half-rhyme, "Shut up!" The deflation of the tone alerts us that we are not meant to take the whole poem seriously, despite its often grim imagery of warfare and brutality.

The poem's meaning may be unclear but Tate's intentions aren't. The poem is a game. When a poem indicates we should approach it primarily as a puzzle, we begin to ask ourselves where the game begins and ends, if our sense of its rules are really its rules. The poem questions the value of rules themselves. The "Guide to the Stone Age" doesn't so much guide us as deflate the efficacy of any guide (much less one to a prelinguistic era). The poem seems to be an instance of "Instructions which ask you to burn other instructions," an unending cycle. By dedicating the poem to the poet Charles Simic, a surrealist realist or realistic surrealist, Tate ups the ante.

Poems such as Tate's have an ancestor in the work of Gertrude Stein (1874–1946), an expatriate American who has been called the "Mama of Dada." Stein spent most of her adult life in Paris as a central part of that city's great artistic and intellectual community; her circle included Pablo Picasso, Henri Matisse, Ernest Hemingway, Mina Loy, Djuna Barnes, and Alfred North Whitehead. She described her writing as a "disembodied way of disconnecting something from anything and anything from something." Here is a short poem that makes up a part of her larger "A Valentine for Sherwood Anderson."

What Do I See

A very little snail.
A medium sized turkey.
A small band of sheep.
A fair orange tree.
All nice wives are like that.   5
Listen to them from here.
Oh.
You did not have an answer.
Here.
Yes.   10

Later in the "Valentine" Stein asks "Why do you feel differently about a very little snail and a big one?" emphasizing her interest in how words affect readers. In writing such as Stein's and Tate's, and in many more poems (consider Stevens's "Gubbinal" and Williams's "The Red Wheelbarrow") words, phrases, images, and whole passages are used as objects for their tone and color, rather than for their representation or for their "meaning."

Since the nineteenth century, the avant-garde has constantly wrestled with notions of "meaning" and "reality." One wave of experimentation has followed another, challenging the notions of some generations while adopting and adapting techniques of others to create their own innovations. (Some of the movements in poetry include Symbolism, Imagism, Modernism, Surrealism, Dadaism, Futurism, Objectivism, Projectivism, Post-Modernism, Beat poetry, the New York School, and Language poetry.) By tapping into the potential of language, poets can suppress the ordinary conscious workings of the mind and allow the profound, subliminal effects of sound, image, and metaphor to confront the reader directly—without a concern for a poem's explicit "meaning." Eliot describes the assumptions behind such poems:

> The chief use of the "meaning" of a poem, in the ordinary sense, may be (for here . . . I am speaking of some kinds of poetry and not all) to satisfy one habit of the reader, to keep his mind diverted and quiet, while the poem does its work upon him: much as the imaginary burglar is always provided with a bit of nice meat for the house-dog. This is a normal situation of which I approve. But the minds of all poets do not work that way; some of them, assuming that there are other minds like their own, become impatient of this "meaning" which seems superfluous, and perceive possibilities of intensity through its elimination.

Eliot's *The Waste Land* is an early example of experimental poetry; it challenges meaning by suppressing the "habits" of narrative and logical argument in favor of a succession of characters, voices, scenes, fragments of scenes, images, quotations, allusions, and snippets. It is as much about itself as an object as about some other "subject."

Like paintings, sculptures, houses, and vases, poems are, first of all, *things* made of other *things* (i.e., words), and we are robbing them of power when we forget that and tie them to the mast of *meaning*. Archibald MacLeish famously asserts in his poem "Ars Poetica": "A poem should not mean / But be."

The Logic of the Analogic

Among its more ordinary—even traditional—functions, the nonrational in literature undermines the barriers normally erected between the normal and abnormal, the real and imaginary, the logical and illogical.

In the following poem, Dara Wier (b. 1949) uses the archetype of the journey to play with the nature of contradiction:

Daytrip to Paradox

Just as you'd expect
my preparations were painstaking
   and exact. I took two

butane lighters and a cooler
   of ice. I knew the route   5
had been so well-traveled

   there'd be a store for necessities
and tobacco and liquor and axes.
   And near the Utopian village of Nucla

   three Golden Eagles watched me   10
from a salt cedar tree. One of them
   held its third talon hard in the eye

of a white Northern Hare. Audubon
   couldn't have pictured it better.
     Everything was perfect. Naturally   15

   it made me think of Siberia,
the bright inspirational star
   that's handed down the generations,

and the long, terrible nights
   of the pioneers' journey to paradise.   20
   The valley on the way to Paradox

   was flat, there would be no choice,
nothing to get me lost.
   Cattleguards, gates and fencing

bordered the open range. Of course   25
   I crossed a narrow bridge
     to get into Paradox proper.

In the store that doubled
as town hall and post office
   there was an account book for everybody   30

laid square on the counter.
  No one was expected to pay
     hard cold cash in Paradox apparently.

If we're going to **Paradox,** which is a contradictory but true statement, this is the way to go. The poem's journey is metaphoric, and in order to arrive at Paradox we must be able to get past contradictions that seem to trip us up. Akin to the logical qualities of a paradox, the speaker's preparations are "painstaking / and exact," and yet they seem to consist of taking only "two / butane lighters and a cooler / of ice." But perhaps she needs them for the "tobacco and liquor" she will apparently pick up at the store, which strangely doesn't seem to carry lighters or ice. She declares that the journey's harsh scenery (which includes a Golden Eagle with its "third talon hard in the eye / of a white Northern Hare") "perfect" then tells us it made her think of Siberia. Of course, eagles and hares fit *perfectly* in Siberia. The valley is, oddly, flat; and, paradoxically, "Cattleguards, gates and fencing" define "open range." A "narrow bridge" leads to "Paradox proper," *proper* as if it were a large town, and *proper* as if narrowness were the correct approach to such an odd place.

    The speaker seems appropriately skeptical. It's only a "daytrip." Nor does she seem persuaded by what she finds: "No one was expected to pay / hard cold cash in Paradox apparently." By connecting the sounds of the final two words, "*Paradox apparently,*" she registers irony. What seems to be *apparent* is that Paradox deceives.

    The fluid form gently supports the poem's wit. Wier deploys the poem in three-line stanzas, but of four different shapes. The pattern of indentations of stanza 1 is repeated in stanzas 6, 8, and 10; that of stanza 2, in stanza 7; that of stanza 3, in stanza 4; and that of stanza 5, in stanzas 9 and 11. The appearance is of logical order, exactness, but the differing stanza patterns fall in place more or less randomly. They seem to point now right (stanzas 2, 7), now left (stanzas 3, 4, 6, 8, 10), and often both ways or neither (stanzas 1, 5, 9, 11). The shifting pattern is never resolved; the impression seems finally to be, if logical, of a jangled logic, going every which way at once—suggesting the experience of a paradox.

    The commonplace framework of narrative or of an argument can offer steady support to a structure built of nonlogical components, a castle in the air. Consider the following poem by John Ashbery (b. 1927), for instance.

At North Farm

Somewhere someone is traveling furiously toward you,
At incredible speed, traveling day and night,
Through blizzards and desert heat, across torrents, through narrow passes.
But will he know where to find you,
Recognize you when he sees you,   5
Give you the thing he has for you?

Hardly anything grows here,
Yet the granaries are bursting with meal,
The sacks of meal piled to the rafters.
The streams run with sweetness, fattening fish;   10
Birds darken the sky. Is it enough
That the dish of milk is set out at night,
That we think of him sometimes,
Sometimes and always, with mixed feelings?

The framework allows this poem to sound as though it makes sense. The end-stopped
lines suggest a series of factual assertions. The vivid imagery creates a convincing
world that is subject to natural law, with cold, heat, floods, and farm products. But
what do the assertions add up to? In the speedy first stanza, "someone is traveling furiously toward you," how can he move toward you if he's not sure where to find you?
Will he not be able to recognize you because he hasn't met you or because you have
changed? And is this "thing" he has for you something real?

The second stanza suddenly slows down; clauses pile up like the abundance they
describe, and the point of view becomes specified as "we." We cannot infer from the
poem who "you" or "he" or "we" signify, so we float in their indeterminacy. Certainly
we feel somehow generally included in this "we" since when we finish the poem we,
too, have "mixed feelings." We simultaneously imagine the scene of plenty while we
ponder its source since "hardly anything grows here." We wonder how the dish is relevant, set out as if for a cat, or Santa Claus. Is the dish for "him"? "Is it enough / That
we think of him" because *thinking of*, imagining, a potential is often its own reward? Is
thinking "sometimes and always" the nature of all imagining, paradoxically sporadic
and constant because we think on many levels at once? The poem resists our questions, even as it plays with our expectations for reasonable answers. The poem's pastoral title "At North Farm" belies the ominous tone that rumbles beneath it like a low
organ note. Ashbery has cited music as analogous to his purposes:

> I feel I could express myself best in music. What I like about music is its ability
> of being convincing, of carrying an argument through successfully to the finish,
> though the terms of this argument remain unknown quantities. What remains is
> the structure, the architecture of the argument, scene or story. I would like to do
> this in poetry.

In a poem called "What Is Poetry," Ashbery speaks of "Trying to avoid / Ideas, as
in this poem." Just as we can string together a perfectly regular syntactic sequence
with nonsense parts ("the cow crawled to conclusions"), so, too, poets can take the
framework of story, description, argument but avoid logical components. As Paul
Carroll suggests in an essay on Ashbery, "multiple combinations of words and images
(islands of significance) continually form, dissolve, and reform." Since meaning is not
fixed, such poems invite the reader to take center stage, to help create the poem. They
are analogous to abstract art where, for instance, a streak of red seems to confront a
field of green paint. Such paintings aren't about the realistic rendering of reality but
about form, shape, color, perception, and paint itself.

Ordinary Strangeness

Our most everyday—or "everynight"—experience of the nonrational comes in dreams. Our dreaming minds seem to translate our conscious experiences and obsessions into a host of symbols and situations. While immersed in a dream, we accept them and feel their significance, but when we wake and our conscious mind tries to sort through them, we often are baffled by them while still feeling their deep relevance. Often we just don't have the language to describe our dream experiences because they occur in our right brain, in our associative faculty, apart from our language abilities. The simple acts of falling asleep or waking up remind us that at times we exist simultaneously on more than one plane of consciousness.

Our senses help us test whether what we are experiencing is really happening. "Pinch me," we say when something seems incredible. But our senses don't always tell the truth. Optical illusions prove that. In our dreams we can experience sensations of waking life—and respond with a racing heart. A dream experience can be so convincing and a waking experience so strange that we might ask, as Keats does at the end of "Ode to a Nightingale," "Do I wake or sleep?"

In this passage from his 1855 *Leaves of Grass*, Whitman captures the frantic energy and heaving confusion of dreams where the divisions between the real and unreal break down, and weird, often erotic, images erupt in our heads:

> O hotcheeked and blushing! O foolish hectic!
> O for pity's sake, no one must see me now! . . . my clothes were stolen
>   while I was abed,
> Now I am thrust forth, where shall I run?
>
> Pier that I saw dimly last night when I looked from the windows,
> Pier out from the main, let me catch myself with you and
>   stay . . . I will not chafe you;   5
> I feel ashamed to go naked about the world,
> And am curious to know where my feet stand . . . and what is this flooding me,
>   childhood or manhood . . . and the hunger that crosses the bridge between.
>
> The cloth laps a first sweet eating and drinking,
> Laps life-swelling yolks . . . laps ear of rose-corn, milky and just ripened:
> The white teeth stay, and the boss-tooth advances in darkness,   10
> And liquor is spilled on lips and bosoms by touching glasses, and the best
>   liquor afterward.

Asleep and dreaming, we assume the genuineness of our fantastic experiences. Images and events open seamlessly into one another. Poems like Whitman's operate through such a self-breeding series of associations. In flash after flash, one image suggests another, and the images in their sequence replace rational and discursive ways of saying something. When the method fails and the poet has not arranged the images so that a reader's responses can glide along with them, impenetrable obscurity results. When association succeeds, it produces poems of great compressive power.

The poet lives in a daydream that is awake, but above all, his daydream remains in the world, facing worldly things.
—Gaston Bachelard

We would be foolish to approach Whitman's dream-vision with only our rational minds, to look simply for its "meaning," for its meaning lies beyond interpretation; it lies within our response to the sensual, frenetic images piling atop one another and within the frenzied pace of its sentences. It recalls to us our own befuddling, even embarrassing, dreams where each element harbors a powerful significance, often a significance beyond our powers to define it. The force of Whitman's images seems primitive. The landscape is biological, perhaps even bio-"logical"; the self is alone, thrust out naked (how many of us have had similar dreams?) to contend with the mysterious pier, with slippery footing, and with the orgiastic imagery of yolks, milky rose-corn, teeth, and liquor.

In both our waking and dreaming lives our bodies act and react without our conscious control; this is perfectly normal. Our lungs expand and contract, our heart beats, our blood circulates, and our synapses fire. We're not aware of these autonomic responses until something out of the ordinary happens, and even then our bodies do most of their work outside our consciousness. After narrowly avoiding a head-on collision, you pull the car over to compose yourself: You realize your heart is pounding, your lungs are straining, your skin is sticky with sweat. However, you still aren't aware of the minute explosions at your nerve endings, for instance, or how your pancreas is operating. This immense nonconscious activity of our bodies—which constitutes what "being alive" literally means—forms the basis of this poem by Nina Cassian (b. 1924):

Ordeal

Translated from the Romanian by Michael Impey and Brian Swann

I promise to make you more alive than you've ever been.
For the first time you'll see your pores opening
like the gills of fish and you'll hear
the noise of blood in galleries
and feel light gliding on your corneas   5
like the dragging of a dress across the floor.
For the first time, you'll note gravity's prick
like a thorn in your heel,
and your shoulder blades will hurt from the imperative of wings.
I promise to make you so alive that   10
the fall of dust on furniture will deafen you,
and you'll feel your eyebrows like two wounds forming
and your memories will seem to begin
with the creation of the world.

This poem's eerie power recalls primitive spells, devised for a particular person or situation but universal in its effects. "Ordeal's" intimate tone suggests the speaker knows the person addressed deeply. She promises to "make you more alive than you have ever been," a promise suggestive of the expansive claims a lover makes. On another level, of course, the poem addresses us.

Through metaphor and a form of **synesthesia** (a mixing of the senses), Cassian creates the ordeal, carrying us into a world so minute that the senses seem to merge, and we arrive at our very creation, as individuals and as a species. The speaker promises that the "you" will be able to see pores opening "like the gills of fish," hear the noise of blood, and feel—not see—the light as it glides across the cornea "like the dragging of a dress across the floor." By magnifying autonomic responses, the speaker seems to imply that the "you" will not only become acutely aware of the microscopic processes of the body but also feel a latent spirituality and realize that within our bodies we harbor the processes of creation itself. Line 9, ". . . your shoulder blades will hurt from the imperative of wings," implies that the aching is caused by one's need to be more than human, to be divine perhaps.

Surreality

Inspired by Freud's excursions into the unconscious, **surrealism,** an artistic movement that began in France in the 1920s, aims at discovering the artistic applications of the unconscious. Through the **surreal,** the unconscious free-associative, nonrational modes of thought (intuition, feeling, fantasy, imagination) awaken us to a surreality, literally, a super reality. Surrealistic poetry merges the inner and the outer world, dream and reality, the flux of sensations or feelings and the hard, daylight facts of experience.

The untutored have often misunderstood surrealism as poetry and art where anything goes; one just puts down whatever pops into one's head. A careful look at the work of the great French Surrealists like André Breton and Paul Éluard tells us otherwise. Paul Auster notes that poems that stick to surrealism's ostensible principle of "pure psychic automatism" rarely resonate. Even poems like those of Breton, which employ the most radical shifts and oddest associations, use "an undercurrent of consistent rhetoric that makes the poems cohere as densely reasoned objects of thought."

In the following poem notice how Paul Éluard (1895–1952) creates a nonrational poem that nevertheless employs familiar modes of logical argument. The first stanza poses a question, and the rest of the poem sets out to answer it.

The Deaf and Blind

Translated from the French by Paul Auster

Do we reach the sea with clocks
In our pockets, with the noise of the sea
In the sea, or are we the carriers
Of a purer and more silent water?

The water rubbing against our hands sharpens knives.   5
The warriors have found their weapons in the waves
And the sound of their blows is like
The rocks that smash the boats at night.

It is the storm and the thunder. Why not the silence
Of the flood, for we have dreamt within us   10
Space for the greatest silence and we breathe
Like the wind over terrible seas, like the wind

That creeps slowly over every horizon.

The phrase that Auster translates as "with clocks / In our pockets" (lines 1–2) in the original poem is "*avec des cloches / Dans nos poches,*" literally, "with bells in our pockets." "Cloche" means the large bell found, for instance, in a belfry; the French words for smaller bells are *clochette* and *sonnette*. We derived our English word *clock* from *cloche*; the earliest clocks—often placed on the town hall—rang out the hour. Sailors still use "bells" to measure time, and when we're "saved by the bell," we're saved by time running out (itself a phrase from the hourglass and its sands).

In trying to keep the sense, spirit, and sound of an original, translators of poetry must weigh literal meanings against considerations of connotation, idiom, form, sound, and rhythm. The translator's choice of "clocks" is shrewd. To the surrealists, a poem's sounds often matter more than one particular meaning. "Clocks" permits an internal rhyme with "pockets," registering Éluard's internal rhyme ("cloches," "poches"), while retaining the absurdity and lucidity of Éluard's first image. Our pockets can't hold something as huge as a town bell (or a clock—we carry watches in our pockets), but on a metaphoric level we might carry along to the sea the weight of regulation and social order, which both town bells and clocks imply. As the scholar Richard Stroik points out, the French have a phrase for parochialism that makes this point: *esprit de clocher*, literally, "spirit of the bell tower." Part of the surrealist agenda is to strip away the layers of received social attitudes to create a fresh realization of language, self, and reality.

Éluard's poem doesn't so much dismiss the rational as transcend or absorb it. The question-answer structure suggests a rational approach toward understanding while the terms of Éluard's argument shift and change. For instance, the sea, the exterior and interior silences, and the flood seem simultaneously to refer to reality and to act as metaphors for our complex experience of that reality. In effect, Éluard makes us question the divisions between our rational and nonrational experiences of reality, and between the reality that exists independently of our senses and the reality we know through our senses. The title helps posit these questions. We know the sea primarily through sight and sound, but how do the deaf and blind experience the sea? Isn't the sea to them an entity different from what the sighted and hearing know? When they touch it and feel its sharpness and coldness, might they think of knives? Yet, no matter who observes it, the sea is still itself; it exists apart.

The poem also suggests that we may be deaf and blind in a metaphoric sense— blinded and deafened by *a priori* knowledge, by preconceptions. Simultaneously the poem may imply a parallel, though inverse, reading: Is the knowledge we carry in ourselves "purer and more silent," perhaps more "real" than the reality we experience around us? Our experience of reading the poem imitates what it seems to be about: the multiplicity, fluidity, and ultimate mysteriousness of physical and metaphysical existence.

Since the origination of surrealism in France, poets have widely adapted its strategies, allowing them to break free of the literal and rational so as to handle experience in fresh and surprising ways. Consider this metaphorical fantasy by Susan Mitchell (b. 1944):

Blackbirds

Because it is windy, a woman
finds her clothesline bare, and without rancor
unpins the light, folding it into her basket.
The light is still wet. So she irons it.
The iron hisses and hums. It knows how to make the best of things.   5
The woman's hands smell clean. When she shakes them out,
they are voluminous, white.

All night my hands weep in gratitude
for little things. That feet are not shoes.
That blackbirds are eating the raspberries. That parsley   10
does not taste like bread.

From now on I want to live
only by grace. In other words, not to deserve things.
Without rancor, the light dives down
among the turnips. I eat it with my stew.   15

Today the woman's hands smell like roots. When she
shakes them out, they are voluminous, green.
All day they shade me
from the sun. The blackbirds have come to sit in them.
Since this morning, the wind has been enough.   20

Instead of finding nothing on the clothesline, the woman discovers what does remain: the sunlight that dries laundry. "Without rancor" she seems to accept this light in terms of the laundry; she unpins it, folds it, feels its dampness, irons it. These actions, both simple and impossible, suggest a kind of mysterious truth to be gained from acquiescence.

In narrating the story of the woman (who perhaps represents a version of herself), the speaker also comes to a decision: "to live / only by grace. In other words, not to deserve things." Through juxtaposition, she likens this state of grace to the light that generously does its work, "dives down / among the turnips," gives us food, without asking for something in return. In the final stanza, Mitchell extends the metaphors to offer a picture of peaceful acceptance: The woman's hands become the sheltering shade trees, the resting places for birds.

By blurring the lines between reality and the imagination, the nonrational poem can register that edge of consciousness where the mind creates its own truth. Sunlight is ironed and plenty exists among scarcity. Eyebrows are wounds, and hands weep.

Like talking to ourselves, fantasy may express our deepest and most serious feelings; we reveal ourselves in daydreams no less than in sleeping dreams.

Poetry has always cast its buckets deep into the human imagination, below the strata of rationality and logic. The subliminal powers of rhythm, image, metaphor, and structure remain as ancient as language itself; the poet-shaman, the bard, is an ancient figure who still lives among us. Poems that bare themselves to the magic of the mind help us appreciate the ordinary work-a-day world as the extraordinary place it is.

QUESTIONS AND SUGGESTIONS

1. Imagine that you are a thistle in a parking lot, a zipper, a brick in a chimney, a mountain, a farm pond, a country on a map, a basketball, or another inanimate object. What might you feel as that thing (consider sensations such as the touch of air, ground, a hand)? What have been your experiences? What might you be aware of? Write a poem in the first person, speaking as that object, and adopting an attitude. Here's an example:

Moon at the Mirror
MICHELLE BOISSEAU (b. 1955)

Location, location, location.
Even when I'm a slivered wafer
blanked out by the big guy, I got pull.

Just a shiny rock? So what. I'm close.
Others triumph in looks and power
but watch them fade as darkness brightens—   5

the big brassy moment I show up
(I adore being a blond), entrancing
homesick soldiers and drowning poets.

2. Use music, food, or another realm to describe to a color-blind person some colorful event or scene, like a carnival, a rock concert, a beach on the Fourth of July, a political rally, or one of your dreams.

3. *For a group.* Each person takes a piece of paper and writes down a noun or verb—something concrete, sensual, resonant, like "plummet" or "biscuit." Pass your word on to the next person who writes down a word that rhymes or off-rhymes with the word, for instance "plunder" with "plummet" and "fist" with "biscuit." Next, fold the paper down so only the second word shows, and pass the paper on to the next person who writes a rhyme or an off-rhyme for it, folds the paper to allow only the last word to show, and passes it on. Continue until every person has written on every piece of paper. Now, using the words on one of the pieces of paper, each of you writes

a poem. Don't try to make sense, but make it sound good. Read over your poem. Does it have anything to do with whatever else you've had on your mind? Take turns reading the poems aloud. Don't be surprised if the group falls into uncontrollable laughter.

4. Write a wild nonsense poem. Coin a few words in a context to let a reader gather their sense: "The flarking car kaffoed beside my window . . ."

5. For several nights place paper and pen beside your bed and record your dreams. Before getting out of bed, write down as much as you remember, paying particular attention to the imagery, but without questioning it. Then in a sonnet or a sonnetlike poem (of roughly fourteen lines that includes a turn—a redirection—somewhere past the midpoint), work the images into a poem in which you are going about your normal life, walking through the supermarket, perhaps, or swimming laps at the pool.

6. Don Kunz at the University of Rhode Island informs us that the town of Paradox really exists: in Colorado near the village Nucla. Its name comes from the Paradox Valley, a geologic oddity that was formed not by a river, but by a combination of rising and later collapsing salts. If you stew over the reality of Wier's poem again, does this information change the poem for you?

7. Here William Carlos Williams (1883–1963) has created a lovers' quarrel in a field; a mullen is a weed that grows an enormous, erect flower stalk with wooly yellow flowers growing out of velvety leaves. Williams explained that "djer-kiss" in line 7 "was the name of a very popular perfume with which ladies used to scent their lingerie." Write a poem that similarly presents a quarrel, or some other intense conversation, through a group of other things: Siblings battling over their inheritance as the trees in the park? Spectators harassing players as canned goods taunting the produce? Try something.

Great Mullen

One leaves his leaves at home
being a mullen and sends up a lighthouse
to peer from: I will have my way,
yellow—A mast with a lantern, ten
fifty, a hundred, smaller and smaller   5
as they grow more—Liar, liar, liar!
You come from her! I can smell djer-kiss
on your clothes. Ha! you come to me,
you—I am a point of dew on a grass-stem.
Why are you sending heat down on me   10
from your lantern?—You are cowdung, a
dead stick with the bark off. She is
squirting on us both. She has had her
hand on you!—well?—She has defiled
ME.—Your leaves are dull, thick   15
and hairy.—Every hair on my body will
hold you off from me. You are a

dungcake, birdlime on a fencerail.—
I love you, straight, yellow
finger of God pointing to—her!   20
Liar, broken weed, dungcake, you have—
I am a cricket waving his antennae
and you are high, grey and straight. Ha!

POEMS TO CONSIDER

Kubla Khan   1816
Or a Vision in a Dream. A Fragment
SAMUEL TAYLOR COLERIDGE (1772–1834)

> In Xanadu did Kubla Khan°
> A stately pleasure-dome decree:
> Where Alph, the sacred river, ran
> Through caverns measureless to man
>   Down to a sunless sea.   5

° Coleridge published a note with the poem. Here is an excerpt:

The following fragment is here published at the request of a poet of great and deserved celebrity [Lord Byron], and, as far as the Author's own opinions are concerned, rather as a psychological curiosity, than on the ground of any supposed *poetic* merits.

In the summer of the year 1797, the Author, then in ill health, had retired to a lonely farm-house between Porlock and Linton, on the Exmoor confines of Somerset and Devonshire. In consequence of a slight indisposition, an anodyne had been prescribed, from the effects of which he fell asleep in his chair at the moment that he was reading the following sentence, or words of the same substance, in *Purchas's Pilgrimage:* "Here the Khan Kubla commanded a palace to be built, and a stately garden thereunto. And thus ten miles of fertile ground were inclosed with a wall." The Author continued for about three hours in a profound sleep, at least of the external senses, during which time, he has the most vivid confidence, that he could not have composed less than from two to three hundred lines; if that indeed can be called composition in which all the images rose up before him as *things,* with a parallel production of the correspondent expressions, without any sensation or consciousness of effort. On awakening he appeared to himself to have a distinct recollection of the whole, and taking his pen, ink, and paper, instantly and eagerly wrote down the lines that are here preserved. At this moment he was unfortunately called out by a person on business from Porlock, and detained by him above an hour, and on his return to his room, found, to his no small surprise and mortification, that though he still retained some vague and dim recollection of the general purport of the vision, yet, with the exception of some eight or ten scattered lines and images, all the rest had passed away like the images on the surface of a stream into which a stone has been cast, but, alas! without the after restoration of the latter!

So twice five miles of fertile ground
With walls and towers were girdled round:
And there were gardens bright with sinuous rills,
Where blossomed many an incense-bearing tree;
And here were forests ancient as the hills,   10
Enfolding sunny spots of greenery.

But oh! that deep romantic chasm which slanted
Down the green hill athwart a cedarn cover!
A savage place! as holy and enchanted
As e'er beneath a waning moon was haunted   15
By woman wailing for her demon-lover!
And from this chasm, with ceaseless turmoil seething,
As if this earth in fast thick pants were breathing,
A mighty fountain momently was forced:
Amid whose swift half-intermitted burst   20
Huge fragments vaulted like rebounding hail,
Or chaffy grain beneath the thresher's flail:
And 'mid these dancing rocks at once and ever
It flung up momently the sacred river.
Five miles meandering with a mazy motion   25
Through wood and dale the sacred river ran,
Then reached the caverns measureless to man,
And sank in tumult to a lifeless ocean:
And 'mid this tumult Kubla heard from far
Ancestral voices prophesying war!   30
  The shadow of the dome of pleasure
   Floated midway on the waves;
  Where was heard the mingled measure
   From the fountain and the caves.
It was a miracle of rare device,   35
A sunny pleasure-dome with caves of ice!

  A damsel with a dulcimer
  In a vision once I saw:
  It was an Abyssinian maid,
  And on her dulcimer she played,   40
  Singing of Mount Abora.
  Could I revive within me
  Her symphony and song,
  To such a deep delight 'twould win me,
That with music loud and long,   45
I would build that dome in air,
That sunny dome! those caves of ice!
And all who heard should see them there,
And all should cry, Beware! Beware!
His flashing eyes, his floating hair!   50

Weave a circle round him thrice,
And close your eyes with holy dread,
For he on honey-dew hath fed,
And drunk the milk of Paradise.

⊞ A Hill   1967
ANTHONY HECHT (b. 1923)

In Italy, where this sort of thing can occur,
I had a vision once—though you understand
It was nothing at all like Dante's, or the visions of saints,
And perhaps not a vision at all. I was with some friends,
Picking my way through a warm, sunlit piazza   5
In the early morning. A clear fretwork of shadows
From huge umbrellas littered the pavement and made
A sort of lucent shallows in which was moored
A small navy of carts. Books, coins, old maps,
Cheap landscapes and ugly religious prints   10
Were all on sale. The colors and noise
Like the flying hands were gestures of exultation,
So that even the bargaining
Rose to the ear like a voluble godliness.
And then, when it happened, the noises suddenly stopped,   15
And it got darker; pushcarts and people dissolved
And even the great Farnese Palace itself
Was gone, for all its marble; in its place
Was a hill, mole-colored and bare. It was very cold,
Close to freezing, with a promise of snow.   20
The trees were like old ironwork gathered for scrap
Outside a factory wall. There was no wind,
And the only sound for a while was the little click
Of ice as it broke in the mud under my feet.
I saw a piece of ribbon snagged on a hedge,   25
But no other sign of life. And then I heard
What seemed the crack of a rifle. A hunter, I guessed;
At least I was not alone. But just after that
Came the soft and papery crash
Of a great branch somewhere unseen falling to earth.   30

And that was all, except for the cold and silence
That promised to last forever, like the hill.

Then prices came through, and fingers, and I was restored
To the sunlight and my friends. But for more than a week
I was scared by the plain bitterness of what I had seen.   35
All this happened about ten years ago,

And it hasn't troubled me since, but at last, today,
I remembered that hill; it lies just to the left
Of the road north of Poughkeepsie; and as a boy
I stood before it for hours in wintertime.   40

Remember the Trains?   1998
MARTHA COLLINS (b. 1940)

The friendly caboose. The whistle
at night, the light across the field.

Not a field: her yard,
its little fountain. Not

a fountain: cattle cars crammed   5
with people. Cattle grazed in the field

of the friendly farmer across the road.
The farmer remembers everything.

She remembers counting the cars,
they were filled with cattle, coal,   10

it would fall on the tracks. The cattle
cars were crammed, he could see the faces

through the cracks, he could hear them cry
for the water he wasn't supposed to give.

She remembers waving, the engineer   15
who waved, the tracks behind her house.

He remembers the bodies, he saw them leap
from the windows, he heard the shots,

and the cars returning, empty,
not a whistle, the single light.   20

The cries she heard were children
at play, friendly children, except the boys

who turned the hose in her face, they said
Come look! she'd almost forgotten.

And the trains kept coming, full,   25
empty, full again, while the fountain

rose like a flower in the yard that was not
a field and the farmer worked

in the field while they wept,
they waited, they asked for water—   30

Nihilist Time   1998
RODNEY JONES (b. 1950)

How stark that life of slouchy avoidance,
Thinking all day and all night of nothing,
Alone in my room with Nietzsche and Sartre.
Nothing is what I'd come from, nowhere
Is where I'd been, and I was nothing's man.   5

Nothing was the matter, I'd not answer
If no one asked, for nothing was the point,
And nothing the view I'd take on faith.
When I died, I'd not be as I had not been
Before I was born, with nothing for a name.   10

Meanwhile I'd cuddle in a vacuum with my abyss,
Whispering endearing stuff: "My darling
Emptiness, my almost electron, my blank pet."
Later with no one, I'd not celebrate
No event, for nothing was what I loved.   15

What I hated were people doing things:
Bouncing balls, counting, squirming into jeans
When oblivion waited in every ditch.
I could hear black motors not starting up,
And zeros going nowhere, nothing's gang.   20

Goat   1998
ANDREW HUDGINS (b. 1950)

You who eat milled grain
may mock the acorn scroungers, mock
the acorn grinders, acorn eaters.
"See how their thin lips twist from chewing
the bitter fruit?" you say, you who've never seen   5
even the milled grain, even the soft
hot loaves shovelled from the oven.
You rip them apart and devour them
without a thought to where they come from,
your sustenance, your pure delight   10
arriving every morning with the dew.

You may mock, deride, despise those
who harvest acorns, shell them, pound them, eat
rough crumbling acorn bread. Mock us,
but not our god, the goat god. Ignore him,   15
pass by his shrines, neglect the gods
with secret names and bestial shapes,

and hunters stumble, horses pull up lame,
the scent hounds fight among themselves,
and your swollen daughters bleed obscenely.   20
Crops wither and collapse into the furrows.
Your woven garments rot and fall
from your white shoulders, which will burn
or shiver according to the season,
and soon you eaters of honied oat cakes   25
will once more, as we do, drape sheepskin
across your shoulders, and roam the farthest woods.
You'll offer in appeasement to the god
your death—thin, unacceptable children,
and you yourselves will eat the scorned offering   30
and with every bitter mouthful you will wish
you were eating at the sufferance of the oak,
wish you were gnawing harsh dry acorn bread,
wish you were choking on it, and not your own blood.

Conception   1998
SUSAN WHITMORE (b. 1962)

There's pasta carbonara in bed
long after the lights go out in the rooms of the house:
we eat bacon, egg, fettucine sweaty and sexy,

sucking on the rind of the grated lemon, aged Parmesan,
and suddenly there's hunger again for that white   5
Cape Cod house seen from the other side

of Beaver Lake, its windows lit at dusk like golden eyes,
sight sprinkled into ribbons across the water
more yellow than the bright trail of moonlight,

and I'm sitting there with my brothers at the table   10
in summer night heat in the screened-in porch by lantern
playing gin rummy and drinking Black Label

as the eels begin to surface on the water with their
scaled and pointed heads and again my first lover
lays me down in Yundt's lily field, saying,   15

Don't expect music or violins, and I'm raising the flute
to my lips as the space in Franck's *Symphonie en D*
falls open for me and the whole orchestra waits

while my little sister holds her baby Andrea, swinging
the rag doll by its worn thin neck like a pendulum   20
in the sleepy grandfather clock in Dr. N.'s waiting room

where I wait until finally my unborn Robert runs me
through Amsterdam rain before breaking me in two
and gluing me back together as I lie on the white,

red, white Venray hospital bed: He comes to me   25
with open mouth and closed fists, fighting,
powerless and angry, bloody and not to blame.

Fruit Flies to the Too Ripe Fruit   1997
MICHELE GLAZER

> *Fruit flies are useful in studies of heredity*
> *because they multiply readily and are easy to keep.*

From a bowl, deeply between green apples some things stir

like inklings of a long secret.

When the boy asks *where do they come from,* say *never.*   5

Not to exist until the fruit rots and then be

ubiquitous is the secret to a long memory.

Some are drawn to the spoiling.

Some sweat out of the smooth-skinned fruit

the way buried in a question is another question.   10

When the boy asks *how do you know*

toss out the hollowed cantaloupe to loosen the flies.

When the boy asks *where do they disappear to* whisper

always

> *Not to exist long but to metamorphose with each*
> *individual extinction is the secret to a long shadow.*   15

In this version of the story the father moves out.

71 Hwy. at the Moment of Change   2002
ROBERT STEWART (b. 1946)

I'd rather lose an hour than gain an hour.
I'd rather be passed than pass.
I see a sign for the Halfway Café,
            too late.
I'd rather turn around than get home.   5

The one-biscuit order of biscuits and gravy
    has two biscuits.
I swear it's a mistake, but she says, No.
    No mistake.
I'd rather be wrong than right.   10

I tip too much rather than sour
    someone's pumpkin smile.
Everyone has idle hands.
My computer at home has set its own
    clock to standard time.   15

Think about what happens in the hour
    that appears one morning.
The hour that flies around the city
    like a bellows.
I'd rather trust than know for sure.   20

Thus it is I discover I am behind.
I'd rather go to the seasons than they
    to me.
I'd rather my computer checked before
    it did things.   25

The sky's bright lanes peak through
    chinks in a barn.
Water towers take to the top of the world.
Streets run to the high one-hundreds.

The Virgin Appears as an Old Gay Man   2001
MICHAEL NELSON*

On the side of the lane that goes
from Kyrkhult to the nursery,
before the darkened woods rise,
an old man, bent to the ground
is picking something. It's too soon   5
in this June, slow to gather heat,
for smultron, the wild strawberry
the Swedes love to hunt and eat
with cream. Against the wind a sweater
covers his back. His body twists   10
like a lichen-encrusted apple tree
that's survived a century of storms.

Through the gray, a ray of light strikes
the gold frame of his glasses.

The thick lenses magnify,   15
as his eye catches mine,
the recognition of another who yearns
for what has more power than shame,
to do what's considered women's work.
The slit in the clouds widens   20
and for a moment he is clothed in white.
He returns to his task with wavering
hands to gather more lily
of the valley. With the devotion
of one who births perfection   25
he adds more stems
to his cluster of white bells
as if their beauty and fragrance
will save the world.

A Man Who Writes   1964
RUSSELL EDSON (b. 1935)

A man had written *head* on his forehead, and *hand* on each hand, and *foot* on each foot.

His father said, stop stop stop, because the redundancy is like having two sons, which is two sons too many, as in the first instance which is one son too many.

The man said, may I write *father* on father?
Yes, said father, because one father is tired of bearing it all alone.

Mother said, I'm leaving if all these people come to dinner.
But the man wrote *dinner* all over the dinner.

When dinner was over father said to his son, will you write *belch* on my belch?

The man said, I will write *God bless everyone* on God.

PART
III

PROCESS

Making the Poem Happen

There is a pleasure in poetic pains
Which only poets know. The shifts and turns,
Th' expedients and inventions, multiform. . . .

—WILLIAM COWPER,
from "The Task"

10

FINDING THE POEM

How do you start a poem? Where does it come from? Like the confluence of streams into the headwaters of a river, many sources flow together to create a poem. Often the sources are hidden, subterranean, difficult to trace. Wade into a river and try to pinpoint where its waters originated. Writing a poem involves finding something to say, and also finding a way to say it.

Many beginning poets start a poem burning to express something in particular, to write about love's sudden coolness or global warming. The urge to write *about* something often gives the poet the first impulse. But poetry isn't primarily "about" something. If it were, a prose summary could fire us up as much as the poem. Louis Simpson cautions:

> Most bad poetry is written because somebody sat down with an idea . . . .
> Somebody has an idea and sits down and writes it out in lines, and maybe
> rhymes, but it's all from a very shallow level of the mind. The thing that comes
> *at* you, when you don't expect it, is the thing you really love.

That *thing* you want is what goes deep: the unexpected connection, the intriguing sentence, the resonant metaphor. You will discover that the most promising poems usually don't start as anything as definite as an idea or a feeling but more as a kind of potential, as an urge to discover what the poem will reveal through language. Yes, it feels fantastic to get off our chests what we truly care about. But to make someone else care, a poem has to move others through language, our common stream. You might, for instance, get others to nod in agreement with you if you say a certain American writer's style annoys you, but you won't capture their attention as this poem does:

Reading the Late Henry James
NATASHA SAJÉ (b. 1955)

is like having sex, tied to the bed.
Spread-eagled, you take whatever comes,
trusting him enough to expect
he'll be generous, take his time. Still
it's not exactly entertainment: 5
Page-long sentences strap
your ankles and chafe your wrists.
Phrases itch like swollen bee stings
or suspend you in the pause
between throbs of a migraine,   10
the pulsing blue haze
relieved. You writhe and twist—
if you were split in half,
could he get all the way in?
When you urge him to move faster,   15
skim a little,
get to the good parts, he scolds,
"It's all good parts."
Then you realize you're bound
for disappointment, and you begin   20
to extricate yourself,
reaching past his fleshy white fingers
for a pen of your own.

Sajé's irreverence for a master writer and her playful language instigates the poem's fun. She connects James's congested syntax with bondage and dashes off the puns that surface ("you realize you're bound / for disappointment"). Her poem also incites parallel questions. Then what is reading Alexander Pope like? Or William Faulkner? Or Jane Austen? Like the "you" of Sajé's poem, you might imagine reaching for a pen of your own.

As painters work with paint, and filmmakers with film, poets work with language—thankfully, our medium is plentiful and free. We feel our way into poems word by word, groping for the right sentence, the magic metaphor—step by step, into the stream.

Imitation and Models

The best advice a beginning poet can get is the simplest: READ. No matter how much you've read, you probably haven't read enough. Often, most of the poems beginning poets have read are tame ones okayed by school boards or the predictable lyrics of popular music that are supported by driving rhythms of drums, guitars, keyboards. But poetry isn't tame or predictable or dependent on an amplifier. Poetry is what disturbs, what disturbs through language. It may be subtle as a gust that sweeps over a pond and rattles the cattails. Your work as a poet includes knowing how other poets have used language; reading their works shows you new ways to use it. We want to write poems in the first place because we have read poems that captivate us. Your notions of what poetry is, or what poems can do, come from the poems you know and admire. The more you know, the more you'll realize where a poem might go. Nothing we or anyone else can tell you about poetry will mean as much to you as what you discover for yourself.

Without your being aware, you have been influenced already by an ocean of voices. These may include an intoxicatingly strange line by Emily Dickinson as well as the entire jingling theme song to a sitcom you loved when you were a kid. Pop culture floods our waking lives. The danger lurks not in being too much influenced by powerful poems but in being influenced too little.

Get under your skin poems of all kinds, old and new, fashionable and unfashionable. Read Shakespeare, Keats, and Dickinson. Read Goethe, Baudelaire, and Lorca. Read poems published this week. Just as essential as poets firmly situated in the literary canon, know the poets experiencing the same world you do—with its SUVs, gene mapping, and body piercing. Don't read *just* what everyone else is reading. Search out poems of other ages and cultures too. Try the hidden corners and odd nooks. Browse. Sniff out. The more you soak up the less likely you'll fix early or fanatically on a single mentor and cling to that one voice, or find the whole truth in one theory or another. Beware of theories: It is *poems* you want.

Look for the poems and the poets who really speak to you. Find poems that make you feel, as Emily Dickinson said, as if physically the top of your head were taken off. Find one poet you love, find another. Look their books up in the library, the bookstore, and

> Imitation, conscious imitation, is one of the great methods, perhaps the method of learning to write.
>
> —Theodore Roethke

on the Internet. Use money you'd spend on a CD to buy their books. Memorize their poems, learn them *by heart*—with all of that phrase's connotations. Make them part of yourself, and you will gain what Robert Pinsky calls the "pleasure of possession—possession of and possession by" another poet's words. These poems will be your models, after which you'll fashion your own poems. Poets' secrets hide in the open, in the poems.

Rather than being a problem, *imitation* makes poets. College basketball players study the reverse lay-ups of the pros. Medical residents stand at the elbows of surgeons. Architecture students crane their necks to take in the cornices of buildings around them. Apprentice poets—all poets—read. As a student, you may write Dickinson poems, Yeats poems, Frost poems, Bishop poems, any number of other poets' poems. As you discover and absorb admiration after admiration, the influences begin to neutralize each other and naturally disappear. The poems you write will begin to be in your own voice, not in Ginsberg's or Plath's. Don't worry about finding your own voice. Like puberty, it will just happen.

Often a poet's love for other poems engenders new poems; Homer inspired Virgil who inspired Dante who inspired Petrarch who inspired Sidney who inspired Herbert who inspired Dickinson who herself inspired a couple generations of poets. Here Donald Justice (b. 1925) takes off on "Piedra negra sobre una piedra blanca," a poem by the Peruvian poet César Vallejo (1892–1938):

Variations on a Text by Vallejo

Me moriré en Paris con aguacero . . .

I will die in Miami in the sun,
On a day when the sun is very bright,
A day like the days I remember, a day like other days,
A day that nobody knows or remembers yet,
And the sun will be bright then on the dark glasses of strangers   5
And in the eyes of a few friends from my childhood
And of the surviving cousins by the graveside,
While the diggers, standing apart, in the still shade of the palms,
Rest on their shovels, and smoke,
Speaking in Spanish softly, out of respect.   10

I think it will be on a Sunday like today,
Except that the sun will be out, the rain will have stopped,
And the wind that today made all the little shrubs kneel down;
And I think it will be a Sunday because today,
When I took out this paper and began to write,   15
Never before had anything looked so blank,
My life, these words, the paper, the gray Sunday;
And my dog, quivering under a table because of the storm,
Looked up at me, not understanding,
And my son read on without speaking, and my wife slept.   20

Donald Justice is dead. One Sunday the sun came out,
It shone on the bay, it shone on the white buildings,
The cars moved down the street slowly as always, so many,
Some with their headlights on in spite of the sun,
And after a while the diggers with their shovels   25
Walked back to the graveside through the sunlight,
And one of them put his blade into the earth
To lift a few clods of dirt, the black marl of Miami,
And scattered the dirt, and spat,
Turning away abruptly, out of respect.   30

Justice's variations on Vallejo's poem—his repetition of phrases, syntax, images, words—create a wholly new poem just as children are separate from their parents though composed of the same genes. As you look at Vallejo's poem, consider how the poems are related:

Piedra negra sobre una piedra blanca

Me moriré en Paris con aguacero,
un día del cual tengo ya el recuerdo.
Me moriré en Paris—y no me corro—
tal vez un jueves, como es hoy, de otoño.

Jueves será, porque hoy, jueves, que proso   5
estos versos, los húmeros me he puesto
a la mala y, jamás como hoy, me he vuelto,
con todo mi camino, a verme solo.

César Vallejo ha muerto, le pegaban
todos sin que él les haga nada;   10
le daban duro con un palo y duro

también con una soga; son testigos
los días jueves y los huesos húmeros,
la soledad, la lluvia, los caminos . . .

Vallejo's first line gave Justice his epigraph which can be translated, "I will die in Paris in a downpour"; Justice adapts the line to fit his own imagined circumstances: "I will die in Miami in the sun, . . . A day like the days I remember." He imagines his death as a returning to his hometown, where the sun shines "on the bay" and "on the white buildings" whereas Vallejo pictures his death far from his native Peru; he will die a stranger. Eerily, Vallejo did die in Paris on a rainy day.

Vallejo's is a spare sonnet-length poem of two quatrains and two tercets. Justice's is longer, denser in detail—three ten-line stanzas. Justice and Vallejo may not have written their revelations about their own deaths all on a stormy day (or in Justice's case with his dog quivering at his feet), but it sounds as though they did. Both poems begin with the future tense and shift to the past tense at about two-thirds into the poems, after the equivalent phrases, "César Vallejo ha muerto" and "Donald Justice is dead." Both poems repeat phrases that include the anticipated death day ("jueves" means "Thursday,") and the words *day* and *today* ("día" and "hoy").

In Justice's poem the gravediggers, who wait for the funeral party to be off, speak the Spanish of the Peruvian poet as if Vallejo's spirit presided over the funeral. The repetitions sound an incantory tone—apropos for someone imagining his own, albeit sun-drenched, funeral. "Variations on a Text by Vallejo" illustrates how many streams flow together in a poem—one's imagination, intuition, ear for language, technical mastery, and knowledge of other poems.

Since reading other poets is such a strong stimulus for poems, many poets begin writing sessions by reading poems for an hour or so, or until some line, some image,

*I think I knew very early on
that if I knew how a poem was
going to end, that poem was not
going to be very good.*
——Michael Ondaatje

some rhythm launches them into a poem's (often provisional) beginning.

Try not to mistake conscious re-creations such as Justice's "Variations" with **parody,** a deliberate, exaggerated imitation of another work or style. Parodies are a form of criticism, exposing weaknesses in the original. Writing a serious parody or an admiring imitation, following mannerisms of style (like Whitman's catalogues or Dickinson's darting dashes) or of subject matter (like Frost's country matters), can let you absorb another poet's technique or style. What, after all, makes Dickinson sound like Dickinson, or Frost sound like Frost? What makes an Elizabeth Bishop poem a Bishop poem?

Watch out for self-parody, the impulse when writing a poem to mock it, turn it against itself. Under the stress of trying to get your poem right, you may subconsciously feel tempted to deflate it, make it into a joke, annul your commitment to it. Be aware of this impulse; ask yourself what issues in the poem are making you uncomfortable and confront them in the poem.

Sources, Currents

As you start a poem, stay open to opportunities; allow early impulses to shift and meander. Maxine Kumin says, "You write a poem to discover what you're thinking, feeling, where the truth is. You don't begin by saying, now this is the truth" and then start writing about it. Often your first notions aren't the richest. They're merely the first. If you stick stubbornly to them, you may miss a more tantalizing direction. Maybe you first thought of a cross-country car trip you took with your mother. Don't let your memory of how bored you were driving the interstate keep you from writing about the graffitied water tower you saw in Iowa or the kid from Honduras you met in a motel pool. Maybe you weren't as bored as you thought—follow the most intriguing phrases and images; don't try to record the trip.

Keeping yourself open to sources means keeping your imagination open. Obviously Justice doesn't *know* he'll die in Miami. He's not a clairvoyant, and Vallejo probably wasn't either. And unlike the reporter whose first loyalty is to the facts—accurately recording the details of an event—the poet's first loyalty is toward making the richest possible poem. Just because something happened a particular way in life doesn't mean it should happen that way in a poem. If your poem ultimately celebrates the way sounds reverberate in a swimming pool at night, that's fine. If the tedium of the interstate asphalt keeps nudging you, you can bring it into another poem.

The rich imagery in this poem by Yusef Komunyakaa (b. 1947) suggests it rose from multiple, even contradictory, sources:

Sunday Afternoons

They'd latch the screendoors
& pull venetian blinds,

Telling us not to leave the yard.
But we always got lost
Among mayhaw & crabapple.   5

Juice spilled from our mouths,
& soon we were drunk & brave
As birds diving through saw vines.
Each nest held three or four
Speckled eggs, blue as rage.   10

Where did we learn to be unkind,
There in the power of holding each egg
While watching dogs in June
Dust & heat, or when we followed
The hawk's slow, deliberate arc?   15

In the yard, we heard cries
Fused with gospel on the radio,
Loud as shattered glass
In a Saturday-night argument
About trust & money.   20

We were born between Oh Yeah
& Goddammit. I knew life
Began where I stood in the dark,
Looking out into the light,
& that sometimes I could see   25

Everything through nothing.
The backyard trees breathed
Like a man running from himself
As my brothers backed away
From the screendoor. I knew   30

If I held my right hand above my eyes
Like a gambler's visor, I could see
How their bedroom door halved
The dresser mirror like a moon
Held prisoner in the house.   35

The children are shut out of the house and shut in the yard, caught in the middle, between the private world of the parents and the dangerous world beyond the yard. They are powerless to enter either, though what holds them is flimsy: only a latched screen door and an admonishment to stay in the yard. And who has locked them out? Komunyakaa intensifies the power the parents hold over the children by identifying them only as "they": the others, the adults, the enemy.

Likely every detail here did not occur in Komunyakaa's childhood precisely as the poem lays it out. That's hardly the point. The details help to evoke the children's pain and confusion. The image of the robin's blue eggs may have flowed into the poem from another day, another experience, and seemed relevant after he came up with the lines "We were born between O Yeah / & Goddammit"; the vandalism of the bird nests implies the boys' anger and confusion over their parents' vacillating intimacy and fights. In this emotional universe, feelings of entrapment spread; Komunyakaa ends the poem with the normally innocuous mirror becoming an imprisoned moon. The simile implies that the children—blinded by anger and confusion—can't comprehend what is really happening in the house.

In starting poems cultivate a fluidity of vision, be receptive to everything. Let impressions, ideas, metaphors, half-forgotten memories, the rhythms of a well-loved poem stream into your poem to enrich your first notions and to surprise you—and your readers. As Frost put it, no surprise for the poet, no surprise for the reader.

When something odd or outrageous enters your poem, allow it to register, to grow and deepen. Don't be quick to judge it. The analytical faculty helps make poems, but don't turn it on too early, lest it dry up your sources. The analytical breaks things down into parts. At this stage you want to pull things together. You want to rouse that part of your brain that says, "What if?" In the earliest stages you want to bring things together, to synthesize, not analyze.

Emotion and Thought

Every poem has a speaker and therefore a voice. Every human voice (even when seemingly unmodulated, level, "emotionless") expresses a tone, an attitude toward the subject. Therefore all poems express some emotion, even if muted, unstated, or matter-of-fact. Handling emotion can trip up an apprentice poet—or any poet. In the earliest stages of some poems, particularly those tossed in an emotional storm, achieving some detachment may be the first step. Before trying to write about some bottomless grief or soaring joy, give yourself some time to gain the control that might shape a poem.

When the sharpness of your emotions has dulled some, you'll be capable of stepping back and taking a look. As Wordsworth notes, poetry

> takes its origin from emotion recollected in tranquillity; the emotion is
> contemplated till, by a species of re-action, the tranquillity gradually disappears,
> and an emotion, kindred to that which was before the subject of contemplation,
> is gradually produced, and does itself actually exist in the mind. In this mood
> successful composition generally begins.

"Emotion *recollected* in tranquillity": We regather the emotion and refeel it, in a new way. The more intense a poem's sources, the longer you may need to channel them into a poem. You don't stop feeling what's driving you to write the poem; your relationship to your emotions changes. You are then able to do more than feel—you can explore, project, discover, discriminate—talk it out. Strong emotions are rarely pure. Grief gets mixed up with guilt and anger; bliss with hope and doubt.

Sorting out our feelings—testing them, wrestling with them—is as much a moral as an aesthetic endeavor. How we come to terms with them stems from what kind of person we decide to be. For the poet, as later for the right reader, the poem (in Frost's words) "ends in a clarification of life—not necessarily a great clarification, such as sects and cults are founded on, but in a momentary stay against confusion."

In the earliest drafts of bringing a powerful emotion to the page, get down in words the emotional nexus that urges you to write. Write images randomly, play out metaphors that occur to you. At first you will likely put down only flat assertions and clichés: "You make me so happy"; "My heart is heavy as lead." Such generalities offer a kind of shorthand to our feelings; we use them automatically without considering what they really mean or what our *particular* feeling is.

To render an emotion your first impulse may be to describe the speaker or character's emotional *response* to a situation—someone weeping or giggling or moaning. But keep in mind that you want to spark a response in the reader. Sure, laughter and tears can be contagious, but novels and films that bring us to tears—or crack us up—don't so much show someone crying or laughing as show someone trying *not* to cry or laugh despite the dire or ridiculous circumstances. The grand comedy, and sadness, of Charlie Chaplin's *Tramp* was his dignity when feasting on a boiled boot or receiving the scorn of the wealthy.

Don't be dismayed if your early drafts are riddled with generalities and clichés. If there wasn't a kernel of truth inside them, we wouldn't use clichés at all. Once every cliché was so bright and memorable that those who heard it adopted it. Eventually through overuse the metaphor became weak and meaningless. If you find yourself drawn to a particular cliché, if you feel you just can't get past it, try delving into it. You may find a way of bringing the dead metaphor inside back to life, as Emily Dickinson does in this poem:

> After great pain, a formal feeling comes—
> The Nerves sit ceremonious, like Tombs—
> The stiff Heart questions was it He, that bore,
> And Yesterday, or Centuries before?
>
> The Feet, mechanical, go round—   5
> Of Ground, or Air, or Ought—
> A Wooden way
> Regardless grown,
> A Quartz contentment, like a stone—
>
> This is the Hour of Lead—   10
> Remembered, if outlived,
> As Freezing persons, recollect the Snow—
> First—Chill—then Stupor—then the letting go—

Out of frustration to describe the pain we suffer, we talk about our heavy hearts, how we can't breathe, how we feel made of stone. But all these feelings remain abstract to someone else and won't affect an objective reader. It doesn't count if your reader is a close friend and knows what you've gone through.

Dickinson's poem makes great pain vivid by reinvestigating the clichés. Lead, that deadly and heavy element, aptly describes how grief and pain weigh on us. But "heavy as lead" means next to nothing. Instead Dickinson uses lead to depict the eerie sense of time pain creates. It shuts us in an eternity where yesterday blurs with the distant past; we exist in an "Hour of Lead." Dickinson's image of lead also excites other senses; we almost taste the dull metal on our tongues.

Another way of achieving emotional detachment from a subject is to consider that the speaker of a poem isn't precisely you, the living poet, but a version of you, an invented *persona*. When we begin a poem, we put on the poet's mask which Yeats talks about to see past the emotional muddle we find ourselves in and gain insight. In the space of their poems, poets become noble, brave, brilliant, tolerant—better people than they normally are. And they can become worse—bitter, jealous, greedy, or vindictive. It's okay not to be "nice" in a poem. Sometimes you must forget good manners and get vicious to be true to the poem.

Besides the mask of the self, try the fiction writer's technique: Focus the poem around another character in the situation. William Carlos Williams (1883–1963) expresses his concern for his newly widowed mother by writing in her voice:

The Widow's Lament in Springtime

Sorrow is my own yard
where the new grass
flames as it has flamed
often before but not
with the cold fire   5
that closes round me this year.
Thirtyfive years
I lived with my husband.
The plumtree is white today
with masses of flowers.   10
Masses of flowers
load the cherry branches
and color some bushes
yellow and some red
but the grief in my heart   15
is stronger than they
for though they were my joy
formerly, today I notice them
and turn away forgetting.
Today my son told me   20
that in the meadows,
at the edge of the heavy woods
in the distance, he saw
trees of white flowers.

I feel that I would like   25
to go there
and fall into those flowers
and sink into the marsh near them.

Taking her perspective, Williams shows the depth of his mother's grief and how negligible his efforts are. To her, the gorgeous spring day loses its luster. The blades of new grass, the masses of plum and cherry blossoms, the forest trees don't touch her; she wants to leave it all. His efforts to cheer her up with tales of the flowering trees he's seen only make her long for obliteration. By allowing her to express what she does feel—instead of how she ought to feel—Williams permits his mother the dignity of her grief.

Inventing a character to speak for you can also give you emotional distance. What might it feel like for another person to feel what you're feeling? Invent a situation, emotionally similar to yours, and speak through that situation. Or become another character entirely. Amy Gerstler speaks in the voice of a mermaid (p. 154), Browning as the Duke of Ferrara (p. 163), Louise Glück as a field of daisies (p. 161). These poets use their understanding of human emotion to create new characters and find the source of a poem.

Using raw emotions risks **sentimentality:** writing that doesn't earn—through imagery, metaphor, detail—the emotion it asks a reader to feel; writing burdened with clichés; writing more interested in self-expression than in making a poem. Most often sentimentality is merely simplistic, cheap, easy: the schmaltz of saucer-eyed urchins in rags and cuddly sad puppies. At its worst, sentimentality masks the truth, especially from the writer. If a writer depicts a ragged child as cute, how much of the child's actual situation has the writer really imagined? Will we be likely to see that child as a real human being instead of merely as a category?

Attendant with sentimentality is **overstatement.** Like the child who cries wolf, a poet who claims more than seems justified risks readers tuning out everything. **Hyperbole,** brash, deliberate overstatement, must seem apt. In Louise Glück's "The Racer's Widow" (p. 38), for instance, hyperbole reveals and measures the violence of the speaker's distress—"Spasms of violets," she says, or "I can hear . . . the crowd coagulate on asphalt." Williams's widow claims "Sorrow is my own yard," and then shows the circumstance which justify her claim.

On the other hand, the calm of **understatement** carries an air of authenticity, like Dickinson's deft touch in depicting death by exposure: "First—Chill—then Stupor—then the letting go—" Your best reader won't miss anything. In the small violence of the following poem, notice how the scene's quietness makes it all the more affecting:

The Hawk
MARIANNE BORUCH (b. 1950)

He was halfway through the grackle
when I got home. From the kitchen I saw
blood, the black feathers scattered

on snow. How the bird bent
to each skein of flesh, his muscles   5
tacking to the strain and tear.
The fierceness of it, the nonchalance.
Silence took the yard, so usually
restless with every call or quarrel—
titmouse, chickadee, drab   10
and gorgeous finch, and the sparrow haunted
by her small complete surrender
to a fear of anything. I didn't know
how to look at it. How to stand
or take a breath in the hawk's bite   15
and pull, his pleasure
so efficient, so *of course, of course,*
the throat triumphant,
rising up. Not
the violence, poor grackle. But the   20
sparrow, high above us, who
knew exactly.

The speaker admits she "didn't know / how to look" at the hawk eating the grackle and doesn't compel us to feel more about this scene than it merits. Nature doesn't sentimentalize its creatures; people do. One task of Boruch's poem includes seeing the predator and prey "exactly," with respect for the precision of the predator, sympathy for the "poor grackle," and acknowledgment that, for once at least, the sparrow's fears were accurate.

A word of caution—or of abandon: A poem that takes no risks is probably not worth writing. The lines can be fine between overstatement and emotional accuracy, between sentimentality and sentiment, between understatement and obscurity. One person's proper outrage over a racist act may seem overblown to someone else. Dickinson's spare style baffled the first editor who published her. Walt Whitman's exhortations shocked some nineteenth-century readers, delighted others. Marvin Bell offers this advice: "Try to write poems at least one person in the room will hate." Not that you need be cruel, but don't try to win a popularity contest (or an unpopularity contest!). A poem burdened with trying only not to offend can harbor little of poetry's power.

Getting into Words

Wherever it originates, the poem begins with a *given* in which the poet becomes aware of the possibility of a poem. Like the speck of dust that water molecules cling to in order to form a rain droplet, a poem needs a given, a speck around which impulses, words, and memories can cohere. Sometimes the seed can be another poem—as with "Variations on a Text by Vallejo."

Feeling for the "given" of a poem, many poets begin by writing randomly, capturing in a notebook (or on a computer or typewriter) whatever swims into their heads:

phrases, rhymes, ideas, images, lists, weird words. Random writing can serve as a writer's practice work, just as the baseball player slugs away in the batting cage or the pianist plays scales. In the free play of the notebook, you can experiment with sentence rhythms, explore images, recollect scenes for future poems, try out new voices. Tracing out a particular image can lead you to details you had forgotten, to a new direction, or to a metaphor, perhaps, that sparks an explosion. Drawing a connection between two or more unrelated passages in your notebook might ignite the elements of a poem. In the following poem, we might suspect that the poet seems to have arrived at his given when he connected a statement by another poet with the image of a wet dog:

To a Stranger Born in Some Distant Country
Hundreds of Years from Now
BILLY COLLINS (b. 1941)

> *"I write poems for a stranger who will be born in some*
> *distant country hundreds of years from now."*
>
> —*Mary Oliver*

Nobody here likes a wet dog.
No one wants anything to do with a dog
that is wet from being out in the rain
or retrieving a stick from a lake.
Look how she wanders around the crowded pub tonight   5
going from one person to another
hoping for a pat on the head, a rub behind the ears,
something that could be given with one hand
without even wrinkling the conversation.

But everyone pushes her away,   10
some with a knee, others with the sole of a boot.
Even the children, who don't realize she is wet
until they go to pet her,
push her away
then wipe their hands on their clothes.   15
And whenever she heads toward me,
I show her my palm, and she turns aside.

O stranger of the future!
O inconceivable being!
whatever the shape of your house,   20
however you scoot from place to place,
no matter how strange and colorless the clothes you may wear,
I bet nobody there likes a wet dog either.
I bet everybody in your pub,
even the children, pushes her away.   25

Linked with the wet dog in the pub, the epigraph provides the poem's seed and part of the poem's good-natured fun. As we read the title, the epigraph, and then the first lines of the poem, we are momentarily suspended as we try to figure out how these elements are related. Part of our pleasure in the poem comes from our "Aha!" as we make the connection: Even strangers in some unimaginable future will still shun a wet dog. Drawing associations between seemingly unrelated notions can give you the controlling metaphor—the seed of the poem—that you can explore through the poem.

Once you have what feels like the *given* of a poem, a number of strategies can help you encourage its growth. One is simply to be very delicate about the moment you commit a line to paper. Poems often begin in the head and continue to develop there in the relatively free-floating mixture of thought, memory, and emotion. Putting something down on paper tends to fix it; in the very earliest stages of a poem, the shoots of the poem may be too tender for transplanting. Words that feel full and grand in the mind may look spindly and naked on the page. All that blankness can be intimidating, swallowing up the handful of words that try to break the silence. Some poets compose scores of lines in their heads before taking up the pen—using meter and rhyme can help in the process. Other poets need to get words down early, when a sentence, line, or just a phrase seems strong enough to withstand the scrutiny of the page.

Consistent writing in a notebook—which Billy Collins calls "keeping a log of the self"—can exercise your linguistic imagination and keep track of your ruminations until you have time for them. Then later, you'll have something to begin with instead of having that oppressive blank page staring back at you.

The more art is controlled, limited, worked over, the more it is free.

——Igor Stravinsky

If you're hooked on a computer and can't fathom going back to pen and paper, regularly print out hard copies. Be generous. If you only print out what you deem worthy, you're letting your analytical mind have too much say too early. For the earliest, sloppiest stages of writing, the notebook has many advantages: It's portable, quiet, always accessible, and no problem during a thunderstorm. Also, unlike the computer that obliterates deletions, the notebook allows you to reconstruct what you've crossed out.

The poet Richard Hugo in *The Triggering Town* advises student poets to use number 2 pencils, to cross out instead of erase, and "to write in a hard-covered notebook with green lined pages. Green is easy on the eyes. . . . The best notebooks I've found are National 48–81." That's what worked for him, and every poet will find a particular system that feels right and swear by it—notebook, computer, index cards with a felt-tip pen. Experiment with many methods, drafting poems on the computer, with paper and pencil, with different colors of ink, with script or printing, with lined and unlined pages, single sheets, tablets, and notebooks. Be loose.

Poets have written with a nursing baby cradled in one arm, by flashlight on an army footlocker after lights-out, and under odder conditions. But the poet is entitled to prefer working wherever it feels right—at a desk or (like Frost) with a lapboard in an easy chair. We know one poet who feels best writing in the bustling anonymity of airport terminals.

When a writing system begins to seem stale, try something else. Write a lot and write often, whether you feel inspired or not. A sculptor who picks up the chisel every day will wield it more nimbly than someone who picks up a chisel once a month. Better to write for an hour a day than eight hours on Sunday or when the feeling grabs you. The feeling may never grab you or, more likely, once you've expelled whatever sparked the desire to write, you'll have little interest in going back to what you wrote, crafting it, making it into a finished poem. Poets who don't revise are as rare as batters who hit every pitch.

Set up a work schedule and stick with it. Try to fence off a particular time of day for writing. When you sit down at your scheduled time, your mind will be alert to poems—your unconscious will have already been getting you ready. Also, be protective of your writing schedule. Unplug the phone, draw the curtains, wake up before anyone else or stay up when they've turned in. Discipline may not be a substitute for talent (however one defines that), but talent evaporates without it.

Most writers go through dry spells. Even the most disciplined come to a point where the wells seem empty and the blank page mocks. This can be particularly aggravating when you have a poem due Monday and don't have a clue where to begin. It sometimes helps to put your mind on something else. Go for a drive, wander around a museum, get a haircut, page through a book of photographs, skim a field guide, and you may find a new way to get started. Or try one of the writing suggestions in this text's Questions and Suggestions or Appendix I. What about writing a sestina? Or an abecedarian? If all else fails, maybe just set out to write a lousy poem. Make it as awful as you can. Really work at that. Revise, expand, make it worse. At least you'll have fun, and you might end up with something appealing.

Keeping a Poem Going

When the poem is coming, when the wind is in the sail, go with it. "And the secret of it all," Whitman says, "is to write in the gush, the throb, the flood, of the moment—to put things down without deliberation—without worrying about their style." Writing the first draft all in one sitting, filling up the page, or pages, from top to bottom, pushing onward when you feel the growing poem resistant, can give a poem coherence and clarity, for you are writing under the influence of a single mood, following the notions of a particular time. Getting a whole first draft early, even if sketchy, sloppy, and wordy, will give you something seemingly complete to work on and puzzle over.

Talking to yourself, *literally*, may also help a poem along. We usually talk to ourselves when we are upset. Worried by some complex choice or problem—like whether to move to a distant city—we weigh the options, "If I do this, then . . . but . . . or . . . then . . . ." Such brainstorming helps you evaluate and project uncertainties. Talking to oneself is often charged with emotion. Upset by injustice, rejection, or an unexpected flout—the niggling bureaucrat, the unfaithful friend—we go off by ourselves and rehearse a speech until we get just the cutting barb our frustration longs for. Of course, the fantasy speech rarely leaves our brains. But we end up with a kind of resolution; we've defined and refocused the situation and our (just) response to satisfy ourselves. Similarly, as your poem develops, talk out your alternatives; verbalize. In the early stages when you don't know what angle your poem will take (unlike, say, the writer of an editorial), literally talking through your choices can guide you toward a solution.

At some stage in the process, seeing the words on the page becomes crucial. Early enough for a poem not to have jelled too much, type it up or print it out. Since we read poems in print, seeing a young poem on the page can help you see clearly how it *looks*. Lines will be longer or shorter than you imagined, for instance, and the poem skinnier or chunkier or more graceful.

Considering its form, even if tentative and provisional, can also help coax out the poem. The very first line you write (which may disappear before the final version) may *feel* right for the poem and provide a norm to build the poem around. You will be looking to discover what visual form the poem will take: A narrow ribbon? A squat, solid poem? Loose? Short? A line that confirms the first shadowy choices can become a standard to measure fresh possibilities, blanks into which you may fit newly arriving inspirations. Determining line and form may open up a stuck poem, allowing it to spread and fill like water into a design.

From these loose impressions he recorded after a visit in 1929 with Olivia Shakespeare (with whom he had been in love as a young man), W. B. Yeats (1865–1939) began to lure the poem out:

> Your hair is white
> My hair is white
> Come let us talk of love
> What other theme do we know
> When we were young
> We were in love with one another
> And then were ignorant

The lines and phrases he began trying out were equally sketchy (and thin). Here are bits of them over several drafts:

> Your other lovers being dead and gone
> Those other lovers being dead and gone

> friendly light
> hair is white

> Upon the sole theme of art and song
> Upon the supreme theme of art and song
> Upon the theme so fitting for the aged; young
> We loved each other and were ignorant

> Once more I have kissed your hand and it is right
> All other lovers estranged or dead

The heavy curtains drawn—the candle light
Waging a doubtful battle with the shade

Gradually Yeats began to find the poem in his phrases and arrived at eight lines of iambic pentameter, rhyming abba cddc. The image of the white hair didn't last, but it lead to a rhyme (*right, night*) which became the opening argument of the final poem:

After Long Silence

Speech after long silence; it is right,
All other lovers being estranged or dead,
Unfriendly lamplight hid under its shade,
The curtains drawn upon unfriendly night,
That we descant and yet again descant   5
Upon the supreme theme of Art and Song:
Bodily decrepitude is wisdom: young
We loved each other and were ignorant.

The writing of even a few lines may be a mingling of a hundred creative and critical acts in rapid-fire, usually invisible, succession. You will find it useful to list several alternatives to a sentence or a word in the margin. Is the tulip *red, streaked, dangerous, deflated, smiling, barbed, bloody, sulking, fisted, squalid, gulping, a striped canopy?* At this stage the standard against which you test possibilities can hardly be more than a sketchy notion of the poem. But as your tentative choices accumulate and the poem seems to materialize on the page, it imposes more and more of its own demands and necessities. Listen to the poem; follow where it wants to lead you.

Put your ear to the poem, too. When a poem seems to peter out, try saying what you have so far aloud, over and over. Through repetition you can reveal both the awkward and graceful parts. Copying out by hand and retyping help, too; don't just use the "copy" and "paste" modes of your word processing program. Repeating the poem from the beginning will improve the continuity of the rhythm as well as the sense. This going back to the poem's first sounds can give you the momentum to get across the hard spot, just as coming upon a ditch you back up and get a running start to leap over.

To clarify the poem's intentions, acting belligerent with your words can pay off. Turn negative phrases into positives, positives into negatives. For instance, if you've written, "I loved him the first night." Why not try, "I wouldn't love him the first night." Or "No one loved him at first." If the peacock's feathers were "beaten metal" try them out as "dragging paper." By challenging your initial impulse, you will test your commitment to your words and may find the opposite assertion more productive or accurate. At least you will stir up the soup pot.

When a poem knots up and won't spool out, you may have before you two (or more) poems. A poem can set off in almost any direction, and in many directions at once; ask yourself if the poem's directions support each other or crowd each other out. "Kill your darlings," Faulkner advised. You must often excise those parts most precious to you before the whole can flourish. Good writing is like good gardening; not only do you yank out the weeds, you thin out perfectly healthy plants to make room for the rest.

Look for the central thrust of the poem and prune what is extraneous. Find the poem's central time and place, its key voice. Ask yourself: Who is speaking? To whom? Why? When? Where? Bring the possibilities into focus. As Yeats drafted "After Long Silence," he sketched out the scene with Olivia Shakespeare—the lamplight, the drawn curtains—and a context ("other loves being dead and gone") and gradually arrived at the final poem.

Every poem comes into its own from a unique set of sources and develops from a unique application of tools. If it comes in a rush, a waterfall down the page, it may then need you to go through it step by step, weighing each word, each sound. If the poem comes slowly, nail by nail and board by board, try working out a new draft in one swift torrent. A strategy that launches one poem may not work for another. Try out several strategies in a different order, at different times. Be elastic in your approach. Writing from formulas will give you formulaic poems.

Every poet has times when after hours of hard, focused work, the poem flops inert on the page. Put it aside then; you may resuscitate it next week or next month. Or maybe not. Let it go then. You have other poems to write. The adventure—and the frustration—begins all over with each poem. But each time you'll have more options to choose from, more experience, and more skills to apply to your poem.

QUESTIONS AND SUGGESTIONS

1. Get up two hours before you usually do—best if it's still dark. Find a comfortable vantage point (window, back steps, bus stop bench) and make *sentences* for everything you notice. Welcome the metaphors ("First light slides a blue flame . . .").

2. Take a poem you admire and type it up. Try memorizing it. See if you can discover its secrets. Then try your hand at a version of the poem, akin to Justice's "Variation on a Text by Vallejo" or Travis Brown's pantoum "At Seventeen," pp. 258, a takeoff on Edward Hirsch's "At Sixteen," p. 257.

3. Below are the opening sentences from short stories, novels, and essays. Take one that pricks your interest and use it as a building block for a poem of your own. The sources are in Appendix II.

   (a) So when I went there, I knew the dark fish must rise.
   (b) Through the fence, between the curling flower spaces, I could see them hitting.
   (c) Now that all the rivers have been named and the woods dying, we look into the territory behind.
   (d) Come into my cell. Make yourself at home.

(e) It wasn't beautiful but he loved his life.

(f) Night fell. The darkness was thin, like some sleazy dress that has been worn and worn . . . .

(g) The car that is chasing me is faster than mine.

(h) There is an evil moment on awakening when all things seem to pause.

(i) Twelve years old, and I was so bored I was combing my hair just for the hell of it.

4. Take a line from another poet—or anyone, for that matter—and see if it might spark a new poem as Mary Oliver's statement does for Billy Collins (p. 249) and Robert Bly's does for R. S. Gwynn (p. 259).

5. Have you ever been boiling mad at someone? Try to recollect the emotion, then write an *understated* poem about that person using details from a context. How would this person seem buying a car? Feeding a dog? Stranded in an oarless rowboat? Remember: *understated.*

6. Translate César Vallejo's "Piedra negra sobre una piedra blanca" (p. 241). If your Spanish isn't strong, ask a friend to do a literal translation, then try to work the poem into idiomatic English, keeping with Vallejo's tone.

7. After reading "A Description of the Morning" (below), Jonathan Swift's view of urban London workers in the eighteenth century, try your own descriptive list of your neighborhood, street corner, or hangout at a particular time of day.

POEMS TO CONSIDER

A Description of the Morning
JONATHAN SWIFT (1667–1745)

1709

Now hardly here and there a hackney-coach°
Appearing, showed the ruddy morn's approach.
Now Betty from her master's bed had flown,
And softly stole to discompose her own;
The slip-shod 'prentice from his master's door   5
Had pared the dirt and sprinkled round the floor.
Now Moll had whirled her mop with dext'rous airs,
Prepared to scrub the entry and the stairs.
The youth with broomy stumps began to trace
The kennel-edge°, where wheels had worn the place.   10
The small-coal man was heard with cadence deep,

1 hackney-coach: horse-drawn taxi   **10 kennel-edge:** curb

Till drowned in shriller notes of chimney-sweep:
Duns° at his lordships' gate began to meet;
And brickdust Moll had screamed through half the street.
The turnkey° now his flock returning sees,   15
Duly let out a-nights to steal for fees.
The watchful bailiffs take their silent stands,
And schoolboys lag with satchel in their hands.

13 Duns: bill collectors   **15 turnkey:** jailer; prisoners were released at night to
earn their maintenance.

Kerosene   1998
CHASE TWICHELL (b. 1950)

Here comes a new storm, roiling and black.
It's already raining up on Cascade,
where lightning makes the clouds look like

flowers of kerosene, like arson at the end
of the match. Lightning comes straight   5

from childhood, where the burned-out storms
still glitter weakly, tinsel on the dead trees
in the January streets. Back there a kid is still

learning why her parents need that harsh
backlight to see each other.   10

Bread and Water   1990
SHIRLEY KAUFMAN (b. 1923)

After the Leningrad trials, after solitary confinement
most of eleven years in a Siberian *gulag*, he told us
this story. One slice of sour black bread a day.
He trimmed off the crust and saved it for the last
since it was the best part. Crunchy, even a little sweet.   5
Then he crumbled the slice into tiny pieces. And ate
them, one crumb at a time. So they lasted all day. Not
the cup of hot water. First he warmed his hands around it.
Then he rubbed the cup up and down his chest to warm his
body. And drank it fast. Why, we asked him, why not   10
like the bread? Sometimes, he said, there was more hot
water in the jug the guard wheeled around to the prisoners.
Sometimes a guard would ladle a second cup. It helped
to believe in such kindness.

⊕ Late Night Drive   1998
DEBORAH KROMAN*

The road unscrolls between flat black fields.
A bolt of lightning backlights a thundercloud

like a memory uncovered by a song on the radio.
In the fissures of the brain the neurons

never touch each other. Filaments   5
with forked tips, they wait for the shock

to leap across, trigger the unstable ions,
illuminate what is hidden. During the eye exam

it startled me to see the veins on my retina
like golden branches. That's why I cast lines   10

across the page—look how the headlights find
the steam ghosts rising from the wet pavement.

⊕ At Sixteen   1997
EDWARD HIRSCH (b. 1950)

I walked under a fire escape splashed with gasoline.
     I walked past a sweatshop buried in a warehouse
where dozens of women were sewing garments.
     I got a job as a waiter in a downtown restaurant.

I walked past a sweatshop buried in a warehouse.   5
     My father lent me the car on Saturday nights.
I waited on tables in a downtown restaurant
     and ate in the kitchen with the other waiters.

My father lent me the car on Saturday nights.
     I took my girlfriend to the beach for parties.   10
I ate in the kitchen with the other waiters.
     Everyone laughed at my enormous appetite.

I took my girlfriend to the beach for parties.
     She wanted to get married, get pregnant.
Everyone laughed at my enormous appetite.   15
     I wanted her so much I thought I'd die of it.

She wanted to get pregnant, get married.
     I wrote a poem about a closing steel door.
I wanted her so much I thought I'd die of it.
     I got a job in a warehouse next to a factory.   20

I wrote a poem about a steel door closing.
    I walked under a fire escape splashed with gasoline.
I took orders in a warehouse next to a factory
    where dozens of women were feeding machines.

At Seventeen
TRAVIS BROWN*

2002

after Edward Hirsch

I slept in vomit in a windowless apartment.
    I drove a Monte Carlo with 103,000 miles
when I was drunk because I couldn't get laid.
    I got a kitchen job in a nursing home off 5th street.

I drove a Monte Carlo with 103,000 miles.   5
    My parents were proud of my grades.
I washed dishes in a kitchen off 5th street
    and ate in the basement with the other aides.

My parents were proud of my grades.
    I cheated on girls and smoked on weekends.   10
I ate in the basement with the other aides—
    each woman had a story about a man.

I cheated on girls and smoked on weekends.
    I wanted to get high, get laid.
Each woman had a story about a man.   15
    I wanted this Asian girl with thick hair.

I wanted to get high, get laid.
    I opened juice tops and milk cartons for old folks.
I wanted this Asian girl with thick hair—
    she got pregnant and vanished from the city limits.   20

I opened juice tops and milk cartons for old folks.
    I slept in vomit in a windowless apartment.
She got pregnant and vanished from the city limits,
    while I was drunk because I couldn't get laid.

Sonnet: To Tell the Truth
ALICIA OSTRIKER (b. 1937)

1979

To tell the truth, those brick Housing Authority buildings
For whose loveliness no soul had planned,
Like random dominoes stood, worn out and facing each other,
Creating the enclosure that was our home.

Long basement corridors connected one house to another   5
And had a special smell, from old bicycles and baby carriages
In the storage rooms. The elevators
Were used by kissing teenagers.
The playground—iron swingchains, fences, iron monkey bars,
Iron seesaw handles, doubtless now rusted—   10
Left a strong iron smell on my hands and in the autumn air
And rang with cries. To me it is even precious
Where they chased the local Mongoloid, yelling "Stupid Joey!
Stupid Joey!"
Now I've said everything nice I can about this.   15

Ballade Beginning with a Line by Robert Bly   2000
R. S. GWYNN (b. 1948)

My heart is a calm potato by day.
My feet are three Belgian nuns by night.
My fingers are speed-bumps in my way
When I'm screwing onions in for light.
My tongue is a shoeless duck; my right   5
Elbow's a celibate tv star.
My navel's a stick of dynamite.
I don't know what my metaphors are.

My son is a half-eaten creme brulee.
My daughters are all under copyright.   10
My wife's a convertible full of hay
In a small, abandoned nuclear site.
My father's a ten-round welterweight fight
With my mother, who isn't a Mason jar.
My family tree is a concrete kite.   15
I don't know what my metaphors are.

My books are chickens who kneel to pray
In a Unitarian solstice rite.
Each page is a prudish manta ray,
Each word an Arabian parasite,   20
Each letter an oyster-knife that might
Plunge fatally into a Hershey bar.
My poems are clocks with an appetite.
I don't know what my metaphors are.

Prince, pray for all those who have to write: 25
My brain is a clam's unlit cigar.
My ear is a cheese with an overbite.
I don't know what my metaphors are.

Good Deeds   2002
ARTHUR SMITH (b. 1948)

> It's easy to forget the bathtub
> I'm scrubbing is the same one
> She once drew hot water in
>
> And undressed me for
> And into which I pooled myself   5
> After a long, down day's work.
>
> Sometimes when I think of her, I remember
> A woman asking the man she loved
> If he thought
>
> She were beautiful—the man   10
> Saying nothing, believing she were the one
> Tried by that question.
>
> A good number of down days would pass
> Before his knowing
> The difference, before his saying   15
>
> She was beautiful, to himself aloud,
> And again, for good measure,
> To the tub.

She Says   1993
LUCI TAPAHONSO (b. 1953)

> The cool October night, and his tall gray hat
> throws sharp shadows on the ground.
> Somewhere west of the black volcanoes,
> dogs are barking at something no one else can see.
>
> His voice a white cloud,   5
> plumes of chimney smoke suspended in the dark.
>
> Later we are dancing in the living room,
> his hand warm on the small of my back.
> It is music that doesn't change.
>
> The ground outside is frozen,   10
> trees glisten with moon frost.
>
> The night is a careful abandonment of other voices,
> his girlfriend's outburst brimming at the edge of the morning,
>
> and I think I have aged so.
> His warm hands and my own laugh are all we share in this other life   15
> strung together by missing years and dry desert evenings.

Tomorrow the thin ice on black weeds will shimmer in the sun,
and the horses wait for him.
At his house around noon, thin strands of icicles drop
to the ground in silence.   20

Early Saturday, the appaloosa runs free near Moenkopi.
The dog yips, yips alongside.

11

DEVISING AND REVISING

Despite all kinds of helpful (and not-so-helpful) technology, new computer hard- and software, the Internet, and countless venues of support and instruction, the secret to writing remains rewriting. To paraphrase W. H. Auden, literary composition in the beginning of the twenty-first century A.D. remains pretty much what it was in the early twenty-first century B.C.: "nearly everything has still to be done by hand." Word by word and page by page, we plunge across known and unknown oceans, revising and tinkering, with each draft trying to get a little closer to landfall. Technique brings inspiration to life; craft makes the magic. Like simplicity, spontaneity and naturalness spring from hard work. "Writing is like evolution," says Forrest Gander, "in that poems are invented . . . as they develop in the act of writing." Poets revise poems because the first draft is just the lump of clay to put on the wheel; revision shapes the material into the poem.

For most poems, the process takes several drafts, often many more. Elizabeth Bishop's "The Moose" took twenty-six years from first draft to finished poem. Carolyn Kizer's "Shalimar Gardens" (p. 203) comes from a group of poems on which she has been working for about thirty years. Richard Wilbur reports that he waited fourteen years, occasionally jotting down a phrase "that might belong to a poem," before he started to write "The Mind-Reader"; he took another three years to finish the poem. Asked how long he was likely to work on a poem, he said, "Long enough."

Exploring

First drafts often mean exploration. The poet holds up a map that's mostly blank, with maybe a few ideas, like the rumor of rivers, sketched in. How can the poem grow out of these notions? How should it begin? Hopeless blunders usually mix with useful clues, and in letting them begin to sort themselves out, the poet becomes an explorer charting uncharted territories.

Let's take a look at an early draft of the poem that became "A Noiseless Patient Spider" (which we talked about in Chapter 2). Here Whitman is sorting out the poem's (sometimes muddled) impulses. He is exploring.

The Soul, Reaching, Throwing Out for Love

The Soul, reaching, throwing out for love,
As the spider, from some little promontory, throwing out filament after
   filament, tirelessly out of itself, that one at least may catch and form a
   link, a bridge, a connection,
O I saw one passing along, saying hardly a word—yet full of love I detected
   him, by certain signs,
O eyes wishfully turning! O silent eyes!
For then I thought of you o'er the world,   5
O latent oceans, fathomless oceans of love!
O waiting oceans of love! yearning and fervid! and of you sweet souls
   perhaps in the future, delicious and long:
But Death, unknown on the earth—ungiven, dark here, unspoken, never
   born:
You fathomless latent souls of love—you pent and unknown oceans of love!

Whitman transforms this material into an entirely new poem:

A Noiseless Patient Spider

A noiseless patient spider,
I marked where on a little promontory it stood isolated,
Marked how to explore the vacant vast surrounding,
It launched forth filament, filament, filament, out of itself,
Ever unreeling them, ever tirelessly speeding them.   5

And you O my soul where you stand,
Surrounded, detached, in measureless oceans of space,
Ceaselessly musing, venturing, throwing, seeking the spheres to connect
   them,
Till the bridge you will need be formed, till the ductile anchor hold,
Till the gossamer thread you fling catch somewhere, O my soul.   10

Despite its obvious weaknesses, the early poem, "The Soul, Reaching, Throwing Out for Love" offers Whitman many clues to his final poem. In the opening lines of the draft Whitman seems to have stumbled upon the *given* of the poem, making the connection between the spider's flinging out of filaments and the soul's groping. The earlier draft doesn't yet apprehend the simile's potential, but in coming back to this draft Whitman must have begun to see—to have "re-visioned"—the possibilities of the spider-soul analogy.

In "The Noiseless Patient Spider," Whitman reshapes this analogy to make it the poem's motivating incident, creating a little fiction that suggests one day the speaker came upon a spider at work. He "marked where on a little promontory it stood isolated," began carefully observing it, then realized how his own soul behaves similarly, "ceaselessly musing, venturing, throwing, seeking."

In the early draft the motivating incident seems to be something entirely different. The speaker says that he first saw "one passing along, saying hardly a word—yet full of love I detected him"; then the speaker describes this person's eyes, thinks of "you o'er the world" (whoever that "you" is), then drifts through references to "oceans of love" and "souls of love." Whitman let go of his first notions of the poem and allowed it develop in a more fruitful direction.

Both poems have about the same number of lines, though the first weighs in at 125 words and the final poem at a slim 87 words. While Whitman jettisons "eyes," "sweet," "delicious," "future," "Death," and "love," he keeps "oceans of" along with a few other words and phrases—"little promontory," "filament," "tirelessly," "bridge," and "catch"—that lead him to the poem's final discoveries. For instance, "filament" is echoed in "ductile anchor" and "gossamer thread"; the phrases "latent oceans," "fathomless oceans of love," and "waiting oceans" develop into the philosophic "measureless oceans of space," akin to the "vacant, vast surrounding" in which the spider finds itself. Whitman further develops this water motif with "launched" and "unreeling," words that help ground the sketchy acts of "musing, venturing, throwing, seeking." These progressive participles (words ending in "-ing"), by the way, stem from the original draft, although in it Whitman does not yet recognize the gerunds' deeper implications, how they celebrate process, trying, *exploration* itself.

> [P]oetry] aims—never mind either *communication* or *expression*—at the reformation of the poet, as prayer does.
> —John Berryman

Appreciating the potential of the spider-soul analogy also helps Whitman refine the shape the poem takes on the page. The two five-line stanzas of "A Noiseless Patient Spider" create a parallel structure that subtly affirms the connection between spider and soul. By pursuing this analogy the poem comes to be about our struggle to be connected and to make connections—how we venture, reach out, till we connect with something in the "measureless oceans of space" around us—which is very like the process of writing: we try and try and try again.

Trying Out

Early stages of writing a poem often involve looking for clues. Before a passage can come right and words click into place, your own dissatisfaction—the cranky sense that something remains vague, weak, or flat—can spur your revision.

We can watch such dissatisfaction at work as John Keats (1795–1821) tries out four successive versions of the opening of "Hyperion," his long poem about the Olympic gods conquering the Titans. Hyperion, the Titan of the sun, was displaced by Apollo, god of poetry; Saturn, the father of the Titans, was replaced by Zeus. Through trial and error, Keats searches for the right image for lines 8 and 9. Here is the passage, with the first attempt in italics:

> Deep in the shady sadness of a vale
> Far sunken from the healthy breath of morn,
> Far from the fiery noon, and eve's one star,
> Sat gray-haired Saturn, quiet as a stone,
> Still as the silence round about his lair;   5
> Forest on forest hung about his head
> Like cloud on cloud. No stir of air was there,
> *Not so much life as what an eagle's wing*
> *Would spread upon a field of green eared corn,*
> But where the dead leaf fell, there did it rest.   10
> A stream went voiceless by, still deadened more
> By reason of his fallen divinity
> Spreading a shade . . . .

Keats presents a gloomy scene of Saturn in the dark, still forest. In line 7, the static internal off-rhyme of "stir-air-there" sharply enough depicts the hush, but Keats was bothered by the simile of the eagle. He discarded the clumsy and unnecessary "what" that merely kept the meter, but instead of taking the easy solution of adding a syllable to describe the eagle (e.g., "Not so much life as a young eagle's wing"), he opted to change the image. Probably he sensed it as too vital for an image of vanquished divinity.

In his next version he tries out a bird with more apt connotations:

> No stir of air was there,
> Not so much life as a young vulture's wing
> Would spread upon a field of green eared corn

Keats apparently intends us to see a large, powerful bird gliding, making not a wisp of motion in the field of delicate grain far below. (In British usage, *corn* is any grain, not American corn.) Perhaps Keats has in mind the shadow of the bird's wing passing over, but not moving, the limber stalks. Perhaps through the *young* vulture he means to accentuate Saturn's age and weakness.

But the image apparently bothered Keats. Carrion or no, the strong, vital bird spoils the mournful tone. And the sunny, spacious "field of green eared corn" detracts from the brooding forest scene of defeated Saturn. Keats scraps the entire image in the next version:

> No stir of air was there,
> Not so much life as on a summer's day
> Robs not at all the dandelion's fleece

Dandelion gone to seed forms a more fitting image than "green eared corn;" and dandelion seeds—easily wafted away—demonstrate how dead the air is and imply through their color "gray-haired Saturn." Following "No stir of air was there," the double negatives "Not . . . not . . ." emphasize the scene's negation, and even the awkward syntax seems, rhythmically, right for air so still it cannot dislodge one wispy seed. For some months Keats let the lines stand this way.

Several problems must have bothered him into another, final, revision. Possibly the lowly dandelion seemed inappropriate for a poem on a classical subject; also, the line must awkwardly emphasize its *seeds* since we often associate dandelions with their bright yellow bloom. More significantly, Keats must have recognized that "fleece," though fluffy like a head of dandelion seeds, doesn't work in this context. For one thing, animal fleece is oily and heavy. For another, a fleece is not easily robbed. Pieces of wool might be snagged from a fleece, but not by a light breeze. Keats may have also been irked by the image's perspective, of the single dandelion seen up close, and so tried moving back:

> No stir of air was there,
> Not so much life as on a summer's day
> Robs not one light seed from the feathered grass

Like the dead leaf in the next line, Keats keeps "seed from the feathered grass" abstract and generic. Visually, nothing competes with the main presentation of Saturn. The rhythm of the revised line is masterful: "Robs not one light seed from the feathered grass." The five even, stressed syllables at the beginning of the line suggest a light, precarious balance. Then the slightest quickening of "from the feathered grass" seems to pass like the absent breath of air. Not the least of Keats's mastery is using spondees for an impression of lightness.

Focusing

As when we look at slides, when we read poems, we want them brought into clear focus. Sharpening fuzzy spots—unintentional ambiguity, exaggerations, private meanings, confusing omissions, and especially purple passages—is part of the poet's job in revising. Since to the poet the words may seem perfectly sharp, noticing the blur is the first step.

Poets' working drafts often capture their struggle to zoom in on the poem. Manuscripts and drafts by hundreds of poets, from Alexander Pope to Julia Alvarez, are reproduced in *The Hand of the Poet: Poems and Papers in Manuscript*; the originals are in the Berg collection at the New York City Public Library. On page after page we see the scrawlings and scratchings of poets working to focus the draft at hand. For instance, in the first draft of "Variations on a Text by Vallejo" (discussed in Chapter 10), written out on a legal pad sheet, we can see Donald Justice teasing the poem from his first notions. The draft has the title from the start and a good feel for the beginning of the poem (Justice started with "I will die in Miami in the sunlight" instead of "sun"), but the draft shows him feeling his way into what became the second stanza. Lines 14 through 17 of the finished poem read

> And I think it will be a Sunday because today
> When I took out this paper and began to write
> Never before had anything looked so blank,
> My life, these words, the paper, the gray Sunday

Justice first wrote these lines:

> because today
> When I got up from my nap & reached for paper
> I could think of nothing else, I could only think
> of how I have been sick for five or six weeks,

Then he seems immediately to have crossed out "I could only think / of how I have been sick for five or six weeks" and wrote "I coughed and could think of nothing else." In the end, Justice abandoned both of these personal explanations and focused the stanza around the larger metaphysical concern of blankness, an astute decision.

Look at the following version of a poem by Michael Burns (b. 1953) which appeared in *The Laurel Review* in 1992.

The First Time

She slapped him. She screamed, Tell me why, why?
And maybe he knew she didn't want an answer,
only the lie that would keep them together,
so he got out of the car and lay down in a dry ditch.

There was sobbing, the quiet headlights in the fog,   5
the motor running. He held his head in his hands
and thought of the other woman's voice, full
of rough pleasure, and the stain
shaped like a ballerina on the motel's ceiling.

Listening to his own weeping, he felt something   10
in him was cast loose, adrift like the wooden boats
of children, or scorched and coasting, falling
like the spent phase of a rocket launched for the moon.

A man has just confessed to a woman, maybe his wife, that he has sexually betrayed her. She hits him and asks him why; since he can't come up with an answer—with a lie that will save their relationship—he retreats to a ditch where he recollects the other woman during sex. As he hears himself cry, he feels something "cast loose" in him like "the spent phase of a rocket." Burns titles the poem "The First Time," implying that this was the first of perhaps many infidelities.

Consider the situation, then ask yourself if any elements of the poem seem gratu-itous. Unnecessary? Do any images seem unrelated to the rest of the poem? Does the tone falter somewhere?

Now take a look at the poem as the poet revised it for his book, *The Secret Names* (1994).

The First Time

She slapped him. She screamed, Tell me why, why?
And maybe he knew she didn't want an answer,
only the lie that would keep them together,
so he left the car and lay down in a ditch.

There was sobbing, the headlights in the fog,   5
the motor running.
He thought of the other woman
As she rode him under the stained motel ceiling.

Listening to his own weeping,
he felt something in him was cast loose,   10
adrift like the wooden boats of children,
or scorched and coasting,
falling like the spent phase of a rocket.

Dropping modifiers (*dry* ditch, *quiet* headlights, rocket *launched for the moon*) sharpens the poem. In the revised poem, no longer do we have an implication that the man had been ambitious, capable of greatness; no longer is the rocket launched for the moon. Instead the revised poem focuses on the falling "spent phase of a rocket," emphasiz-ing his failure. The deep cuts Burns makes in the second stanza make the tone harsher, complicating our view of the man. In the earlier version, the man "held his head in his hands," suggesting he is suffering, perhaps feeling remorse, for his behavior. In the revision such implication is gone. Also in the earlier version he remembers the other woman as having enjoyed the act; her voice was "full / of rough pleasure," a depiction further softened by the image of the ballerina. In the final version these somewhat tender details become the starker, bestial "she rode him under the stained motel ceil-ing." In the revision, Burns's tone and point of view—a distant third person from the start—become even more remote and cool. The revised character is less thoughtful than the first, making him all the more a person at the mercy of his impulses.

In terms of form, Burns appears to have made a trade-off. In the earlier version he established a symmetrical stanzaic pattern of 4-5-4 lines, but his deletions in the second stanza have broken the symmetry. His final version is asymmetrical, putting the greater weight on the longer, closing five-line last stanza. This slightly off-balance form emphasizes the man's sense of being "cast loose," "scorched and coasting."

At times the smallest tinkerings with a poem allow for a brilliant stroke that oth-erwise might never have come to the poet. Consider the fourth stanza of a 1924 revi-sion of Marianne Moore's "My Apish Cousins," which she retitled in 1935:

The Monkeys

winked too much and were afraid of snakes. The zebras, supreme in
their abnormality; the elephants with their fog-colored skin
and strictly practical appendages
  were there, the small cats; and the parakeet
    trivial and humdrum on examination, destroying   5
  bark and portions of the food it could not eat.

I recall their magnificence, now not more magnificent
than it is dim. It is difficult to recall the ornament,
  speech, and precise manner of what one might
    call the minor acquaintances twenty   10
      years back; but I shall not forget him—that Gilgamesh among
  the hairy carnivora—that cat with the

wedge-shaped, slate-gray marks on its forelegs and the resolute tail,
astringently remarking, "They have imposed on us with their pale
  half-fledged protestations, trembling about   15
    in inarticulate frenzy, saying
      it is not for us to understand art; finding it
  all so difficult, examining the thing

as if it were inconceivably arcanic, as symmetrically frigid as if it had been carved out of chrysoprase   20
  or marble—strict with tension, malignant
    in its power over us and deeper
      than the sea when it proffers flattery in exchange for hemp,
  rye, flax, horses, platinum, timber, and fur."

Whether ordinary, odd, or noble, the zoo animals are handled affectionately. The admired big cat seems a Gilgamesh—that is, like the Babylonian epic hero.

At line 14 the poem takes a stunning leap, for the cat turns out to be summarizing the paralyzing attitudes of certain art critics. Moore's admiration for the cat aligns her with its angry statement, and with the common readers whose portraits she has been amusedly sketching in the guise of zoo-creatures who turn out to be not so ordinary after all. The poem argues against the notion that art is some "inconceivably arcanic" thing, "malignant / in its power over us," which like the sea can take our practical goods in exchange for mere prettiness that deceives.

Moore's poem first appeared in 1917 with this fourth stanza:

As if it were something inconceivably arcanic, as
Symmetrically frigid as something carved out of chrysoprase   20
  Or marble—strict with tension, malignant
    In its power over us and deeper
      Than the sea when it proffers flattery in exchange for hemp,
  Rye, flax, horses, platinum, timber and fur."

Besides dropping the lines' initial capitals, Moore's only change occurs in lines 19 and 20. Especially after "thing" in line 18, the repetition of "something" in both lines no doubt seemed redundant. Since the poem is in syllabics, she couldn't simply drop "something" unless she wanted to recast the whole poem. And in line 20 inserting "if"—"frigid as if carved . . ."—would still leave the line a syllable short.

Moore's solution repairs the syllable count of line 20 by inserting "if it had been" and moving the first two syllables of "symmetrically" up to restore the syllable count of line 19. In the move she trades off the off-rhyme of "as-chrysoprase," for the enactment of crabby rigidity itself, dividing the word "symmet- / rically." Some close tinkering leads to a moment of wit.

Shaping

Another essential part of composition is *shaping*. As the words of a poem come, they must be deployed into lines. Sometimes the earliest verbalization carries with it an intuitive sense of form—as Whitman's earlier draft was similar in length and number of lines to his final "A Noiseless Patient Spider." But often the first phrases are a scattering, fragments with no certainty even as to which should come first. As a poem grows, the poet opts for some possible form, however tentative, which can be tested and altered as draft leads to draft. Meter? Rhyme? Free verse? Longer lines? Stanzas? The initial preference may be habitual, as Dickinson or William Carlos Williams instinctively worked in very short lines, or Whitman in very long lines. But a given poem may want a different sort of form. In "The Yachts," for instance, Williams elected to write in lines much longer than was his custom: "Today no race. Then the wind comes again. The yachts // move, jockeying for a start, the signal is set . . . ."

In choosing stanzaic forms, whether in free verse or in meter, the poet looks for a pattern that can be used fully, without slackening, in subsequent stanzas. Of "I Hoed and Trenched and Weeded," A. E. Housman commented: "Two of the stanzas, I do not say which, came into my head. . . . A third stanza came with a little coaxing after tea. One more was needed, but it did not come: I had to turn to and compose it myself, and that was a laborious business. I wrote it thirteen times, and it was more than a twelve-month before I got it right." Poems don't always unwind from the top. Robert Lowell recalled that his well-known "Skunk Hour" was "written backwards," the last two stanzas first, then the next-to-last two, and finally the first four in reverse order. Similarly, many poets don't come to a final title until they have finished the poem.

Along with a tentative choice of form, shaping involves the experimental sculpting or fitting of further parts to the developed design. In the published versions of Marianne Moore's "The Fish," we can trace her shaping her poem to its final form. Here is an early version that appeared in a magazine in 1918:

The Fish
Wade through black jade.
Of the crow-blue mussel-shells, one

Keeps adjusting the ash-heaps;
Opening and shutting itself like

An injured fan.   5
The barnacles undermine the
Side of the wave—trained to hide
There—but the submerged shafts of the

Sun, split like spun
Glass, move themselves with spotlight swift-   10
Ness, into the crevices—
In and out, illuminating

The turquoise sea
Of bodies. The water drives a
Wedge of iron into the edge   15
Of the cliff, whereupon the stars,

Pink rice grains, ink-
Bespattered jelly-fish, crabs like
Green lilies and submarine
Toadstools, slide each on the other.   20

All external
Marks of abuse are present on
This defiant edifice—
All physical features of

Accident—lack   25
Of cornice, dynamite grooves, burns
And hatchet strokes, these things stand
Out on it; the chasm side is

Dead. Repeated
Evidence has proved that it can   30
Live on what cannot revive
Its youth. The sea grows old in it.

As usual, Moore has devised a poem with a novel form. Unmistakable rhyme-pairs (wade-jade, keeps-heaps, an-fan, and so on) *begin* and end lines 1 and 3 of each stanza. Self-enclosed in sound, tightly laced, these lines seem to resist the otherwise fairly straightforward movement of the sentences, so that the poem alternates between the rigidity of rhyme and the fluidity of enjambment (even over stanza breaks), mimicking the stiff surfaces within the water and the flowing water itself.

But Moore was dissatisfied with the poem's shape, as this 1924 version makes clear from its appearance alone:

The Fish

wade
through black jade.
  Of the crow-blue mussel shells, one
    keeps
      adjusting the ash heaps;   5
  opening and shutting itself like

an
injured fan.
  The barnacles which encrust the
    side   10
    of the wave, cannot hide
  there for the submerged shafts of the

sun,
split like spun
  glass, move themselves with spotlight swift-   15
    ness
    into the crevices—
  in and out, illuminating

the
turquoise sea   20
  of bodies. The water drives a
    wedge
    of iron through the iron edge
  of the cliff, whereupon the stars,

pink   25
rice grains, ink-
  bespattered jelly-fish, crabs like
    green
    lilies and submarine
  toadstools, slide each on the other.   30

All
external
  marks of abuse are present on
    this
      defiant edifice—   35
  all the physical features of

ac-
cident—lack
  of cornice, dynamite grooves, burns
    and   40
      hatchet strokes, these things stand
  out on it; the chasm side is

dead.
Repeated
  evidence has proved that it can   45
    live
      on what cannot revive
    its youth. The sea grows old in it.

Moore sharpens her images with two verbal changes: "The barnacles *undermine* the /
Side of the wave—trained to hide / There—*but* . . ." becomes "The barnacles *which
encrust* the / side / of the wave, *cannot* hide / there *for* . . .". The physical image of
encrusting replaces the notion of undermining, and clearly focuses the wit of revers-
ing the usual way of seeing barnacles as belonging to, being attached to, the rock surface. The change also makes moot the possible questions of "trained to hide," how, by
whom?—a training which, in any case, doesn't prevent the shafts of sunlight from
spotlighting them.

In stanza 4, "Wedge of iron *into* the edge" becomes "wedge / of iron *through* the *iron*
edge . . ." The repetition of "iron" makes the opposing forces—sea against cliff—
equal; the denser sound suggests iron's heaviness.

As you saw immediately, the most dramatic change is visual: Moore opens up the
earlier boxy stanza and devises a pattern of indentation. The relining *in effect* moves
each flush-left rhyme-syllable up to a line of its own. So,

An injured fan

becomes

an
injured fan

This slight adjustment, making both words *end*-rhymes, relieves the odd pressure in
the 1918 version of the rhymes' seeming to frame each line tightly. The 1924 stanzas
rhyme *a a b c c d.*

The result might have been merely:

an
injured fan.
The barnacles which encrust the
side
of the wave, cannot hide
there for the submerged shafts of the

But Moore varies the indenting rhymed and unrhymed line pairs, and thereby creates a more flexible stanza shape that moves in and out like the sea shifting against
the shore. "The Fish" in 1924 exemplifies great fluidity and, in the unvaried syllabics and unremitting rhyming (which incorporates any word, however unimportant), great rigidity.

Reprinting the poem in 1935, with no verbal changes whatever, Moore made one further adjustment: moving the single-syllable lines 4 up to the end of lines 3, making a five-line stanza: *a a b b c*. Thus:

The Fish

wade
through black jade.
   Of the crow-blue mussel-shells, one keeps
   adjusting the ash-heaps;
      opening and shutting itself like   5

an
injured fan.
   The barnacles which encrust the side
   of the wave, cannot hide
      there for the submerged shafts of the   10

sun,
split like spun
   glass, move themselves with spotlight swiftness
   into the crevices—
      in and out, illuminating   15

the
turquoise sea
   of bodies. The water drives a wedge
   of iron through the iron edge
      of the cliff, whereupon the stars,   20

pink
rice grains, ink-
   bespattered jelly-fish, crabs like green
   lilies, and submarine
      toadstools, slide each on the other.   25

All
external
   marks of abuse are present on this
   defiant edifice—
      all the physical features of   30

ac-
cident—lack
   of cornice, dynamite grooves, burns and
   hatchet strokes, these things stand
      out on it; the chasm side is   35

dead.
Repeated
   evidence has proved that it can live

on what cannot revive
    its youth. The sea grows old in it.   40

The poem becomes less fussy, by avoiding the *two* monosyllabic rhyming lines of the 1924 stanza, which—as in the unindented form of it printed above—make the pattern of lines 1 through 3 and 4 through 6 rhythmically redundant. The 1924 stanza, by contrast, seems perhaps more exacting, more brittle. In the 1935 version, stanzas cast in progressive indentations shape the most flexible and expressive of Moore's attempts, and demonstrate how even small adjustments in a poem's shape give a poem resonance.

Drafts

Most working drafts are much messier than the fair copies or transcriptions from poets' manuscripts that we have been discussing. These days many poets do write on a computer, but for many acts during revision, a hard copy and a pen or pencil are superior tools. They easily allow for many possibilities at once, the scribbles and scrawls, sketches, arrows, jottings, marginal lists, doodles, and even coffee stains, that help the poet tease out the poem. Besides, writing poems is such an intense mental activity that the physicality of paper and pen can give some relief. Sometimes, actually sketching out, drawing a picture of something you're trying to depict, can help you see it. And, frankly, hitting the delete button is no substitute for those times when a stubborn poem is really driving you nuts. You can cross the page out with big black lines, crumple it into a ball, and try to sink it in the trash can (and later fish it out).

> *I*t is no accident that book, sentence, and pen are the terms not only of artistic profession, but of penal containment.
> —Heather McHugh

    Let's look at a couple early drafts of one of Robert Wallace's poems, "Swimmer in the Rain," about a bay-creek behind one of New Jersey's sand-spit islands. Like most poems, the poem gathered over many years. Drawing on memories going back to his childhood and physical sensations that he hadn't consciously thought of in more than twenty years, the first draft of the poem arrived, but then he got stuck, and the rest of the page is covered with doodles:

```
No one but him to see
                  a
the rain begin fine scrim
                    slow
far down the bay, like smoke,

smoking and hissing its way
              then   (into  marsh
toward, and then{up the creek

where he drifted swam, waited

           a suit  clad in
cold,      thin
   supple, green glass

to his neck.
```

The draft shows him scrutinizing his choices, exploring and focusing his material. One change he made immediately, as he was typing, was in the sixth line; "drifted" became "swam," which clarifies just what this man is doing. When Wallace came back to the typed draft he replaced by hand a simile ("like smoke") with the more exact "slow smoke" and modified "creek" with "marsh" to help us visualize how the rain approaches and where we are. The draft shows him looking very carefully at what he has on the page. He has noticed, and underlined, rhymes that appeared in the draft: "him-scrim-in" and "bay-way." With an eye to these rhymes, he launched into another draft. In trying to set up the "him" rhymes he shifted from a three-beat line to a two-beat line, and, after a fitful start, he abandoned the rhyme altogether. But with the two-beat line established, something clicked, and the poem began to flow out onto the page, reaching fifty-two lines in about an hour.

Watching a poem flow out like that is a poet's rare reward for years of stubborn starts and stuck corners. Here, somewhat simplified, is the first part of that second draft:

```
                    No one but him
      to see/      seeing the rain
                              , ~~like~~ smoke,
      start/       ~~begin~~, a scrim,

                    far down the bay,
                         ing        in a line
                  ~~and~~ advances ~~till~~,
           till  ←——————————————— between two grays
              , the salt-grass rustles

                    and the ~~marsh~~ creek's mirror

              ?  → in which he stood--
          (green, cold, ~~gr~~ and supple/—
                    to his neck, like clothing--
      ripple/      begins to dimple.
```

As he generated this draft he dropped several directions the poem had been heading in. In the first, he had included a metaphor for the sound of the rain coming on, "hissing." Although rain on water does seem to hiss, the implication of a snake would misdirect the poem. He uses "hissing" later in the poem, but when it appears there, the other imagery will be so sharp that it will screen out the snake suggestion. He also abandoned the "marsh creek" for "creek" that he had first off: He doesn't need the clarifying "marsh" once the image of the rustling salt-grass locates us. He had fiddled with the word "glass" and then went with "mirror," which includes glass but offers other opportunities for the poem. He has set in the left margin alternative words with slash marks and made other changes by crossing out and inserting. The blurry image of the rain "advancing / between two grays," which came to him as he returned to the draft, nicely sets up the contrast between the ill-defined clouds and the silvery rain.

On the first draft Wallace became stuck because his three-beat lines were too *horizontal*—too slow, too paced—for the fast-paced, ever-changing rain. In adopting the two-beat line, Wallace reported he wasn't imposing a pattern on it; he was listening to and learning from the poem how it should move: *vertically*. In general, the lines are iambic, but in such short lines, substitutions produce a varied, shifting rhythm without seeming too loose or uncontrolled. Here is the poem:

Swimmer in the Rain

No one but him
seeing the rain
start—a fine scrim
far down the bay,
smoking, advancing   5
between two grays
till the salt-grass rustles
and the creek's mirror
in which he stands
to his neck, like clothing   10
cold, green, supple,
begins to ripple.

The drops bounce up,
little fountains
all around him,   15
swift, momentary—
every drop tossed back
in air atop
its tiny column—
glass balls balancing   20
upon glass nipples,
lace of dimples,
a stubble of silver
stars, eye-level,
incessant, wild.   25

White, dripping, tall,
ignoring the rain,
an egret fishes
in the creek's margin,
dips to the minnows'   30
sky, under which,
undisturbed, steady
as faith the tide pulls.
Mussels hang
like grapes on a piling.   35
Wet is wet.

The swimmer settles
to the hissing din—
a glass bombardment,
parade of diamonds,   40
blinks, jacks of light,
wee Brancusi's°, chromes
like grease-beads sizzling,
myriad—and swims
slowly, elegantly,   45
climbing tide's ladder
hand over hand
toward the distant bay.

Hair and eye-brows
streaming, sleek crystal   50
scarving his throat—
no one but him.

42 **Brancusi's:** modern sculptures like those of Constantin Brancusi (1876–1957).

Wallace believed that the "quick, two-beat rhythmic pattern and the quick, balancing, piling-up, syntactical elaboration of the multiplying images . . . were the necessary technical discoveries" that allowed the poem to come forth. Much of revision is listening to the poem.

QUESTIONS AND SUGGESTIONS

1. Here is an early and a later draft of a student's poem. How do they demonstrate the poet discovering, focusing, shaping, and tightening her material? What about the nature of her line and stanza did she seem to discover as she drafted the poem? If she were a member of your class, what suggestions could you give her for further revision?

Van Gogh Gets Lost in the Starry Night
ASHLEY KAINE*

The palette is bleeding with colors:
blues, purples, greens.

I pick up the blue, mix it with green,
primary and secondary feeling become
the tumultuous swirling sky.   5

The day nearly gone and three people;
Margaret, Katherine, and Richard,
all believe me to be an artist (I am a
man) like they believe in the Savior
or three meals a day.   10

There is wind sweeping through my sky.
I will put a sun in the upper right, but the
moon will be placed in the sun, a meager
orange, whispering that it's barely there.

A shadow in the city of the world I've   15
created. I am a man asleep, blankets
pulled tightly to the chin in one of the
cottages in the right forefront of the
painting.

I am in the darkness of the black paint   20
(you do not see me) of my creation,
stuck in the bristles of the brush that
won't wash clean.

The three believe me to be an artist,
(I want to be an artist painted in red,   25
not black.) I am Van Gogh a no one
who created a something,
that people love with a brush stroke.

I have lost myself in the blackness
of the Starry Night. In the assumption   30
that I am more than I am. I am a man
hiding in the painting, not the artist
who painted it.

Van Gogh Inside the Starry Night

The palette is bleeding:
I pick up the blue, infect it with green,
primary and secondary feeling become
the sky that swirls like smoke.

I will put a sun in the upper right   5
but place the sun in the moon as a reminder
that art brings happiness, a meager orange,
will whisper of the heat of the night.

I am a man asleep, blankets pulled tight
in one of the cottages in the right   10
forefront of the painting. I hide so that you
will not see the artist, but see the art.

The chaos of the night is stuck in the hard
bristles of my brush that will not wash clean.
I work the bristles back and forth in my palm,   15
my hands have become a stained palette.

The color is persistent in its dark demeanor
and I want the depressive black to wash clear,
but the night is hot and I am hiding in the city
that I created so that I can be alone,   20

To find a quiet light blue or off white,
a pastel pink, that I may paint in a red,
that is as lustful and living, and find
relief in the colors that bleed here through
these finger tips and onto this palette.   25

2. Take a completed but somehow still unsatisfactory poem of yours and take
   another stab at revising it. Read it aloud several times. Does something
   make you wince? Does something thud? That might be the trouble spot.
   Take out the phrase. Recast the sentence in another syntax. Or rethink the
   metaphor. Or try taking a couple syllables out of each line; does that open it
   up? Look back through the drafts for a dropped word, image, or detail that
   might reinvigorate the poem.

3. Wander around an art museum or if you really can't get to one, page through
   a book on the Prado, the Louvre, the Uffizi, the Met, or another great
   museum (not as good, but a substitute, are their Web sites). Find a painting
   that really strikes you. Spend some time with it and let it soak into you.
   Then write a poem that "tours" the painting. When you return to your first
   draft to revise, cue in on its words and lines and see if you can tease out a
   fresh draft from them.

4. Try your hand at an **abecedarian,** a variant of an acrostic, in which each line
   begins, in order, with a letter of the alphabet. Copy the letters of the alphabet down the left side of a blank page, and begin filling in the lines, using
   each next letter as a clue for what might come next. Or try a shorter version; Robert Pinsky in his "ABC" (p. 285) set himself the extra challenge of
   writing an abecedarian in which the *words* of the poem are alphabetical:
   "Any body can die, evidently," the poem opens. Similarly, some recent student poems have begun: "Abused beauty craves death" and "Asphyxiate /
   breathing ceases. / Decapitate / ecstatic flail."

5. Here are the first six drafts of the opening lines of Richard Wilbur's "Love
   Calls Us to the Things of This World." Examine how they show the poet
   exploring, trying out, focusing, and shaping ways to begin the poem. What
   losses and gains does he make as he drafts the stanza? The finished poem
   appears on page 282.

Draft 1

My eyes came open to the squeak of pulleys
My spirit, shocked from the brothel of itself

Draft 2

My eyes came open to the shriek of pulleys,
And the soul, spirited from its proper wallow,
Hung in the air as bodiless and hollow

Draft 3

My eyes came open to the pulleys' cry.
The soul, spirited from its proper wallow,
Hung in the air as bodiless and hollow
As light that frothed upon the wall opposing;
But what most caught my eyes at their unclosing   5
Was two gray ropes that yanked across the sky.
One after one into the window frame
. . . the hosts of laundry came

Draft 4

      The eyes open to a cry of pulleys,
And the soul, so suddenly spirited from sleep,
   Hangs in the air as bodiless and simple
   As morning sunlight frothing on the floor,
     While just outside the window   5
The air is solid with a dance of angels.

Draft 5

      The eyes open to a cry of pulleys,
And spirited from sleep, the astounded soul
Hangs for a moment bodiless and simple
As dawn light in the moment of its breaking:
    Outside the open window   5
The air is crowded with a

Draft 6

      The eyes open to a cry of pulleys,
And spirited from sleep, the astounded soul

Hangs for a moment bodiless and simple
As false dawn.
       Outside the open window,   5
The air is leaping with a rout of angels.
  Some are in bedsheets, some are in dresses,
    it does not seem to matter

POEMS TO CONSIDER

Love Calls Us to the Things of This World   1956
RICHARD WILBUR (b. 1921)

    The eyes open to a cry of pulleys,
And spirited from sleep, the astounded soul
Hangs for a moment bodiless and simple
As false dawn.
          Outside the open window
The morning air is all awash with angels.   5

    Some are in bed-sheets, some are in blouses,
Some are in smocks: but truly there they are.
Now they are rising together in calm swells
Of halcyon feeling, filling whatever they wear
With the deep joy of their impersonal breathing;   10

    Now they are flying in place, conveying
The terrible speed of their omnipresence, moving
And staying like white water; and now of a sudden
They swoon down into so rapt a quiet
That nobody seems to be there.
                The soul shrinks   15
  From all that it is about to remember,
From the punctual rape of every blessed day,
And cries,
      "Oh, let there be nothing on earth but laundry,
Nothing but rosy hands in the rising steam
And clear dances done in the sight of heaven."   20

    Yet, as the sun acknowledges
With a warm look the world's hunks and colors,
The soul descends once more in bitter love
To accept the waking body, saying now
In a changed voice as the man yawns and rises,   25

"Bring them down from their ruddy gallows;
Let there be clean linen for the backs of the thieves;
Let lovers go fresh and sweet to be undone,
And the heaviest nuns walk in a pure floating
Of dark habits,
                keeping their difficult balance."   30

⊡ The Edge of the Hurricane   1983
AMY CLAMPITT (1920–1994)

Wheeling, the careening
winds arrive with lariats
and tambourines of rain.
Torn-to-pieces, mud-dark
flounces of Caribbean   5

cumulus keep passing,
keep passing. By afternoon
rinsed transparencies begin
to open overhead, Mediterranean
windowpanes of clearness   10

crossed by young gusts'
vaporous fripperies, liquid
footprints flying, lacewing
leaf-shade brightening
and fading. Sibling   15

gales stand up on point
in twirling fouettés
of debris. The day ends
bright, cloud-wardrobe
packed away. Nightfall   20

hangs up a single moon
bleached white as laundry,
serving notice yet again how
levity can also trample,
drench, wring and mangle.   25

⊡ And Sweetness Out of the Strong   2000
JENNIFER ATKINSON (b. 1960)

From the rocks—fire, sheen, sheer stealth
released to strength—the lioness
sprung, and huntress by hunted

(the hero) was stopped midflight,
wrung, wrecked, rent wholecloth, and left   5
to rot in the desert sun.

Three days passed. One imagines
a whirlwind of flies, spirals
of vultures, black grace reeling

down on the lion's updrafted stink.   10
But no. Or not only what
one would imagine occurred.

When Samson returned, he turned
back the plush tawny pelt (why?
to judge the work of the world?)   15

and found sweet geometry,
a full hive. There in the rank
gap in the lion carcass

a cold golden spirit whirred.
One imagines forgiveness   20
like that—honey to the brim

of the wound—impossible,
rich, a ruinous riddle,
worth (do you still think, my love?)

betrayal to taste again.   25

Trompe L'oeil: Slovenia   1998
COLLEEN J. McELROY (b. 1935)

This first glimpse of the eastern side of the Alps
and the driver turns his movie profile to the rear

view mirror dancing on the neap and ebb of springless
seats where I ride shoaling waves of cobblestones.

I am new at this—the chauffeured car, the driver   5
whose face I've only dreamed of outside GQ magazines.

He is taking me to the edge of tourists' maps
where, he grins, the sights are oldest and best.

We whisk by streets of handsome men in throaty shirts,
occasional statues of lock-jawed poets and patriots, all   10

men; this country is all about men—the driver's sly smile,
the sidewalk Lotharios, their women bent under strong bread

and onions, and children trying to live up to the legend,
staring as if it is their nature to be stupid.

I am just a break in their routine—my black face   15
despite the familiar car, a foreign blur racing by.

Inside hairpin curves, the driver's smile is slower:
with each casual roll of the wheel against his thumb

my heart turns in my mouth—he is taking me to see
the sights but what I see is another sad town strung out   20

in ever-thinning mountain air while the car,
German-made despite its lumpy seats, eats up the climb.

At the top I take his hand, half-grateful for its firm hold,
and the ground. Before me the usual castle dungeon awaits.

Below, a postcard town. I sigh, hurry in, hustled along by   25
another tourist wearing a zoom lens camera like a penis.

ABC   1998
ROBERT PINSKY (b. 1940)

Any body can die, evidently. Few
Go happily, irradiating joy,

Knowledge, love. Many
Need oblivion, painkillers,
Quickest respite.   5

Sweet time unafflicted,
Various world:

X=your zenith.

Woman on Twenty-Second Eating Berries   1990
STANLEY PLUMLY (b. 1939)

She's not angry exactly but all business,
eating them right off the tree, with confidence,
the kind that lets her spit out the bad ones
clear of the sidewalk into the street. It's
sunny, though who can tell what she's tasting,   5
rowan or one of the service-berries—
the animal at work, so everybody,
save the traffic, keeps a distance. She's picking
clean what the birds have left, and even,
in her hurry, a few dark leaves. In the air   10

the dusting of exhaust that still turns pennies
green, the way the cloudy surfaces
of things obscure their differences,
like the mock-orange or the apple-rose that
cracks the paving stone, rooted in the plaza.   15
No one will say your name, and when you come to
the door no one will know you, a parable
of the afterlife on earth. Poor grapes, poor crabs,
wild black cherry trees, on which some forty-six
or so species of birds have fed, some boy's dead   20
weight or the tragic summer lightning killing
the seed, how boyish now that hunger
to bring those branches down to scale,
to eat of that which otherwise was waste,
how natural this woman eating berries, how alone.   25

Romance in the Old Folks' Home   2001
MICHAEL WATERS (b. 1949)

First he offered to read to her,
but she was afraid
he spoke as Bible-thumper, so declined.

Then he steeped several
herbal teas for her table—   5
she sipped without looking up.

He scissored photos from weeklies
and taped them to her door,
little windows into the past:

couples skating on Highland Pond,   10
dancing four days in a marathon,
sleeping on roofs above Flatbush Avenue.

She knew she was being spoken to
in a language long forgotten,
like Latin lost after school.   15

When she found the horned shell
near her lounge on the lawn,
she pressed it to her ear

to hear the ceaseless *hush*,
knowing longing had replaced   20
the sluggish creature housed there.

The next evening she appeared
with freshly washed hair
pinned with an ivory comb,

and brought that shy spirit   25
her favorite book—
The Marble Faun by Nathaniel Hawthorne

who liked to brood on sin—
while the faint widows flushed
and whispered her name—oh Anna!—   30

and she asked him please to begin.

Eggs   1991
SUSAN WOOD (b. 1946)

for Stephen Dunn

        Morning broke like an egg
on the kitchen floor and I hated
        them, too, eggs, how easily they broke
and ran, yellow insides spilling out, oozing

        and staining, the flawed   5
beneath what's beautiful. And I hated
        my father, the one cock
in the henhouse, who laid the plate

        on the table and made me
eat, who told me not to get up   10
        until I was done, every bite. And I hated
how I gagged and cried, day

        after day, until there was no time
left and he'd give in and I'd go off
        to school like that, again, hungry.   15
But why did I hate eggs

        so much? Freud, old banty rooster, who knew
a thing or two about such things, might say
        I hated myself, hated the egg
growing in secret deep inside my body,   20

        the secret about to be spilled
to the world, and maybe I did.
        Or maybe it's the way the egg
repeats itself again and again, a perfect

oval every time, the way I imagined myself,   25
furious, standing by my own child's bed
     holding a belt, and saw her face
dissolve in a yolk. But that doesn't say

     enough about why we hoard
our hurts like golden eggs and foolishly   30
     wait for them to hatch, why
we faced each other across the table,

     my father and I, and fought
our battles over eggs and never fought
     with them, never once picked up   35
those perfect ovals and sent them singing

     back and forth across the room, the spell
broken like shells, until we were
     covered with them, our faces golden
and laughing, both of us beautiful and flawed.   40

The Man. His Bowl. His Raspberries.   1994
CLAUDIA RANKINE (b. 1963)

The bowl he starts with
is too large. It will never be filled.

Nonetheless, in the cool dawn,
reaching underneath the leaf, he frees
each raspberry from its stem   5
and white nipples remain suspended.

He is being gentle, so does not think
I must be gentle as he doubles back
through the plants
seeking what he might have missed.   10

At breakfast she will be pleased
to eat the raspberries and put her pleasure
to his lips.

Placing his fingers beneath a leaf
for one he had not seen, he does not idle.   15
He feels for the raspberry. Securing, pulling
gently, taking, he gets what he needs.

Laws   1984
STEPHEN DUNN (b. 1939)

A black cat wanders out into
an open field. How vulnerable it is,
how even its own shadow
causes it to stop and hunch.
Mice come, hundreds of them,   5
forming a circle around the cat.
They've been waiting for months
to catch the cat like this.
But the cat is suddenly unafraid.
Though the mice have their plans,   10
have worked on tactics and tricks,
none of them moves.
The cat thinks: all I have to do
is be who I am. And it's right.
One quick move   15
and the mice scatter, go home.

After humiliation, home is a hole
where no one speaks. Mouse things
get done, and then there is
the impossibility of sleep.   20
They curse nature, they curse
their small legs and hearts.
We all know stories of how, after
great defeat, the powerless rise up.
But not if they're mice.   25
The cat waits for them in the tall grass.
The mice are constantly surprised.

12

BECOMING A POET

"A writer's life is lived," says J. D. McClatchy, "not in bed or on the road but at the desk." And that's where one becomes a poet. Liking poems leads to trying to write one's own; urged on by these poems, the beginning poet reads more poets and, influenced by them, experiments with new poems and in struggling to get each new poem right, learns draft to draft, poem to poem. And in working on poems and reworking poems, one becomes a poet.

Eventually the beginner shows some work to a friend or a teacher, enrolls in writing classes, finds a writing group, perhaps has a few poems published in the school or college literary magazine. Then one day, with some encouragement and determination, the poet takes a chance and sends some poems off to one of the literary magazines he or she has been reading. And probably the editor sends the poems back because they aren't quite good enough—yet. And sometimes—only sometimes—despite all the discouragements . . . .

What drives poets to write? Is it a love of words, of ideas, of the gorgeousness of language? Is it because nothing else is quite as challenging and fulfilling? Is it because they can always imagine a better poem? In her Nobel Prize address, the Polish poet Wisława Szymborska says poets like scientists are "questing spirits," and like scientists

Poets, if they're genuine, must also keep repeating, "I don't know." Each poem marks an effort to answer this statement, but as soon as the final period hits the page, the poet begins to hesitate, starts to realize that this particular answer was pure makeshift, absolutely inadequate. So poets keep on trying, and sooner or later the consecutive results of their self-dissatisfaction are clipped together with a giant paperclip by literary historians and called their "oeuvres."

A poet develops over years, and if the poet is lucky and determined that growth continues. Reading the early writing of poets like Dickinson and Whitman can be tremendously reassuring. One of Dickinson's earliest poems, written when she was about nineteen, is an unremarkable valentine. Here are a couple of lines:

Oh the Earth was *made* for lovers, for damsel, and hopeless swain,
For sighing, and gentle whispering, and unity made of twain.

Damsel, swain, sighing, whispering: the poem's saccharine images, slack lines, wooden rhythms, and pedestrian or inflated diction make it typical of the drawing-room poems of its time and in many ways typical of most poets' early work. It merely makes pretty a commonplace notion. It doesn't grapple. It certainly doesn't make a reader, as Dickinson later defined poetry, "feel physically as if the top of my head were taken off." Reading it, one could not predict that in her early thirties she would be writing some of the most powerful and distinctive poems in our language.

> *A real writer is always shifting and changing and searching. The world has many labels for him, of which the most treacherous is the label of Success.*
> —James Baldwin

Whitman's early poems are as slight as Dickinson's valentine. Here is a stanza of "Our Future Lot," published in a newspaper in 1838 when Whitman was nineteen:

O, powerless is this struggling brain
    To pierce the mighty mystery;
In dark, uncertain awe it waits,
    The common doom—to die!

This doggerel hardly anticipates the poet who would pierce the mystery in poems like his elegy for Lincoln, "When Lilacs Last in the Dooryard Bloom'd" (even the title tells us how far Whitman had come from his "Our Future Lot"). Dickinson's and Whitman's early work share at least one problem: The poems aim to decorate a fact or a feeling rather than to discover or explore. They don't take chances. They are unadventurous. Language appears to act as a servant to a preordained "meaning." The poems are written from the outside in, not from the inside out: from that sense of curiosity, that "I don't know" Szymborska cites as the motive for poems.

Obviously both beginning poets grew dissatisfied with their early efforts; they wrote more poems and read more poems. They read the journals of their age and immersed themselves in the world around them—even if that world, in Dickinson's case, remained a house and garden in Amherst, Massachusetts. Dickinson found guides in Shakespeare, George Herbert, and her older contemporary, Elizabeth Barrett Browning. Whitman found guides in the Bible, Shakespeare, and his older contemporary, Ralph

Waldo Emerson. They grew up and became, in the great mystery of such things, the great foremother and forefather of American poetry.

The Growth of a Poet

Don't be too hard on yourself when a poem fails. Poets learn from their failed poems. And don't be embarrassed to be a beginner. All poets begin as beginners. Had creative writing classes been around in the sixteenth century, who knows, the student passing around a recent poem might have been a sophomore named Will Shakespeare.

Draft by draft, poets grow in the struggle to make each poem fulfill itself. "Fixing" a poem may not be the answer. Often, as Marvin Bell remarks, "revision means writing the next poem." In a looping progress from poem to poem, sometimes two steps forward and one back, the poet develops.

It's how we become proficient at anything. You may discover a new way of handling metaphor, only to find that the voice in your poems has become flat. You may suddenly be able to write in blank verse only to find the imagination seems to have evaporated from your poems. But try not to be dismayed, and don't give up. Like perfecting a tennis serve or a high dive, we'll have awkward stretches as we bring in new skills, but as we continue to practice—and writing is the poet's practice—we accommodate the new skills and begin to move gracefully again.

Let's follow one student poet, Carrie Klok, as her work develops over about a year. Here is one of Klok's earliest poems—although not an early draft. Out of frustration, she labeled this "revision #1,203."

The Voyeur: Third Day

Yellow-slickered and rubber-booted
he and his mother own the soaked streets.
Outside she holds her head up instead of down.
There are no eyes or fists to catch her here.
First there is only walking, little hand in big.   5
She stops under a narrow eave, leans into an old building—
she watches him watching her as he jumps into a puddle.
He squats down then and traces his fingers over a mini-oil slick.
The rain comes harder and he stands,
holds his arms out at his sides, tilts his head back, eyes closed,   10
mouth wide
to catch the rain.

A drip finds its way onto her forehead, zigzags
to the top of her nose, she tastes
salt muted from her skin.   15
Her but not her. Her but something more.
Stepping out from the chalky brick she tosses

her arms out, elbows crooked, head thrown back,
like a very tall bird that has lost its wings.
But the rain has stopped.   20

The poem shows an appreciation for language, detail, and implication. The first two
lines give us a bright interplay of sounds which seems to match the colorful image of
mother and son wearing slickers on the wet streets. Notice the "o" sounds repeated in
"yellow," "own," and "soaked," the "u" in "rubber" and "mother," and the hard "k" in
"slickered" and "soaked."

The poem hones in on one significant scene, using details to imply that the mother
has somehow been harmed—even if only psychologically—perhaps by her husband,
by the boy's father. Whatever the threat—we don't need an exact cause for it—she
feels safer outside where "no eyes or fists can catch her." Mother and son don't speak
to each other, yet they're keenly aware of each other, of themselves, and of what seems
to threaten them. They watch each other watch each other. Although the boy's
actions, and later the mother's, suggest playfulness, they behave too self-consciously
to be having much fun. The somewhat strained metaphor in line 19 of a bird that has
"lost its wings" implies that the mother has somehow been robbed of flight. She is
stuck in her situation.

The poem presents a situation clearly but also misses opportunities. First notice how
little the poem pays attention to its lines. After the relatively normal line length of
nine syllables which opens the poem, by the sixth line, the poem swells into a sluggish
fifteen-syllable line that isn't counteracted by a powerful momentum in the syntax.
Each line begins merely to equal the sentence until line 11 where the poem suddenly
seems to consider enjambment and delivers the strangely emphatic lines of "mouth
wide / to catch the rain." The second stanza adopts a more varied lineation strategy
which invigorates the poem a notch, but, in the end, the poem remains static.

Examining the diction and syntax we see other missed opportunities. The core sentences of lines four and five ("There are" and "there is") do little more than act as
markers. An easy revision might read: "No eyes or fists can catch her here," but the
generality of the image dulls the threat the mother and son feel. The succeeding verbs
("stops," "leans," "watches," "jumps," "squats") yield a sharper description, but the per-
functory syntax ("she stops," "he squats," "he stands") snuffs whatever energy Klok is
trying to ignite. Sure, she wants to imply that mother and son are slow and cautious,
but she doesn't want the poem to poke along.

In the second stanza when the point of view shifts to the mother, we move closer
to her feelings, and the poem gives us a moment of discovery: "Her but not her. Her
but something more." But the poem doesn't delve into this contemplative moment.
Besides, what's the point? Isn't the "something more" she tastes just the rain? The
poem's attention seem to wander. The participial phrase that starts line 17 ("Stepping
out from the chalky brick") attempts to invest the action with anticipation, but the
return is meager: the mother finally lets down her defenses and mimics her son's
playfulness only to find it's too late; the rain has stopped. Part of the problem may be
that the poem banks too much on the rickety vehicle of the rain stopping to signal

disappointment or squelched joy. The mother and son are already generalized and the speaker a vanilla narrator; the soft metaphor of playing in the rain as representative of spontaneous joy is asked to work harder than it can. The title, on the other hand, does little work besides, perhaps, perplex us. Who is the "voyeur"? How is this the *third* day? Our fumbling for answers to such basic questions short-circuits the poem's energy.

Here is a draft of a poem Klok wrote soon afterward; already we can see a new liveliness has entered her work:

Untitled

It's not the stars falling or the aurora borealis
dancing across the sky that makes the house feel
insignificant, even the stone. Or opening the door
to a crowded room—just a crack—and seeing slivered
fragments of conversation, slices of suits and faces   5
that makes me look around to see if I am really alone.

And on nights when it's cold and the dogs snuffle
next to the fire, I wonder about next year and why my bones
feel damp and heavy. The dogs look at me with wet eyes
and I think they must know everything and God   10
has given them the gift of irrefutable muteness.

It was a night when the cold makes the stars slivers of ice,
How they glitter and mock—I heard
A muted shuffle and a knock. The dogs sniffed the air
And looked over at me mumbling to myself in my chair.   15

I didn't much care who stood in the dark waiting
for me to come to the door. It was too late
For time and passion—too soon for death and passion.
The fire crackled, shot stars and I heard feet moving
Away. I felt sorrow then and knew that tomorrow would   20
    be the same as today.

Let's put aside for a moment the poem's infelicities of phrasing and those elements that don't seem to add up. Instead notice the poem's intricacy. Compared to her earlier poem this poem feels more adventurous and ambitious. Many of the poem's ingredients show Klok trying out new techniques and embracing language's fluid potential. Inventiveness flashes throughout the poem, for instance in phrases like "slices of suits," "the gift of [irrefutable] muteness," "glitter and mock." Syntax and lineation have taken on a clearer purpose. The opening sentences sweep us into the poem, and enjambment and caesura work together to produce a varied rhythm that suggests the speaker's meandering thought.

We are also more likely to be curious about this speaker than her earlier one. Klok brings us in closer to the poem by casting it in first person, creating a particular narrator, and giving us a room on a cold night with dogs by the fire. Grounded in this scene, the poem can investigate the questions of vulnerability and isolation that it presents. Klock also repeats imagery—like the stars—and thereby gives the poem continuity.

And yet, this poem, too ends anticlimactically. Its initial spirited impulses are undermined, even contradicted, by its ending—and the sparks from its imagery, diction, syntax, and lineation dim. After leading us to a moment when the speaker's sense of isolation will be challenged by the caller at the door, the poem seems to experience a failure of nerve. The speaker ignores the knock, claiming "I didn't much care who stood in the dark waiting / for me to come to the door." Her explanation ("It was too late / for time and passion—too soon for death and passion") may be weirdly appealing—or confusing—but it doesn't really satisfy; it sounds more like a dodge. The poem avoids confronting what lies beneath its surface, the tensions between stressful interaction and comfortable loneliness.

Part of Klok's difficulty may be that she is trying to do too much at once in the poem. Look at the first stanza, for instance, where she sets up competing sets of images (the stars falling and the aurora borealis dancing opposed to the fragments glimpsed of a crowded room). Although the stars reappear later in the poem, the imagery of bits of people isn't brought to bear on the scene that follows, and so seems extraneous, diminishing some of the speaker's credibility: the speaker oddly "look[s] around to see if [she is] really alone" after she has just shown us a crowded scene. The core of the poem lies in the last three stanzas. The first stanza might easily be dropped, and Klok could concentrate on developing that part of the poem. Oftentimes, the opening of a poem can be cut, particularly in early drafts, where it often merely supports the developing poem as we test where it might go. Once the poem is on its feet, the opening can be pulled down like scaffolding.

In following the many threads that a poem offers, we may end up with a tangle, and as we revise we may decide, as Klok did, that we have more than one poem before us; sorting out the multiple directions can awaken you to a poem's potential. When Klok began to rework the poem above, she realized that the image of peering through the door kept tugging at her. Pursuing this direction, she arrived at an entirely new poem (pieces of the original which she reused are in italics below).

All of You

There is something deep and secret
about *opening the door*
to a crowded room—just a crack—
and seeing slivered fragments of expression,
slices of suits and curls *and faces—*   5
Half mouths are softer than whole mouths
and eyes should be seen completely alone, the nose
usually ruins everything. God intended
wisps of hair to be seen from behind ears; other
than hearing that is their sole purpose. Snatches   10
of clothing are usually better than entire

ensembles: the *mock* part of the turtleneck, the pleat
of trousers, stray straps and laces. And then
there is the half-smile, the quarter-sneer. I
do not think that we were meant to be seen all at once.   15

This time Klok takes advantage of the opportunity a title offers. The shrewd title "All of You," which recalls the jazz standard "All of Me," seems to belie the poem's celebration of fragments and so injects the poem with irony. The "you" can simply be read as "one": "All of You" might imply that we can know all of another only through bits and pieces. The "you" might also imply a particular "you," someone addressed surreptitiously, someone the speaker prefers to know only partially. Perhaps—as the image of peeking through a crack in the door suggests—the speaker is spying on this other; the person addressed may be someone the speaker doesn't trust, especially in a crowd. Certainly, through phrases such as "the mock part of the turtleneck" and "the half-smile and quarter-sneer" the poem hints that insincerity and animosity lurk behind human relationships. The title also helps us linger on the poem's final line and question the speaker's motives as she hides behind a door and claims, "I / do not think that we were meant to be seen all at once."

In the poem, we can see how phrases from the original became a launching pad for the new poem, with a sound, form, and direction very much its own. Klok has permitted the poem to find its own way rather than bullying it to go in a preconceived direction; it moves naturally from the assertion that "There is something deep and secret / about opening a door . . ." to the examples of snippets.

Stronger attention to syntax and line exploits the discrepancy between what the speaker claims and how she makes her claim. Look, for instance, at Klok's handling of caesura and radical enjambment. After the relatively shorter and balanced phrasal lines of the opening, stops begin to occur within, especially near the end of, lines, accentuating the fragmentation the speaker identifies. Notice, too, how the lines sharply break natural phrase groups:

than héaring thát is their sóle púrpose. ‖ Snátches   4/1

of clóthing are úsually bétter than entíre   4

ensémbles: ‖ the móck párt of the túrtlenéck, ‖ the pléat   1/4/1

of tróusers, ‖ stráy stráps and láces. ‖ And thén   1/3/1

there ís the hálf-smíle, ‖ the quárter-snéer. ‖ Í   3/2/1

The lurching effect of this rhythm helps convey the speaker's mounting anxiety as the "softer" mouths she first identifies give way to the closing more ominous images of "the half-smile, the quarter-sneer."

As Klok continued struggling from poem to poem, writing and revising and reading more poetry, her poems grew in scope and took more risks. Here's a poem she wrote at the end of her first year of writing poems seriously:

Stillness

It seems for a moment there is no motion
　but the unraveling shadows of late morning
over patched fields of lulled green and spun yellow.
　I am at rest next to the woodpile
like the fox far in the distance—　　　　　　　　　　　　　5
　head cocked, one foreleg held up, poised.
Like the farmer bent over, gazing
　into the hole he has just dug
where he will bury last year's dried potato root.
　The wind that never gives up is suddenly gone　　　　10
leaving the trees modest and a hawk gliding.

　But there is underneath it all some movement—
mist dissolving to air, worms turning the earth—
　and before the fox leaps and the farmer stands,
before the wind starts singing again,　　　　　　　　　　15
　I can feel the movement under the movement
that makes heat, that makes air,
　that makes the earth breathe.

This poem resembles a fluid, natural utterance; the dancer is learning how to move to the music; self-assurance hides the stretch and strain. What accounts for that assuredness? First notice how Klok's attention to syntax and proportion helps her convey the poem's discovery of the motion inside stillness; indeed, such attention probably lead her to that discovery. Lines are mostly end-stopped or phrasal, mirroring the poem's sense of achieved understanding.

In its overall form, the poem's two stanzaic divisions follow the two stages of the poem's revelation: "It seems . . . there is no motion . . . . ‖ But underneath it all . . . ." An eleven-line stanza is followed by a seven-line stanza. This 11/7 proportion resembles the sonnet's form where a larger opening establishes a situation, and a shorter and more intense closing section comments upon or contradicts the opening.

On the level of sentence and line we see a similar congruency of content and form. The first sentence presents the scene, with the first line establishing the motionlessness ("It seems at first there is no motion"), and the next two lines qualifying the stillness: "but the unraveling shadows . . . over patched fields . . . ." The second sentence also equals three lines, introducing the speaker in the first and the fox in the next two lines. The third sentence, a fragment, gives us in three lines the farmer and his task. The symmetry of these three-line groups interweaves speaker, fox, and farmer and makes more emphatic the shorter two-line sentence that closes the stanza: "the wind which never gives up is suddenly gone / leaving the trees modest and a hawk gliding."

The single long sentence of the second stanza implies the unbroken flow of the world. This compound-complex sentence offers first an assertion in its first line ("there is underneath it all some movement") that the speaker, after suspending time for a moment, registers herself in the poem's final clause, in "the movement that makes heat, that makes air, / that makes the earth breathe." The emphatic shorter phrasal lines which close the poem ring with the power of revealed truth.

We also see Klok's growing sophistication in how the poem's camera work subtly supports its discoveries. The poem begins with a panorama shot of the fields, shifts to the speaker, fox, farmer, then the hole he has dug. From the ground we climb to the sky and the image of the gliding hawk. In the second stanza, we begin in the clouds, in the dissolving mist, then drop to the earth with the worms. In line 14, a freeze frame image suspends action ("before the fox leaps") and builds tension. In this moment of stopped time, the speaker "feel[s] the movement under the movement," a current enlivening all things from the smallest worm to the earth itself.

Is the poem finished? Are some lines gangly? Are some passages flat? Could it benefit from more revision? Probably, and from week to week, even day to day, the places a poet might take a poem will change. No one way is right, although some directions might be unfruitful. The key is writing consistently, keeping your poetic nerves, so to speak, tingling, so you'll be able to recognize a likely trail and follow where it leads. Developing as a poet means gaining experience about which direction might take you to the most fertile terrain, and nurturing your intuition so you'll know when to abandon a trail and blaze a new one.

As a poem might go in countless directions, so too a poet might develop in countless ways. It doesn't happen overnight; don't expect to wake up one morning singing like Yeats. But it does happen that one day, after challenging your poems, your ear, your intuition, you'll find yourself writing a poem that seems to shimmer before you. Where'd it come from? Don't ask. And it's probably not a good idea to decide unequivocally the kind of poet you want to be. Early on, William Carlos Williams and Wallace Stevens wrote poems modeled on Keats. Keats guided them through much they had to learn—and he taught each different things—but had Williams and Stevens clung to their Keatsian aspirations, neither would have been able to forge the particular poems that spoke to their particular time (and still to us), the poems that critics coming along afterward lump together under "Modernism."

Going Public

Mull over this tiny essay by Robert Francis.

Professional Poet

Someone the other day called me a professional poet to my face.

"Don't call me that," I cried. "Don't call anyone that. As well talk about a professional friend."

"Oh!" he said.
"Or a professional lover."
"Oh!"

Most poets and readers share Francis's reverence for poetry's intimacy and its often lonely devotion to truth. But, like any art, poetry has a practical side we should consider when we take it from the private place where the poem lives with us to the world outside where it might live with readers. As we have been saying all along, respect for the poem means getting it right. To make it new, as Pound urges, you must learn not only the trade or craft, but also the traditions that gave birth to the poets who preceded you. Dickinson, Whitman, Williams, and Stevens became the poets they became partly because they knew earlier traditions so well that they could challenge them, change them, and bring other traditions to bear on them and create new traditions.

Poets such as Forrest Hamer, Joy Harjo, Derek Walcott, Garrett Hongo, M. Scott Momaday, and Wanda Coleman have found new ways to marry the European traditions of poetry to the oral and musical traditions of their ancestral cultures—to line singing, jazz rhythms, ceremonial chants—and the protean aspects of the world's traditions, past and present. Knowing the great (and not-so-great) work of other poets both humbles and thrills any poet. John Dryden scolds poets who, rashly deciding they know all about poetry before they have immersed themselves in it, conclude that "Virgil, compared to them, is flat and dry; / And Homer understood not poetry." Don't be too quick to grab a theory about poetry; theories—like the knowledge of craft—must be earned through practice. And remember not to be in a rush, either, to finish a poem and judge it. As William Stafford remarks, "Writing is a reckless encounter with whatever comes along. . . . A writer must write bad poems, as they come, amongst the better—and not scorn the 'bad' ones. Finicky ways can dry up the sources." If you write enough poems, good ones will happen. Try having several poems going at once; then, as a class due date approaches, you'll have choices. Pounding out a poem the night before will usually produce something misshapen or frail and likely to wither under the strong light of public scrutiny.

Respect for the poem also includes finding for it the readers who complete the equation. Later, as you grow as a poet, you will think of submitting your work to magazines and journals, perhaps eventually of gathering your poems in a book. For now, though, your audience is your class. Your poems are published—made public—as soon as the class reads them. Put your best foot forward. Type or print out the poems neatly. Proofread—carefully—to prevent mistakes from creeping in and to check for oversights. Anything that distracts for even the tiniest flicker of a second—a grammatical error, mispunctuation, cloudy bit of syntax, misspelling, typo—will cost your poem a momentary loss of your reader's attention. Do a surgical job. Don't leave clamps in the patient.

When you discuss another poet's work in class, be fair. Give the poem and the discussion your honest attention. You will learn much, almost by osmosis, by listening to others talk about a fellow poet's work and by trying to articulate your response to it. Read the poem on its own terms. What is the poem trying to do? What are the ways it is trying to do it? How are they working? Be honest, but never cruel or patronizing.

Your responsibility as a poet-reader means you respect and trust the poet's effort. By the same measure, when your poem comes up for discussion, do hear what people are saying. Some of it won't be helpful, but you can think that through later. And don't rush to explain or defend. A poem that needs explaining isn't doing its job.

Writing Communities

Because the poem that seems great today can seem dumb tomorrow and wonderful again the day after, poets need honest, thoughtful readers: other members of a writing class, other poets, and eventually editors. An observation obvious to someone else, though not to the poet, may reignite the poet to the poem, or provide the clue to patching a thin spot or avoiding a clunker.

A facsimile of Draft 15 of Donald Hall's "Ox Cart Man" is shown on page 301. The comments, originally in longhand, are those of poet Louis Simpson, to whom Hall had sent the draft. Both of Simpson's insightful suggestions prompted good revisions by Hall. The awkward "He walks by ox head," perhaps natural enough in earlier versions where the poem was cast in first person as spoken by the character, becomes "He walks by his ox's head." (Why might Hall have preferred this to "by the ox's head"?)

When Hall saw that the activities that would complete the cycle in stanza 6 (back to potatoes, where the poem began) are already implied, he dropped the stanza. Dissatisfied with the rhythm of "to build the cart again" for concluding the poem, however, he tried out several alternatives: "to make the new cart," then "building another cart," "building the cart again," and "building the new cart." He finally settled on "building the cart again," a quiet iambic trimeter line whose initial reversed foot (buíldĭng) emphasizes the farmer's steadfast work.

Good readers for your poems aren't those who love everything you write (or love you!), nor are good readers those who slash it to ribbons. Praise, however, can be more ruinous than tart criticism. If a reader showers your poem with praise, you will feel reluctant to change it, less likely to hold under the microscope places which require close scrutiny and that will lead you to a better poem. You want a sharp, disinterested eye. In general, be suspicious of praise, and, certainly, don't write for it. On the other hand, ignore readers who make personal attacks or who come after a poem with a bulldozer. Good readers help you find the gold seam in the rock—they don't blow up the mountain. And if readers seem uninterested in a poem, take that response into consideration. What in your poem might attract someone outside your poem, outside the intricacies of your own life?

Your class will likely act as one of your earliest groups of readers. Before the term finishes, you may want to make sure you have traded phone numbers and e-mail addresses to continue exchanging poems with members of your class. You may also find fellow poets in the community around you. Check your local and regional papers and Web sites for writing groups and literary readings—you'll find them everywhere from bars and coffee shops to museums and bookstores. Regularly attending poetry readings, by those with many published books and by those just starting out, will put you in contact with the variety of poetry and poets out there.

Besides the writing programs at local colleges and universities, many cities and towns have literary centers and libraries that hold workshops, sponsor readings, publish

Ox Cart Man

In October of the year,
he counts potatoes dug from the brown field,
counting the seed, counting
the cellar's portion out,
and bags the rest on the cart's floor.

He packs wool sheared in April, honey
in combs, linen, leather
tanned from deerhide,
and vinegar in a barrel
hooped by hand at the forge's fire.

He walks by ox head, ten days
to Portsmouth Market, and sells potatoes,
and the bag that carried potatoes,
flaxseed, birch brooms, maple sugar, goose
feathers, yarn.

An odd phrase.
Is it better than
"by the ox's head"?

When the cart is empty he sells the cart.
When the cart is sold he sells the ox,
harness and yoke, and walks
home, his pockets heavy
with the year's coin for salt and taxes,

and at home by fire's light in November cold
stitches new harness
for next year's ox in the barn,
and carves the yoke, and saws planks
to build the cart again

This strikes me as
the place to stop.

and in March taps sugar trees,
and in April shears wool
from sheep that grew it all over again,
and in May plants potatoes
as bees wake, roused by the cry of lilac.

omit

Very well finished. No big cracks that I can see.
I'm pretty sure about omitting the last stanza—
it's fidgety. And redundant.

literary calendars/newsletters, and provide space for poets to meet. These centers often rely on the help of volunteers. Good citizenship in your writing community will help you learn. You may also find helpful the writing conferences throughout the United States and abroad that for a couple days or weeks generally offer workshops, readings, lectures, receptions, and individual conferences with poets. With some careful homework you can find one within your budget (some offer scholarships or work opportunities) that will give you the kind of help you're seeking. National organizations devoted to supporting poets and poetry include the Associated Writing Programs (AWP, to which your school may belong), Poets and Writers, The Poetry Society of America (PSA), The Academy of American Poets, and PEN (Poets, Essayists, and Novelists).

Since the development of the Internet, someone with access to the Web can have readers all over the globe. You can find poetry chatrooms at many sites, from small groups that started in a college writing class to groups allied with large literary organizations. Like the rest of the Web, these sites are very fluid, but a little surfing, particularly starting with links from large reputable sites will lead to a variety of inspiring (and irritating) sites. Start surfing with Poets and Writers (www.pw.org), Poetry Society of America (www.poetrysociety.org), Associated Writing Programs (awpwriter.org), Academy of American Poets (www.poets.org), Webdelsol (webdelsol.com), Poetry Daily (www.poems.com), and Verse Daily (www.versedaily.org). As with all parts of the Web, the user should be cautious about sharing personal information and remain skeptical about the expertise (or sincerity) of anyone you happen to meet.

Getting Organized

Keep the drafts of your poems; you never know what will be useful. Clip the sheets together, latest version on top. Always keep a hard copy when you submit poems for class (or to a magazine).

As poems multiply, a system of manila folders will keep things straight: a folder labeled NEW for poems you are currently working on, one marked FINISHED, and maybe one for NOTES that contains ideas, stray lines or images, interesting words, clippings, and so on. Soon an OLD MSS folder will be useful to collect fragments and poems that seem no longer promising; it may relinquish a treasure on a rainy Saturday morning when you are looking for ideas. And soon, too, perhaps a folder marked PUBLISHED. Some poets find it useful to think of their work in an assembly line with poems moving along it in all the varying stages of the process. Most poets have devised one system or another. Ask your teacher, who is likely a publishing writer, how he or she manages the "professional side" of writing poems.

When should a beginning poet start sending poems to magazines? If your school has a literary magazine, start readying a group of poems now—apply the finishing touches, check the journal's deadlines—and away they go!

How about the larger journals? As soon as you have three or four good, polished poems and know several magazines or journals that would be appropriate for the poems, send them out. Stick to magazines you have read. If you like the poems in a magazine, odds are that you and the editors have a similar bent. If you don't like the poems in a magazine, you would probably be wasting stamps to send a manuscript there. Your first task is getting acquainted with magazines that publish poetry including literary quarterlies, poetry journals, little magazines (we offer a list of some titles in "Questions and Suggestions," p. 304) as well as *The New Yorker, The Atlantic,* and

The Nation. Start browsing at the library, pick up some literary journals in bookstores, surf the Net, and subscribe to a few that feature work you like. Literary magazines remain some of the great bargains on the planet, and your support can help them stay around.

Writer's Digest Books publishes *Poet's Market*, an annual, which lists about two thousand periodicals and presses that print poems, specifying the kind of poetry each wants, what they pay, and how to submit manuscripts. Dustbooks' *The International Directory of Little Magazines and Small Presses* lists thousands of markets. In the journals *Poets & Writers* and *The Writer's Chronicle* you'll find announcements from editors wanting poems. If you can't find a magazine, send for a sample copy (enclosing the single copy price).

When you are ready, send three or four poems to the first magazine on your list. Check the magazine or its Web site for submission guidelines; if it doesn't offer any, follow these as a rule of thumb: Each poem should appear cleanly printed or typed, single-spaced, on one side of a sheet of regular 8½-by-11-inch bond paper, with your name, address, phone, and e-mail address in the upper left corner. You needn't include a cover letter—although some poets like to drop a note to editors thanking them for their consideration—but *always* enclose a self-addressed, stamped envelope (SASE) for a response from the editors. If you want your copies back, include enough postage for their return; otherwise, ask the editors to recycle them. Some journals read only at specified times of the year; find out when you should submit your work. Address the packet to the editor by name if you know it, or to Poetry Editor. Keep a log of poems, date sent, and, later, the response. A few journals have begun to accept only electronic submissions; check the latest guidelines.

Practice patience. Editors of small journals receive thousands of submissions a year. Expect to wait a few months before you hear anything. The probability, at least at the beginning, is rejection. And the rejection will probably be a short form letter that thanks you for sending your work and tells you the editors cannot use it. Even very good poets receive enough rejection slips to wallpaper a den. But don't be easily discouraged. Read the poems over again as objectively as you can. New ways to revise might now become clear to you. If the poems still look good to you, put them in another envelope and ship them off to the next magazine on your list. Sooner or later, a rejection slip will carry a scribbled note: "Sorry" or "Came close" or "Liked 'Guapo'." Sooner or later, a letter of acceptance will arrive and perhaps a check. (Checks for poems are usually small.)

Sending poems around may be exciting as well as part of learning the ropes. And it can be a stimulus to finishing poems. Never mind Horace's classical advice to wait nine years before publishing. Learning from mistakes may be more useful in the long run than trying not to make them.

If anyone wants money to publish or consider your poems, beware. Odds are, unless you know the journal or press to be reputable, it is a scam. Several outfits offer grand prizes for winning poems. Once you enter, they will send you a letter celebrating how your poem

> *To earn a living is needful, but it can be done in routine ways. One writes because one has a burning desire to objectify what it is indispensable to one's happiness to express.*
>
> ——Marianne Moore

has been accepted, and offer you the chance to send them money for the hardcover book where you can see yourself in print. Or you'll be invited to a pricey conference where you'll be acknowledged with hundreds of other novices. Don't be impressed. They take anything sent to them, and make a profit with those they've seduced. Avoid them.

Recent copyright law gives copyright protection to a work created since 1978 for the author's lifetime plus seventy years. That protection begins with its creation, so the penciled poem on your desk is included. You may register unpublished work (Form TX, one copy of the work, and the fee), but you needn't bother. The publisher of any reputable periodical or book will register the work on publication. Even though the registration is made in the publisher or magazine's name, the copyright belongs to the author, unless there is a written agreement to the contrary. In the absence of such a written agreement, a magazine acquires only the right to initial publication in one of its issues. The author retains copyright and full control. So don't sign anything, except a check. If in doubt, consult someone who knows about such things. (For information or forms: U.S. Copyright Office, Library of Congress, Washington, DC 20559–6000, www.loc.gov/copyright.)

Very few poets earn a living through poetry. Williams was a doctor, Moore a librarian and editor, Stevens an attorney for an insurance company, and Frost did a lot of teaching (he also tried poultry farming and failed). Today, many poets teach, and many others are park rangers, researchers, attorneys, physicians, managers, motel maids, ranchers, nurses, therapists, journalists, union organizers—just about anything you might think of to make a living. Writing poems itself doesn't pay much money.

More important than money, though, is freedom. In our society, poetry doesn't pay much, but poets are free to write pretty much as they want. And more important still is the art of poetry. While we're writing, we join the company of Shakespeare, Whitman, and Dickinson.

QUESTIONS AND SUGGESTIONS

1. In the library browse among the poetry in magazines such as *Poetry, Gettysburg Review, Callaloo, Ploughshares, Field, American Poetry Review, Shenadoah, North American Review, New Letters, Cream City Review, Iowa Review, Georgia Review, River Styx, Green Mountains Review, Prairie Schooner, Poet Lore, Missouri Review, New Republic, Hudson Review, Paris Review, Agni, Tar River Poetry, Southern Review, Crazyhorse, Boulevard, Threepenny Review, Yale Review, Quarterly West, Laurel Review, DoubleTake, Five Points, Pleiades, Salamagundi, Witness, Crab Orchard Review,* or *Zzyzyva.*

2. Buy a book of poems. Buy another.

3. *For teams.* In small groups, meet at the library to examine a few journals listed above. Look over the issues for the past two years or eight issues. For

each journal, get a strong impression of the kinds of poems it publishes and select at least one poem that particularly attracts you, and make a copy of it. Then create a list of each journal's submission policy, editorial staff, address, Web site. Each team reports what it learns to the class and shares the sample poems.

4. Write a poem about writing poems. Use metaphors and detailed images to realize it. Is it like planning, planting, tending, and harvesting a garden? Like snow boarding? Rock climbing? Playing a high-stakes poker game? Making a kite? Perhaps focus on a single detail in the process of writing: The miles of words stored in the cylinder of a pencil lead? The little fox trot your fingers do on the keyboard?

5. Look over three or four poems you have written during the past few months. What has changed in your work? How have you grown as a poet? In what ways would you like to see your work develop further?

6. What have you felt you couldn't write about? Write it.

7. Prepare and send out a group of poems to the first magazine on your list.

POEMS TO CONSIDER

Dancing with Poets   1987
ELLEN BRYANT VOIGT (b. 1943)

"The accident" is what he calls the time
he threw himself from a window four floors up,
breaking his back and both ankles, so that walking
became the direst labor for this man
who takes my hand, invites me to the empty strip of floor   5
that fronts the instruments, a length of polished wood
the shape of a grave. Unsuited for this world—
his body bears the marks of it, his hand
is tense with effort and with shame, and I shy away
from any audience, but I love to dance, and soon   10
we find a way to move, drifting apart as each
effects a different ripple across the floor,
a plaid and a stripe to match the solid navy of the band.
And suddenly the band is getting better, so pleased
to have this pair of dancers, since we make evident   15
the music in the noise—and the dull pulse
leaps with unexpected riffs and turns, we can hear
how good the keyboard really is, the bright cresting

of another major key as others join us: a strict
block of a man, a formidable cliff of mind, dancing   20
as if melted, as if unhinged; his partner a gift of brave
elegance to those who watch her dance; and at her elbow,
Berryman back from the bridge, and Frost, relieved
of grievances, Dickinson waltzing there with lavish Keats,
who coughs into a borrowed handkerchief—all the poets of exile   25
and despair, unfit for this life, all those who cannot speak
but only sing, all those who cannot walk
who strut and spin until the waiting citizens at the bar,
aloof, judgmental, begin to sway or drum their straws
or hum, leave their seats to crowd the narrow floor   30
and now we are one body, sweating and foolish,
one body with its clear pathetic grace, not
lifted out of grief but dancing it, transforming
for one night this local bar, before we're turned back out
to our separate selves, to the dangerous streets and houses,   35
to the overwhelming drone of the living world.

If You Don't Force It   2000
MICHAEL S. HARPER (b. 1938)

He's talking about interpolations
riffs that come in the midst

of action, responding to the line,
accommodating the blues

and note neglecting the melody   5
refusing to smother beauty

with too many chords
to show off is to bungle

the melody with chordal blocks
not building anything to your baby   10

hiding the melody
like only the young can do

Lester Young would watch the dancers
moving into his vernaculars

with rhythms augmenting the melody   15
Herschel would set the pace

Pres would follow
Count would comp time

as though you could improve
on stride piano   20

Ben Webster could do stride
when you get possessed with wild chords

tie your left hand behind your back
then play the melody with one finger

on your right hand: 25
put the melody on your heart

❖ The Purpose of Poetry   1993
JARED CARTER (b. 1939)

This old man grazed thirty head of cattle
in a valley just north of the covered bridge
on the Mississinewa, where the reservoir
stands today. Had a black border collie
and a half-breed sheep dog with one eye.   5
The dogs took the cows to pasture each morning
and brought them home again at night
and herded them into the barn. The old man
would slip a wooden bar across both doors.
One dog slept on the front porch, one on the back.   10

He was waiting there one evening
listening to the animals coming home
when a man from the courthouse stopped
to tell him how the new reservoir
was going to flood all his property.   15
They both knew he was too far up in years
to farm anywhere else. He had a daughter
who lived in Florida, in a trailer park.
He should sell now and go stay with her.
The man helped bar the doors before he left.   20

He had only known dirt under his fingernails
and trips to town on Saturday mornings
since he was a boy. Always he had been around
cattle, and trees, and land near the river.
Evenings by the barn he could hear the dogs   25
talking to each other as they brought in
the herd; and the cows answering them.
It was the clearest thing he knew. That night
he shot both dogs and then himself.
The purpose of poetry is to tell us about life.   30

Rain   1997
SIDNEY WADE (b.1951)

It so happens I'm tired of desire,
of the mouths of the thousand things endlessly calling,
of the tongues of lemons, the voices of men,
the taste of iron and salty linen.
It so happens I'm tired of the pulling,   5
the vigorous dance of the charming ego,
the songs of the kitchen, the boiling sonata,
bite of the tweezers, the plumbing's whine.
I'm tired of passion, counterfeit or otherwise,
tired of prices, of heft and of gain,   10
of the towering columns, the whole archipelago
of plummeting bridgework and dangerous vines.
I want to lie down and transmogrify sentences,
I want to dissolve on a cool, gray cloud.
When the sky bends down to pleasure the ground,   15
the rain is cool; it's dark and it rains.

Buffalo   1997
MARK IRWIN (b. 1953)

They are the earth we have forgotten.
And the great continent of the head knows this
and will look right through you from the brown stones
of the eyes. And I would know them as a child knows
the brown-humped land that listens   5
for the prairie wind that is the bellows of their lungs.
A friend and I once stopped, astonished by the mile-long
herd, and by the slow train of the hooves
drumming up an expiring music like wind like God like sun.
Still I marvel as the late Nebraska light gilds the horns   10
and the ponderous mass of fur, while the foothills blue,
recalling the cold declining length of the rifle's bore.
They are the color of the earth thrust up, and history
still roams in the matted rags of hair, in the bleached litter
of bones, and in the chalky cliffs of the skull.   15

La Muerte, Patron Saint of Writers   1993
CLARISSA PINKOLA ESTÉS

Here buses rattle like buckets
of bolts; brake drums made stronger
by prayers to Santiago. The paint of these buses

regalo blue, cielo red, tierra y sanguine.
Up front Old Virgin Mother rides lookout,   5
and it is the law: all bus tires must be square,
all drivers must be certifiably blind,
all riders must have springs in their necks
and their ass cheeks.
The men wear their hats extra jammed on.   10
The women tie the live chickens together loosely
on purpose, just to make trouble. And the old
toothless one sags next to me. She has always
just eaten a tub of garlic, she has always just rubbed
her armpits and genitals with vinegar and goat cheese.   15
She is always leaning toward me, never away.
And I am always her seat mate, or that of her older sister
or her aged father. Always I am sitting thigh to thigh
with La Muerte. Now this La Muerte, this old one, laughs
maniacally at absolutely nothing, and over and over,   20
and always right in my face. Her breath fogs my vision, wilts
my hat brim, makes my nose cry. I work hard to stay by her,
to love her, love her cackle, love her odor, to love the pain
that I feel. If I can love her, if I can stand this pain,
of being near what others flee,   25
I will be able to write tonight,
and maybe for as long as a month.

Ah La Muerte, patron of las chupatintas, the pen-pushers,
you who only travel by bursting bus or teeming train or
broken car or bombed-out lorry, you who run   30
all over my page, screeching, "Catch me if you can,"
you who hide between the lines as though they are hedges,
peering over like some old baby in a macabre peek-a-boo.
Ah La Muerte, my love, my lover, pray for us, your writer children.
Give us all those acrid, sour, dour, and sickeningly sweet   35
smirks and smells, exactly the ones we need to write right.
Please, I beg you in all my authorial insanity, sit beside us
now and forever, fertilize our writing for ever and always
with the holy compost of your smiles.

Riverside Ghazal   2002
PATRICIA CLARK (b. 1951)

Most watery of all the trees, these willows
stand in water. Ice pools around the ankles of willows.

A tree's name should reveal its nature.
Salix babylonica: the first word is for willow.

Doesn't it sound stretchy and pliable?   5
Babylonica is for the weeping part of willow.

From a quotation in Psalms: by the rivers of Babylon
we wept. The people hung harps on willows.

The weight gave them a bent, permanent shape.
A girl flings her hair down, a young willow.   10

A golden color, like a shout, all the length
of the fronds. They light up the willow.

Nearby on the concrete ramp, an ice-filled boat
waits for the sun to unmoor it, sail it past the willows.

In the season of thaw, this ice giving way.   15
By the rivers of America, we wept these willows.

Under the Oaks at Holmes Hall, Overtaken by Rain   1999
GARRETT HONGO (b. 1951)

A desert downpour in early spring,
and I'm standing under California oaks,
gazing through rain as the gray sky thunders.
I don't know why the nightingale sings
to Kubla Khan and not to me, nineteen   5
and marked by nothing, not even ceremony
or the slash of wind tearing through trees.
I don't know why Ishmael alone is left
to speak of the sea's great beast, why
the ground sinks and slides against itself,   10
why the blue lupines will rise and quilt
through the tawny grasses on the hillsides.
I can't explain the garment of rain on my shoulders
or the sour cloth of my poverty unwinding
like a shroud as the giant eucalyptus   15
strips and sheds its gray parchments of skin
and stands mottled and nude in the shining rains.
I want something sullen as thundering skies,
thick as earthmilk, brown and sluicing
across the streets, grievous as the flood of waters.   20
I want unfelt sorrows to give away and wrought absence
to exchange for the imperfect shelter of these oaks,
for the froth of green ivy around my feet,
for the sky without gods and the earth without perplexity.
I want to have something like prayer to pay   25

or a mission to renounce as a fee
for my innocence under cloud-cover
and these furious nightingales of thunder,
companions of song in this untormented sea
of memory uncrowded with bliss or pain.   30

Improvisation   2001
ERIC PANKEY (b. 1957)

The only bridge across Wind River is the wind.

This is not a poem, not a suture of words, not a voice without accompaniment.

The poem is what silence instigates: a sanctuary between "The Temptation" and "The Expulsion" furnished with footfalls and echoes, a way station between *rapture* and *rupture*.

Beneath the chandelier, a single wooden chair with a braided velvet cord draped over its arms. The poem is not the chair, but the reconfigured function of the chair: *to be seen.*

The wind rattles around in the heart like a janitor with nothing left to clean but hours to go on the time clock.

Desire and its generation, its preservation, its fulfillment, its deterioration, its vanquishing, its loss, are the residue of the poem and not its source. When I say *the wind*, I mean *the poem*. When I say *the poem*, I mean *a variable in an equation*. When I say *I*, I mean *a voice without accompaniment*.

No one looking in the goat's eye mistakes it for a human eye. The devil's, perhaps. Close enough to be the devil's eye. The little horns and the tuft of a beard complete the mask. The poem is the expression of the actor behind the mask. The poem is the human eye that, from the theater's back row, seems goat-like in the devil mask.

Put a line through it. X it out: *The wind over the lip of the green bottle. The wind-frayed stamen.*

Writer in Exile   2000
RAFAEL CAMPO (b. 1964)

I've wished that I were born a Soviet,
so that my presence in America
would cause as greatly dignified regret
as leads to literary coups d'état—

but I am merely Cuban, dark and small   5
as any from a hundred nations which
exist for other's domination. All
I say is colonized, if not by rich

"protectors," then by communists who redden
on Varadero Beach; my poetry,   10
if plagued by form, otherwise does not threaten
(conveniently) the New-World-Orderly

procession of the vanquished. Hear my voice,
my queerly Spanish intonation, hear
the perfect sound of banishment. Rejoice!   15
I'm nothing yet, although tomorrow's near.

The Next Poem   1985
DANA GIOIA (b. 1950)

How much better it seems now
than when it is finally done—
the unforgettable first line,
the cunning way the stanzas run.

The rhymes (for, yes, it will have rhymes)   5
almost inaudible at first,
an appetite not yet acknowledged
like the inkling of a thirst.

While gradually the form appears
as each line is coaxed aloud—   10
the architecture of a room
seen from the middle of a crowd.

The music that of common speech
but slanted so that each detail
sounds unexpected as a sharp   15
inserted in a simple scale.

No jumble box of imagery
dumped glumly in the reader's lap
or elegantly packaged junk
the unsuspecting must unwrap.   20

But words that could direct a friend
precisely to an unknown place,
those few unshakeable details
no confusion can erase

And the real subject left unspoken   25
but unmistakable to those
who don't expect a jungle parrot
in the black and white of prose.

How much better it seems now
than when it is finally written.   30
How hungrily one waits to feel
the bright lure seized, the old hook bitten.

APPENDIX I

A BRIEF GLOSSARY OF FORMS

See also the Index of Terms.

abecedarian   A variant of the acrostic in which each line begins with a successive letter of the alphabet. Robert Pinsky's "ABC" (p. 285) is a variant whose words are alphabetical: "Anybody can die, evidently," the poem opens. (See also p. 280.)

acrostic   A poem in which the initial letters of each line spell out a name or message. In Michael Heffernan's "Acrostic on a Line from Tom T. Hall," this sentence reads vertically: "Something is going to kill us."

ballad   A narrative poem typically written in stress meter in quatrains of 4/3/4/3 beats with an exact or slant rhyme on the second and fourth lines (*a b c b*). Keats ("La Belle Dame Sans Merci"), Coleridge ("The Rime of the Ancient Mariner"), and contemporary poets such as Dudley Randall and Marilyn Nelson have written successful literary ballads, but most ballads were anonymous creations. **Folk ballads** were passed down orally from generation to generation and usually saw great change over time. "Bonnie Barbara Allen" apparently developed in the Scottish Highlands and was carried with immigrants to the Appalachian mountains where versions of the ballad are still sung; this version is from the collection of G. Ronald Dobler.

> In Scarlet Town where I was born,
> There was a fair maid dwelling,
> Made every youth cry "Well a-day!"
> Her name was Barbara Allen.
>
> In the merry month of May,
> When green buds they were swelling,
> Sweet William on his death-bed lay,
> For love of Barbara Allen.
>
> He sent his servant to the town,
> To the place where she was dwelling.
> "My master is sick and sent for you
> If your name be Barbara Allen."

Then slowly, slowly she got up,
And slowly she came nigh him,
And all she said when there she came,
"Young man, I think you're dying."

"Don't you remember the other day
When you were in town a-drinking,
You drank a health to the ladies all around
And slighted Barbara Allen?"

"Oh, yes, I remember the other day
When I was in town a-drinking,
I drank a health to the ladies all around,
But my love to Barbara Allen."

He turned his pale face to the wall
And death was in him dwelling;
"Adieu, adieu, to my friends all,
Be kind to Barbara Allen."

When she got in two miles of town
She heard the death bells ringing;
They rang so clear, as if to say,
"Hard-hearted Barbara Allen!"

"Oh, mother, oh, mother, come make my bed,
Oh, make it both soft and narrow,
For sweet William died today
And I will die tomorrow."

She was buried in the old churchyard
And he was buried a-nigh her;
On William's grave there grew a red rose,
And out of hers, a briar.

They grew and grew to the old church tower
Till they could grow no higher;
And at the end tied a true lovers' knot,
The rose wrapped around the briar.

ballade   A form developed in medieval France of three eight- or ten-line stanzas followed by an **envoy**, or short concluding stanza, usually dedicated to an important person. The last line of the first stanza acts as a refrain in a typical rhyme scheme of *a b a b b c b* C with the envoy rhyming *b c b* C (the uppercase letter indicates the refrain). The ten-line version rhymes *a a b a b b c d c d* D, and the envoy *c c d c* D. The example by R. S. Gwynn (p. 259) shows how in English poets have often used the form for comic verse.

ballad stanza   A quatrain in stress verse of 4/3/4/3 beats with an exact or slant rhyme on the second and fourth lines (*a b c b*), or, in syllable-stress verse, in alternating tetrameter and trimeter lines, a stanza popular with Dickinson.

blank verse   Unrhymed iambic pentameter. Since the seventeenth century, it has been a formal workhorse for longer poems, including Shakespeare's tragedies, Milton's *Paradise Lost*, Wordsworth's *The Prelude*, and Browning's and Frost's dramatic monologues. Howard Nemerov's "Learning by Doing" (p. 75) and Henry Taylor's "Barbed Wire" (p. 74) are in blank verse.

couplet   The most elementary stanza, two lines; when rhymed, *a a*, called a **heroic couplet**. Flexible, it has served for narrative (Chaucer's *The Canterbury Tales*), but is also capable of succinctness and punch, as in this epigram by Anonymous:

> Seven wealthy towns contend for Homer dead
> Through which the living Homer begged his bread.

ghazal   From the Arabic, a lyric poem composed of at least five closed couplets that rhyme *aa ba ca*, etc., and often at the end include the poet's name. Popular also in Persian, Urdu, Hindi, Turkish, Pashto, and other languages, like Spanish, with Arabic influences. Ghazals are often sung at public gatherings. When the form is translated into English, the scheme often involves repeating the final word of the opening couplet as the last word of the succeeding couplets and an internal monorhyme in the couplets' second line. Patricia Clark's "Riverside Ghazal" (p. 309) repeats the word "willow"; Carolyn Kizer's "Shalimar Gardens" (p. 203) is a variation.

haiku (hokku)   A Japanese form composed of three lines, of five, seven, and five syllables. The essence of the haiku, however, is not its syllabic form (which is virtually meaningless in English), but its tone or touch, influenced by Zen Buddhism. Haiku are, in general, very brief natural descriptions or observations that carry some implicit spiritual insight. Robert Bly captures this insight (but not in syllabics) in his translation of a haiku by Kobayashi Issa (1763–1827):

> The old dog bends his head listening . . .
> I guess the singing
> of the earthworms gets to him.

nonce stanza   A stanza created for a particular poem, like that invented by Marianne Moore for "The Fish" (p. 270) or by George Herbert for "Easter Wings" (p. 105). The challenge is to repeat the form naturally and effectively throughout the poem.

ottava rima   An eight-line stanza, *a b a b a b c c*, adopted from Italian, and used most memorably, and comically, by Byron in *Don Juan*.

quatrain   In general, a stanza of four lines, but the term often implies a rhymed stanza. Francis's single rhyme is unusual:

Cadence
ROBERT FRANCIS (1901–1987)

Puckered like an old apple she lies abed,
Saying nothing and hearing nothing said,
Not seeing the birthday flowers by her head
To comfort her. She is not comforted.

The room is warm, too warm, but there is chill   5
Over her eyes and over her tired will.
Her hair is frost in the valley, snow on the hill.
Night is falling and the wind is still.

Other schemes are *a b c b* (often used in ballads, hymns, and popular songs); *a a b b*; *a b a a* (Erin Belieu's "Her Web," p. 73); *a b a b* (Lizette Woodworth Reese's "Crows," p. 70), *a b b a* (when written in iambic tetrameter also called the "In Memoriam" stanza after Tennyson's use of it in that elegy).

pantoum   A Malayan form: an indefinite number of *a b a b* quatrain stanzas, with this restriction: lines 2 and 4 of each stanza, *in their entirety*, become lines 1 and 3 of the following stanza, and so on. The carry-over lines are called **repetons.** The sequence is ended in a quatrain whose repetons are lines 1 and 3 of the *first* stanza *in reversed order*. Edward Hirsch's "At Sixteen" and Travis Brown's "At Seventeen" (pp. 257–258) are versions of this form.

rime royal   A seven-line stanza of iambic pentameter, *a b a b b c c*, used by Chaucer, Shakespeare, and occasionally by modern and contemporary poets.

sestina   A French form of six six-line stanzas and an envoy of three lines. Instead of rhyme, the *six words* at the ends of lines in the first stanza are repeated in a specific, shifting order as line-end words in the other five six-line stanzas. Then all six words are used again in the final triplet, three of them at line ends, three of them in mid-line. The order of the line-end words in the stanzas may be transcribed this way: 1-2-3-4-5-6, 6-1-5-2-4-3, 3-6-4-1-2-5, 5-3-2-6-1-4, 4-5-1-3-6-2, 2-4-6-5-3-1; and in the triplet, (2)-5-(4)-3-(6)-1. Poets in English since Sir Philip Sidney have explored the sestina's potential, including notably Marilyn Hacker, David Lehman, James Cummins, as well as Michael Heffernan in "Famous Last Words," (p. 119).

sonnet   A poem typically written in fourteen lines of iambic pentameter (see also discussion on p. 36). The **Shakespearean** (or **English**) **sonnet** is commonly rhymed in three quatrains and a couplet: *a b a b, c d c d, e f e f, g g.* Shakespeare's Sonnet 73 (p. 34) is a good example in which the sense corresponds to the four divisions. Marilyn Nelson's "Balance," p. 71, manages a story within the sonnet's strictures. The **Italian** (or **Petrarchan**) **sonnet** is typically rhymed in units of eight (**octave**) and six lines (**sestet**): *a b b a a b b a, c d e c d e* (or *c d c d c d*). The sense, statement, and resolution usually conforms to this division. Poets have worked any number of successful variations on the rhyme schemes of both kinds of sonnet. Edmund Spenser used an interlocking *a b a b, b c b c, c d c d, e e*. Frost, who wrote more sonnets than might be supposed, tried numerous variations, including: *a a a b b b c c c d d d e e*.

Spenserian stanza   A nine-line stanza, eight lines in iambic pentameter and the last iambic hexameter, *a b a b b c b c c*; Spenser developed it for *The Fairie Queen* and Keats mastered it in "The Eve of St. Agnes".

stichomythia   A device developed from Greek drama, in which two characters speak in exactly alternating lines of verse, as in this poem by Christina Rossetti (1830–1894), question and answer:

Up-Hill

Does the road wind up-hill all the way?
   Yes, to the very end.
Will the day's journey take the whole long day?
   From morn to night, my friend.

But is there for the night a resting-place?   5
   A roof for when the slow dark hours begin.
May not the darkness hide it from my face?
   You cannot miss that inn.

Shall I meet other wayfarers at night?
   Those who have gone before.   10
Then must I knock, or call when just in sight?
   They will not keep you standing at that door.

Shall I find comfort, travel-sore and weak?
   Of labour you shall find the sum.
Will there be beds for me and all who seek?   15
   Yea, beds for all who come.

syllabics   A poem that counts the number of syllables in each line instead of another quality such as stresses. Syllabics can offer a poet limitations in which to deploy the poem and create tension. Marianne Moore's "To a Steam Roller" (p. 89) and "The Fish" (p. 270) are two examples of poems composed in syllabics (as is the familiar haiku).

tercet   A stanza of three lines, sometimes called a **triplet,** which can rhyme *a a a, a b b, a b a,* or *a a b*.

terza rima   An Italian form of interlocking tercets (three-line stanzas) following an *a b a* scheme and using the unrhymed line for the double rhymes of the next stanza: *a b a, b c b, c d c*, and so on. The form is most closely associated with Dante's *Divine Comedy*. Familiar examples in English are Shelley's "Ode to the West Wind" and Frost's "Acquainted with the Night." See Geoffrey Brock's "Move" (p. 73) and Molly Peacock's, "Putting a Burden Down" (p. 194).

villanelle   From the French, a poem of six stanzas—five triplets and a quatrain. It employs only *two* rhymes throughout: *a b a, a b a, a b a, a b a, a b a, a b a a.* Moreover, the first and third lines are repeated entirely, three times, as a refrain. Line 1 appears again as lines 6, 12, and 18. Line 3 appears as lines 9, 15, and 19. Dylan Thomas's "Do Not Go Gentle" is a famous example, but many contemporary poets have worked with the form; see Allison Joseph's "The Payoff" (p. 75).

APPENDIX II

NOTES TO THE QUESTIONS AND SUGGESTIONS

Chapter 2

1. (a) **Night Winds**
ADELAIDE CRAPSEY (1878–1914)

The old
Old winds that blew
When chaos was, what do
They tell the clattered trees that I
Should weep?

(b) **Liu Ch'e**
EZRA POUND (1885–1972)

The rustling of the silk is discontinued,
Dust drifts over the court-yard,
There is no sound of foot-fall, and the leaves
Scurry into heaps and lie still,
And she the rejoicer of the heart is beneath them: 5

A wet leaf that clings to the threshold.

3. **IBM Memo: Mouse Balls Available as Field Replacement Unit (FRU)** 1996
JEFF WORLEY (b. 1947)

(a found poem)

Mouse balls are now available as FRU. Therefore,
if a mouse fails to operate or begins to perform
erratically, it may need a ball replacement.
Because of the delicate nature of this procedure,

replacement of mouse balls should only be attempted   5
by properly trained personnel. Before proceeding,
determine the type of mouse balls by examining
the underside of the mouse. Domestic balls will be
larger and harder than foreign balls. Ball removal
procedures differ. Foreign balls can be replaced   10
using the pop-off method. Replace domestic balls
using the twist-off method. Mouse balls are usually
not static sensitive; however, excessive handling
can result in sudden discharge. Upon completion of
ball replacement, the mouse may be used immediately.   15
It is recommended that each replacer have a pair
of spare balls for maintaining optimum customer
satisfaction, and that any customer missing his
balls should suspect local personnel of removing
these necessary items for their own unofficial use.   20

Chapter 3

p. 53

Thăt tíme | ŏf yéar | thŏu máyst | ĭn mé | bĕhóld

Whĕn yél | lŏw léaves, | ŏr nóne, | ŏr féw, | dŏ háng

Ŭpón | thŏse bóughs | thăt sháke | ăgáinst | thĕ cóld

Báre rú | ĭned chóirs | whĕre láte | thĕ swéet | bírds sáng.

p. 57

Lícked | ĭts tóngue | (́)íntŏ | thĕ cór | nĕrs óf | thĕ éve | nĭng,

Língĕred | ŭpón | thĕ póols | thăt stánd | ĭn dráins, |

Lét fáll | ŭpón | ĭts báck | thĕ sóot | thăt fálls | frŏm chím | nĕys,

Slípped bў | thĕ tér | răce, máde | ă súd | dĕn léap,

Ănd sée | ĭng thát | ĭt wás | ă sóft | Óctŏb | ĕr níght,   5

Cúrled ŏnce | ăbóut | thĕ hóuse, | ănd féll | ăsléep.

6. (a) **Delight in Disorder**

Ă swéet | dĭsór | dĕr ín | thĕ dréss

Kíndlĕs | ĭn clóthes | ă wán | tŏnnéss;

Ă láwn | ăbóut | thĕ shóul | dĕrs thrówn

Íntŏ | ă fíne | dĭstrác | tĭ ón,

Ăn ér | rĭng láce, | whĭch hére | ănd thére,   5

Ĕnthrálls | thĕ crím | sŏn stóm | ăchĕr,

Ă cúff | nĕgléct | fŭl, ănd | thĕrebý

Ríbbănds | tŏ flów | cŏnfús | ĕdlý,

Ă wín | nĭng wáve, ‖ dĕsér | vĭng nóte,

Ín thĕ | tĕmpés | tŭoŭs pét | tĭcoát,   10

Ă cáre | lĕss shóe | -stríng, ĭn | whŏse tíe

Ĭ sée | ă wíld | cĭvíl | ĭtý,

Dŏ móre | bĕwítch | mĕ thán | whĕn árt

Ĭs tóo | prĕcíse | ĭn év | ĕry párt.

(b) **A Bird came down the Walk**

Ă Bírd | cáme dówn | thĕ Wálk—

Hĕ díd | nŏt knów | Ĭ sáw—

Hĕ bít | ăn Áng | lĕ wórm | ĭn hálves

Ănd áte | thĕ fél | lŏw, ráw,

Ănd thén | hĕ dránk | ă Déw   5

Frŏm ă | cŏnvén | ĭ ĕnt Gráss—

Ănd thén | hópped síde | wĭse tŏ | thĕ Wáll

Tŏ lét | ă Bée | tlĕ páss—

Hĕ glánced | wĭth ráp | ĭd éyes

Thăt húr | rĭed áll | ăróund—   10

Thĕy lóoked | lĭke fríght | ĕned Béads, | Ĭ thóught—

Hĕ stírred | hĭs Vél | vĕt Héad

Lĭke óne | ĭn dán | gĕr, Cáu | tĭous,

Ĭ óf | fĕred hím | ă Crúmb

Ănd hé | ŭnrólled | hĭs féath | ĕrs   15

Ănd rówed | hĭm sóft | ĕr hóme—

Thăn Óars | dĭvíde | thĕ Ó | cĕan,

Tóo síl | vĕr fŏr | ă séam—

Ŏr Bút | tĕrflíes, | óff Bánks | ŏf Nóon

Léap, plásh | lĕss ăs | thĕy swím   20

(c) **Anecdote of the Jar**

Ĭ pláced | ă jár | ĭn Tén | nĕssée

Ănd róund | ĭt wás, | ŭpón | ă híll.

Ĭt máde | thĕ slóv | ĕnlў wíl | dĕrnéss

Sŭrróund | thăt híll.

Thĕ wíl | dĕrnéss | rósĕ úp | tŏ ít.   5

Ănd spráwled | ărŏúnd, | nŏ lóng | ĕr wíld.

Thĕ jár | wăs róund | ŭpón | thĕ gróund

Ănd táll | ănd óf | ă pórt | ĭn áir.

Ĭt tóok | dŏmín | ĭon év | ĕrywhére.

Thĕ jár | wăs gráy | ănd báre.   10

Ĭt díd | nŏt gíve | ŏf bírd | ŏr búsh,

Lĭke nóth | ĭng élse | ĭn Tén | nĕssée.

(d)   **For My Contemporaries**
J. V. CUNNINGHAM (1911–1985)

Hŏw tíme | rĕvér | sĕs

Thĕ próud | ĭn héart!

Ĭ nów | mãke vér | sĕs

Whŏ áimed | ăt árt.

Bŭt Í | sleep wéll.   5

Ămbí | tĭŏus bóys

Whŏse bíg | línes swéll

Wĭth spír | ĭtŭal nóise,

Dĕspíse | mĕ nót!

Ănd bé | nŏt quéa | sȳ   10

Tŏ práise | sŏmewhát:

Vérse ĭs | nŏt eá | sў.

Bŭt ráge | whŏ wíll.

Tíme thăt | prŏcúred | mĕ

Góod sénse | ănd skíll   15

Ŏf mád | nĕss cúred | mĕ.

Chapter 4

5. **In One Place**
    ROBERT WALLACE (b. 1932)

            —something
    holds up two or three leaves
    the first year,

                and climbs
    and branches, summer   5
    by summer,

                till birds
    in it don't remember
    it wasn't there.

Chapter 5

3. The rain it raineth every day,
    upon the just and unjust fella,
    but more upon the just, because
    the unjust hath the just's umbrella.
                    ANONYMOUS

    Leo
    BOB McKENTY (b. 1935)

    Leo doesn't give a damn.
    He won't lie down beside the lamb.
    He's too preoccupied, my guess is,
    Lying with the lionesses.

Chapter 6

3. **In Her Parachute–Silk Wedding Gown**
   MICHELLE BOISSEAU (b. 1955)

She stands at the top of the aisle
as on a wing. The white paper
carpet is cloud
spilled out. The pillbox hats

turned to her are the rows   5
of suburbs she falls into.
She is our mother,
or will be, and any of us

stumbling upon this scene
from the next generation, would fail   10
to notice what makes even her
tremble, with her silver

screen notions of marriage—
where all husbands scold
to hide their good natures, and wives   15
are passionately loyal.

Her groom, after all, is just a boy
home from the war,
his only trophy, the parachute
she's made into her dress. It's a world   20

of appetites, she knows
all too well, waiting there
watching the flowers
bob in her hands, dizzying.

Despite herself, she's not thinking: 25
Go slowly, pace it,
a queen attended to court,
Bette Davis. Nor of the $20 bill

her mother safety-
pinned to her underpants.   30
But: My God,
a room full of men, looking,

each will ask me to dance—
your hand tingles
when you touch their close-clipped   35
heads. And the men,

nudged to turn around
and watch the bride descend,
see a fellow parachutist
as they all drift   40

behind enemy lines,
stomachs turning over as they fall
into the horizon, into the ring
of small brilliant explosions.

Chapter 8

The original words are in italics.

(a) "A clear *fretwork* of shadows / From huge umbrellas *littered* the pavement,"
    "A Hill," Anthony Hecht (p. 228).
(b) "The sky's bright *lanes* peak through / chinks in a bar," "71 Hwy. at the
    Moment of Change" Robert Stewart (p. 232).
(c) "Miraculous water, God's *emissary*," "Shalimar Gardens," Carolyn Kizer
    (p. 203).
(d) "The road *unscrolls* between flat black fields," "Late Night Drive," Deborah
    Kroman (p. 257).
(e) ". . . lightning makes the clouds look like / *flowers* of *kerosene*," "Kerosene,"
    Chase Twichell (p. 256)
(f) "The great *continent* of the head knows this," "Buffalo," Mark Irwin
    (p. 308).

Chapter 10

3.   The lines originally came from:
     (a) Louise Erdrich, "Saint Marie"
     (b) William Faulkner, *The Sound and the Fury*
     (c) Hilary Masters, "So Long, Natty Bumppo"
     (d) Walker Percy, *Lancelot*
     (e) Rosellen Brown, "Cecil and Amelia"
     (f) Eudora Welty, "The Whistle"
     (g) Italo Calvino, "The Chase"
     (h) Kay Boyle, "The Astronomer's Wife"
     (i) Charles Baxter, "Snow"

APPENDIX III

FURTHER READING

Anthologies

Susan Aizenberg and Erin Belieu, *The Extraordinary Tide: New Poetry by American Women*, Columbia, 2001.

Gerald Costanzo and Jim Daniels, eds., *American Poetry: The Next Generation*, Carnegie Mellon, 2000.

Philip Dacey and David Jauss, eds., *Strong Measures: Contemporary American Poetry in Traditional Forms*, Harper & Row, 1986.

Sascha Feinstein and Yusef Komunyakaa, *The Jazz Poetry Anthology; Second Set: The Jazz Poetry Anthology, Vol. 2*, Indiana, 1991, 1996.

Annie Finch, ed., *A Formal Feeling Comes: Poems in Form by Contemporary Women*, Story Line Press, 1994.

Ray Gonzalez, ed., *After Aztlan: Latino Poets of the Nineties*, Godine, 1992.

Michael S. Harper and Anthony Walton, eds., *Every Shut Eye Ain't Asleep: Poetry by African Americans Since 1945*, Little, Brown, 1994.

Garrett Hongo, ed., *The Open Boat: Poems from Asian America*, Anchor, 1993.

Mark Jarman and David Mason, eds. *Rebel Angels: 25 Poets of the New Formalism*, Story Line, 1996.

David Lehman, series ed., *The Best American Poetry*, annual, Simon & Schuster, 1988 to present.

Phillis Levin, ed., *The Penguin Book of the Sonnet*, Penguin, 2001.

Czeslaw Milosz, ed., *A Book of Luminous Things: An International Anthology of Poetry*, Harcourt Brace, 1996.

Duane Niatum, ed., *Harper's Anthology of Twentieth-Century Native American Poetry*, Harper & Row, 1988.

Kevin Prufer, ed. *The New Young American Poets*, Southern Illinois, 2000.

Jahan Ramazani, Richard Ellmann, and Robert O'Clair, eds., *The Norton Anthology of Modern Poetry and Contemporary Poetry*, 3d. ed., Norton, 2003, Vol. 1: Modern Poetry, Vol. 2: Contemporary Poetry.

Kenneth Rosen, ed., *Voices of the Rainbow: Contemporary Poetry by Native Americans*, Arcade, 1993.

Jerome Rothenberg and Pierre Joris, eds., *Poems for the Millennium: The University of California Book of Modern & Postmodern Poetry*, Vol. I, 1995, Vol. II, 1998.

Stephen Tapscott, ed., *Twentieth-Century Latin American Poetry, Bilingual Anthology*, Texas, 1996.

Michael Waters and Al Poulin Jr., eds., *Contemporary American Poetry*, 7th ed., Houghton Mifflin, 2001.

On Poetry, Writing Poetry, and Poets

Derek Attridge, *Poetic Rhythm*, Cambridge, 1995.

Gaton Bachelard, *The Poetics of Space* (trans. Maria Jolas), Beacon, 1969.

David Baker, ed., *Meter in English: A Critical Engagement*, Arkansas, 1996.

Robin Behn and Chase Twichell, eds., *The Practice of Poetry*, HarperPerennial, 1992.

Eavan Boland, *Object Lessons: The Life of the Woman and the Poet in Our Time*, Norton, 1995.

Eavan Boland and Mark Strand, *The Making of a Poem: A Norton Anthology of Poetic Forms*, Norton, 2000.

Sharon Bryan, ed., *Where We Stand: Women Poets on Literary Tradition*, Norton, 1993.

Alfred Corn, *The Poem's Heartbeat: A Manual of Prosody*, Story Line, 1997.

Annie Finch and Kathrine Varnes, *An Exaltation of Forms: Contemporary Poets Celebrate the Diversity of Their Art*, Michigan, 2002.

Alice Fulton, *Feeling as a Foreign Language: The Good Strangeness of Poetry*, Graywolf, 1999.

Robert Francis, *The Satirical Rogue on Poetry*, Massachusetts, 1968.

Paul Fussell, *Poetic Meter and Poetic Form*, rev. ed., Random House, 1979.

Robert Hass, *Twentieth Century Pleasures*, Ecco, 1984.

John Hollander, *Rhyme's Reason*, Yale, 1991.

Richard Hugo, *The Triggering Town*, Norton, 1982.

Randall Jarrell, *Poetry and the Age*, Knopf, 1953.

Mary Kinzie, *A Poet's Guide to Poetry*, Chicago, 1999.

Stephen Kuusisto, Deborah Tall, and David Weiss, eds., *The Poet's Notebook: Excerpts from the Notebooks of 26 American Poets*, Norton, 1995.

Martin Lammon, ed., *Written in Water, Written in Stone: Twenty Years of Poets on Poetry*, Michigan, 1996.

Robert McDowell and Harvey Gross, *Sound and Form in Modern Poetry*, Michigan, 2000.

Mary Oliver, *A Poetry Handbook*, Harcourt Brace, 1995.

Robert Pack and Jay Parini, eds., *Introspections: American Poets on One of Their Own Poems*, Middlebury, 1997.

Rodney Phillips, et al., *The Hand of the Poet: Poems and Papers in Manuscript*, Rizoli, 1997.

Robert Pinsky, *The Sounds of Poetry*, Farrar, Straus & Giroux, 1998.

Alex Preminger and T. V. F. Brogan, eds., *The New Princeton Encyclopedia of Poetry and Poetics*, Princeton, 1993.

Rainer Maria Rilke, *Letters to a Young Poet* (trans. Stephen Mitchell), Vintage, 1986.

Barbara Herrnstein Smith, *Poetic Closure: A Study of How Poems End*, Chicago, 1968.

Timothy Steele, *All the Fun's in How You Say a Thing*, Ohio, 1999.

Lewis Turco, *The New Book of Forms: A Handbook of Poetics*, New England, 1986.

Miller Williams, *Patterns of Poetry*, Louisiana State, 1986.

Clement Wood, *The Complete Rhyming Dictionary*, rev. ed., Doubleday, 1992.

Also bear in mind literary journals (some are listed on p. 304) and writing organizations (p. 302); these often have Web sites. Stroll through a library or bookstore (physical or virtual), and you'll find books by many poets included in this text—and by many others.

ACKNOWLEDGMENTS

Alexander, Pamela, "Look Here." Copyright © 1994 by Pamela Alexander. First appeared in *The Atlantic*. Reprinted by permission of the author.

Andrews, Tom, "Cinema Vérité: The Death of Alfred, Lord Tennyson." Copyright © 1993 by Tom Andrews. First appeared in *Field*. Reprinted by permission of the author.

Ashbery, John, "At North Farm." From *A Wave*. Copyright © 1981, 1982, 1983, 1984 by John Ashbery. Reprinted by permission of Georges Borchardt, Inc., for the author.

Atkinson, Jennifer, "And Sweetness Out of the Strong." From *The Drowned City*. Copyright © 2000 by Jennifer Atkinson. Reprinted by permission of Northeastern University Press.

Ball, Angela, "Difficult Daughters." Copyright © 2001 by Angela Ball. First appeared in *Denver Quarterly*. Reprinted by permission of the author.

Barrax, Gerald, "The Guilt." Copyright © 1992 by Gerald Barrax. First appeared in *The Gettysburg Review*. Reprinted by permission of the author.

Becker, Robin, "When Someone Dies Young." From *All-American Girl*, by Robin Becker. Copyright © 1996 by Robin Becker. Reprinted by permission of University of Pittsburgh Press.

Belieu, Erin, "Her Web" (originally titled "Brown Recluse"). From *One Above & One Below*. Copyright © 2000 by Erin Belieu. Reprinted by the permission of Copper Canyon Press.

Bennett, Bruce, "Smart." Copyright © 1978 by Bruce Bennett. From *Taking Off*, Orchises Press. Reprinted by permission of the author.

Bishop, Elizabeth, "First Death in Nova Scotia." From *The Complete Poems: 1927–1979* by Elizabeth Bishop. Copyright © 1979, 1983 by Alice Helen Methfessel. Reprinted by permission of Farrar, Straus & Giroux, LLC.

Bly, Robert, "Looking at a Dead Wren in My Hand." From *The Morning Glory* by Robert Bly. Copyright © 1970 by Robert Bly. Translation of haiku by Issa. Copyright © 1969 by Robert Bly. Reprinted by permission of the author.

Boisseau, Michelle, "In Her Parachute–Silk Wedding Gown." From *No Private Life*, Vanderbilt University Press. Copyright © 1990 by Michelle Boisseau. "Moon at the Mirror." Copyright © 2001 by Michelle Boisseau. Reprinted by permission of the author.

Boruch, Marianne, "The Hawk." From *A Stick That Breaks and Breaks*. Copyright © 1997 by Marianne Boruch. Reprinted by permission of Oberlin College Press.

Brock, Geoffrey, "Move." Copyright © 1998 by Geoffrey Brock. Originally appeared in *Mississippi Review*. Reprinted by permission of the author.

Brown, Fleda, "Kitten." Copyright © 1994 by Fleda Brown Jackson. First appeared in *Indiana Review*. Reprinted by permission of the author.

Brown, Travis, "At Seventeen." Copyright © 2003 by Travis Brown. Reprinted by permission of the author.

Bryan, Sharon, "Sweater Weather: A Love Song to Language." From *Flying Blind*. Copyright © 1996 by Sharon Bryan. Reprinted by permission of Sarabande Books.

Buckley, Christopher, "Perseid Meteor Shower." From *Dark Matter*. Copyright © 1993 by Christopher Buckley. Reprinted by permission of Copper Beech Press.

Budy, Andrea Hollander, "Giving Birth." Copyright © 2002 by Andrea Hollander Budy. First appeared in *Field*. Reprinted by permission of the author.

Burns, Michael, "The First Time." From *The Secret Names: Poems*. Copyright © 1994 by Michael Burns. Reprinted by permission of the University of Missouri Press and the poet.

Campo, Rafael, "Writer in Exile." From *Ploughshares*. Copyright © 2000 by Rafael Campo. Reprinted by permission of the author.

Carter, Jared, "The Purpose of Poetry." Originally published in *Images*. Copyright © 1981, 1993 by Jared Carter. From *After the Rain*, Cleveland State University Poetry Center, 1993. Reprinted by permission of the author.

Cassian, Nina, "Ordeal." Translation copyright © by Michael Impey and Brian Swann. Originally published in *An Anthology of Contemporary Romanian Poetry*, London. Reprinted by permission of Michael Impey.

Cherry, Kelly, "Battle Scene." From *Rising Venus: Poems*. Copyright © 2002 by Kelly Cherry.

Reprinted by permission of Louisiana State University Press.

Chun, Ye, "For Hai Zi ..." Copyright © 2002 by Chun Ye. Originally appeared in *New Letters*. Reprinted by permission of the author.

Citino, David, "Cycladic Island Female Statue, British Museum." From *The Invention of Secrecy*, 2001. Copyright © 2001 by David Citino. Reprinted by permission of the Ohio State University Press.

Clampitt, Amy, "The Edge of the Hurricane." From *The Collected Poems of Amy Clampitt*, by Amy Clampitt. Copyright ©1997 by the Estate of Amy Clampitt. Used by permission of Alfred A. Knopf, a division of Random House, Inc.

Clark, Patricia, "Riverside Ghazal." From *The Atlantic Monthly*. Copyright © 2002 by Patricia Clark. Reprinted by permission of the author.

Collins, Billy, "To a Stranger Born in Some Distant Country Hundreds of Years from Now." From *Picnic, Lightning*, by Billy Collins. Copyright © 1998 by Billy Collins. Reprinted by permission of the University of Pittsburgh Press.

Collins, Martha, "Remember the Trains." From *Some Things Words Can Do*, Sheep Meadow Press. Copyright © 1998 by Martha Collins. Reprinted by permission of the author.

Cunningham, J. V., "For My Contemporaries." From *The Exclusions of a Rhyme*. Copyright © 1960 by J. V. Cunningham. Reprinted by the permission of the Ohio University Press.

Daniels, Jim, "Short-order Cook." From *Places/Everyone*. Copyright © 1985 by Jim Daniels. Reprinted by permission of the University of Wisconsin Press.

Dickinson, Emily, Poems #328, 341, 465, 986. Reprinted by permission of the publishers and the Trustees of Amherst College from *The Poems of Emily Dickinson*, Thomas H. Johnson, ed., Cambridge, Mass.: The Belknap Press of Harvard University Press. Copyright © 1951, 1955, 1979, 1983 by the President and Fellows of Harvard College.

Doty, Mark, "No." From *My Alexandria: Poems*. Copyright ©1993 by Mark Doty. Reprinted by permission of the author and the University of Illinois Press.

Dove, Rita, "The House Slave." From *The Yellow House on the Corner* by Rita Dove. Copyright © 1980 by Rita Dove. "A Hill of Beans." From *Thomas and Beulah*. Copyright © 1986 by Rita Dove. Reprinted by permission of Carnegie Mellon University Press.

Dunn, Stephen, "Laws." From *Not Dancing*. Copyright © 1984 by Stephen Dunn. Reprinted by permission of Carnegie Mellon University Press.

Eady, Cornelius, "The Wrong Street." From *The Gathering of My Name*. Copyright © 1991 by Cornelius Eady. Reprinted by permission of Carnegie Mellon University Press.

Edson, Russell, "A Man Who Writes." From *The Tunnel: Selected Poems, Field Poetry Series*, v. 3, Oberlin, OH, Oberlin College Press. Copyright © 1994 by Russell Edson. Reprinted by permission of Oberlin College Press.

Eimers, Nancy, "A Night without Stars." From *No Moon*, Purdue University Press. Copyright © 1997 by Nancy Eimers. Reprinted by permission of the author.

Éluard, Paul, "The Deaf and Blind." Translation by Paul Auster in the *The Random House Book of Twentieth Century French Poetry*. Copyright © 1982 by Paul Auster. Reprinted by permission.

Emanuel, Lynn, "The White Dress." Copyright © 1998 by Lynn Emanuel. Reprinted by permission of the author.

Espada, Martín, "A Cigarette's Iris in the Eye of a Candle." Copyright © 1999 by Martín Espada. Reprinted by permission of the author.

Estés, Clarissa Pinkola, "La Muerte, Patron Saint of Writers." Copyright © 1990 by Clarissa Pinkola Estés. First appeared in *Colorado Review*. Reprinted by permission of the author.

Fantauzzi, David A., "Moorings" and draft of same. Copyright © 1977 by David A. Fantauzzi. Reprinted by permission of the author.

Francis, Robert, "Cadence." From *Butter Hill*. Copyright © 1984 by Paul W. Carman. Reprinted by permission. "Professional Poet" and "The Indecipherable Poem." From *The Satirical Rogue on Poetry*. Copyright © 1965 by Robert Francis. Reprinted by permission of the University of Massachusetts Press. "Excellence" and "Glass." From *Robert Francis: Collected Poems, 1936-1976*. Copyright © 1976 by Robert Francis. Reprinted by permission of the University of Massachusetts Press.

Friman, Alice, "Diapers for My Father." First appeared in the *Ohio Review*. Copyright © 1998 by Alice Friman. Reprinted by permission of the author.

Frost, Carol, "Moon." First appeared in *Gettysburg Review*. Copyright © 2001 by Carol Frost. Reprinted by permission of the author.

Gerstler, Amy, "Siren." From *Bitter Angel*. Copyright © 1990 by Amy Gerstler. Reprinted by permission of the author.

Getsi, Lucia Cordell, "Meeting the Occasion." From *Intensive Care*. New Rivers Press. Copyright © 1992 by Lucia Getsi. Reprinted by permission of the author.

Gibson, Margaret, "Amaryllis." From *Icon and Evidence: Poems*, by Margaret Gibson. Copyright © 2001 by Margaret Gibson. Reprinted by permission of Louisiana State University Press.

Gioia, Dana, "The Next Poem." Copyright © 1985 by Dana Gioia. First appeared in *Poetry*. Reprinted by permission of the author.

Glazer, Michele, "Fruit Flies to the Too Ripe Fruit." From *It Is Hard to Look at What We Came to Think We'd Come to See*, by Michele Glazer.

Copyright © 1997 by Michele Glazer. Reprinted by permission of the University of Pittsburgh Press.

Gleason, Kate, "After Fighting for Hours." Copyright © 1995 by Kate Gleason. First appeared in *Green Mountains Review*. Reprinted by permission of the author.

Glück, Louise, "The Racer's Widow." Copyright © 1968 by Louise Glück. Reprinted by permission of the author. "Daisies" from *The Wild Iris* by Louise Glück. Copyright © 1993 by Louise Glück. Reprinted by permission of HarperCollins Publishers Inc.

Greenway, William, "Pit Pony." From *Where We've Been*. Copyright © 1987 by William Greenway. Reprinted by permission of Theodore W. Macri, agent for Breitenbush Books.

Gwynn, R. S., "Ballade Beginning with a Line by Robert Bly." Copyright © 2000 by R. S. Gwynn. Reprinted by permission of the author.

Hall, Donald, "Names of Horses." From *Kicking the Leaves*. Copyright © 1978 by Donald Hall. Reprinted by permission of the author. Draft of "Ox Cart Man." From *A Piece of Work: Five Writers Discuss Their Revisions*, edited by Jay Woodruff. Copyright © 1993 by Jay Woodruff and Donald Hall. Reprinted by permission of the University of Iowa Press and Donald Hall.

Harper, Michael S., "If You Don't Force It." From *Songlines in Michaeltree: New and Selected Poems*. Copyright © 2000 by Michael S. Harper. Reprinted by permission of the author and the University of Illinois Press.

Harrison, Jeffrey, "Rowing." From *Feeding the Fire* by Jeffrey Harrison, Sarabande Books, Inc, 2001. Copyright © 2001 by Jeffrey Harrison. Reprinted by permission of Sarabande Books and the author.

Hayden, Robert, "Those Winter Sundays." From *Collected Poems of Robert Hayden*, edited by Frederick Glaysher. Copyright © 1966 by Robert Hayden. Used by permission of Liveright Publishing Corporation.

Hecht, Anthony, "A Hill." From *Collected Earlier Poems*, by Anthony Hecht. Copyright © 1990 by Anthony E. Hecht. Used by permission of Alfred A. Knopf, a division of Random House, Inc.

Heffernan, Michael, "Famous Last Words." From *The Cry of Oliver Hardy*, The University of Georgia Press. Copyright © 1979 by Michael Heffernan. Reprinted by permission of the author.

Hilberry, Conrad, "Storm Window." Copyright © 1980 by Conrad Hilberry. Reprinted by permission of the author.

Hirsch, Edward, "At Sixteen." Copyright © 1996 by Edward Hirsch. First appeared in *Five Points*. Reprinted by permission of the author.

Holmes, Elizabeth, "What She Could Do." Reprinted from *The Patience of the Cloud Photographer*. Copyright © 1997 by Elizabeth Holmes. Reprinted by permission of Carnegie Mellon University Press.

Hongo, Garrett, "Under the Oaks at Holmes Hall, Overtaken by Rain." First appeared in *Southern Review*. Copyright ©1999 by Garrett Hongo. Reprinted by permission of the author.

Hudgins, Andrew, "Goat." Copyright © 1998 by Andrew Hudgins. First appeared in *The Hudson Review*. Reprinted by permission of the author.

Irwin, Mark, "Buffalo." Copyright © 1997 by Mark Irwin. First appeared in *The Nation*. Reprinted by permission of the author.

Jackson, Richard, "Antigone Today." From *Heartwall*. Copyright © 2000 by Richard Jackson. Reprinted by permission of the University of Massachusetts Press.

Jarman, Mark, "Ground Swell." Copyright © 1991 by Mark Jarman. First appeared in *New American Poets of the 90s*. Reprinted by permission of the author. Account of the writing of "Ground Swell," copyright © 2003 by Mark Jarman. Used by permission of the author.

Jones, Hettie, "April." From *All Told*, Hanging Loose Press, 2002. Copyright © 2002 by Hettie Jones. Reprinted by permission of the author.

Jones, Rodney, "Nihilist Time." Copyright © 1998 by Rodney Jones. Reprinted by permission of the author.

Joseph, Allison, "The Payoff." Copyright © 2000 by Allison Joseph. First appeared in *Pleiades*. Reprinted by permission of the author.

Justice, Donald, "Variations on a Text by Vallejo." From *Selected Poems*. Copyright © 1979 by Donald Justice. Reprinted by permission of the author.

Kaine, Ashley, "Van Gogh Inside the Starry Night" and draft. Copyright © 2003 by Ashley Kaine. Reprinted by permission of the author.

Kaufman, Shirley, "Bread and Water." From *Rivers of Salt*, Copper Canyon Press. Copyright © 1990 by Shirley Kaufman. First appeared in *Ploughshares*. Reprinted by permission of the author.

Kennedy, Sarah, "In the Beginning." From *Flow Blue*. Copyright © 2002 by Sarah Kennedy. Reprinted by permission of Elixir Press.

Kirschbaum, Roger, "My Attempt to Slow Down the World." Copyright © 2003 by Roger Kirschbaum. Reprinted by permission of the author.

Kizer, Carolyn, "Shalimar Gardens." Copyright © 1998 by Carolyn Kizer. First appeared in *New Letters*. Reprinted by permission of the author.

Klok, Carrie, "The Voyeur: The Third Day," "Untitled," ("It's not the stars"), "Stillness," "All of You." Copyright © 2003 by Carrie Klok. Reprinted by permission of the author.

Knight, Etheridge, "A Poem of Attrition." From *The Essential Etheridge Knight*. Copyright © 1986 by Etheridge Knight. Reprinted by permission of the University of Pittsburgh Press.

Komunyakaa, Yusef, "Sunday Afternoons." From *Magic City*. First appeared in *New American*

Poets of the 90s. Copyright © 1991 by Yusef Komunyakaa. Reprinted by permission of the author.

Kostova, Elizabeth, "Suddenly I Realized I Was Sitting." Copyright © 1996 by Elizabeth Kostova. Reprinted by permission of the author.

Kroman, Deborah, "Late Night Drive." Copyright © 1998 by Deborah Kroman. Reprinted by permission of the author.

Kumin, Maxine, "The Long Marriage." Copyright © 1997 by Maxine Kumin. First appeared in *The Georgia Review*. Reprinted by permission of the author.

Larkin, Philip, "First Sight." From *Collected Poems of Philip Larkin*. Copyright © 1988, 1989 by the Estate of Philip Larkin. Reprinted by permission of Farrar, Straus and Giroux, LLC.

Lattimore, Richmond, "Catania To Rome." From *Poems of Three Decades*. Copyright © 1972 by Richmond Lattimore. Reprinted by permission of the University of Chicago Press.

Lee, Li-Young, "One Heart." From *Book of My Nights*. Copyright © 2001 by Li-Young Lee. Reprinted by permission of BOA Editions, Ltd.

Levine, Philip, "The Return: Orihuela, 1965." Copyright © 1994 by Philip Levine. First appeared in *The Nation*. Reprinted by permission of the author.

Lyons, Richard, "Lunch by the Grand Canal." Copyright © 1998 by Richard Lyons. First appeared in *Paris Review*. Reprinted by permission of the author.

MacDonald, Cynthia, "Celebrating the Freak." From *(W)holes* by Cynthia MacDonald. Copyright © 1980 by Cynthia MacDonald. Used by permission of Alfred A. Knopf, a division of Random House, Inc.

Mann, Randall, "Fiduciary." From *Poetry*, May 2002. Copyright © 2002 by Randall Mann. Reprinted by permission of the author.

Matthews, William, "Men at My Father's Funeral." Copyright © 1992 by William Matthews. First appeared in *The Ohio Review*. Reprinted by permission.

McElroy, Colleen J., "Trompe L'oeil: Slovenia." From *Travelling Music*. Copyright © 1998 by Colleen J. McElroy. Reprinted by permission of Story Line Press.

McHugh, Heather, "Sizing." From *The Father of the Predicaments*. Copyright © 1999 by Heather McHugh. Reprinted by permission of Wesleyan University Press.

McKenty, Bob, "Leo." From *Lighten Up*. Copyright © 1994 by Bob McKenty. Reprinted by permission.

Miles, Josephine, "David." From *Collected Poems, 1930-83*. Copyright © 1983 by Josephine Miles. Reprinted by permission of the estate of Josphenine Miles and the University of Illinois Press.

Milosz, Czeslaw, "Realism." Copyright © 1994 by Czeslaw Milosz. First appeared in the *New Yorker*. Reprinted by permission of Robert Hass.

Mitcham, Judson, "An Introduction." Copyright © 1996 by Judson Mitcham. First appeared in *The Georgia Review*. Reprinted by permission of the author.

Mitchell, Susan, "Blackbirds." From *The Water Inside the Water*, Wesleyan University Press. Copyright © 1983 by Susan Mitchell. Reprinted by permission of Wesleyan University Press.

Nelson, Marilyn, "Balance" and "Minor Miracle." From *The Fields of Praise*. Copyright © 1997 by Marilyn Nelson. Reprinted by permission of Louisiana State University Press.

Nelson, Michael, "The Virgin Appears as an Old Gay Man." Copyright © 2003 by Michael Nelson. Reprinted by permission of the author.

Nemerov, Howard, "Power to the People," "Learning by Doing," "The Fourth of July." Copyright © 1973 by Howard Nemerov. Reprinted by permission of the author.

Newton, Linda, "Sheep." Copyright © 2003 by Linda Newton. Reprinted by permission of the author.

Niedecker, Lorine, "Laundromat." From *Collected Works*, ed. by Penberthy Jenny Lynn. Copyright © 2002. Reprinted by permission of University of California Press.

Nye, Naomi Shihab, "Famous." From *Hugging the Jukebox*. Copyright © 1982 by Naomi Shihab Nye. Reprinted by permission of Theodore W. Macri, agent for Breitenbush Books.

Oliver, Mary, "Music at Night." From *The Night Traveler*. Copyright © 1978 by Mary Oliver. Reprinted by permission of Bits Press and the poet.

Olsen, William, "The Fold-Out Atlas of the Human Body." From *Trouble Lights*. Copyright © 2002 by William Olsen. Reprinted by permission of TriQuarterly Books/Northwestern University Press, 2002.

Ortiz Cofer, Judith, "Cold as Heaven." From *Reaching for the Mainland & Selected New Poems*. Tempe, AZ: Bilingual Press/Editorial Bilingüe (1995). Copyright © 1995 by Judith Ortiz Cofer. Reprinted by permission of Bilingual Press/Editorial Bilingüe.

Ostriker, Alicia, "Sonnet: To Tell the Truth." From *A Dream of Springtime*. Copyright © 1979 by Alicia Ostriker. Reprinted by permission of the author.

Pankey, Eric, "Improvisation." First appeared in *Gettysburg Review*. Copyright © 2001 by Eric Pankey. Reprinted by permission of the author.

Pape, Greg, "My Happiness." Copyright © 1978 by Greg Pape. From *Border Crossings*, University of Pittsburgh Press, 1978. Reprinted by permission of the author.

Peacock, Molly, "Putting a Burden Down." From *Cornucopia* by Molly Peacock. Copyright ©

2002 by Molly Peacock. Used by permission of W. W. Norton & Co., Inc.

Phillips, Carl, "X." From *In the Blood* by Carl Phillips. Copyright © 1992 by Carl Phillips. Reprinted with the permission of Northeastern University Press.

Pinsky, Robert, "ABC." Copyright © 1999 by Robert Pinsky. Reprinted by permission of the author.

Plath, Sylvia, "Balloons." From *Ariel* by Sylvia Plath. Copyright © 1965 by Ted Hughes. Reprinted by permission of HarperCollins Publishers, Inc.

Plumly, Stanley, "Woman on Twenty-second Eating Berries." Copyright © 1990 by Stanley Plumly. First appeared in *Antaeus*. Reprinted by permission of the author.

Rankine, Claudia, "The Man. His Bowl. His Raspberries." From *Nothing in Nature Is Private*, Cleveland State University Poetry Center. Copyright © 1994 by Claudia Rankine. Reprinted by permission of the author.

Reese, Lizette Woodworth, "Crows." From *White April*. Copyright © 1930. Reprinted by permission of Henry Holt and Company, LLC.

Reeves, Trish, "The Elements." From *In the Knees of the Gods*, BkMk Press. Copyright © 2001 by Trish Reeves. Reprinted by permission of the author.

Roethke, Theodore, "My Papa's Waltz." Copyright © 1942 by Hearst Magazines, Inc. From *The Collected Poems of Theodore Roethke* by Theodore Roethke. Reprinted by permission of Doubleday, a division of Random House, Inc.

Rogers, Pattiann, "On the Way to Early Morning Mass." From *Song of the World Becoming: New and Collected Poems 1981-2001*. Minneapolis: Milkweed Editions, 2001. Copyright © 2001 by Pattiann Rogers. Reprinted with permission from Milkweed Edition.

Rosenberg, Liz, "The Silence of Women." From *Children of Paradise*. Copyright © 1994 by Liz Rosenberg. Reprinted by permission of the University of Pittsburgh Press.

Rukeyser, Muriel, "A Simple Experiment." From *Out of Silence*, TriQuarterly Books. Copyright © 1991 by William Rukeyser. Reprinted by permission of International Creative Management.

Ryan, Kay, "Don't Look Back." From *Say Uncle*. Copyright © 2000 by Kay Ryan. Reprinted by permission of Grove Press Poetry Series.

Sajé, Natasha, "Reading the Late Henry James." From *Red under the Skin*. Copyright © 1994 by Natasha Sajé. Reprinted by permission of the University of Pittsburgh Press.

Shomer, Enid, "Among the Cows." From *This Close to Earth*. Copyright © 1992 by Enid Shomer. Reprinted by permission of the University of Arkansas Press.

Simpson, Louis, "American Classic." From *Caviare at the Funeral*. Copyright © 1981 by Louis Simpson. Reprinted by permission of Grolier Publishing/Scholastic Library, Inc.

Smith, Arthur, "Good Deeds." Reprinted from *The Late World*. Copyright © 2002 by Arthur Smith. Reprinted by permission of Carnegie Mellon University Press.

Smith, R. T., "Scavenging the Wall." From *Brightwood: Poems*, by R. T. Smith. Copyright © 2001 by R. T. Smith. Reprinted by permission of Louisiana State University Press.

Song, Cathy, "Primary Colors." From *Picture Bride*. Copyright © 1983 by Cathy Song. Reprinted by permission of Yale University Press.

Spires, Elizabeth, "Letter in July." Copyright © 1992 by Elizabeth Spires. First appeared in *Poetry*. Reprinted by permission of the author.

Stafford, William, "Traveling through the Dark." From *The Way It Is: New & Selected Poems*. Copyright © 1962, 1998 by the Estate of William Stafford. Reprinted by permission of Graywolf Press, Saint Paul, Minnesota.

Stanton, Maura, "Handwriting." Reprinted from *Glacier Wine*. Copyright © 2001 by Maura Stanton. Reprinted by permission of Carnegie Mellon University Press.

Steele, Timothy, "Epitaph." From *Uncertainties and Rest*. Copyright © 1979 by Timothy Steele. Reprinted by permission of the author.

Stewart, Robert, "71 Hwy. at the Moment of Change." Copyright © 2002 by Robert Stewart. Reprinted by permission of the author.

Tapahonso, Luci, "She Says." From *Sáanii Dahataal/The Women Are Singing: Poems and Stories*, by Luci Tapahonso. Copyright © 1993 by Luci Tapahonso. Reprinted by permission of the University of Arizona Press.

Tate, James, "A Guide to the Stone Age." From *Absences*. Copyright © 1972 by James Tate. Reprinted by permission of Carnegie Mellon University Press.

Taylor, Henry, "Barbed Wire." From *The Flying Change* by Henry Taylor. Copyright © 1985 by Henry Taylor. "Understanding Fiction." From *Understanding Fiction*. Copyright © 1996 by Henry Taylor. Reprinted by permission. Both reprinted by permission of Louisiana State University Press

Tomes, Marta, "The Kiss." Copyright © 1995 by Marta Tomes. Reprinted by permission of the author.

Tran, Janine, "Early Dawn." Copyright © 2003 by Janine Tran. Reprinted by permission of the author.

Trowbridge, William, "Slug." From *O Paradise*. Copyright © 1995 by William Trowbridge. Reprinted by permission of the University Of Arkansas Press.

Twichell, Chase, "Kerosene." From *The Snow Watcher*. Copyright © 1998 by Chase Twichell. Reprinted by permission of Ontario Review Press.

Updike, John, "Player Piano." Copyright © 1958 by John Updike. Reprinted by permission of the author.

Vando, Gloria, "Ronda." Copyright © 1995 by Gloria Vando. First appeared in *Paper Dance: 55 Latino Poets*, 1995, eds., Virgil Suarez and Juan Felipe Herrera. Reprinted by permission of the author.

Voigt, Ellen Bryant, "Dancing with Poets." From *The Lotus Flowers*. Copyright © 1987 by Ellen Bryant Voigt. Reprinted by permission of W. W. Norton & Company, Inc.

Wade, Sidney, "Rain." From *Green*. Copyright © 1998 by Sidney Wade. Reprinted by permission of University of South Carolina Press.

Wallace, Robert, "Swimmer in the Rain," "In One Place." Copyright © 1979 by Robert Wallace. From *The Common Summer: New and Selected Poems*, Carnegie Mellon University Press, 1989. Reprinted by permission.

Waters, Michael, "Romance in the Old Folks' Home." From *Parthenopi: New and Selected Poems*. Copyright © 2001 by Michael Waters. Reprinted by permission of BOA Editions, Ltd.

Webb, Charles Harper, "Charles Harper Webb." From *Tulip Farms and Leper Colonies*. Copyright © 2001 by Charles Harper Webb. Reprinted by permission of BOA Editions, Ltd.

Whitmore, Susan, "Conception." Copyright © 1998 by Susan Whitmore. First appeared in *The Georgia Review*. Reprinted by permission of the author.

Wier, Dara, "Daytrip to Paradox." From *The Book of Knowledge*. Copyright © 1988 by Dara Wier. Reprinted by permission of Carnegie Mellon University Press.

Wilbur, Richard, "Hamlen Brook." First appeared in *The New Yorker*. Copyright © 1985. Reprinted by permission of the author. "Love Calls Us to the Things of This World." From *Things of This World*. Copyright © 1956 and renewed 1984 by Richard Wilbur. Reprinted by permission of Harcourt, Inc. Six drafts of the opening lines of "Love Calls Us to the Things of This World." Copyright © Richard Wilbur. Reprinted by permission.

Williams, Miller, "The Curator." From *Adjusting to the Light*. Copyright © 1992 by Miller Williams. Reprinted by permission of the University of Missouri Press.

Williams, William Carlos, "Poem (As the cat)." From *Collected Poems: 1909-1939, Volume I*. Copyright © 1938 by New Directions Publishing Corporation. Reprinted by permission of New Directions Publishing Corporation.

Wiman, Christian, "Poŝtolka (Prague)." From *Atlantic Monthly*. Copyright © 2002 by Christian Wiman. Reprinted by permission of the author.

Wood, Susan, "Eggs." From *Campo Santo: Poems*. Copyright © 1991 by Susan Wood. Reprinted by permission of Louisiana State University Press.

Worley, Jeff, "IBM Memo . . ." Copyright © 1995. First appeared in *Southern Poetry Review*. Reprinted by permission of the author.

Wormser, Baron, "Mulroney." From *Mulroney & Others* by Baron Wormser, Sarabande Books, Inc, 2000. Copyright © 2000 by Baron Wormser. Reprinted by permission of Sarabande Books and the poet.

Wright, C. D., "Personals." Copyright © 1991 by C. D. Wright. First appeared in *String Light*, University of Georgia Press, 1991. Reprinted by permission of the author.

Wright, Charles, "January II." Copyright © 2002 by Charles Wright. First appeared in *Field*. Reprinted by permission of the author.

Young, Al, "Détroit Moi." First appeared in *Michigan Quarterly Review*. Copyright © 1999 and 2001 by Al Young. Reprinted by permission of the author.

Young, Gary, "The still born calf . . ." From *Days*. Copyright © 1997 by Gary Young. Reprinted by permission of Silverfish Review Press.

INDEX OF AUTHORS AND TITLES

INDEX OF TERMS